RENEWALS 691-4574

DATE DUE

APR 1 9			
APR 1 9			
DEC 0 1			

EUGENE V. DEBS
SPOKESMAN FOR LABOR AND SOCIALISM

EUGENE V. DEBS
Blue Denim Reformer
1855-1926

Eugene V. DEBS

Spokesman for Labor and Socialism

Bernard J. Brommel

1978 Chicago
CHARLES H. KERR PUBLISHING COMPANY
Published for the Eugene V. Debs Foundation

Copyright © 1978

Charles H. Kerr Publishing Company

Printed in the United States of America

LC 75-23910

ISBN 0-88286-006-2

Graphic Design: Pamela Rice and Leo Tanenbaum

478

Foreword

In *Eugene V. Debs: Spokesman for Labor and Socialism*, Bernard J. Brommel makes a major contribution to an understanding of his subject, and a good knowledge of Debs is necessary to comprehend fully the history of the American Left and at least an aspect of American labor history. Dead for half a century, Debs continues to be the nation's foremost radical hero, the most popular leader of a Marxist movement, the Left's most beloved personality. Neither his successor as leader of the Socialist Party, Norman Thomas, nor any of the Communist leaders since World War I, nor the often colorful and sometime bizarre characters of the New Left of the 1960's and early 1970's even approach Debs as a radical heroic figure.

Attractive to his own generation, Debs has excited the creative attention of several historians and biographers since his death, particularly since 1945. Some of these books about Debs are quite good. Carefully reasoned, clearly written, and well researched as they are, however, Professor Brommel adds new information and insights in his work because he has combed the already known sources so finely and has used manuscript sources heretofore unavailable. Indeed, Brommel had a major role in making these new Debs sources available.

For eight years Brommel was a member of the faculty of Indiana State University, which is in Debs' home city, Terre Haute, and in recent years the university has expanded to surround the home where Debs lived most of his adult life. He, some of his faculty colleagues, and some labor leaders, notably Walter Reuther of the United Auto Workers and Patrick Gorman and Hilton Hanna of the Amalgamated Meat Cutters, joined forces to restore and preserve the Debs home on the Indiana State campus. The home is now a small museum and library operated by the Eugene V. Debs Foundation, and the surprising number of visitors to it each year is another measure of the continuing appeal of its former occupant.

In the course of restoring the home, Brommel came to know Mrs. Marguerite Debs Cooper, the daughter of Debs' younger brother Theodore, who until Eugene's death in 1926 served his brother as a secretary and general helper in Debs' causes. Incidentally, the brothers looked so much alike that those who did not know them well frequently mistook Theodore for Eugene. In fact, during the 1908 presidential campaign, when the Socialists had enough funds to sponsor a national campaign train called the Red Special, Theodore occasionally substituted for his brother, who needed sleep, and made the appearances at short whistle-stops. Theodore had kept many of Eugene's papers in the basement of his home, and

Brommel arranged for the Debs papers to be deposited in the library of Indiana State. It is these Debs papers which are the major new sources used in this book. Brommel was also successful in finding long-forgotten Debs material in the archives of local labor organizations, papers that illuminate the Socialist leader's early career.

Scholars and others interested in the Socialist part of the American past have a debt of gratitude to Bernard J. Brommel for digging out these lost sources, making them available, and writing this book.

— David A. Shannon

Dr. Shannon, formerly professor of history at Columbia, Wisconsin and University of Virginia, now serves as Vice President and Provost at the University of Virginia. He wrote the distinguished book, *The Socialist Party of America.*

Table of Contents

Chapter   Page

Foreword	5
Introduction	9
Acknowledgments	11
I Early Life and Education of a Spokesman	13
II Blue-Denim Spokesman	23
III The Pullman Ordeal	35
IV Shifting Tides	41
V The First National Campaign	59
VI Uniting the Party	67
VII A Willing Candidate	79
VIII The 1908 Red Special Campaign	91
IX A Limited Success	127
X Militant Pacifist	147
XI Delay and Dissillusionment After the Campaign	159
XII Citizen of the World	167
XIII A Half-Century Milestone	181
XIV Setting the Record Straight	189
XV In Retrospect	199
List of Illustrations	107
Illustrations	108-126
Chapter Notes	229-259
Index	260-265

Dedicated to
Grace Laird, friend and teacher

Introduction

As a spokesman for labor and socialism, Eugene V. Debs delivered over six thousand speeches and wrote an even larger number of pamphlets, magazine articles, and newspaper editorials between 1872 and 1926. During this period no other advocate for these interests gained as much prominence, created as much controversy, or attracted as many followers. Debs served as a writer and speaker in important strikes, union organizational battles, five Socialist presidential campaigns, cases defending imprisoned workers, free speech contests, and anti-war disputes. Since past biographers such as David Karsner (*Debs, His Authorized Life and Letters,* 1919, and *Talks with Debs,* 1922), McAlister Coleman (*Eugene V. Debs, A Man Unafraid,* 1930), and Stephen Reynolds (*Debs, His Life, Writings and Speeches,* 1908), and Ruth Le Prade (*Debs and the Poets,* 1919), have ignored most of Debs' rhetoric supporting these causes, I plan to focus my study upon what he said and wrote in order to better evaluate the influence, or lack of it, that he had in his time. Other biographers such as Alexander Trachtenberg (*The Heritage of Gene Debs,* 1918), Henry T. Schnittkind (*The Story of Eugene Debs,* 1929), Scott Nearing (*The Debs Decision,* 1919), Herbert Morais and William Cahn (*Gene Debs, The Story of a Fighting American,* 1948), and H. Wayne Morgan (*Eugene V. Debs: Socialist For President,* 1962), have written about certain years and events in Debs' career. With the exception of Morgan and Ray Ginger (*The Bending Cross,* 1949), Debs' biographers have been close political friends or former party associates who broke with Debs in his later years when he refused to join the Communist Party. In addition to manuscripts of his addresses in libraries, I found accounts of his speeches and copies of them in both large and small newspapers throughout the country. I located his essays in not only the once popular *Pearson's Magazine* and *Everybody's Magazine,* but in obscure journals devoted to labor, women's rights, socialism, and birth control.

By documenting many aspects of Debs' career that have been overlooked, I hope to separate the facts about his life from the legends that have been told about him. Debs captured people's imagination and inspired some men to work diligently for him and tell stories of his greatness. Other men feared him and worked equally hard to counter the evils they thought he represented. Some union writers referred to Debs as the Abe Lincoln of labor while more conservative journalists described him as the Aaron Burr of labor. Countless stories have been told of Debs' generosity. For example, Debs did give his watch to a railroader who needed a timepiece to get a certain job on the Illinois Central and on another occasion he insisted that a poor man take his overcoat in Indianapolis, but Debs could not possibly have owned as many watches and overcoats as his admirers say that he gave away. The same kind of discrepancy can be found in other reports about more crucial events in Debs' life, including his home life, his drinking, his non-attendance at party meetings, and his role as a policy maker: first, as a labor leader, and later as a Socialist Party official.

No previous biographer has footnoted with sufficient primary sources his generalizations about Debs. These writers largely ignored documentation or cited only a few readily available pamphlets, often those published by the Socialist Party. Debs' most accurate biographer, Ray Ginger, used more extensive resources, but he only cites at the ends of his chapters a list of the sources that he used, frequently including anonymous informants.

In recent years, and since the publication of Ginger's book, several important collections of papers of prominent people associated with Debs in the Socialist Party and labor movement have become available. For example, Rose Pastor Stokes, Victor Berger, Robert Hunter, Ryan Walker, Morris Hillquit, Adolph Germer, Mabel Curry, Job Harriman, George and Grace Brewer, and George Herron. In addition, papers of many lesser known but important supporters or opponents of Debs have been acquired and processed by libraries. The bulk of Debs' own papers and those of his brother, Theodore, have been located. At the time of Eugene's death, Theodore, who had served for over twenty years as his brother's secretary, acquired his papers. He stored them in their original letter boxes in his basement where they remained until the summer of 1967 when his daughter, Marguerite Debs Cooper, granted me permission to read the collection. She said that her father had kept the letters thinking that he might write a biography of Debs. Before his own death in 1945, Theodore did show several letters to Irving Stone when he came to Terre Haute to research his fictionalized life of Debs, later titled *Adversary in the House*. According to his daughter, Theodore selected the letters Stone read and permitted no one else to read or to go through the papers. After his death, Mrs. Cooper, tired of curiosity seekers and publicity, refused interviewers' requests for materials and information.

During the eight years that I taught in Debs' hometown, I interviewed many people who remembered Debs and some who had worked with him. From my questioning, I learned that several men had borrowed books from a lending library that Debs once maintained in some union hall. After a search I discovered a significant part of Debs' personal library in the basement of the Labor Temple. Late in his life Debs gave to Rand School in New York City, a Socialist college for leadership training, approximately half of his library, but he kept this part for the use of local laborers. Ned Bush, a Terre Haute union leader and a man who knew Debs, helped me find the minutes of the early union in which Debs had served as secretary and president for several years. Some former members of Debs' union evidently had joined the Steamfitters' Local and had stored these ledgers in their vault for safekeeping. With all of these sources, plus the insights gained from reading the papers of others working for or against the same causes that Debs advocated, I hope to trace with more care the chronology of the influences upon Debs' life and answer some of the questions about why Debs played the effective yet sometimes vacillating role that he did in both labor and Socialist causes. I will maintain that Debs knew far more about party matters than past biographers have given him credit for and that his actions, radical in some cases and noncommittal in others, were planned and deliberate. In many difficult situations Debs, as a tactician, made effective and rational choices of his available means of persuasion.

Acknowledgments

The writer acknowledges his debt to the people he interviewed and corresponded with; to other scholars for materials used in the content and footnotes. Librarians at Library of Congress, Washington; Tamiment Library, New York City; Lilly Library, Bloomington, Indiana; Chicago Public Library, Newberry Library, Chicago; Chicago Historical Society Library; Milwaukee Historical Society Library; John Whitcomb's private collection of Rose Pastor Stokes, et. al. papers in Dedham, Massachusetts; Indiana State Historical Library, Indianapolis; Henry Huntington Library, San Marino, California; Houghton Library, Harvard, Cambridge, Massachusetts; New York City Public Library; Wisconsin Historical Library, Madison; Massachusetts Historical Society Library, Boston; Eugene V. Debs Foundation Library, Emmeline Fairbanks Library, and Indiana State University Library, Terre Haute, Indiana, provided valuable assistance. Indiana State University gave the writer a faculty research grant for study in New York and Boston. The University of North Dakota provided a grant for research in Wisconsin and Illinois libraries. Special thanks to Professor Robert G. Gunderson, Indiana University, for his encouragement; Joan Young and Gertrude Edelheit, typists; Barbara Hunter, Elizabeth Hampsten, and Reba Reynolds for reading the manuscript; Wilma and our children for the time to pursue this study.

Northeastern Illinois University

Chicago, Illinois

May, 1978.

Bernard J. Brommel

Chapter I
Early Life and Education
of a Spokesman

On November 5, 1855, Jean Daniel and Marguerite Debs anxiously awaited the birth of their fifth child. Since their first four children had all been girls, they wanted a son. More importantly, and especially for the sake of his wife, Jean Daniel wished that the child would be healthy because two of their daughters had died at birth. In the late afternoon when their first son arrived in excellent health, both parents rejoiced. Jean Daniel celebrated the news by inviting neighbors into their old weather beaten frame house at 447 North Fourth Street, Terre Haute, Indiana, for a glass of wine. He proudly announced that he would name the boy Eugene Victor after two of his favorite authors, Eugene Sue and Victor Hugo.

The past seven years had been difficult for the Debses. Jean Daniel, called Daniel by his friends, had left Colmar Alsace, France, on November 10, 1848, after his father's death and a family dispute over his property. His father had planned that Daniel would manage a clothing factory he owned. In order to learn the business Daniel had worked in the mill, and there he met his future wife, Marguerite Bettrich. But his socially prominent family objected to this romance for two reasons: Marguerite represented a lower class and she belonged to the Catholic church. Neither Marguerite nor Daniel forgot or forgave his family for their callousness and avariciousness.[1]

The cash settlement from his father's estate enabled Daniel to come to America. Unfortunately, an engaging American businessman travelling on the same boat swindled Daniel out of his legacy. This "businessman" sold Daniel a partnership in his store. After his arrival in New York City on January 20, 1849, Daniel spent several days searching for his non-existent partner and his store. Penniless, he worked hard at various odd jobs and began to save money for Marguerite's fare. Daniel didn't mind the menial jobs but he found the separation from Marguerite unbearable.

After receiving a particularly depressing letter in which Daniel spoke of suicide, Marguerite decided to join him. She sailed on August 7, 1849, although in earlier letters to Daniel she stated that perhaps he had given up too much for her and should keep his money to start a business and then, if he still cared, she would come to America. They married on September 13, two days after her arrival.[2]

A year later, after the death of a daughter, the young couple decided to move to Cincinnati. But they were disappointed with job opportunities in Cincinnati and left on May 20, 1851, for Terre Haute, Indiana. Daniel knew of other Alsatians who had settled in the French colony in Terre Haute. Soon after arriving, Daniel secured permission from Jacob and

Samuel Early, who ran a large slaughter house, to open a meat packaging and shipping business adjacent to their plant. By 1851, Terre Haute had become a thriving trade center for shipping East and West. The Wabash River and Canal provided cheap water transportation, and railroads soon linked the city to Indianapolis and St. Louis.

In March 1854, an ague [a malarial fever] epidemic broke out in Terre Haute, and many died. Mrs. Debs feared that their second daughter, Marie, would not survive the dreaded chills and fever that accompanied the disease. So the family sold their small business and fled to Brooklyn, New York. Six months later, after four moves in four years, the Debses returned and settled permanently in Terre Haute. Daniel took a job in the Early packing plant where he often worked sixteen hours a day processing pork.

After two years, Daniel's health broke under the strain of the long hours, heavy lifting, and poor working conditions. He lost his job. Later, he found work laying ties and rails for the Vandalia Railroad but a recession forced his layoff. Against Daniel's wishes, Mrs. Debs took their last few dollars and started a grocery store in the front room of their small four room house. Other French people who had settled in Terre Haute patronized the grocery, and this business helped the family avoid starvation. Daniel began to import from Europe special products, including French wines, that his customers liked. While the parents managed the store, the younger children played in the upstairs. Daniel put slats on the windows of the two rooms to prevent his children from falling out. Years later Eugene quipped that he grew up behind bars.[3]

Between 1855 and 1865 the Debses had five more children, but only three—Eugenia, Emma, and Theodore—survived. The family lived in close harmony. In an interview, Harley Pritchett, a lifelong friend of Gene and Theodore, said that the neighbors thought the Debses too clannish. Pritchett romped with the two boys during the week, but Sundays the Debs family spent together. Although Pritchett frequently visited the Debs home, both as a child and an adult, he commented that a visitor would not know much about their lives personally. According to Pritchett, they were "close-mouthed" and the father dominated most conversations. The mother, "a little bit of a woman," always agreed with the father whose word ruled. Daniel disciplined the boys, but they did not resent it. Pritchett described the mother as kind and sympathetic.[4] He characterized Daniel as a man who lived his own life and cared nothing for outward show but everything for inner worth. Because Daniel loved literature, art, and music, he encouraged his children to study in each of these areas. He corresponded with his friend, August Bartholdi, sculptor for the Statue of Liberty. He played the cornet with skill and memorized the works of the great composers.[5] The Debs' children appreciated their parents' concern for their well being. Affectionately, the Debs' children used the nicknames of "Daisy" and "Dandy" when referring to their parents.

Religion was not a vital factor in the Debs' home. During Eugene's boyhood his parents deliberately avoided church. Daniel could make nothing out of the hell-fire preachings of the local Protestant parsons. His wife had insisted upon baptizing her first four children as Catholics, but discontinued the practice at the time of Gene's birth.[6] She gradually stopped attending Mass and other services. Although customarily a Catholic child was baptized at two weeks, Mrs. Debs had Louise baptized at a year—on May 22, 1855, preceding Eugene's birth in November.

As a boy Eugene attended St. Joseph's on one occasion. "I went to hear a sermon one Sunday," he related, and "the priest delivered an address on hell. I shall never forget it as long as I live. He pictured a thousand demons and devils . . . threatening to consume all who did not accept his interpretation of Christianity. I left that church with a rich and royal hatred for the priest as a person, and with a loathing for the church as an institution. I vowed I would never go inside a church again."[7] Eugene kept this promise, but later in life often referred to God as an agitator who sought justice and equal rights for all. "I don't subscribe to any creed," he asserted, "I believe in the religion of the Golden Rule. I wouldn't if I could disturb anyone's religion. If he sincerely believes it, it is the right creed."[8] Rather than attend church on Sunday mornings, Daniel regularly took his two sons hunting while Marguerite and the four daughters prepared an elaborate dinner. Daniel, a skilled marksman, hunted frequently. The boys took pride in their father's skill. At one time he served as president of the Terre Haute Gun Club.

Daniel Debs began the literary indoctrination of Eugene at an early age. On Sunday evenings the family discussed literary works. When the father could get away from his grocery, they spent other evenings in the same way.[9] During his school days in Paris and Le Bau la Roche at Walderbach, Daniel studied many classic writers. He insisted that his children read the works of Hugo, Goethe, Moliére, and Schiller. As an adult Eugene declared that *Les Misérables* impressed him more than any other book, and excerpts from this book and others appeared in his speeches and writings. As soon as he could read, his father helped him memorize excerpts from it. Neighbors of Daniel Debs admired his huge library which he eventually gave to the Terre Haute Public Library. A neighbor remarked that Daniel's collection contained not only many volumes of French literature, but French history as well.[10]

From 1860 to 1867 Eugene attended the Old Seminary School. Daniel sent him to the private school because he admired the headmaster, Benjamin Hayes. Also, Daniel distrusted the Terre Haute public schools because they closed frequently between 1855 and 1860 for lack of consistent state support. In 1847 Hayes started a boys school that he described as an intermediate seminary between district school and the university. A strict disciplinarian, Uncle Benny Hayes, as he was locally known, advocated thoroughness and insisted upon high standards. In arithmetic, his favorite subject, the schoolmaster strongly maintained that a boy must go through the book three times before he could be called a cipherer.[11] For a staff Hayes hired four other teachers, Messrs. Probst, Seifert, Treplo, and Abbie Flagg, who agreed upon the importance of drill and discipline.

Although Debs' parents had a difficult time starting their grocery, it provided enough extra money for Gene's tuition. For each of two terms of twenty-two weeks, Hayes charged sixteen dollars for classics, and thirteen dollars for the lower grades.[12] Dr. W. W. Parsons, first president of Indiana State Normal, who studied under Uncle Benny at the same time as Debs, described the school they attended: "We studied the three R's and something called parsing. It was a 'lickin and larning' program. Hayes was the crowned head of the pedagogues about 1857, and a conscientious votary of the rod for the government of the child."[13] In later years when Debs became a controversial public figure, his enemies charged that he had never respected any authority or order. They forgot or did not know about Hayes' discipline requirements. Others might say Debs rebelled because of harsh discipline both at home and at school, but Debs' remarks as an adult indicated that he appreciated his teachers and his father.

George Scott attended the public school across the street from the Old Seminary at the time Debs entered the upper grades. Scott remembered the competitive program between the schools. Public school children could not play with Benny's boys. Their teachers told them that only naughty, bad boys went to the Old Seminary. Since the public school had the only playing field, Hayes stood out in the street with a switch and marked the boundaries. Students and teachers in each school thought themselves superior to the other. Photographs frequently appeared in store windows to present to the public the scope of the work done in each school.[14] W. H. Wiley, public school superintendent who later hired Hayes, reported that the sharp competition between the schools in the 1860-1867 period forced them both to offer similar courses.[15] Both schools offered German in the lower grades.[16] The Old Seminary claimed that it specialized in copperplate handwriting, spelling, theology, and arithmetic. Occasionally the school scheduled public speaking programs which consisted of debates, declamations, and essay readings. Debs' name did not appear on any of the programs.[17]

When laws passed in 1867 guaranteed state aid to public schools, Debs transferred from the Old Seminary School into the public school.[18] In the recession after the Civil War, the Debs' store lost money. In 1858 Daniel had built a larger store and home at 11th and Wabash, the edge of the prairie surrounding Terre Haute. The loss of income due to the depression may have forced Eugene to change schools.[19] Most private school pedagogues accepted positions in the public system for better pay. Eugene Debs' name appeared in the "Terre Haute Monthly Records of the Relative Standing of Pupils in Deportment for the School Year 1868," the only known school record with his name on it. As an eighth grader, he compared favorably in deportment with his classmates.[20] When this record was mentioned to a man who knew and admired Debs, he incorrectly surmised, "I'll bet even in school he raised hell."[21] Each month in 1868 Miss Abbie Flagg, Debs' teacher, rated all of her pupils in deportment. A student could attain a maximum of 240 deportment merits in one month. The chart below indicated how Debs compared with his sister, Louisa, and Annie Gehman, teacher's delight.

	September		October		November	
Number in class	68		69		75	
	Merits	Rank	Merits	Rank	Merits	Rank
Louisa Debs	233	6	200	30	210	24
Eugene Debs	225	13	221	17	224	15
Annie Gehman	238	1	239	1	228	11

Because of stern discipline at home, Debs respected authority at school.

What kind of teacher was Abbie Flagg? She was the only teacher, other than Benny Hayes, that Debs mentioned in later life. Since Debs had her for a teacher for two years in high school in addition to the seven years she taught in the Old Seminary School, she undoubtedly had an influence upon Debs. In 1867 she gave Eugene a Bible for not missing a spelling word during the second twenty-two week term. Her terse note to Debs on the flyleaf read, "Read and Obey." A half century later Debs retorted, "I never did either."[22] Abbie's superintendent regarded her as an excellent teacher. When in the fall of 1867 Superintendent Olcott started a series of monthly teachers' meetings, stalwart Abbie never missed a meeting, and appeared more frequently on the programs than other teachers. She gave demonstrations in teaching reading and arithmetic, plus talks on a variety of subjects.[23]

In her teaching, Miss Flagg stressed drill in oral as well as written communication. On November 9, 1867, she presented the monthly lecture, "What Are the Advantages of Oral English?" She advised her colleagues to "fix the attention of their scholars upon the oral subject so that grammar was something practical, and not an occult science." Debs' instructor continued, "If these oral lessons are accompanied with frequent criticisms at any and all times, they . . . form early habits of correct speaking." Perhaps Debs as a future spokesman profited from her tutelage, and received his first formal speech training from her.[24]

During Debs' high school days, the Board of Trustees ordered monthly oral and written reviews and examinations. As students advanced in school, the examinations became more comprehensive. Sometimes Superintendent Wiley, Olcott's successor, constructed questions for the written tests at the close of the term. In 1869, he announced that he had available questions for Debs' high school classes. Debs disliked these examinations but knew better than to cut classes because the school rules required that truants on test days take "double exams" on their return to school. Prominent local citizens presided over the oral quizzing. Wiley disliked this practice because the examiners often knew the students and picked the questions accordingly.[25]

Debs learned French at home. His parents spoke French as much as English. The high school he attended offered Latin or German. Since he took German in the Old Seminary School, and since his father also spoke and read German at home, he continued German in high school. In addition, a notation on the curriculum sheet announced "exercises at regular intervals in composition, rhetoric, and declamation."[26]

Literary societies flourished in Terre Haute around 1870. At least one of these, the Philomathean Literary Club, met at the high school and had high school members. On one program several names from Abbie Flagg's class appeared. Frank McKeen, a close friend and later a banker from whom Debs borrowed money for both labor and Socialist causes, gave an oration titled "Honor." Two debates completed the program: "Resolved, that Benedict Arnold was a greater traitor than Aaron Burr," and "Resolved, that Columbus was a greater American than Washington."[27] Debs attended these programs with his friends.

While in high school, Eugene started his own library. His father gave him the first book, Voltaire's *Philosophical Dictionary*. He assiduously read this volume and quoted from it. "Voltaire! What a Titan upon the world's vast stage! The American people are pitifully ignorant of him," Debs asserted. "His towering figure is too tall for them to see above his shoe tops."[28] During these years Debs read also the plays of Moliére and the poetry of Burns and Whitman. The combination of teachers who placed an emphasis upon literary activities and a father who stressed the same, placed Debs in an environment in which he could explore ideas.

In May 1870, the fourteen-year-old Debs quit school and joined a railroad yard crew. His parents opposed this decision, but Eugene insisted upon helping support the large family. "I need not tell you we were comparatively poor," Debs later stated. "I voluntarily quit school and went to work to learn the painter's trade."[29] In the year that Debs quit school, Superintendent Wiley expressed concern over the large number of absences on Friday afternoons and over the number of dropouts. "Make an attractive and interesting program for all days," he advised, "and show the necessity for attendance at the last as well as the first of the week."[30] Few students in Debs' class finished high school. Only thirteen names appeared on the graduation list of his class.[31] Flagg's deportment records indicated sixty-eight to seventy-five attended in 1868. Debs also probably left school because he had neither the means nor the desire to go on to college.[32] There were a number of courses available in areas that Debs had not studied. Surely several had valuable subject matter for him. The logic, rhetoric, philosophy, and political economy courses might have changed or modified his future opinions.[33] Like most schoolboys who quit school, he frequently expressed regret over the decision. Once he remarked that he felt keenly "his lack of knowledge," especially the power of expression, both oral and written. He tried to improve these skills by studying the structure of sentences and memorizing those he thought striking.[34]

Gene secured his first job in the Vandalia Railroad yards through a friend of his father's. Pierre Solomon, also from Alsace, visited frequently with Daniel and agreed to introduce Gene to his boss, known only as Old

Man Peddle. On May 23, 1870, Debs went to work scraping paint and grease off locomotives for fifty cents a day. It took his first two day's wages to pay for the scraper. When a drunken fireman failed to report for duty in early December 1871, Debs got his advancement to the rails.[35] This position paid one dollar a day. With the additional income, the sixteen-year-old fireman enrolled in the afternoon and evening classes of Garwin's Business College. After classes he would go to work and fire the switch engine in the local yards. Debs took courses in telegraphy, penmanship, bookkeeping, correspondence, account writing, and commercial calculations.[36] From this business college, he received instruction that helped him in his later work as a union clerk, secretary, and president. He left the railroad for a year and worked in a wholesale grocery but the proprietor became irked at Debs' inability to refuse anyone credit. He returned to the railroad and fired the night train to Indianapolis. From these experiences as a student, clerk, and railroad worker, Debs gained his first impressions of the working world and social injustice. He also became independent of his parents and experienced the loneliness of growing up.

He held his railroad job until the recession of 1873 caused a layoff which forced him to seek work outside of Terre Haute. He knew that he could not find railroad work in town and took the first opportunity to "hop a ride" to Evansville. Lacking the money for a ticket, Debs lingered around the railroad yards until a train came through that carried a fireman that he knew. Unable to find a job in Evansville, he went to St. Louis. He spent several anxious weeks seeking work. In a letter to his family, he apologized to his mother for leaving home without saying farewell. "I am so homesick," he admitted, but he added that he hoped after "I get to work I will get a little accustomed to being away from home."[37] He wrote his parents that it made his "heart ache to go along some of the main streets in the city and see men, women and children begging for something to eat,"[38] and he confided to his sisters and brother that they should appreciate their comfortable home and understanding parents. "I did not," he confessed, ". . . until I came over here."[39] While out looking for a job, he discovered that Tom McCabe, a machinist who formerly worked at Seath and Hagers in Terre Haute, had a job as foreman on the St. Louis, Belleville, and Southern Illinois Railroad. He showed him his letter of recommendation. McCabe was impressed with the letter and introduced him to the master mechanic, who promised Debs the next opening.

When his parents found out that Gene had not found work, they quickly advised him to come home. Gene replied that "this winter will see this country in the worst pecuniary embarrassment possible. I can see it better than I could in Terre Haute, for if you had any idea of the hundreds of starving people that I see daily you would not urge me to return to Terre Haute . . . at least as long as I have prospects of an occupation at which I can at least support myself." He assured his parents that he did not want to remain away from home permanently but only asked for time "to save a little money and to prove that I can act manly . . ." Again he acknowledged his loneliness but added that he had met a French family by the name of Duches. "We all speak French," he related to his parents. He also commented that the Duches had a seventeen year old daughter, Lena.

Before concluding Debs replied to his mother's question about whether he knew a young man by the name of Stewart who had been killed in a railroad accident near Terre Haute. Evidentally he had kept the news of the accident from his apprehensive mother because he replied, "I suppose I was aware of this before you. I knew him, and to tell you the truth, I do not sympathize with him a particle as he was a genuine dead beat of the first order. The road that I intend working on is safe as a bed, never having had any ill luck."[40] Whether Debs cared this little for Stewart or indirectly tried to placate his mother by suggesting that Stewart had been careless and that he would not be, is not known. Debs also sent a tip to his sister, Eugenia. He mentioned that Johnie Clay, who had attended a dance in their home, had come to St. Louis and stolen $160 from the bank where he worked and left town. If Eugenia met him again, he warned that she should "stay away from him."

When he received letters from his family, Eugene read them on the St. Louis Post Office steps because he could not wait until he returned to his boarding house. He did find odd jobs around the railroad yard on a day-by-day basis. His parents wrote frequently, inquiring about his job opportunities and health, but his sister Eugenia primarily wanted to know all about Lena, the Duches' young daughter. Debs sent her Lena's picture and hoped that it would answer most of her inquiries. In a note to Theodore, he lamented that bedbugs bothered him greatly. "The other night I killed 37 in my bed in a few minutes," he reported.[41]

In mid-October Debs, then nineteen, secured a position on the regular run of the seventy-eight-mile Belleville Line. He continued railroading until the fall of 1874. He never forgot the difficult time he had finding work. He saw how workers struggled, and he observed that other cities had slums worse than those in Terre Haute. In later life he frequently described the suffering he witnessed during this depression.

Railroads then used unsafe equipment to cut costs. Rails seldom received adequate repairs. Boilers often exploded, burning the wooden coaches. Weak bridges collapsed, and poor couplings smashed men between cars. Railroad deaths became so common that newspapers carried casualty notices only when an accident killed several passengers or crewmen. In 1874 Debs watched in horror as a backing locomotive crushed a friend to death. According to Debs, this death, plus his mother's continuing concern for his safety, prompted him to quit the railroad.[42]

After returning home, he again secured, with his father's help, a position as a warehouseman with Henry Hulman, wholesale grocer. Contrary to other published reports, Debs did not serve as a bookkeeper, but as a loader and packer of orders. His bookkeeping was only incidental to his filling orders. Coleman erroneously called Debs a bookkeeper in his early Debs biography, and other writers repeated the error.[43] Theodore Debs insisted that his brother never held a white-collar job with Hulman's.[44] At Hulman's while lifting barrels of kerosene, he sprained his back. This injury bothered Debs for many years.[45] Although Debs had quit railroading, he continued to attend all local train workers' meetings because he remembered the conditions under which he had worked. If as a young fireman Debs had not experienced the dangers and problems of railroaders, he would never have returned to their meetings or to work later as their organizer.

In 1874 Eugene and a group of friends started the Occidental Literary Club because none of the organized clubs in Terre Haute were willing to invite controversial figures of that time as speakers. As president of the new club, Debs quickly invited Robert Ingersoll to be a guest lecturer. Ingersoll required a fee so large that each member had to advance five dollars in case local citizens refused to buy tickets. Debs eagerly looked forward to the visit of the popular orator. At this time, Debs' highest ambition was to be an orator. He had concluded that the "power of the speaker was infinitely greater than that of the writer."[46] Ingersoll's visit marked the beginning of a lasting friendship and correspondence, and, indeed, Ingersoll became Debs' speaking idol. Debs later recalled that "never until that night had I heard real oratory; never before had I listened enthralled to such eloquence." Ingersoll's speech that so impressed Debs was his famous "Liberty of Man, Woman, and Child."[47] When Ingersoll left on the midnight train for Cincinnati, Debs joined him so that they could continue talking.[48] The financial success of Ingersoll's lecture before a packed house helped the club. They bought clubroom furniture with the profits.[49] Inspired by Ingersoll and convinced of the power of the spoken word, Debs delivered his first public speech before this group. "Everything that was revolutionary appealed to me," Debs recalled. "Thus Patrick Henry and Robert Emmett became my heroes. They were the inspiration for my maiden speech before the Occidental Literary Club. Never shall I forget that racking but memorable occasion. It was then that I realized my need of education and training; so I set to work in earnest to learn what I needed to know. I bought a set of *Appleton's Cyclopaedias* on the installment plan, one volume each month, and began to study seriously."[50] In an interview in 1922 with David Karsner, a friend and biographer, Debs remembered more details about his first speech: "The little room was crowded, and how the cold sweat stood in beads upon my brow when I realized the awful plight I had invited upon myself and the utter hopelessness of escape. The spectacle I made of myself that evening will never be effaced from my memory." At the close of the speech, club members assured Debs that he had not failed. This sympathy did not relieve the keen sense of humiliation and shame he felt for the disgrace he had brought upon himself and his "patron saint, Patrick Henry." Before the speech, Debs asked his parents to attend. This he regretted. When he looked at his father, he knew his opinion of the speech. He had failed. After the meeting, Debs remarked that he hoped his hero's ears "were not attuned to the affairs of this earth, at least not that evening."[51]

In subsequent meetings Debs debated with older members, and frequently made speeches before members and any outsiders who might care to listen. The youthful president persuaded the club to bring to Terre Haute important speakers who spoke as prophets of their time. Through this club, Debs met Wendell Phillips and Susan B. Anthony. When the club balked at sponsoring the "radical" Miss Anthony, Debs asked Mrs. Ida Husted Harper, a Terre Haute woman who later became Miss Anthony's biographer, to help him sponsor the speech. He frequently recounted this memorable occasion: "She seemed completely absorbed in her mission. She scarcely spoke of anything else. The rights and wrongs of her sex seemed to possess her completely."[52] When Debs and Miss Anthony walked along the street, he recalled resentfully that Miss Anthony was an object of derision and contempt. Few attended Miss Anthony's lecture because they thought it was improper for women to speak in public on political issues. Debs admitted that "it wouldn't have taken any great amount of egging-on to have excited the people to drive her from the community."[53] Two years later Debs requested Miss Anthony to return, and the hall overflowed. Attitudes toward women speakers had changed, and Anthony's fame attracted an audience.[54]

Born just a block away from the taverns and whorehouses of early Terre Haute, Debs at twenty knew only a few railroaders outside of his home city. His boyhood coincided with the Civil War and two depressions. His father supported the Union cause, but many local citizens refused to do so. Fourth of July celebrations required two separate parks during the war. Debs saw troops move through Terre Haute and later the wounded returned to a local hospital. After the war he observed crippled men idle in the streets. The depressions indelibly imprinted upon his mind the plight of the working man in economic crises.

During Debs' formative years, his parents exerted a firm yet understanding control over his activities. Although the father wanted his son to join him in the grocery business, he did not force this choice. Free to make his own decisions, Debs at twenty had gained experience as a paint scraper, a railroader, and warehouse laborer. A family friend later reported that "it was a wonderful family into which Debs was born. It was wonderful because of the affection that the children gave to their parents and to each other."[55] Debs echoed this sentiment in a speech at the 50th wedding anniversary banquet of his parents: "There are two words in our language forever sacred to memory—Mother and Home!"[56] Debs made the most of the advantages of poverty and a mediocre education. Poverty reinforced his instincts of human sympathy and close family feelings—instincts he later relied upon and found valuable. When his railroad friends told him about a forthcoming meeting possibly to organize a union, Debs promised to attend. Although no longer a railroad fireman, he agreed that such an organization might help his friends.

Chapter II
Blue-Denim Spokesman

It took little persuasion by Joshua Leach, an Eastern labor organizer, who came to Terre Haute on February 27, 1875, to get Eugene V. Debs to join his first labor union, the Brotherhood of Locomotive Firemen. "Old Josh Leach, a typical locomotive fireman of his day, founded the Brotherhood," Debs recalled, "and I was instantly attracted by his rugged honesty, simple manner, and homely speech." Because of Debs' interest in the problems of trainmen, his former co-workers recommended to Leach that he appoint Debs as organizer. Leach said to Debs, "My boy, you're a little young but I believe you will make your mark in the Brotherhood."[1]

Immediately Debs began to organize other Terre Haute firemen. He established headquarters in a rented room at Seventh and Wabash.[2] After work at Hulman's, he would rush to the office to answer the mail. In the evening he would go to the pool halls and taverns where the railroaders congregated and encourage them to join Vigo Lodge, Number 16. Three months after the February 27 meeting and after receiving many new membership cards from Debs, Mr. Leach told an audience in St. Louis, "I put a tow-headed boy in the Brotherhood at Terre Haute not long ago, and some day he will be the head of it."[3] Later that same year Debs helped P. J. McGuire organize a local for the Brotherhood of Carpenters and Joiners in Terre Haute.[4]

In addition to his duties as local organizer, the railroaders elected Debs recording secretary. He carefully kept records and entered into the minutes only the essential items of business. From these minutes, however, one can gain insights into what interested Debs and what he thought important enough to record. These minutes reveal a sympathetic, if somewhat self-righteous, young Debs. He included little of the members' discussion.[5] From the beginning, the lodge members, who referred to one another as brothers, concerned themselves with providing aid for those who were injured and for widows whose husbands were killed. Since dues never covered all of the expenses in the first years of the union, members accepted additional assessments to assist their injured brothers. In addition to helping sick members pay their bills, the lodge sometimes loaned money. Often the loans and death assessments were only for ten or twelve dollars. For example, death assessments No. 11 and No. 12 were $10.25 each; sick benefits for W. Fluegge $10, M. Cadle $5, J. Benz $5.[6] When a member died, the lodge helped make arrangements for the funeral and attended en masse. For example, when William Saunders, a friend of Debs', was killed in an engine collision on the Vandalia Railroad, a union committee headed by Debs, sent $5 for flowers and paid $15 for music and a minister.[7]

Members attempted to improve their image as workers by policing and barring from lodge meetings those men who drank excessively, visited houses of prostitution, or cursed in public. Charles A. Baker, the first "black-balled" member of Vigo Lodge No. 16, was dismissed for drunkenness.[8] In all such cases demanding censure of members, the union master appointed a committee which investigated the charges, interviewed the accused, and reported at the next meeting. Debs frequently served on these committees. In one case, the lodge permitted a member to tend bar only until he could find a better second job.[9] The lodge approved moonlighting if the job was considered respectable. On another occasion when David De Wolf "engaged in the sale of intoxicating liquors," he applied for a withdrawal card which the lodge promptly granted.[10]

Another committee which Debs participated in reported that they had given Bill Snodgrass "a fair and impartial trial," and, since Snodgress refused to apologize to J. Benz for "slanderous remarks," they recommended expulsion. After a long discussion, the members expelled Snodgrass. At a later meeting Debs moved for Snodgrass' reinstatement and read a letter in which Snodgrass apologized to Benz.[11] Debs often introduced motions that enabled repentant members to rejoin.

Although Debs staunchly supported the idea of health benefits, he objected to R. Snabley's request for total disability benefits from the order. He demanded proof that Snabley's disability had not been "brought about by his immoral conduct." Debs implied that venereal disease rather than a railroad injury caused Snabley's ill health. The members passed his motion and selected a Dr. Roberts as examiner. Another member, J. D. White, charged William Payne for "associating with prostitutes contrary to the teaching of the order." The committee appointed to investigate these charges later dropped them for lack of proof.[12] This action did not deter Debs' moral righteousness campaign, because he later accused Brother Dearman of disgracing the order by failing to pay his board bill, saloon bill, and "acting unbecoming conduct."[13] Debs never elaborated upon the curious last charge.

Other items in the minutes indicate Debs' early concern about safety. Debs recorded with the death notices comments on how the accident happened. In the interest of safety, sometimes the union aided the railroad company. When Gorm Smith attempted to become an engineer, in spite of his "enlarged heart and valve trouble," Debs headed a committee that investigated the matter and advised railroad officials not to hire Smith. Debs continued as secretary for eight years until the members elected him master of the lodge on July 22, 1883, a position he held for five years.[14]

Debs took vacation time to attend national meetings of his Brotherhood. In 1876 he attended the session in New York and saw this city for the first time. He wrote his eleven year old brother how lonesome he felt in the large city and promised never to leave home again. "There are thousands of little boys here of your age who are working hard almost for nothing and have no place to go when the cold night comes," he reported. "You ought to see how sad they look and you ought to be happy."[15] At the convention a year later he began to work on committees and take an active part in the running of the national organization. He also found time to enjoy a ball and no longer mentioned being lonesome at conventions. This year when he wrote his younger brother he said: "I am playing the gentleman. I have also been to the theatre twice this week and two evenings I worked on committees until 2 A.M."[16] Shortly after this convention Debs began to write articles for the union's magazine. Two years later at the 1878 Buffalo, New York, meeting, the Brotherhood of Locomotive Firemen delegates elected Debs associate editor of their magazine.

In all of these activities, Debs at twenty-four had impressed his local firemen brothers. They recognized his leadership potential and insisted that he run in 1879 as a Democrat for Terre Haute city clerk. He left Hulman's to campaign and began his career as a political figure. He won and soon incurred the disfavor of the strong party machine by insisting upon his own appointments. Debs refused to use patronage and insisted upon merit and qualifications as criteria for his office help. He fulfilled his clerk duties well and made his office a model of efficiency and service to taxpayers.[17] Only one other Democrat in 1881 won re-election, and Debs' vote margin led the field of local candidates.[18] Debs' victory gave him the leadership of the local Democrats, and the weakened party machine made no new patronage demands upon him.

In addition to his political duties, Debs had accepted the editorship of the *Firemen's Magazine* in 1880. He spent most of his salary as clerk in securing the debt of the National Brotherhood of Locomotive Firemen and its magazine so that they would not go bankrupt.[19]. The total expenses of the journal and the benefit payments often exceeded the dues and subscription income. The officers of the First National Bank in Terre Haute came to know Debs and trust his judgment.

In 1883, Debs disappointed his supporters when he refused to run for a third term as city clerk. He declined because he wanted to work full time as an organizer and editor. By spending all of his time writing for the journal and soliciting members, Debs hoped to improve the Union's finances. In 1884, however, his political friends persuaded him to run for the Indiana General Assembly. Debs viewed this as an opportunity to secure needed legislation for the railroads. He made a brief campaign and won easily. On January 8, 1885, Debs at thirty took his seat in the Indiana House of Representatives. He received the committee assignments that he wanted: railroads, corporations, and engrossed bills.[20] On January 12, 1885, Terre Haute's young representative introduced his first two bills, which closely related to his earlier concerns about workers' safety. House Bill No. 91 concerned the classification and grading of locomotive engineers by railway corporations and rules in declaring an emergency. House Bill No. 92 pertained to the liability of corporations for injuries sustained by their employees.[21] He introduced other bills, but concentrated his efforts upon getting these two passed. Although he succeeded in the House with these bills, the Senate added crippling amendments. Debs regretfully withdrew the bills. The young legislator attracted some further attention as a speaker in this session when he nominated Daniel W. Vorhees of Vigo County for United States Senator.[22]

Discouraged with politics, he adamantly refused a second term. Years later Debs summed up his feelings toward his legislative experience when he said: "There was a time in my life, before I became a Socialist, when I permitted myself as a Democrat to be elected to a state legislature. I have been trying to live it down. I am as much ashamed of that as I am proud of having gone to jail."[23]

Between his union and legislative duties in 1885, Debs found time to do some dating. For several years rumor had circulated in Terre Haute that Debs planned to marry Katherine Metzel, whom he met through his sister Marie. The two young ladies often attended local concerts and meetings together. At first Debs would walk Katherine home when she came to visit Marie and his parents. In 1882, townspeople noticed that Katherine occasionally accompanied Debs to plays and lectures at the old Opera House. Katherine, like Eugene, had known hardship as a child. Her father died when she was seven, leaving her mother with two children to rear. Later her mother married John Baur, a widower with four children, and they moved from Louisville to Terre Haute. The Baurs had four more children and Katherine spent her days helping her mother cook, clean, and sew for the large family. Although Baur established what became a profitable drug business in Terre Haute, Katherine grew up with few luxuries. Mr. Baur insisted upon college educations and travel for his sons but saw no need for his daughters to do the same.

After Eugene proposed in February, 1885 Katherine spent months planning their wedding. She insisted upon going to Louisville to shop for her trousseau. To symbolize the beginning of their new life together, they decided to marry at dawn on June 9, 1885. Debs' labor friends as well as John Baur's prosperous business friends attended the large wedding in St. Stephen's Episcopal Church. After a two week honeymoon in the East, the young couple returned to Terre Haute and rented a small three room apartment at 323 South Sixth Street. Debs, broke from the expenses of the trip, quickly went back to work and soon found himself on a cross-country union organizing tour. Katherine protested the separation but failed to dissuade Eugene.

In addition to the firemen, Debs assisted at this time in the organization of Terre Haute and other Indiana unions for carpenters, printers, and miners. He began to travel extensively to help organize the Brotherhood of Railroad Brakemen, the Switchmen's Mutual Aid Association, the Brotherhood of Railway Carmen, and the Order of Railway Telegraphers. The Western Federation of Miners and the United Mine Workers employed Debs as a special organizer for difficult areas.[24] "My grip was always packed," he asserted, "and I was darting in all directions. To tramp through a railroad yard in the rain, snow or sleet half the night, or till daybreak, to be ordered out of the roundhouse for being an agitator, or put off the train, while attempting to deadhead over the division, were all part of the program and served to whet my appetite to organize the railroad workers."[25] Through these travels Debs became well known in the increasing number of locals in his union. In 1886, his Brotherhood of Locomotive Firemen elected him national secretary-treasurer, and editor-manager of the *Firemen's Magazine*. He continued in these capacities until 1892.[26]

When called upon to speak as a national officer, Debs often proclaimed that "the labor question was born of the first pang of protest that died unvoiced in the breast of unrequited toil, and the labor movement of modern times is the product of past ages."[27] Through his work as an organizer and editor, Debs hoped to establish unions where laborers could voice their protests. "The wrongs in labor I knew from having experienced them, and the irresistible appeal of these wrongs to be righted determined my destiny," Debs wrote. "The high ambition and controlling purpose in my life has been the education, organization and emancipation of the working class. . . . In this there was no altruism, no self-sacrifice, only duty. I could not have done otherwise."[28]

The following statistics indicate the scope of the problems Debs faced and why he felt challenged to work hard to establish unions. America's rapid industrial growth in the 1880's had increased labor's problems. The number of wage earners in manufacturing increased from 2,750,000 in 1880 to 5,880,000 in 1890. The railway mileage of the United States expanded from 93,239 miles to 163,579 in the decade 1880-1890.[29] In this period when Debs started speaking for labor, the trust became the most popular form of industrial combination. The number of patents increased from 13,000 in the seventies to 21,000 annually in the eighties.[30] New patented machines replaced workers faster than they could find re-employment.

These conditions convinced Debs that labor had to organize or suffer. The United States census of 1870 estimated the average annual income at slightly over $400 per capita. The census of 1880 placed it at $333. By 1890, railroad engineers received $957; conductors, $575; firemen, $337; brakemen, $212; switchmen, $294; flagmen, $224; baggagemen, $311; laborers, $124; telegraph operators, $235.[31] Engineers received "preferential" pay and refused to unionize. Debs deplored this practice. Railroad management set the engineer's scale high enough to prevent their gaining by organizing with other railroad trades. Editor Debs printed these figures and remarks in the January 1894, issue of the *Locomotive Firemen's Magazine*: "According to Interstate Commerce Commission's reports, there were 2,070 workers killed and 20,148 injured on the railroads in 1880; 2,554 killed and 28,267 injured in 1892; and 2,727 killed and 31,729 injured in 1893. This means one railroad worker was killed out of every 115 employed, and one injured out of every ten employed."[32] Railroad managers continued to reduce their working force and required men to do double duty; the resulting loss of rest and sleep increased injuries and deaths.

Debs charged that the greed of the corporations indirectly caused accidents. In many factories workers spent fifteen and sixteen hours at their jobs, from five in the morning until nine at night. Some workers saved both time and rent by sleeping on bundles of goods in the shop. A New York garment maker earned nine dollars a week for six working days of fifteen hours each.[33] These working conditions in America in the late 1800's help explain why large audiences gathered to hear Debs speak on labor questions, and why workers from Colorado to New York invited Debs to help them organize.[34] In a speech before a large Southern crowd, the young labor spokesman declared, "Every age has its problem to solve. The labor question is the question of the world today. The amassing of great wealth of late in the United States has been without parallel. Labor has organized in self-defense." Debs told this audience that "if all employers had always treated their employees fairly, there would never have been a single labor union in the world." "A businessman picks up his morning paper and reads that there is a strike," Debs stated. "He has some goods on the road and he says, 'Damn those strikers!' He never takes time to think that probably the other side is to blame."[35]

Since Debs had little money, he begged rides on the engine, and shared food with the trainmen. While en route to the next speaking engagement, Debs talked to the railroaders instead of sleeping. He did some effective organizing from the engine to the caboose, convincing workers that they needed the Brotherhood's plan for mutual aid in case of accidents or death.[36] When he reached his destination, he cleaned up as best he could and proceeded with caution "to look up 'the boys', careful to elude the vigilance of the boss, who had no use for a worthless labor agitator."[37] Under these conditions, Debs served his apprenticeship as a spokesman for labor.

From the founding of the Brotherhood of Locomotive Firemen in 1873 until July 1887, when the firemen struck the Brooklyn Elevated Railroad, the organization had never authorized a strike. "Strikes are the knives with which laborers cut their own throats," Debs wrote in the *Firemen's Magazine* in 1883.[38] Although the Brotherhood of Locomotive Firemen's constitution permitted strikes in 1885, Debs failed to mention them in his address to the annual convention that year. Instead he advocated "honesty, purity, and sobriety" as a motto for the firemen. "To drink and carouse has been shown to be incompatible with good health, a good conscience and honest toil," he declared. "Our fundamental principle is justice," continued the young organizer. "In times of disaster and depreciation of values we will not mistake unavoidable depression for tyrannical imposition. But in prosperity we expect our due share."[39] During these years Debs believed in arbitration as the answer to conflicts between management and labor. If workers could gain recognition and respect at the bargaining table, Debs saw no need for strikes.

Katherine became accustomed to Eugene's frequent absences. She had long dreamed of her own home and frugally saved from Eugene's salary for this purpose. On March 20, 1889, Debs paid $4,000 for a lot on North Eighth Street in a fashionable section of Terre Haute. Katherine drew preliminary plans for a large eight room house with full basement and a third floor for storage of Eugene's growing collection of newspapers and magazines. He liked to keep copies of what he read and made large scrapbooks of clippings reporting his speeches. She imported Italian tile for the fireplaces in each room and Honduras mahogany for the library cabinets and mantel. When the house was finished in 1890, Katherine held an open house. In answer to critics, who soon began to say that a labor leader had no business living in such a fine house in a wealthy neighborhood, Debs replied honestly that they had built the house out of his savings and a legacy Mrs. Debs received when an aunt died in Louisville.

By 1890, Debs had a staff of eleven workers and 18,000 members in the Brotherhood. He proposed these terms to the workers: Every member pays an annual fee of $20; in case of death the society pays the heirs $1,500; and in all cases of disability from accident or sickness a weekly allowance is made. An additional $1.50 goes to the Grand Lodge. Admission must be preceded by one year's work as a fireman.[40] Through speaking and writing Debs increased interest in the *Firemen's Magazine,* and although Brotherhood membership totaled only 18,000 in 1890, the organization printed and sold 28,000 magazines.[41] At Debs' request, Ida Harper directed the women's section of the magazine.[42] The Brotherhood also had problems. Prior to 1885, in what Debs called "forty nine contests" with railroad managers, the Brotherhood had never won a complete victory. After 1885, the Brotherhood authorized four strikes and lost two of them. They lost the Burlington and the Ann Arbor strikes but won the New York Elevated and the Carondelet and East St. Louis strike. Striking, fired or laid-off workers lacked funds to pay fees and created another problem. Debs strongly objected to the organization's policy of expelling men who could not keep up their insurance assessments,[43] and succeeded in getting the rule changed.

Three events in 1892 convinced Debs that the craft union method of organizing laborers had limitations. At Carnegie Steel in Homestead, Pennsylvania, Henry Frick with the aid of Pinkerton detectives and eight thousand state troops enforced a lockout that destroyed one of the strongest craft unions in America. In the silver miners' strike at Coeur d'Alene, Idaho, President Benjamin Harrison ordered federal troops to restore order. This federal intervention on the side of management defeated the craft unionists. Strikebreakers with New York court support broke the Buffalo Switchmen's Strike. What caused these strikes? Each of these companies suffered when the recession of 1893 started, and consequently wages dropped, part time work replaced full time, and unemployment increased. Union members led strikes to regain their losses.

The idea of one large combined union for all employees in an industry had fascinated Debs for some time. "Federation means unity and strength," he declared. "It is many in one."[44] In discussing federation, Debs stated,

"It should be understood that the proposition is power versus power." In this same 1890 article the Firemen's secretary-editor lamented that labor had no other choice: "I see little opportunity for sentiment. I recognize the fact the battle is on."[45] Since the other officers of the Brotherhood of Locomotive Firemen believed in the craft type union, Debs submitted his resignation at the Cleveland convention in 1892. The delegates protested, but Debs insisted upon his freedom to pursue this new idea. They voted him a $2,000 gift for a European trip as a reward for his services. Although appreciating their generosity, he told them to put the money in their welfare fund. He gave up the $3,000 a year post as secretary-treasurer of the organization but continued at the delegates' insistence as editor of their journal for $1,000 a year.[46]

Debs decided to attend a meeting of fifty concerned and irritated railroaders in Chicago on June 20, 1893.[47] At this meeting he convinced these delegates from various craft unions of the merits of federation. If all railroad employees joined a single union, he pleaded, management would have to arbitrate their demands, or cease to operate. Later Debs stated, "The Panic of 1893 had come. It was an opportune time to organize the American Railway Union. This was done. I became its head."[48] He accepted a salary of $75.00 a month.

As the new union's leader, Debs left Chicago and started on a speaking tour to organize and federate railroaders into one big union. In this position he now had a chance to spread his ideas, not only about federation but about welfare benefits, to more than just firemen. Within twenty days after the first lodge started in Fort Madison, Iowa, thirty-four ARU locals received charters. Debs interrupted his organizing to accept an invitation from Henry Demarest Lloyd to speak at the Columbian Exposition in Chicago.[49] In this speech Debs proclaimed his new philosophy that labor could assert its independence by combining into an organization that capitalists had to recognize. "What can labor do for itself?" he challenged. "Labor can organize, it can unify, it can consolidate its forces. This done, it can demand and command."[50]

Since few newspapers in 1893 printed Debs' speeches or writings, he had them privately published in Chicago and Terre Haute. About this time Debs published a pamphlet titled, *You Railroad Men*.[51] In this pamphlet he stated that he wanted the American Railway Union to embrace all railway workers, so that the engine wiper and section men might come in for their share of consideration as well as the engineer and conductor. "That is where I broke with the railway officials," Debs wrote. "They were perfectly willing that we should have a firemen's union, but they were not willing for us to have a union that would unite all employees in the equal interest of all."[52] In a speech in Spokane, Washington, Debs effectively summarized his federation idea in these analogies: "I liken this form of organization to a great roundhouse. One roof covers all, but there are different compartments for different departments." Each branch had exclusive supervision of all interests pertaining to the trade or occupation that it represented. "I use this figure frequently—separate as the waves, yet united as the seas."[53] In all addresses he argued that management gained with craft unions because they used these separate unions to keep the workers divided. He thought it unfair for management to use one part of the working force to conquer and crush another part. Within less than one year of the founding of the ARU in Chicago in 1893, the organization faced its first strike tests. Certainly the new union found early a formidable opponent in James J. Hill and his Great Northern Company.

In March 1894, the Union Pacific secured an injunction forbidding a strike by the American Railway Union. During the first week of April, 1894, the ARU in its first test case, won a court hearing in Omaha against this railroad. The judge ordered old pay schedules restored, and declared the injunction illegal. Two weeks later James J. Hill, owner of the Great Northern, ordered a series of wage cuts which forced the average income of all workers on that line to $40 per month. While Hill reduced wages, he never lowered passenger and freight rates. This especially irritated the wheat farmers who depended upon the railroad.[54] On April 13, 1894, the ARU called for a strike. Debs went to St. Paul and took charge of the strike. Immediately Debs called representatives of the strikers into conference to hear their grievances firsthand. After other meetings with the presidents of the Brotherhood of Locomotive Firemen, Brotherhood of Carmen, Brotherhood of Locomotive Engineers, he received assurance that their unions would not meddle in the strike if Hill would arbitrate.[55] To unify the strikers Debs spoke before groups of workers in and around St. Paul. In St. Cloud, he said that he "preferred to agitate rather than stagnate" until every laboring man received an adequate wage. He asked his listeners not to deprecate strikers because every star and stripe in the flag represented a successful strike for liberty. In this address, as in all other telegrams, interviews, and speeches, Debs urged his supporters "to be firm but commit no violence."[56]

Hill circulated the rumor throughout Minnesota and North Dakota that the ARU planned to end the strike. He did this because he did not want the strike to spread north of St. Cloud. In the first two weeks of the strike, Hill had succeeded in partially curbing the extent of the strike by hiring strike breakers and by convincing Grover Cleveland to send troops from Fort Snelling to maintain order. Two of Minneapolis' leading newspapers supported Hill and printed distorted reports of the strike.[57] According to the pro-Hill papers, the Great Northern trains ran with little or no interference. Although Hill obviously had this influence over Minneapolis presses, *The St. Paul Globe* and newspapers along the line overwhelmingly supported the ARU.[58] By April 27, the entire Great Northern system had been affected. When Debs heard of Hill's rumors, he countered with telegrams to the newspapers and local ARU branches along the line. Debs knew that he had a strong supporter in Editor A. W. Edwards of the

Fargo Forum and could count upon him to spread the news in his popular and widely circulated paper in both Minnesota and North Dakota. Edwards had formerly worked for the *Fargo Argus,* a newspaper that Hill owned. "Absolutely no truth in the reports of my withdrawal. Am here to stay," Debs wired Edwards, "until the men secure their rights. The situation is extremely favorable and success is assured."[59] Hill persisted in trying to run the trains by putting eight to ten deputy marshals on board. Hotel managers and storekeepers along the Great Northern line refused to rent rooms or sell groceries to these men they called "scabs." In fact the owners of the O'Brian Hotel in Moorhead, Minnesota, went so far as to change the name of their hotel to "The Debs House" to honor the ARU men.[60] To counter this reaction Hill had to add dining cars and carry food supplies. In spite of Debs' admonitions to commit no damage, several raidroad bridges between Minot, North Dakota, and the Montana border were burned. Each side in the controversy blamed the other for the burning and no later investigations settled the question. ARU members sometimes fooled Hill and his deputies by various maneuvers, especially abandoning trains on the main line on the vast open prairies of North Dakota. For example, when Hill demanded that additional federal troops sent to Grand Forks, North Dakota, go on to Devils Lake and Minot, North Dakota, and Great Falls, Montana, the trainmen willingly cooperated. But after fifteen miles of the one hundred mile trip to Devils Lake, the crew abandoned the train west of Grand Forks and suggested the soldiers would enjoy walking the rest of the way to Devils Lake.[61] In other towns switchmen in the yards refused to turn the trains around, and they forced some trains to run backward if they ran at all. Federal officers operating under orders from Attorney General Olney made numerous arrests, especially in Grand Forks and Barnesville, Minnesota. Local judges consistently dismissed the charges for insufficient evidence. The editor of the Jamestown *Capitol* summarized the sentiments of the anti-Hill forces when he wrote: "This would not be so if the people did not believe the men had justice on their side. The people are disposed to look upon such matters from the standpoint of common sense justice and not with prejudice against the railroads."[62]

When the strike began to affect business in the Twin Cities, the Board of Trade there appointed a conference committee to sit as a court to hear both sides of the dispute. By the last week in April many mills along the Great Northern line had closed down, including those owned by Charles Pillsbury. The fact that Pillsbury became chairman of this committee did not surprise Debs or his supporters! Pillsbury, largest of the mill owners, stood to lose even more money if the strike continued into the harvest season. By the time the conference committee met, Debs had consolidated his forces, especially his liaison with other railroad unions. Since the ARU at this time consisted largely of firemen members, this liaison was important. In the first meeting, after Debs had made his presentation, Hill arose and said, "I guess you have played your last card—haven't you?" "No," replied

Debs quietly. "I think I can play another, if necessary." "Do you mean that you can call out the engineers?" "Yes, I can call them out in five minutes, if I want to."[63] Hill knew Debs well enough by this time to know that this was not an idle threat and decided to cooperate with this committee.

The strike ended after eighteen days when Hill agreed to restore wages to the approximate level of August of 1893.[64] By comparison the earlier Union Pacific victory attracted little national attention compared to the publicity after the Great Northern strike. Newspaper reporters proclaimed the Great Northern settlement on April 29, 1894, as the first ARU victory.[65] When Debs returned to Terre Haute, the Brazil Cornet Band, followed by members of the Typographical Union, the Cigar Makers Union, and the local ARU, led a parade of four thousand people to meet the train. On an improvised platform behind the Terre Haute Hotel, Debs told the crowd, "One of the remarkable features of this victory is that the great idea of arbitration has been firmly established in America. Arbitration means mutual concessions; it means peaceful adjustment of all difficulties between the employee and the employers. These men on the Great Northern made a noble stand. The solid ranks of capital were met with solid ranks of labor."[66] As a result of this strike the Great Northern workers gained $146,000 more each month, or 97.5% of what they demanded. With pride Debs asserted: "Another remarkable feature of this victory is that not a drop of blood was shed on the system . . . this fact triumphantly proves that great permanent reform can be achieved without violence and force."[67] After the speech Debs answered a reporter's question about his opinion of James Hill. Debs praised Hill as a man willing to change when forced to arbitrate and stated that he felt sure the railroad men of the Great Northern would have no more trouble. The young ARU spokesman concluded: "The strike was admirably conducted. The men guarded the company's property night and day, and not a pin was pulled or a pound of freight stolen."[68] Because of this strike, Debs modified his earlier view that arbitration alone could settle differences. He recognized that arbitration worked with Hill because the strike was successful.

Although Debs spoke enthusiastically of the terms of the settlement, Hill's officers did not immediately carry out the terms of the agreement. Debs interrupted an organizing tour in the Chicago area and returned to Minneapolis on May 15, 1894. By the time that he arrived, representatives of the railroaders from the Western divisions of the line had decided that the managers had taken advantage of them. Tempers flared and the Western contingent declared that one of their leaders, Ben Hogan, was more aggressive than Debs and should meet Hill. Debs maintained that he and vice-president Howard of the ARU could settle the issue, for he had no indications that the officers of the Great Northern would not keep their promises to the arbitration committee. The management was guilty of slowly implementing the agreement and had not rehired some men involved in the strike, including the men who had abandoned their trains between stations. Another objection that affected many more workers was that clerks and other general office workers had not had their pay restored. In the debate over these issues, Debs cautioned some of those present "against allowing their indignation to overcome their prudence."[69] Debs reiterated that he expected Hill to keep his word. Further meetings with the officials of the Great Northern led to an amicable settlement of all the issues.[70]

Certainly Hogan, noted for his fiery temper and outspoken manner, could not have stepped into the situation and commanded the respect of Hill or other members of the committee. Debs and Howard appealed in a rational way to the committee and succeeded in pointing out that Hill indeed had an ethical responsibility to keep his word. Years later James Hill remarked, "Gene Debs is the squarest labor leader I have ever known. He cannot be bought, bribed or intimidated. He never deals under the table, and his spoken word is as good as his bond or signed contract. I know. I have dealt with him and been well spanked."[71]

Chapter III
The Pullman Ordeal

Success in the Great Northern strike caused membership in the ARU to increase rapidly. It also created in other railroad unions the desire to correct their grievances immediately through strikes. This pressure under the fire of increasing worker protests further tested and modified the ideas and techniques that Debs used as a leader. On June 26, 1894, the Pullman strike started. The strike edict followed a committee investigation made during the ARU convention in Chicago. Since so many of the members were new to the organization, Debs feared that they would lack the discipline, cooperation with other unions, and resources to carry out what could develop into a long strike against an obstinate and wealthy opponent, George Pullman. Delegates listened to Debs' counsel and might have agreed with his caution if a young girl, Jennie Curtis, who worked in the Pullman laundry shops, had not asked to address the convention. Without embellishment she told the delegates that her father, although a skilled mechanic, had found it impossible, with sickness in his family, to keep both ends even. He died owing the company $65 rent after having worked for it eleven years. In tears the girl stated that immediately after his death she received written notice that she could not remain with the company unless she agreed to pay the debt in installments out of her pay—money she needed to support herself and other family members. "It was this case that decided the union to give their aid to the oppressed Pullman workers," Debs later declared.[1] Delegates representing 465 local unions and 150,000 employees voted to strike.[2] Although Debs had opposed this strike because he thought the odds too great, once the organization made its decision, he joined the battle.[3]

This strike which became famous in the annals of labor history did not simply happen. It had been years in the making and like the earlier ARU strikes, including the Great Northern, represented a breaking out by the workers from the pressures of management. In 1893 labor and capital battled with such great fury because it was a showdown of forces. Laborers felt they had little to lose under the system that operated. They were disillusioned with their share of the profits and sensed that the industrialists cared little for their welfare. These labor troubles followed years of mutual hate and distrust. Attempts to unionize resulted in workers being dismissed and then blacklisted from finding further work. Too many managers had the opinion that they should set the hours, wages and working conditions, and labor had to accept or starve. The hours were excessively long, health and safety measures inadequate and although wages increased from 1860 to 1890, the commodities and services workers had to buy increased at a far greater rate. Wage cuts and layoffs in this period made it impossible for workers to make ends meet. They were simply caught in an economic squeeze play that made them desperate.

This was all certainly true of the activities of George Pullman. Although he built an attractive model village for his workers to live in, he had ulterior motives for doing so. He wanted to keep his workers under his control, including no drinking, and everything he established in the village, from the store to the library, turned a profit. Workers had to buy library cards! He bought utilities from the city of Chicago and dispensed them to his workers' homes at exorbitant profits. Pullman consistently paid a dividend to his shareholders. He saw his first and primary obligations to his shareholders and he never wanted them to lose faith in his company. He did this at the expense of his workers.

George Pullman, creator of the Palace Car Company, hoped to save the huge profits gained from the World Fair traffic of 1893. Early in the recession that started in 1893, he discharged one-third of his workers and cut the wages of those remaining thirty per cent. Rents and grocery prices in Pullman, a company town, remained the same.[4] Debs never forgot the fact that Pullman reduced the wages and refused to lower the rent and price of groceries. He frequently retold this story in his speeches. Rent in comparable housing in nearby Roseland was one-half the price in Pullman. When Pullman refused to arbitrate, Debs, as president of the ARU, gave financial aid to the strikers. Debs ordered all members on twenty-five different railroad lines to refuse to work on any train that used Pullman cars and equipment. The railways quickly hired men to replace the strikers, but non-striking engineers and firemen refused to risk their lives by working with the "green hands." The General Managers Association, whose membership included twenty-four railroads, backed Pullman and ordered their employees to pull his coaches. During this strike the Association, known as the G.M.A., opened offices for hiring men; furnished lawyers for legal advice to members; released daily press reports; maintained constant contact with the civil and military authorities involved. With fewer funds, Debs organized a small staff that kept sending countless telegrams to the strikers scattered over 4,500 miles of rail lines. Later, through pressure from the G.M.A., federal court officials issued subpoenas requiring local telegraph companies to produce the messages.[5] In a typical telegram Debs wrote, "I realize tremendous pressure laid on you, but this is the hour of all times when determined manhood must prevail. Cincinnati, Toledo, St. Paul, St. Louis, Duluth, Council Bluffs with many other important points are more determined than any time since inagurated. Newspapers and rumors would have you believe business has been resumed in these places as usual. The fact is they are paralyzed . . ."[6]

Most Chicago newspapers supported Mr. Pullman. Nym Crinkle's account typified the reporting:

Forty eight hours ago nobody outside of the ARU ever heard of Mr. Eugene V. Debs . . . Westward from Chicago, Mr. Debs' imperious hand stretched, Kansas was dumb and trade stood still . . . The U.S. mail for six hundred miles had to catch the local trains from town to town. . . The mysterious Mr. Debs, like the Black Death, was spreading over the continent and there was no escape from him. . . Mr. Debs. . . leans too decidedly to the side of revolution, and there is a suspicion that he may be a Caesar in his ambition.[7]

After the strike one reporter for the *Chicago Journal* wrote Debs: "I fear I wrote you up somewhat harshly, for I represented a sheet that was decidedly antagonistic to labor."[8]

Following Cleveland's edict that the trains must run because the mail service had been interrupted by violence, the Federal Court in Chicago issued an injunction against the ARU. Cleveland ordered federal troops to Chicago to enforce his edict. Throughout the strike, Debs talked daily to the workers and had insisted upon no violence.[9] Since Debs denied any connection with any disorder and blamed company strike-breakers for the trouble, he defied the injunction on July 12, and called for labor leaders to continue the strike—an action which led to his arrest and six months imprisonment in Woodstock Jail. The Chicago Chief of Police in his report supported Debs' contention: "It is a notable fact there was no trouble where there were no troops. In all cases where the police were left to themselves peace was preserved, property was kept uninjured and interference with non-union workers was trifling . . . The U.S. troops came near being held responsible for the entire trouble."[10] Debs refused to turn over the books of the ARU because he knew that the membership lists would be used for blacklisting purposes.[11]

After tedious trial preparations and days in court, Debs never received a jury verdict. Magnate Pullman ignored a court order to appear and answer questions from Debs' lawyer, Clarence Darrow. Pullman left town and went East to attend his business interests. In challenging Thomas Milchrist, the federal attorney, to prove that Debs and his officers had conspired to destroy property or obstruct the mails, Darrow remarked, "This is a historical case that will count much for liberty or against liberty." Darrow relinquished a promising career as a corporation lawyer to plead the case because he thought Debs innocent and the strikers justified in demanding a redress. When a juror became ill, Judge William A. Woods cancelled the trial after repeated delays, but sentenced Debs and six other ARU officers for contempt.

Reaction continued in the press. "But now that it is all over and you are willing to let the government of the United States continue business at the old stand," the editor of the *New York Tribune* addressed Debs, "do you think that it was really worth while?" "You have been lucky," he continued. "They hanged a man in Chicago for committing only one murder. He knew less than you do."[12] Other journalists disagreed. The *Chicago Times* published an editorial stating that justice had been slighted. The editor of *The Nation* denounced the trial even though he detested "this dangerous union man." "The belief that the courts have allied themselves with corporate interests," the editor wrote, "should have no sound basis." He concluded, "There is reasón for contending that this caution has been disregarded in the recent injunctions."[13] Attempts by Debs to gain a new trial failed.

On January 9, 1895, Debs made this press statement before he entered the McHenry County Jail at Woodstock, Illinois: "In going to jail for participation in the late strike we have no apologies to make nor regrets to express. I would not change places with Judge Woods, and if it is expected that six months, or even six years, in jail will purge me of contempt the punishment will fail."[14] While in prison Debs had many visitors, including Socialists Victor Berger, Keir Hardie, and Thomas J. Morgan. The judge had sentenced Debs and his ARU colleagues to this remote county jail, fifty-five miles from Chicago, in an attempt to prevent union rallies and visitors. Berger spent one afternoon lecturing Debs on the merits of socialism and left behind a copy of Marx's *Das Kapital*.[15] Hardie gave Debs a copy of Karl Kautsky's book on socialism. Debs later wrote Kautsky, "It was from you that I learned some of my earliest and most precious lessons in socialism. I have always felt myself in debt to your gifted pen for having opened my eyes to the light . . ."[16] Debs also read in Woodstock Jail the following books: *Intellectual Development of Europe* by John W. Draper, *Social Problems* by Henry George, *Coin's Financial School* by W. H. Harvey, *Civilization Civilized* by Stephen Maybell, *Holy Bible*, *Textbook of Rhetoric* by Grenville Kleiser, *Better Days* by C. Fitch, *The Cooperative Commonwealth* and *Our Destiny* by Lawrence Gronlund, and volumes by Hawthorne and Shakespeare.[17] "Coin" Harvey brought his book to Debs and spent the afternoon. Thereafter Debs read Harvey's writings and followed his career.[18]

With unrestricted writing privileges Debs continued his organizing and agitating activities. In the first few months he estimated that he wrote fifteen hundred letters and twenty articles. In these writings Debs attempted to counteract the adverse publicity he and the ARU had received. Nym Crynkle might have recognized some of his journalism techniques in this letter Debs sent to a newspaper: "I speak as a victim from a dungeon tomb, as one who loved his fellow men and dared to raise his voice to mitigate the pangs of famine in a suburb of hell, known as Pullman, and all over this once favored land men are imprisoned or are driven into idleness and 'beg-abondage', blacklisted and exiled because they had the courage to teach trampled hearts to feel the curses that their plutocratic masters were heaping upon them."[19] Actually Debs did not suffer many privations during his stay in prison, except most importantly his loss of freedom.

In a letter to his parents, he wrote that he was housed in "the best jail in the state, out in the country, where we eat with the sheriff's family and have clean comfortable beds." For his parents' solace, he included this additional remark: "Would you believe it? The sheriff, Mr. Eckert, is an Alsatian and a noble man."[20] Even in prison Debs maintained close ties with his family. His mother had worried even more about his strike activities than she had about the dangers on the railroad. In his letters, Gene always assured her that he was all right. On another occasion he said that he had "a good dinner of stuffed roast chicken." Governor Waite of Colorado had visited that day and stayed for dinner. He told his father that Waite was "a fine old man of about your age who is chock full of fight and one who did not care what the plutocratic press" said about him.[21]

The excellent food the prisoners received can be explained. In a letter to Theodore, in addition to asking numerous questions about the growth and problems of the ARU, Gene also included this request: "Send me a draft for $60 payable to George Eckert to pay for our board for 3 weeks . . .Hereafter when you send your weekly statement enclose with it a draft for $20 for one week's board. This will only last six weeks as the time for all but myself expires then."[22] He obviously read carefully the reports on union activities that Theodore sent to him and from his cell directed the ARU. For example, he ordered that "if Wild and Shannon show no returns" to not advance them any more money. Concluding he stated that he had written Benedict, another union official, to inform these ARU organizers of this intention.

To overcome the monotony of prison life Debs and six ARU prisoners organized "The Cooperative Colony of Liberty Jail" and set up a daily schedule of physical exercises and study. Their officers consisted of an inspector, a colonel, a professor, and a teacher. Debs filled the latter position. Their rules forbade talking during the sessions assigned to reading. From eight until ten every evening the group held a debate or discussion. They locked any violator of their code of rules in his cell. "Best lot of prisoners I ever had to handle," the jailer told a reporter. "They all have a wheel in the head on social subjects and you can't sidetrack them when they get on the strikes and labor questions."[23] Since Judge Woods gave Debs a six-month sentence and the other ARU officers only a three-month sentence, Debs spent a lonely final three months in jail. Debs called this additional sentence from the judge a "special favor" and hypothesized that the judge suspected his "contempt for him" was twice as great as that of his fellow prisoners.[24] During these months the rapidly declining ARU membership worried Debs. Finally he sent this notice to the directors: "I am compelled to ask that as far as possible each director support himself during the next two or three months. At this writing there is not only not a dollar in the treasury but I shall have to make a loan to meet the bills and expenses due on November 1."[25]

Debs devoted the last few weeks to working on a speech celebrating his release. He knew that he had to create the most publicity possible out of the event, for he needed public understanding and workers' support to continue his ARU campaign. Two weeks before his release labor groups in Chicago issued invitations for a reception "in testimony of their sympathy with Debs for unjust and unlawful imprisonment."[26] Newspapers provided vivid accounts of a huge, cheering crowd at the reception and speech on

November 22, 1895. In an interview Harley Pritchett, who heard the speech, agreed: "Never did I hear such enthusiasm during a speech! They would hardly let him continue."[27] *The Chicago Chronicle,* controlled by John R. Walsh, powerful Chicago banker who had strongly supported Pullman, described the event in Battery D, an armory: "Never did men strive and struggle so to demonstrate their love for a fellowman just released from a convict's cell. Theirs was no outward show alone." While marching into the armory to hear the speech, the crowd sang: "We'll hang Judge Woods to a sour apple tree, As we go marching on . . ."[28]

Governor "Bloody Bridles" Waite of Colorado and Henry Demarest Lloyd gave introductory speeches. Debs spoke from manuscript and titled his address "Liberty." He did not focus his attack upon Pullman or tell of his days in prison. Instead he stressed the need for justice in labor cases, and indirectly the necessity of rebuilding the ARU: "The theme tonight is personal liberty, or giving it its full height, depth, and breadth . . . Thousands of Americans do not recognize the truth that in the imprisonment of one man in defiance of all constitutional guarantees, the liberties of all are invaded and placed in peril."[29]

All of the events related to the Pullman strike, trial, and jail sentence have importance because they provided the material for many examples that Debs used in his later writings and speeches. The results of this strike sharpened the issues that he championed. His rhetoric after the Pullman strike included more invective and less hope for justice. He no longer had faith in his earlier contentions that arbitration would solve the differences between labor and management, and that strikes should be avoided. This strike also made the name Debs famous — or infamous — throughout the country. The publicity created a larger potential audience for Debs. Devoted laborers clamored to hear him, and others followed to see the "agitator" in action. When the committee of investigators appointed by President Cleveland released their report on the Pullman strike, Debs' appeal to workers was further enhanced because the committee condemned the tactics of the General Managers Association. The report stated that "the courts, the jury, and the District Attorney came dangerously near, if they have not committed a violation of the Constitution in their eagerness to obey the General Managers Association."[30] C. H. Chappell, vice-president of the association, claimed that Debs wrote the report! Debs quickly retorted: "Any intimation that I wrote the report or any part of it, or that I had anything to do with its preparation is totally false . . . I never met or corresponded with any member of the board either before or after my testimony was given."[31] An interesting postscript to this chapter is the story of the fear that George Pullman had of unions and workers after this strike. Prior to his death from a heart attack on October 19, 1897—two years after the strike report—Pullman left careful instructions for his burial because he believed workers would steal his body and mutilate it. At Graceland cemetery in Chicago grave diggers spent three days digging a huge hole and then covering his casket with layers of asphalt, railroad ties and concrete![32]

Chapter IV
Shifting Tides

When Debs left prison in 1895, a $40,000 debt faced the ARU. Available records do not indicate the total amount of money the union spent on the strike, especially wages paid to strikers. Prior to the strike however, Debs had built up the treasury from bankruptcy in 1880 to $66,557.61 in 1894.[1] Although not liable, Debs promised to pay back the $40,000 debt. In order to repay the debt, Debs readily accepted speaking engagements and turned the proceeds over to the ARU. No records show exactly how many times Debs criss-crossed America, or how many speeches he delivered before he repaid the debt.

In his scrapbooks Debs pasted newspaper clippings about speeches that he gave in thirty states. During an average month he delivered as many as twenty-two speeches. Most of Debs' speaking invitations came from labor organizations. Sylvester Keliher, one of the six who had received a jail sentence in Woodstock with Debs, served as Debs' advance publicity man and visited each town several days before Debs' arrival. Keliher checked final arrangements and made sure that everything from a union greeting committee at the station to a farewell group was prepared. These unions rented the largest hall in town and sold tickets, usually twenty-five cents a seat, in advance of Debs' arrival. In addition to the expense of debt repayment, Debs incurred the costs of rebuilding the ARU. The blacklist kept many railroaders from joining the union.

More than repaying the debt, Debs knew that he needed to convince railway employees and men in other industries that by uniting they could achieve improved wages and working conditions. In these lectures he hoped to overcome the demoralizing effect of the failure of the Pullman strike. Without new confidence, the ARU could not be rebuilt and established as a bargaining power. Repeatedly he attempted to convince his audiences that he spoke on behalf of a just cause, for many listeners believed the biased newspaper accounts they had read during the Pullman strike. Before a Lansing, Michigan, crowd the labor spokesman avowed that cooperation between capital and labor could prevent future strikes. He enhanced his ethical appeal by insisting that changes must come by law, not by force.[2] A Lansing newspaper editor summarized Debs' speech: "A fine lecture in which the pathetic, humorous, and serious were well blended." He complimented Debs for a concise statement of a question about which the majority of the people know but one side. "Many who came out of curiosity felt the justice of his claim," he wrote. "They expected to hear the capitalist arraigned and abused, but departed feeling none could take offense."[3] Another minister stated: "I was pastor at Pullman and know from experience the truth of all Debs said about that place. He might have said much more and still been within the truth." Instead, the Lansing editor declared, "The agitator was a plain gentle soul pleading for the rights and fairness of his fellow men."[4] Obviously Debs had the ability to ingratiate himself with his listeners and then gain sympathetic ears for his discussion of workers' right to join unions and bargain collectively. When Debs toured the areas adjacent to the Great Northern railroad line, he met enthusiastic crowds. He often titled his speech, "Who are the Conspirators?" Keliher had a difficult time keeping Debs on schedule, for he often stayed extra hours—missed train connections—but revitalized or organized new ARU locals.[5]

In this period after the Pullman strike, Debs became concerned about machines replacing workers. Although he admired American inventive genius, he lamented that labor-saving machines did not get weary or feed and clothe workers or their families. With the increasing number of machines he predicted that the "only remedy" would be a reduction of hours. This he feared would result in idleness. "Idleness is a colossal calamity," he warned, for he suspected laborers would not know how to use leisure time.[6] In another statement Debs declared, "The machine is invading every department and it is only a question of a short time when trades, in so far as they represent skill, will disappear."[7]

In most lectures he repeated an idea from the "Liberty" speech which stressed the importance of the ballot. "What remains worth saving of the liberties of Americans?" he asked. "I answer—the ballot. It is a powerful weapon if the American people can be persuaded to unify and wield it in defense of their rights."[8] He also consistently suggested that women should have the right to use the ballot.[9]

In 1895, Debs shifted his focus from primarily speaking for labor issues and made a vigorous appeal for Populist support.[10] After hearing Debs give a speech that year, a newspaper reporter commented: "The labor leader said that his work for the People's Party is secondary to his work for the railway union, but it is so closely allied that it is hard to say where his agitation for a closer union of railroad employees ends and agitation for the People's Party begins."[11] Debs proclaimed to this same audience of six thousand people that the "money question is the vital, and almost only, question. All the others are subsidiary and their solution will follow the solution of the great question naturally and without trouble." He observed that the Republicans could not unite on the tariff issue, and neither could the Democratic Party. "A principle is involved in the money question and this is one of justice to those who produce the wealth, but are not permitted to enjoy it," Debs declared. "The People's Party," the enthusiastic labor-Populist announced, "was the only organization as an entity that had declared itself prepared to deal with the principle on any definite plan."[12] Evidently Debs did not always know who sponsored his stump speeches in the political arena. In Spokane, Washington, he opened a speech with this remark: "I assume that this meeting is held under the auspices of the

People's Party. I need not say that I am with you heart and soul. If ever we hew out labor's emancipation, it will be by using our best endeavors for the only party of the people."[13]

Debs received offers for political office in both the Democratic and Populist Parties. In both 1894 and 1896, Indiana Populists urged the labor leader to run for governor.[14] Henry Demarest Llyod actively supported Debs for political office in other Populist conclaves.[15] In 1896, a Southern newspaper sent a reporter to find out Debs' political aspirations. He answered, "Under no circumstances would I become a presidential candidate on the People's Party or any other ticket. Such aspirations would ruin my usefulness in advancing the interests of the working people."[16] But Debs failed to convince some of his followers that he had no ambitions for high political office.

When the Populists convened in St. Louis in 1896, Debs' supporters opened an official headquarters and passed out pamphlets and Debs buttons. Reporters noted that vast numbers of delegates who wore "Middle of the Road" badges also wore the large Debs pin. The Ohio delegation endorsed Debs early in the convention. Ignatius Donnelly and William Jennings Bryan actively campaigned for the nomination. On the second day Bryan supporters offered Debs' backers the second place on their ticket. In refusing, the Debs delegates claimed that they had taken a poll of twenty-two states and found the majority favored Debs.[17] That night at eight o'clock the lights in the auditorium mysteriously went out. After some delegates bitterly shouted that Bryan had turned them off, the crowd began to sing and banter in the darkness. Debs' followers yelled from one end of the hall to other supporters in the distance. They shouted, "No trimming" and "One, two, three, who are we? We are for Debs, Eugene V." Later, a convention officer in asking for adjournment, stated that none of the officers could attend the evening session; that the credentials committee had not finished its work; and, that the delegates might like to attend the Silver Convention in session at Exhibition Hall. Ten minutes after the delegates left the lights flashed on.[18] No available records prove which side plunged the assembly into darkness or whether it was a power failure. Many Debs delegates thought the Bryan forces had plotted the delay to gain time and to rethink their strategy.

Another possible answer is that Debs' chief promoters wanted time to convince Debs to run. Victor Berger and Henry Demarest Lloyd did telegraph Debs to come quickly to St. Louis. If Debs would leave Terre Haute on the late train, these men hoped that they could persuade him to accept the nomination the next morning. Debs hesitated, for he remembered his earlier dissatisfaction with politics in Indiana and his remarks to reporters. On the fourth day of the convention Debs still had an impressive number of pledged votes. Twenty-two states still favored him and sixteen of these states announced pledged votes for him. Reluctantly Lloyd asked for the floor and read a telegram in which Debs declined to run. Debs wrote that he preferred to remain out of active politics so that he could devote all of his energies to labor reforms.[19] No other candidate had sufficient delegates to oppose Bryan. The convention delegates proceeded to name Tom Watson of Georgia as their vice-presidential choice and endorse Bryan, who had won the Democratic party nomination three weeks earlier.

In the late summer Debs felt obligated to help the campaign. He made seventy-seven speeches for Bryan. At Bryan's request Debs remained in Illinois in the closing days of the campaign. Bryan knew of Debs' immense popularity with workers and asked that he concentrate his speaking in the larger cities in Illinois. "Mr. Bryan wanted all the support I could bring him," Debs commented, "but he was careful all through the campaign and ever afterwards to remain a stranger with me, lest any recognition of me cost him some votes."[20] Months prior to election day Debs predicted the outcome. When a reporter asked him about the Republican convention, he replied: "McKinley will be nominated; in fact I believe he is already practically nominated, and there is little doubt he will be elected. The Democratic party is completely annihilated."[21] If Debs sincerely meant his remark, he contradicted himself by actively campaigning for the Democrats and Populists. The campaign came at a time in Debs' life when he was unsure as to what specific role he should play in politics. He believed that laborers had to take an active part in political affairs and had no hesitation in opposing Samuel Gompers and other conservative labor leaders who thought otherwise. Before blue-denim audiences Debs often discussed the relationship of politics to labor in detail. "The working men are beginning to think and will win not by crime or injunction but by a united ballot," Debs declared.[22] The election results in 1896 convinced Debs that none of the major parties could play the political role that he envisioned necessary for the reforms laborers needed.

During the years following his release from Woodstock Jail, Debs continued his wide reading on socialism. He especially enjoyed reading *The Coming Nation,* the first popular propaganda paper for socialist causes. J. A. Wayland, who started the paper in 1893, wrote provocative editorials that Debs admired.[23] He began to correspond with Wayland. Debs' speaking tours also enabled him to meet members of the Socialist Labor Party, including Daniel DeLeon who led the party in the 1890's. This party publicly claimed Debs long before he even became a Socialist. In 1895, the Socialist Trade and Labor Alliance, a trade union group formed out of the Socialist Labor Party, planned to help reorganize labor organizations and possibly take over the Populist Party with Debs as leader, but Debs refused the assignment.[24]

At this important time in Deb's life when he sought ways to be more effective politically, he certainly knew about DeLeon's rise to leadership within the Socialist Labor Party. In 1890 DeLeon, a Columbia University lecturer in international law, gave speeches for the Socialist candidate for mayor of New York. Prior to that he had campaigned in 1886 for Henry George for mayor. Almost an instant success as a leader of Socialists "boring from within" the trade unions and taking them over, DeLeon became editor of *The People,* the party's English language weekly, and the recognized intellectual leader of the Socialist movement in the United States. DeLeon tangled with Samuel Gompers and succeeded in the 1894 A.F. of L. convention in helping John McBride of the mine workers win the presidency from Gompers. By 1895 Gompers had regained the presidency and had sufficient power to refuse to seat Lucien Sanial, DeLeon's hand-picked Socialist Labor Party delegate.

Although DeLeon failed in his fight with Gompers, he earlier had succeeded in 1893 in uniting forces with John R. Sovereign, a Populist Iowa farmer editor, and removing Terrance V. Powderly from control of the Knights of Labor. In order to do this DeLeon and his Socialist Labor Party followers had taken over the strongest unit in the New York Knights' organization, the District Assembly 49. Sovereign and DeLeon parted company when Sovereign reneged on his promise to appoint Sanial editor of the *Journal of the Knights of Labor.* When DeLeon arrived at the 1895 convention of the Knights, as delegate of the 13,000 members of District Assembly 49, he was refused a seat. Sovereign had consolidated successfully his supporters against DeLeon. Thereafter DeLeon abandoned efforts to overtake the A.F. of L. or the Knights of Labor and decided to concentrate on establishing a new revolutionary union demanding the overthrow of capitalism.

He formed this new union, the Socialist Trade and Labor Alliance, by bringing together various unions including the Central Labor Federation, some German and Jewish Unions, plus athletic and burial societies. His District Assembly 49 group had control. In the 1896 Socialist Labor Party convention, DeLeon requested all Socialists to carry the revolutionary spirit to all workers' organizations and bring them into the Alliance. Thus his new organization was to be a dual union of those socialists within the A.F. of L. and those outside it. From the beginning DeLeon had troubles within the Alliance because he derided and disregarded those Socialists who remained within their old unions. Within three years the arguments over an active revolutionary union dedicated to overthrowing capitalism and Socialists taking over A.F. of L. trade unions and seeking immediate reforms for workers had dissipated much of the strength of the group. DeLeon's arbitrary manner and ruthless condemnation of any who disagreed with him added fire. He had figured out what he called Marxian scientific solutions to the problems workers faced in America and demanded adherence to this fixed dogma. Other solutions by Socialists were unscientific and thus unworthy of consideration. Morris Hillquit, a Russian born attorney, successful corporation lawyer in New York City, and ardent Socialist emerged as the leader of those who opposed DeLeon.

Hillquit gained control of the daily German *New Yorker Volkzeitung* and used its editorial pages to counter DeLeon's charges. Newspapers played a big role in the movement because membrs got their information on these idealogical arguments from these sources. By 1898 DeLeon's *The People* had 10,000 subscribers but *Volkzeitung* sold 18,000 copies. At this time

Debs kept his distance from DeLeon but recognized the impact that he had upon socialism developing in this country. He watched closely this struggle between Hillquit and DeLeon.

Debs had admitted his growing interest in socialism in a letter to Henry Demarest Lloyd in the early part of 1896. In this letter Debs also protested against Thomas Watson's article in the *People's Party Paper*. "I agree with you entirely that Mr. Watson has no rational conception of what socialism really is," Debs wrote, "and it is not likely his tirade will injure those against whom it is directed. . . . I do not permit myself to be much disturbed by self-appointed censors."[25]

On January 1, 1897, Debs officially announced that he had resigned from the People's Party and had become a socialist, but he did not immediately endorse Berger, Heath and Stedman's group or DeLeon's Socialist Labor Party. In a letter to ARU members he declared that although the common people supported the free silver issue in the '96 campaign, "the money power" had won. He asked laborers to join the ranks of socialism in order to put into office men who would represent their interests. In a traditional way, and without American modifications, Debs defined socialism in this letter as a more perfect and equitable distribution of the products of labor; cooperation instead of competition; collective ownership of land and all means of production and distribution.[26] "I convinced myself," he later related, "that there had to be some other way than strikes."[27] Thus Debs left the Populists without ever really understanding or becoming deeply involved in their movement. Debs had the desire and naive assumption that workers, farmers, and radicals could drop their differences and band together into an effective political party. When they didn't, Debs became impatient. Unfortunately Debs was more sentimental and rhetorical in his view of the Populists than he was resourceful as a leader and strategist to bring about a possible successful merger of joint interests. Certainly such a merger would have taken more time than Debs wanted to give to it. In his judgment socialism in 1897 offered a quicker and better way than populism. Several years later Debs took this view of the Populists: "As the populist and prohibition sections of the capitalist party represent minority elements which propose to reform the capitalist system without disturbing wage slavery, a vain and impossible task, they will be omitted from this discussion with all the credit due the rank and file for their good intentions."[28]

As a new Socialist, Debs became fascinated with the idea of developing a cooperative commonwealth colony for unemployed workers and Socialists. If the idea worked with a pilot group, Debs contemplated organizing thousands of workers into a cooperative that would set up factories in basic industries, control them, and return the profits to laborers. Debs hoped to start the experiment in some Western state so that, if it succeeded, Socialists in large numbers could migrate to the state and take over the political offices.[29] One reporter dubbed Debs "the Moses of the labor people" and suggested that moving the unemployed didn't solve the

46

basic problems.[30] Debs issued a circular that explained the plans for this big project and asked members of the ARU to pledge from ten cents to ten dollars monthly to help get the venture underway. "Until they can raise their own food and provide necessities," Debs wrote, "they will need aid." If contributions would average $1.00 a month, and the brotherhood would continue to grow, Debs promised that $25,000 would be available monthly to support the project.[31]

To further his plans for a workers' utopia, Debs called for a convention of workers to meet in Chicago on June 15, 1897. In the meantime Debs and his friends formed the Brotherhood of the Cooperative Commonwealth and elected Reverend Myron Reed of Denver as temporary president. Because Debs had not finished repaying the ARU debt, he declined to serve as organizer. Before the convention opened, this group decided that the first colony should settle in the Southwest and specialize in fruit raising. Later the group planned that the Western Miners' Association would sponsor a colony that would organize and develop a mine.[32]

At this special convention called under the auspices of the ARU, Debs made two speeches to the delegates gathered in Uhlich's Hall in Chicago. In his remarks Debs asserted that the project would not result in "another Coxey's movement" and dared the government to intervene. "If in defiance of the federal Constitution, they send federal troops to suppress us," he declared, "they will find 300,000 at the state line ready to receive them."[33] Debs promised to draft a constitution for the commonwealth with this philosophy: "That government is best which governs least." Without giving credit, Debs had borrowed this quote from Henry David Thoreau's "Civil Disobedience." Perhaps credit also should have been paid to his father who introduced Debs to Locke, Thoreau, and other important writers.

This group meeting in Chicago became known as the Social Democracy of America. The delegates elected Debs chairman of the project and party despite his objections. Four of his Woodstock jailmates held other offices: William E. Burns, vice chairman; Sylvester Keliher, secretary; Roy M. Goodwin, treasurer; James Hogan, organizer. Debs proclaimed that the colonization idea would help the Social Democracy group to grow and that in 1900 the party would slate candidates for state and national offices. "We do not say we will elect a president," Debs declared, "but it would not surprise me if we did."[34] The convention approved Debs' request to turn over the ARU membership lists to the new party. Since only about fifty delegates attended this convention, it was not surprising that Debs succeeded in this action. Interest in the ARU had steadily declined since the election of 1896. Debs and his supporters optimistically thought that the commonwealth idea and the new political party would appeal to more workers. Hereafter the ARU members belonged to the new organization called the Social Democracy of America and received their *Railway Times* under a new title, *Social Democrat*.

After the convention Debs and his officers set to work to collect the needed money. From the beginning it was a difficult task. Large audiences attended Debs' talks about the cooperative commonwealth plan but came more out of curiosity than as avid supporters of this new cause. Many of the old ARU members still lacked money and full time jobs. Others who had jobs saw no need for a colony for the unemployed or disagreed with the colony idea. Henry Demarest Lloyd, Victor Berger, and other past supporters of Debs refused to endorse the project.

These men thought that the colonization scheme attracted too much attention away from the party's plans for a socialist nation. Berger especially felt that Debs should direct his energies toward a more permanent solution for the unemployed than colonization. Debs attempted to placate the powerful Berger and his active group of Milwaukee supporters by going to their city and giving a speech in which he declared that the new party would develop into more than "a colonization scheme."[35] He insisted that the colonization idea represented only a "detail of his general plan." After discussing at length ways to organize local party branches in each ward to support the commonwealth plan, and how to then consolidate these locals into a state organization, Debs declared that he hoped to update the Declaration of Independence by restoring the land and all the means of production, transportation and distribution to the people as a collective body, and to substitute a cooperative commonwealth for the "present state of planless production, industrial war and social disorder."[36] Certainly Berger agreed with parts of these statements, but he did not change his mind and back Debs' colonization efforts. Instead the pragmatic Berger spent his time organizing Wisconsin workers into an effective political machine which soon demonstrated its strength by electing men to office, especially in the City of Milwaukee. While Debs gave lip service at this time to such political action, he devoted his energies to eliciting support for the commonwealth colony.

In order to secure land, Debs asked the Union Pacific for several thousand acres suitable for agriculture. Although this railroad had encouraged immigrants to move West via land grants, the officers refused Debs' request.[37] Debs had expected this refusal and continued his search for land for a colony. Rumors circulated that Utah had been selected as the state for the first group. Debs stated to a reporter that he admired the Mormons for the way they had successfully organized a "commonwealth." However, because of the Mormons' strength and number in Utah, Debs decided upon Washington as better suited for the first colony. His plans called for spending $50,000 in Washington for irrigation, agriculture implements, seed, and housing. In the same interview Debs also announced that a second colony would start in Colorado to manufacture men's clothing and later shoes, plus women's and children's clothing.[38]

Women, according to the constitution of the commonwealth, were politically equal to men and had the right to vote and hold office. Debs recognized that women were not physically equal to men and planned so that women would not suffer unnecessary hardships in establishing the colonies. Because of the hard work necessary to establish the colonies, Debs insisted that women not accompany the men. After the colonies had been operating for a brief period of time, women could join their husbands and find work, if they desired, in the clothing factories. When a woman reporter inquired if women in the factories would wear bloomers, Debs replied, "I will always remain neutral on that point. I say if a woman wants to wear bloomers, let her, but if she doesn't show any such inclination, so much the better." Although Debs promised that the "new woman" could do just as she pleased in the matter, he hoped that women would be concerned about more important political matters. Under closer questioning he did say that he preferred that women not entirely discard petticoats and "the thousand and one lace befrilled odds and ends that constitute the charm of femininity."[39]

While publicly Debs continued in July of 1897 to explain the details of the cooperative commonwealth plan to numerous audiences, privately he became increasingly concerned about the West Virginia coal miners' strike. He decided to go to Wheeling, center of the strike. After failing to convince the operators to restore the wage cuts, he stopped speaking for the colony project and devoted full time to aiding the strikers. Upon investigation Debs found that many miners, in spite of working full time, owed the company stores more than they earned. "The only way to get even is to quit," he wrote. "I wish every foe of labor agitation could see the poverty I have seen in the last week."[40]

In speeches to the strikers, Debs warned them not to drink whiskey until the strike ended. "If you drink, you will do just what the operators want," he cautioned. "You'll commit violence and lose the support of the American people. What you men want is more books and less booze."[41] Debs called upon all miners in West Virginia to strike in sympathy with the Monongah Coal Company workers. "Slaves were worth $1,500," he shouted. "You miners are not worth fifteen cents a shipload. You have allowed other people to do your thinking for you so long that your brain has become petrified," he continued, "and if you were to have an idea it would cause you pain."[42] The local police had informed Debs before he started speaking that if the crowd gathered on any public road, he would be arrested. Instead of the highway Debs chose a spot beneath a weeping willow tree in a large pasture adjacent to a cemetery. After the speech Debs led the miners to the next camp and again encouraged other miners to strike and join them. During this strike Debs met the father of Victor and Walter Reuther. They became close friends since Valentine Reuther, a union miner, admired Debs and appreciated his leadership. Debs accepted their hospitality and stayed several nights in their home. Thereafter whenever Debs visited the Wheeling area, he visited the Valentine and Anna Reuther family. Walter treasured these memories and acknowledged Debs' influence upon his life.[43]

Each day Debs addressed different groups of miners in the Monongahela District begging them to support the strikers. Pinkerton detectives hired by the coal companies made sure that Debs did not speak on company property.[44] Because of an arduous schedule Debs suffered a sunstroke after speaking two hours in stifling heat at Montana, a camp in the lower end of the district.[45] This stroke, which happened during the third week of the strike, curtailed Debs' activities for several days.

Gradually the sympathy strike spread into other states. Debs regained his strength and began to speak in nearby states to encourage support. In western Pennsylvania 22,600 miners left their shafts; 28,000 in Ohio; 8,000 in Indiana; 37,000 in Illinois. Although organizers assisting Debs and the strikers encouraged workers in Kentucky, Tennessee, Iowa, and Missouri to join the strike, they hesitated because coal operators in these states had quickly granted pay advances.[46]

Encouraged by the miners' support in other states, including those that would not strike but promised aid, and by the growing unity among the strikers in West Virginia, Debs thought the strike would soon end. But the coal company owners had one other strategy they planned to try. In early August, after receiving a request from James Stern of Baltimore, a stockholder in the Monongah Company, Judge Jackson of the United States District Court of West Virginia issued an injunction forbidding anyone "in any way from inciting employees to strike or interfering in any manner, whatever, either by word or deed in the company's affairs." Immediately the United Labor League of Western Pennsylvania made arrangements for an open air demonstration at nearby Duquesne Wharf. Twenty thousand heard Debs and Mother Mary Jones, colorful heroine of miners throughout the country, demand free speech and the right of peaceable assembly.[47] After Mother Jones' husband and her four children died of the yellow fever in 1867 she had left Memphis for Chicago and devoted her life to organizing workers. An indomitable woman, she repeatedly defied police orders and spent many nights in jail. She and Debs had frequently met wherever miners were striking. By the injunction's provisions, Debs declared, "I am enjoined from walking on the public highways which lead to the mines, and all highways lead to mines." He told the crowd that he understood why people demanded "Judge Lynch" since they had lost confidence in the courts.[48] Governor George W. Atkinson of West Virginia also protested against the injunction and asked in a public letter why the "legal instead of judicial remedy" was used.

Tension mounted as the strike continued. Seventeen miners from Latimer, Pennsylvania, died when Sheriff D. Martin and his deputies fired into a marching crowd.[49] Indiana's governor, James A. Mount, became alarmed that violence also might break out in his state. He decided to conduct an investigation into mining grievances in Debs' home state. Mount appointed Judge Thomas J. Terhune of Lebanon to conduct the probe.

Judge Terhune reported that a miner's wage in Indiana had dropped in the last few years from $1.25 a ton to 35 cents per ton. This investigation revealed conditions similar to those in West Virginia. Since a good miner could dig only three tons a day in the coal veins of Southern Indiana, he often had no take home pay after he paid for rent and groceries at exorbitant prices at the company store. Two-room shanties that cost the operators $100 to build rented for $5 a month. Terhune also noticed that the furniture in most homes consisted of boxes for tables and chairs and old rags piled up for beds. "The blackberries which are plentiful in that part of the state have been a great blessing," he stated. "Some strikers' families have lived for days with nothing to eat but berries."[50]

Unfortunately, violence continued throughout West Virginia and Pennsylvania. In numerous conferences, representatives of both sides failed to reach agreement. Debs, forced to stay out of these two states because of injunctions, sent President William McKinley a telegram asking him to end the strike and to inform the operators that they must grant the miners "living wages" or have their mines seized by the government in forty-eight hours and operated in the interests of the people.[51] McKinley ignored the message. Debs continued speaking on behalf of the miners throughout the Midwest. After one speech an Ohio editor commented: "Today there is more sympathy for the struggling miner in Columbus than had ever been hoped for . . ." At the conclusion of this speech, the audience, like many other groups Debs addressed, voted to send a telegram of protest to West Virginia coal operators and state officials.[52]

In September, a committee reached a settlement in the Pittsburgh district. This agreement gave the miners sixty-five cents more a ton and three-fifths of that amount where companies used machine loaders.[53] All miners refrained from work for an additional ten days to allow strikers in other districts to confer with their operators and attempt to gain the same price. By late September the strike ended and Debs was disappointed because all strikers did not get the same terms as those in Pennsylvania. The strike had been more successful than the Pullman strike and it had continued after the injunction. However, piecemeal settlements and the fact that miners in Kansas, Missouri, Iowa, and northwest Kentucky had worked throughout the strike and supplied coal to eager buyers had diminished the effectiveness of the strike. In this dispute, Debs again sensed the need for greater unity among workers, for legislation to protect their rights, and for larger union funds to prevent employees and their families from starving during long strikes. By comparison to the needs for a commonwealth colony, Debs began to realize that these union needs demanded more consideration, and he decided to shift his energies from the colony project to more union organizing.

In his writings and lectures during the following months, Debs decried the weaknesses of small union funds and little worker solidarity in organized labor and devoted little energy to the cooperative colony project. However, Debs did spend the last week in September investigating a 250,000 acre site for a colony near Sparta, Tennessee. He had made this commitment months earlier but could not go until the settlement of the West Virginia strike. After four days of carefully examining the "timber, soil, waterways and kinds of crops produced in the different neighborhoods as well as the character of the improvements,"[54] Debs advised the committee in charge of colonization that "a more desirable body of land probably could not be found."[55] Two coal companies owned the land and wanted $1,300,000 for it. Debs included the price in his report, knowing better than any other party fund raiser the overwhelming odds against raising such a sum. The officers decided to try and buy the property. From the beginning the slowness in accumulating funds for the project discouraged Debs. The blacklisting of the old ARU members continued. These members who could be depended upon in the past lacked any salary to contribute. Because of insufficient funds the Tennessee project was dropped but enough money had been collected to start two colonies at Edison and Olalla, Washington, each planned for two hundred families.[56]

Debs also began to realize that successful colonies, such as New Harmony, Indiana, or Nauvoo, Illinois, had been dominated by a central religious figure who cohesively bound the people together. He had no desire to play such a role. His admired friend, Julius A. Wayland, had started a private socialistic colony in Tennessee in 1894. Wayland abandoned it in 1896 when he recognized that he had to exert full time leadership and control or the operation would fail.[57] Debs could foresee the same happening to him because no other leader of the party seemed willing to accept the responsibility. If the money had been easily raised, Debs probably would have overlooked these obstacles. His report on the Tennessee site revealed his enthusiasm for the project. This colony scheme which he had labeled "a detail in his general plan," however, required more attention than Debs wanted to give it. Basically, Debs envisioned socialism spreading throughout the United States instead of just developing in a few colonies in certain states. Although he energetically promoted the idea of a socialist colony, he reached the conclusion that labor needed greater strength immediately in legislative halls. This meant organizing masses of workers in the more populous states. If Debs had to devote his energies exclusively to colonization, he could not further these aspirations. With these thoughts firmly in mind, Debs decided to announce his decision at the next party convention.

On June 10, 1898, the Social Democracy of America Party met in Uhlich Hall in Chicago. In the opening session the delegates asked Debs to serve as chairman of a committee to draft a resolution noting Edward Bellamy's death. In this resolution Debs paid tribute to Bellamy for popularizing the ideas of socialism in America. Bellamy's death depressed Debs, because he had avidly read his writings, kept a scrapbook of his activities, and believed that Bellamy "filled a despairing world with hope."[58] On the second day the delegates quickly divided over a minority report of the platform committee that favored colonization over political action by a vote of 52-36. The heated debate started at 5 p.m. and ended at 2:30 a.m. with the adoption of the plank. Debs immediately announced his resignation, and he and his supporters left the hall.

At this famous meeting Debs broke with many men who had backed him in the Brotherhood of Locomotive Firemen and the ARU, including four of his cellmates at Woodstock. Although Debs was ill at his hotel the next day, the dissidents met at Hull House and organized themselves into the Social Democratic Party. They elected the following executive committee: Eugene Debs, Victor Berger and Frederick Heath of Milwaukee, Seymour Stedman and Jesse Cox of Chicago.[59] After Debs declined the chairmanship, the group elected Jesse Cox as chairman and William Mailly as secretary. After ten speakers from the newly formed party had denounced the Uhlich Hall contingent as anarchists and paid henchmen of political parties, the Hull House delegates settled down to developing their own platform.[60] This 1898 platform, broad in perspective, became a model for subsequent ones and foreshadowed many welfare issues and laws that required years for realization. Dividing the platform into two divisions, one for city dwellers and the other for farmers, the committee based both on an old Debs premise that since labor created all wealth, all returns rightfully belonged to labor. Planks for laborers contained the following demands: 1. Public ownership of all industries controlled by monopolies, trusts and combines; 2. Public ownership of all railroads, and all other means of transportation, water works, gas and electric plants, and other public utilities; 3. Public ownership of all mines, gas and oil wells; 4. Reduction of the hours of labor in proportion to the increasing use of machines; 5. The inauguration of a system that used government funds for public works and improvements for hiring the unemployed; 6. All inventions free to the public and the inventor remunerated by the public; 7. The public to provide honorable maintenance for the aged and disabled workers; 8. National labor legislation instead of local; 9. National insurance for workers against accidents and unemployment; 10. Equal civil and political rights for women; 11. Adoption of the initiative and referendum and right to recall representatives; 12. Minorities to be represented according to their number voting; 13. Abolition of war and use of international arbitration instead.

In the farmer's platform, the new Social Democratic Party members hoped to unite the workers on the farm with those in the city. Although their problems differed, the platform committee attempted to attract rural supporters by specifically recognizing some of the difficulties farmers encountered. For farmers, Debs' group asked: 1. Nationalization of all mortgages on loans and lowering the rate of interest to cost; 2. National credit to be available to farmers for land improvement to the extent of half its value. (Money repaid from these loans was to be destroyed!); 3. No more selling of public land because such land should be utilized by the federal or state government directly for public benefit or leased to farmers in parcels of not more than 640 acres. The state should make regulations regarding improvements and cultivation. All forests and waterways were to be under federal control; 4. Erection of grain elevators and cold storage facilities by the government for use by farmers at cost; 5. A uniform rate for the transportation of agriculture products by railroads; 6. Public credit to be at the disposal of counties and towns for improving roads, soil, irrigation and drainage.[61] This ambitious program contained demands and ideas that supported arguments Debs had been advocating for years. No records indicate the origin of each plank. Probably Berger influenced those regarding public ownership and Debs those on labor, civil rights, and natural resources. The agrarian planks reflected the persuasion of the Populists who had joined the Socialist movement. Regardless of authorship, Debs enthusiastically endorsed the platform and gained increased notoriety in ensuing years by his explanation and defense of it.

The new party officers claimed that they represented 4,000 members but the Social Democracy party leaders disagreed. After the convention many branches repudiated their delegates that followed Debs. Some did the opposite. Because of the split both factions abandoned plans for a political ticket in the fall election. "No use," Jesse Cox, the new chairman, declared, "unless we can get enough votes to make a big showing."[62] Later Republican party officials in Cook County asked Debs if he would campaign for a state and county Socialist ticket and draw votes away from the complacent Democrats' majority. Debs refused.[63]

After helping to draft the platform at the convention, Debs returned to Terre Haute and announced his intentions to retire from labor and party positions. "For twenty years I have worked for fraternal organizations," Debs declared. "For five years I had the responsibilities of leader of a vast organization (ARU) and during that time was engaged in the greatest struggle between labor and capital the world has ever seen. Meanwhile I have neglected my home duties and have had no income." He and Katherine planned a two month trip to Europe and after that Debs hoped to start a newspaper.[64] Before they could take the trip, Debs promised to finish his lecture commitments which extended into early fall. By that time the seriousness of the split in the party forced him to cancel his travel plans and accept responsibility for building his faction of the party into a stronger political unit. Repeatedly he insisted to audiences of supporters and non-supporters that the labor movement must be "dual in character": economic and political.[65] "The laboring man," he asserted, "has found that in unions he can win his fight for existence, but now he is beginning to learn that success in his battle is impossible without unity in politics."[66] Debs' speeches did not pass unnoticed. A prominent Kansan, Judge P. S. Grosscup's remarks typify the "establishment" reaction Debs provoked: "The methods now being pursued by Mr. Debs and his followers will not bring the relief which they are demanding. They are proceeding in the wrong direction. Mr. Debs is a malcontent." According to Grosscup, labor organizations succeed when they are conservative and confine their work to their own craft.[67] Workers must have disagreed because increasing numbers turned out to hear Debs speak.

To gain political strength several hundred members of Debs' party attended the American Federation of Labor convention in December. They introduced a resolution that endorsed socialism as the eventual goal of labor. Samuel Gompers, irritated by the motion, spoke against it. "Either the trade union principles are right, and trade unionists must declare for them without frills and furbelows, or wrong, and the adoption by us of the theories suggested will be a confession that we are wrong," he declared. "The men who advocate this socialistic amendment have done all men can do to frustrate the aims of the organizations of wage earners."[68] The assembly defeated the motion 1,923 to 492. Although Debs and Gompers had met and worked together during strikes in previous years, hereafter they openly opposed one another. Gompers particularly irked Debs when he announced that organized labor "simply viewed trusts as their employers," and that experience had proven that laborers secured no greater advantages through "cooperative schemes" than under the wage system.[69] Failing to make any headway with the AFL, Debs kept seeking ways for his group to assert itself politically. He soon had another opportunity when he decided in March to meet in New York with representatives of the Silver Clubs, Populist Party, and other reform groups.

At this convention Reverend W. S. Rainsford presided and urged the formation of a new party. George P. Kenney, delegate from the National Association of Silver Clubs, predicted that the Democrats and Republicans would split at their conventions and a reform party could win. Debs disagreed and announced that such an "amalgamation" would require each group to sacrifice its principles. Rainsford replied that although he saw a need for radical action, history proved all great reforms required compromise. "I would rather have 10,000 Socialists . . . who knew what they wanted," Debs retorted, "than millions of men of varying opinion held close together with the hopes of making a step at a time."[70] Little resulted from this meeting because too few of the groups represented were willing to relinquish any of their autonomy.

Debs' new party was also having difficulty with Daniel DeLeon and his followers in the Socialist Labor Party. This problem further complicated any immediate plans for merging with other organizations. Although Debs disagreed with Rainsford, he recognized that the radical DeLeon's idea of immediate revolution was not the answer either. In a later meeting in New York City, Debs and Berger led a group that attempted to secure a majority vote and oust DeLeon.[71] When the motion failed, Debs, Berger, and their followers made another dramatic exit from a meeting.[72] Within a year the Debs group had gained many new adherents and prevented further factions from developing. They also attracted part of DeLeon's supporters back into their party.

During these same years in which Debs was involved in mining strikes, repaying the ARU debts, and building the Social Democratic Party, he began to protest against America's intervention in Philippine and Cuban affairs. He accused business interests of making war to gain an economic stranglehold on the islands. "Our treatment of the Philippines," he berated, "was one of the most cruel, diabolical and damnable outrages ever perpetuated upon any people in all history."[73] In another speech before a Saginaw, Michigan, crowd, Debs stated, "I have no sympathy with the expansion policy." The inhabitants of Cuba, he believed, had been for years the victims of tyranny and exploitation for years by the Spanish rulers and American businessmen. "If we get complete control of Cuba," he asserted, "it will not be five years before it will be Mark Hanna's private plantation."[74]

Debs also found time to include in his addresses remarks on prison reform. Although his own days at Woodstock had been tolerable, he became interested in this issue and sympathized with those less fortunate. His descriptions of prison life must refer to the brief time he spent in the Chicago city jail following his arrest, rather than to his Woodstock experience. Debs maintained that "if one half of the money spent in punishing crimes was spent in preventing it, the question would soon be solved."[75] Debs particularly deplored the use of prison labor in competition with other workers. He gave his first complete address on this subject when he was asked to address the elite Nineteenth Century Club at Delmonico's in New York City. "The pernicious effect of prison contract labor upon 'free labor', so called, when brought into competition with it in the open market, is universally conceded," Debs orated, "but it should not be overlooked that prison labor is itself an effect and not a cause, and that convict labor is recruited almost wholly from the propertyless, wage-working class. . ."[76] Mary Elizabeth Lease, vituperative Populist speaker, heard this address. She described the audience as follows: "The cultured East, self-satisfied and self-satiated, effete immorals, Europeanized in methods, had just received from the West the breath of its prairies. . ." In her account of Debs' address she included this statement that other writers later often used to describe Debs' rhetoric: "Presenting first the thought side and then directly the heart side of the economic questions of the hour, he does not excite that unreasoning enthusiasm which causes swarms of unthinking political devotees to view questions of right and wrong through the medium of a fanatical egotism, but his hearers are impelled to think and conviction follows investigation." After the talk, Mary Lease joined the two daughters of Robert Ingersoll, Mary Donovan Hapgood, and the widow of General Custer, for a long visit with Debs.[77]

To further all of these issues, Debs decided to start his own publishing business in Terre Haute. He had local printers do the typesetting, especially Bert Viquesney, T. S. Moore, E. O. Langen, and E. J. Langen, but these men did not wish that their firms gain a reputation for publishing Socialist literature. To overcome this problem, Debs suggested using the name of "E. V. Debs Publishing Company." This satisfied the local printers, who welcomed the business. Publishing materials for workers would help spread Debs' ideas, for he took seriously his announced mission to educate the working class. He advocated that every worker have a library in his home in which he could read every evening. Following the reading, Debs suggested that the worker conduct discussions within his own household and with his neighbors. If a man had a neighbor who could not read, Debs pleaded that this man had an obligation to teach his neighbor how to read.[78] "Books are better than beer," Debs maintained. "Under the new system you will become a man. The people collectively can do all things," Debs promised, "I can sum it up in these three words—read, think, and study."[79] Debs had learned something about the value of spreading ideas through print with his experiences as editor of the Brotherhood of Locomotive Firemen's magazine, *Railway Times*, and from his fellow Hoosier, Julius Wayland. Wayland had made a fortune in publishing and banking in Pueblo, Colorado. Suspecting an economic crash in the early 1890's Wayland sold everything prior to 1893, and returned to Greensburg, Indiana, where he decided to renounce the Republican party and publish *The Coming Nation*, a newspaper for the discussion of social and economic problems. Wayland soon had 50,000 subscribers. From funds accumulated from this enterprise, he decided to start his colony in Tennessee. In 1896, he returned to publishing and in Kansas City started *The Appeal to Reason* (later moved to Girard, Kansas), a newspaper soon noted for its blazing headlines and militant appeals for reforms. No records indicate how much advice Wayland gave Debs at this time, but they did meet frequently and Debs always read Wayland's publications.

Debs started his own magazine in 1899. He called it *Progressive Thought, A Radical Monthly*. In addition, Debs' publishing firm issued such items as the following: *Air-Brake Practice* by J. E. Phelan; *Alexander's Ready Reference; Burning Soft Coal Without Smoke;* M. N. Forney's *Catechism of Electricity* and *Catechism of the Locomotive;* G. R. Kinne's *Catechism of the Steam Plant,* and *Engineers' Guide, Time and Pocketbook;* Robert Grimshaw's *Locomotive Catechism,* L. C. Hitchcock's *Locomotive Running Repairs,* etc. Later reprints included such items as: Edward Aveling's *Students' Marx;* Robert Bax's *Ethics of Socialism;* Richard T. Ely's *Labor Movement in America* and *Socialism and Social Reform;* Frederick Heath's *Socialism in America;* Emile Vandervelde's *Collectivism;* Mills' *Socialism;* and J. Ritchie's *Darwinism and Politics.* Obviously Debs attempted to publish a combination of practical and political books for workers. His ideas on home libraries and the importance of education for workers closely paralleled those of Josiah Holbrook who started the lyceum movement in New England in the late 1820's. Holbrook formed Worker Institutes—an idea which originated in England—to better train unskilled laborers.[80] Although no evidence indicates that Debs knew about Holbrook's work, Debs certainly extended Holbrook's ideas of self-education by advocating that social and political action result from reading and attending lectures. Holbrook avoided all political and religious topics in his lyceum programs because he feared controversy would destroy the lyceum. In contrast Debs stimulated interest in unions and socialism with his lectures and publishing enterprise.

In October Debs announced that the Social Democratic Party planned to nominate a national ticket in 1900.[81] In November of 1899, the party had tickets in three states: Massachusetts, Maryland, and California. Other states had slates of candidates in some counties. This political activity encouraged Debs. He eagerly looked forward to the coming convention and announced the slogan for the campaign: "No fusion; no compromise."[82]

Chapter V
The First National Campaign

For several years Debs had worked toward the day when he thought the socialists would be unified and strong enough to field a national ticket. In January Debs succeeded in getting some members of the Socialist Labor Party to agree to meet with Debs' Social Democratic Party and talk about unity. Complete harmony still did not exist between all of the diverse elements within the country advocating socialism but Debs hoped that their differences could be settled in the discussions at the convention called for March 6, 1900, in Indianapolis, Indiana.

In the opening session, Theodore Debs, serving at that time as secretary of the Social Democratic Party, announced that the sixty-two delegates present represented 4,426 members in 226 branches in thirty-two states.[1] Since Debs had done more speechmaking, writing and travelling than any other figure in the party, he took pride in these figures. In bringing these party branches together in this convention, Debs and other party officials recognized that compromise would be difficult because some of the delegates thought that the party should be more radical and other delegates thought the opposite. Trouble between the factions started when J. F. Carey, newly elected Socialist member of the Massachusetts legislature, moved that the Milwaukee group led by Victor Berger and Frederick Heath be censured for taking over the central labor union in that city. An angry floor debate followed. Carey and his supporters advocated "education rather than conquest." This moderate group believed socialists could make more rapid political advances by endorsing existing unions. They cited the recent union elections in St. Louis as a case in which the unions had organized against the Socialist candidates. As the arguments continued, Debs became increasingly irritated, for he saw his wing of the party dividing over this issue. He feared that the eastern DeLeon faction, which was far more aggressive than Berger's faction, would counter with more radical motions. Debs counseled Carey to withdraw the motion. When Carey refused, Debs quickly suggested that a committee investigate the matter. Later in the convention, after tempers had calmed, the committee reported. Debs spoke against the motion and succeeded in tabling it 31 to 23.

Most delegates assumed that Debs would seek the nomination as the party's first candidate for president. He surprised his supporters by refusing to run. "There are conditions of health known to me which make it necessary for me to decline," he announced to the assembly.[2] Job Harriman, a former New York lawyer who had moved to California, implored Debs to accept for the sake of socialism. He offered him a recuperative trip to his home. Debs shook his head. In addition to this concern for his health,

Debs replied that he had to finish paying the ARU debt and that he feared his candidacy would focus attention upon him and not on the goals of the party.[3] His refusal to run started a new fight within the party.

Delegates proceeded to nominate Reverend F. O. McCartney who also refused. Next they named Theodore Debs, but he laughed and protested that he was too young. DeLeon's group, known as the Socialist Labor Party, nominated Job Harriman for president and Max Hayes, a Cleveland printer, for vice-president. Harriman, born in Indiana and educated for the ministry at Butler University in Indianapolis, had many supporters in the western states because he had campaigned on the Socialist Labor Party Ticket for the governorship of California in the 1898 election.[4] Berger and Debs supporters certainly disapproved of Harriman and Hayes. After a quick adjournment, representatives of both factions met in a strategy meeting. Since both of the men proposed as candidates represented the opposition wing, Debs' supporters insisted upon the use of their Social Democratic party label as a united party name. Berger, a shrewd bargain maker, still hoped to convince Debs to accept the nomination, so he proposed using the Social Democratic name and running Harriman for vice-president on the ticket. After considerable haggling, the Harriman supporters agreed. No sooner had Berger gained this compromise than word came that others working for Berger had secured Debs' consent to run.[5] Late on March 8, 1900, Eugene V. Debs reluctantly agreed to have his name placed in nomination for president on the Socialist Democratic Party ticket. Debs accepted more to achieve unity in his party than for any other reason. His friends convinced him that he could best lead the party and win votes in November.

On March 9, Debs and Harriman for vice president received the nominations by a vote of acclamation. In his acceptance speech Debs assured delegates that he had been sincere in his reasons for not wanting the nomination. "But now with your united voices ringing in my ears. . .," he stated, "I am brought to realize that in your voice is a supreme command of duty."[6] After the convention he met with the campaign committee and planned for the months ahead.

William McKinley represented the Republicans and William Jennings Bryan the Democrats in the 1900 election. Debs expended more oratorical energy than either of his opponents in his first campaign to occupy the White House. He attempted to cover a majority of the states and made two rail tours from coast to coast. Debs spoke largely to a beer drinking, frankfurter eating crowd dressed in their Sunday best, including bowler hats, rather than their usual blue denim trousers and shirts. Some more prosperous listeners, dressed in straw boaters, striped blazers, and white flannels, came to satisfy their curiosity or to find some entertainment other than the weekly summer band concerts in the park or vaudeville troupes in the fall.[7] Debs spoke consistently to large audiences, regardless of their reasons for coming to hear him, and he carefully explained the party's platform for the future.

The 1900 Social Democratic Party platform, an extension of the 1898 statement, listed two long-range goals: first, the organization of the working class into a controlling political party, and second, the abolition of wage slavery by establishing a national system of cooperative industry based on common ownership.[8] To implement these goals the party listed twenty demands, most of them similar to the 1898 platform. In addition, the new platform proposed public ownership of trusts and reduction of working hours in proportion to the increasing use of machines. Although not new to Socialists, this radical program attracted wide attention. Historically, the document gained significance as Americans started thinking and arguing about welfare legislation.

Although Debs had given many addresses after the closing of the convention in March, the formal opening of the national campaign took place in Chicago Music Hall on September 29, 1900. In the first speech of the evening, Debs' friend, Professor George D. Herron, Christian Socialist from Grinnell College in Iowa, spoke of his conversion to socialism and challenged his listeners to quit "asking what Lincoln would do, or what Jefferson would do, or what Moses would do, or what Marx would do, and decide for themselves, and by their own original inspirations what they were going to do in the face of the world problem that confronted them."[9] In his opening statement Debs declared: "The one vital issue in the present campaign springs from the private ownership of the means of production and it involves the whole question of political equality, economic freedom and social progress."[10] Parties, like individuals, he continued, acted from motives of self-interest. In his judgment, the Republican party represented the capitalists and their desire to expand into Asia; the Democratic party— the middle class and small capitalists; and the Socialist Party—the exploited wageworkers.

Although the platform did not include a statement on the Philippines, Debs spent considerable time midway in his opening speech on this issue. He upbraided the Republicans for favoring the acquisition of foreign territory, focusing his criticism upon a fellow Hoosier, Albert J. Beveridge. Sarcastically, Debs stated: "Senator Beveridge says that they take this land because they are the trustees of Jehovah!" In Debs' estimation, Senator Chauncey Depew better revealed the truth when he admitted: "The markets for the products of our farms and factories accessible by the Atlantic Ocean will soon be filled, but across the Pacific are numberless opportunities." In the Democratic opposition to this issue, Debs saw a desire for self-preservation. He insisted that they had no real power against the large capitalists. Further, he declared that, once the vast foreign trade was secured, Republican business interests would "crush out their small competitors in the middle class." In the main body of his address that followed the Philippine argument, Debs demonstrated a careful study of the platforms and acceptance speeches of both McKinley and Bryan. He quoted issues from each opponent's platform and address, and then explained how the Socialists took what he called a superior stand on the same issues. Throughout the speech he enhanced his status by comparing his cause to that of William Lloyd Garrison, Elijah Lovejoy, and Wendell Phillips. Because these men had new ideas, Debs asserted, they failed to receive immediate acclaim. Like these other causes, he said, socialism would eventually gain respect. Before Debs concluded he confronted those who thought that a vote for him wasted a vote: "Let me say to you that it is infinitely better to vote for freedom and fail than to vote for slavery and succeed."[11] In a final prediction, Debs proclaimed that he could see "the first struggling sun rays of a cooperative commonwealth in which men and women would enjoy equality in a land without a master—a land without a slave."[12]

This opening speech served as a pattern for the many that followed. In addition to his usual discussion of the issues in the platform, Debs sometimes liked to compare himself to Jefferson. "Jefferson was right in his day," he asserted. "He stood for the individual man and his right to use the implements of that industrial environment. Socialism is the evolution of Jeffersonian democracy. . ."[13] He continued his argument by asserting that the individual has been crushed rather than strengthened by competition. On October 29, 1900, *The Boston Globe* reported Debs' plea urging the middle class to join the Social Democratic party: "This class is doomed to disappointment. . . They tried the Republicans three times in twenty years and the Democrats twice." In Debs' opinion, the people had changed musicians repeatedly but heard the same music: "They tried Cleveland but the tunes were just the same, 'Over the Garden Wall' and 'Pop Goes the Weasel.' They tried Harrison but out came the same tunes, and now they think if Bryan is elected that he will give them symphonies."[14] Debs spoke in three different Boston halls on October 29 to overflow audiences. Before each address he spoke first to a street crowd and then to those inside. *The Boston Herald* reviewed these rallies and stated that Mr. Debs made "a good figure on the platform, controlled a pleasing voice," and used "an epigrammatic way" of saying such "striking thoughts" as "it is a case of lead vs. bread; which diet do you want?" The reporter concluded that "the agitator" had an "engaging presence, smiled kindly on the men who shook his hand, but still preached a strenuous doctrine."[15] On the next day when Debs spoke at Taunton, Massachusetts, his Social Democratic backers expected the strong local Socialist Labor Party to cause trouble. According to the newspaper, "nothing happened at the rally. The speaker was not interrupted for a single question."[16] There could have been trouble because members in this local, like several others with ties to the old Socialist Labor Party, refused to endorse Debs and maintained that DeLeon's more revolutionary ideas had been unfairly ignored at the nominating convention.

Throughout the campaign the party factions continued feuding. One side refused to collect funds for the other. As a result two national campaign committees opened headquarters in Chicago. Thomas J. Morgan, representing what he called the United Socialist Democratic Party composed of old Socialist Labor Party members, headed one group. Morgan's group wanted their funds used only to support the candidates their faction endorsed.

Seymour Stedman, backed by Victor Berger and Theodore Debs, led the other. Because of misinformation, Debs assumed that both groups were supporting him and so he publicly backed the Morgan group. He had to take time midway in the campaign to go to Chicago and settle the squabble.[17] By stressing the advantages of unity and the fact that the Socialist Labor supporters did not have candidates for national offices, Debs convinced Morgan's group to close their office. In addition to arbitrating party disputes, Debs repeatedly had to deny that he planned to quit and aid Bryan. Other rumors alleged that Senator Mark Hanna, prominent Republican Party boss, sent money to Debs to defeat Bryan.[18]

Near the end of the campaign Bryan and Debs spoke the same day in Philadelphia to separate audiences. The *North American* gave the two equal front page coverage and spoke of huge throngs greeting both speakers. Since Mother Mary Jones had spoken with Debs in Pennsylvania and West Virginia during several strikes, Debs had asked her to come to Philadelphia and introduce him. In a brief speech that warmed up the audience she stated: "I am glad to be here but it was hard to leave those men and boys, slaves in the truest sense of the word, waiting for the capitalist to say that their iron hand shall be a little relaxed for the time being. . ." After the applause ended for Mother Jones, Debs explained why he thought the old parties had nothing to offer the working class. In this address he discussed the surplus produced by American industries and their demands for new markets while most workers needed many necessities. Since neither of the two old parties had destroyed the trusts, the Socialist candidate asked his listeners why they perpetuated the present system.[19] Morris Stempa, who later became a close friend of Debs, heard the candidate speak on this occasion at the Philadelphia Academy of Music. "I was a young man at that time and had heard good speakers before," he avowed, "but Debs was something out of the ordinary. He held the audience in a trance with his tall figure and long arms waving."[20]

Not all reporters and editors responded as enthusiastically as Stempa to Debs' speaking. Late in the campaign, Debs complained about unfair newspaper coverage. He noted that the Republican papers published Bryan's speeches in full, and the Democratic, Roosevelt's in full, but none of them published his speeches. Roosevelt's speeches appeared in the newspapers because McKinley stayed home and let Teddy do the speaking. "During the past few weeks we have had most extraordinary demonstrations, but you have heard nothing of them," Debs charged. "We also have held a series of meetings here in the East of which you have heard little. Evidently the capitalist class is class conscious."[21] On the other hand many of Debs' addresses received considerable publicity and editors printed large sections of them. Debs could claim the coverage had not been equal—inch for inch of type—but he could not claim he had been ignored.

At the conclusion of this eastern campaign tour, Debs returned to Terre Haute and waited for the election returns. He received 96,116 votes, or three times more votes than any other Socialist candidate had ever garnered.[22] The result encouraged party supporters and they immediately began to plan ahead for future elections. Party adherents became convinced that socialism would soon triumph. This optimism, based on less than one hundred thousand votes, partially explained why many people in the movement sacrificed what little security they had to work for the cause.[23] Of course, Debs heightened this optimism by repeatedly stating in his speaking that success fast approached. He wrote his brother after the campaign and declared, "I am serene for two reasons: First, I did the very best I could for the party that nominated me and for its principles. Second, the working class will get in full measure what they voted for. And so we begin the campaign for 1904.[24]

In this same letter Debs asked Theodore to tell Seymour Stedman, member of the party's executive committee, that he opposed an immediate national conference and that he needed time to rest. In planning any meetings, Debs warned that if there was any attempt "to placate (factions within the party), *count me out* (underscored by Debs). We must go forward on our own lines. . . There must be no wobbling at this time."[25] Debs told Theodore of a long board meeting he attended in October in which party direction had been decided. "Hell! Don't we know what we want? Or are we crazy?" Debs wrote.[26] He asked Theodore to read his letter to Stedman, including this remark: "Stedman makes actually too much of the 'unaffiliated and unattached.' I would not cater to them a damned bit. We have invited them to a convention and if they don't come, let them stay out. A thousand men organized are better than ten times that number unorganized. Let's take care of the organized and the rest will take care of themselves."[27] Although the convention had been planned for three weeks after the election, it was repeatedly postponed. Stedman and other board members desired more time to bring the factions together. Stedman feared Debs' hard line approach would lose valuable supporters for the party, but Debs believed that compromise, especially with the Socialist Labor Party, was an impossibility. Debs had grown tired of appeasement, but other Party leaders had not.

On March 29, William Butscher, secretary of the eastern branch of the party, wrote Morris Hillquit that he had heard from George Goeble who had recently seen several National Executive Board (NEB) members in Chicago. Goeble confided to Butscher that "all are for union except Victor Berger, but do not want the convention before September."[28] In another letter to Hillquit, A. M. Simons, editor of the *International Socialist Review* in 1901, advised that Hillquit get the other New York delegates to accept unification. Since several groups had expressed a willingness to unite, Simons asked what Hillquit proposed to do with such men. He quipped, "Borrow DeLeon's 'gaspipe' or hire Hickey (who I understand is for sale at a bargain) to chase them back?" "Or shall we welcome them," he questioned, "and then get to work on their education?"[29]

Simons was also writing Hillquit to tell him that he intended to go to the conference and that a group of dissatisfied workers and reformers had organized to meet in Detroit in June. Simons hoped that this gathering of dissidents could be prevented from forming any national organization until after they held their meeting. "There will probably be 1,000 people there. Of these, there will be perhaps 50 of the type represented by Pomroy and Bliss, and 25 or 30 more of the radical democracy, such as Jones, Johnson, Williams, etc.; this will leave 700 or 800 who do not know what they want, but as soon as they do know, should want socialism," he declared.[30] Hillquit opposed Simons going to the meeting because he thought that he would have to compromise too much and use "tricks, conspiracies or schemes" to succeed.[31] To counter Simon's efforts, Hillquit proposed to send a letter to be read at the conference stating that their supporters would make no concessions. Simons sternly inquired by whose authority would Hillquit address such a letter. "You certainly have no business to affix your name to it, or that of any other member of the NEB officially without a referendum as this is an action far beyond any powers ever conferred upon a national body," Simons warned.[32] Finally Simons assured Hillquit that he would lead a fight to leave their party if any of the groups within the party ever tried to "turn the party from the position of clear-cut class conscious socialism."[33] After all of this behind the scenes politicking, the majority of the NEB members finally agreed to call the convention. Debs remained doubtful that unification could be achieved.

Chapter VI
Uniting the Party

The modest success of Debs in the 1900 campaign did more than any other factor to encourage unification. He demonstrated that he had more power at the polls than any leader in the other factions. On July 29, 1901, all elements in the party, except the New York representatives of DeLeon's Socialist Labor Party, met in Indianapolis for the expressed purpose of uniting. The delegates represented 10,000 members. Prior to the 1900 convention Debs had spent considerable time in getting DeLeon's followers to merge with his own. Their absence indicated that Debs' statements that he was no longer willing to compromise had reached their ears. Both sides recognized that their differences could not be reconciled at this time. An even more disturbing party division to Debs was the growing split with the Springfield group. The expense and confusion of two national headquarters in Springfield, Massachusetts, and Chicago, Illinois, could end if the delegates would agree upon a constitution and a platform. The Springfield or more conservative faction, led by James Carey, had been more successful in securing proxies and delegates than the Chicago faction. Carey's followers held 4,798 "credentials" and were represented by sixty-eight delegates. The Chicago group, led by Berger, George Herron, and Theodore Debs, held 1,396 proxies and had forty-eight delegates.[1] Seven unpledged delegates held 382 votes. Berger had obviously been right in assessing the opposition's strength and in hoping to delay the convention. Theodore Debs didn't seem as concerned about the opposition.

Certainly Debs could have taken any one of several trains that daily made the seventy-mile trip to Indianapolis and appeared briefly at the convention. He chose not to attend the convention. He said that illness in his family prevented his coming to Indianapolis. Both his wife and aged mother-in-law, who now lived with the Debses, were ill and suffering from the extreme heat. Since Debs did not state this reason in his telegram to the assembly, gossip spread that Debs had avoided the convention because the Springfield group had a majority of the votes.[2] A curious reporter checked and found both women ailing; however, Debs worked daily in his office and visited about town.[3] Since the delegates at all previous national meetings had engaged in numerous bitter disputes, Debs reasoned that he had nothing to gain in prestige by becoming involved. Since his brother Theodore served as secretary of the Chicago faction, he knew his interests would be represented. The second rumor that Debs had opposed the convention was not true. After a favorable vote of the membership of Debs' wing of the party in March 1901, Theodore Debs had written to William Butscher, secretary of the Springfield faction, and announced a date to plan the meeting and requirements for joining with the Chicago faction in sponsoring a convention. Although Eugene did not attend the planning session for this convention, Theodore did. After the invitation for the convention had been issued, Debs appealed to both groups to settle their disagreements.[4]

By avoiding this convention Debs set a precedent which he would follow in future years. His non-intervention in public conventions would become a habit. He evidently sensed that his value to the party would be in the role of a leader who remained above the annual conflicts. The many aggressive individualists and dissenters from other parties who joined the Socialists were bound to disagree over party strategy. Debs had learned from experience that when these strong-willed people argued about the policies that would guide the party, they often became irritated and vindictive toward those who opposed them. These personal attacks made permanent enemies. Debs as the recognized leader in the party had to work with all of these men, and he knew that he would lose part of the appeal and strength that he had if he identified too closely with his faction or openly fought any other. Also, he remembered earlier conventions in which he had tried to secure compromise and failed. He viewed this 1901 convention as the legislative session of the party and envisioned himself as the executive officer who would have to carry out the decisions.

In the opening business session, Theodore Debs, after reading his official report as secretary for the Chicago group, submitted his resignation and asked that he not be reelected in any subsequent merger. He wanted to be free to support Eugene without the responsibility of serving as a party official. He felt one spokesman in their family was sufficient. Although his request disappointed Berger and others in the Chicago group, they recognized the wisdom of his decision. Theodore feared his brother would receive unwarranted criticism if he continued in this strategic position.

After settling routine matters on the first day of the convention and selecting a committee to find a successor to Theodore, the delegates started discussing a party platform. Several delegates lost sight of their unity goal and began a dispute over including a plank in the platform that requested immediate political and economic changes. The Springfield delegates preferred a general revolutionary plank, even if it took years to achieve. This group opposed the Berger-Debs faction's immediate demands of public ownership of all means of transportation and communication, public utilities, industries controlled by trusts; reduction of hours of labor; state or national insurance for unemployment, sickness and old age; the initiative and referendum.[5] A. M. Simons, Gaylord Wilshire and others argued for the Berger-Debs faction that conditions in the United States favored immediate adoption of socialism and that their new party should not try to outpromise other political parties attempting to modify capitalism. During this controversy word spread that the Sprngfield group also planned "to shelve" Eugene Debs as party leader. Since they controlled the convention, Debs' supporters had a difficult time securing recognition. After failing in three attempts to gain the floor, C. G. Clemons, delegate from Kansas, and cousin of Mark Twain, shouted, "I know the Chicago faction is down, never to regain prestige; I know that the end of the brilliant leadership of Eugene V. Debs has come."[6] Prior to the convention the Springfield faction had agreed to follow the practice of the Chicago faction that all decisions had to be submitted via ballot to all the members for final approval. Berger, who had insisted upon this procedure of all members voting, warned his opposition: "You may drown us here, but I want you to understand that it is here alone, because the action of this convention must go back to the members. . . . Through this medium, if through no other we can prevent unity."[7]

The rumored threat of dropping Debs as chief party spokesman served as a catalyst to gain compromise. Although many leaders in the Springfield faction disagreed with Debs, they recognized his strength with the rank and file Socialists. At the next session, delegates debated a resolution that denied the newspaper report that Debs was ousted. Since the majority of the delegates did not want to confirm the newspaper story with a formal vote, they voted instead to send Debs a telegram which assured him of the "respect of the members and that the convention was progressing to its purpose."[8] After receiving the telegram Debs stated in an interview: "This is an important convention from every standpoint. The delegates who have been divided upon questions relating not to principles but to tactics will doubtless find a way of uniting. I do not doubt the severity of the debate. It will sometimes seem as if factional dissension were to continue."[9] Another important factor that helped gain compromise was the fact that delegates switched back and forth on various issues, especially on the immediate demands. Hillquit, prominent New York leader in the Springfield faction, saw the practicality of the immediate demands. "If . . . the working class wait six or ten years and see no chance of its (cooperative commonwealth) realization, then we will be much worse off for they will lose faith in your propaganda," he declared.[10] His view prevailed. The delegates in a final hassle selected St. Louis as the new party headquarters and Leon Greenbaum, a little known party neutral, as national secretary. Soon after the close of the convention Debs related his pleasure with their actions: "The Socialist delegates. . . are entitled to the thanks and congratulations of every Socialist in the country. . . They accomplished more than could have reasonably been expected."[11] He proceeded to praise the party name, Socialist Party of America, platform, new headquarters and secretary. Debs' tactic of avoiding the convention and letting the delegates fight over the issues had worked reasonably well. The delegates had created a platform that Debs could support and the annoying problem of duplication between two national headquarters ended with the opening of the St. Louis office. With the vote of confidence from the assembly and a better unified party, Debs set to work to increase membership and to create public understanding of the party and its program.

In the years between 1900 and 1904, Debs continued lecturing throughout the country under the sponsorship of several national lecture bureaus.

After closing the party headquarters in Chicago, his brother Theodore returned with his wife and daughter to Terre Haute and organized a Labor Lecture Bureau with Eugene as the principal speaker. He also joined Eugene in an office at 11th and Wabash and became his fulltime secretary and adviser. In the evening Eugene would often drop by to visit Theodore and his wife Gertrude, and plan the next day's work. He became especially fond of his niece, Marguerite. Since he and Kate did not have any children, he enjoyed his niece and remembered her with cards and gifts when he travelled. Theodore scheduled Gene to speak for one lecture bureau one month and for their own Labor Lecture Bureau the next month. Since the other bureaus, especially those with Chautauqua circuits, guaranteed higher fees, Debs could earn under this arrangement the dollars he so desperately needed to repay the ARU debt and yet serve labor and Socialist Party interests as a speaker and organizer.[12]

Debs especially enjoyed the Chautauqua assignments. Before these crowds of curious faces Debs pleaded for understanding of laborers' rights to organize for financial reasons and to join the Socialist party for political reasons. He also discussed current events of the day and gave his frank opinion of them. For example, Andrew Carnegie's philanthropy irked Debs. In 1901 he admonished his listeners not to forget that "the soulless millionaire" had hired "Pinkerton assassins" to force laborers to accept his terms.[13] In every town where Carnegie offered a library, Debs encouraged the central labor body to form a protest committee and refuse the gift. "They may have to work for Carnegie," he admitted, "but they are not compelled to recognize as a gift the pennies he throws them in return for the dollars he stole from them!"[14]

In addition to his attacks upon Carnegie, Debs had little good to say about John Mitchell, the powerful leader of United Mine Workers of America who advocated craft unionism. Mitchell feared the drift toward socialism in many of the mining unions, especially those in Illinois, West Virginia and Pennsylvania. Debs' past work on behalf of the miners during strikes in these states had made him a favorite with many miners. Mitchell thought the Socialists were too radical and that labor would make greater gains by supporting other political parties. Adolph Germer, influential Illinois miner and organizer who also did "trouble shooting" and consulted on difficult organizing problems throughout the country, kept Debs informed of activities within the mining unions. Germer, who later became secretary of the Socialist party, often became discouraged in his work since he believed as Debs did. Debs counseled Germer to "not take those people too seriously." "They are doubtlessly honest, but they are fanatics," he wrote. "I have no time to waste on them. Some of them are not open to reason. Thomas Paine said: 'To argue with a man who has renounced his reason is like administering to the dead.' "[15] In another letter, Debs stated to Germer that "President Mitchell's oftrepeated statement that 'there is no necessary antagonism between capital and labor' meets its denial in every hour of the present hostilities." In articles in the *Social Democratic Herald*

Debs continued his attacks upon Mitchell. In 1903 and 1904 when the Miners Union accepted reductions in wages to reach settlements on a two year contract, Debs accused Mitchell of abusing the powers of his office to force settlements rather than strike for benefits and higher wages. Debs felt the coal operators had taken advantage of the recession in 1903 and could afford better terms.[16] Finally Mitchell became so irked with Debs that he maneuvered a resolution through the national miners convention denouncing Debs and specifically condemning his articles.[17] Germer continued to enlighten Debs about activities within the miners' union, even the secret sessions held at the national conventions. After receiving the 1904 convention proceedings from Germer, Debs replied: "I shall look them over carefully and may have occasion to refer to them in dealing with those who hide behind secret proceedings to keep up their apostasy to labor."[18] Debs further suggested to Germer that "if you get a copy of a complete roster of all locals with names and addresses of officers I can make it serve a good purpose. Go to no trouble. I am very thankful for what you have already sent."[19] Obviously Mitchell's denouncing Debs did little to deter his efforts to infiltrate the miners' organization. Perhaps it challenged him.

Unions increased in number and Debs found it less difficult to convince workers of the necessity of unions. Just as the conflict between Mitchell and Debs continued so did the disagreements between management and labor. There were many strikes between 1901 and 1904, and workers readily joined the picket line when thwarted. The recession in 1903 heightened the struggle, with management blaming the unions for it. In 1904, Senator Marcus (Mark) Hanna, formerly a manufacturer and national campaign manager but then a senator from Ohio, said to a reporter that the recession was only temporary and that labor should not be blamed for it. However, he opined that, "In New York and Chicago and one or two other places a depression has been created by the troubles in the building trades."[20] Debs followed Hanna's remarks closely and often attacked Hanna's views in his speeches. In answer to another question from the interviewer, Hanna gave a reply that reflected the gradual change in attitude that some management spokesmen were beginning to take toward unions. When asked if he thought that organized labor had come to stay, Hanna replied: "Yes, it is a condition and should be treated accordingly. . . such things as shorter working hours and rising pay regulate themselves. The movements are perfectly natural ones. The capitalist tries to get all he can out of his share of the business and so does the workman. With our enormous immigration and restricted supply of work, there have been plenty of laborers and the capitalists have had the upper hand. Within the past three years there have been two men for every job. . ." He continued by stating that he could understand why workers needed unions under these conditions. "If I were a working man, I would belong to a union," he admitted, "but I would do all I could to bring capital and labor together."[21] Debs doubted his sincerity because Hanna's record in Congress had not been pro-labor. Whether

Hanna played the politician's role of gaining laborers' votes with these statements or not is unknown. They do indicate some perception of the problems labor faced and some tolerance of these problems. But Hanna's views did not represent all of management. David M. Parry, president of the National Association of Manufacturers in 1904, called organized labor a mob. "I believe many of the labor leaders would guillotine us if they could. It is not right to look upon the unions as representatives of American labor. 85% of our working men do not belong. . . . $25,000,000 lost in wages during the coal strike; $125,000,000 added to consumers' coal bills. Labor agitators have put a check to a period of unparalleled prosperity," he declared.[22] Furthermore he believed that "ten hours a day of work is required to satisfy the needs of humanity."[23] Debs had other interpretations of these figures and other ideas on what was required to satisfy human needs. According to Parry, the question of whether or not an employer could employ a man who did not belong to a union was absurd. "It is revolutionary," he declared. In an attack upon those in management, such as Hanna, who took a more conciliatory view, Parry exclaimed: "How public men can lend their voices and influence to arbitration is beyond me. . . The present depression is caused by the exorbitant demands of labor."[24] As he traveled, Debs clipped out newspaper articles on Hanna's and Parry's views and sent them to Theodore to read and file.[25]

Between 1901 and 1903, Debs strongly advocated Negro rights. His speaking tour through the South in 1903 made him more acutely aware of racial inequality. In January 1903, at the annual Socialist convention held in St. Louis, Debs finally secured enough support after years of agitation to get the party to adopt a special Black resolution. In this resolution the party welcomed Blacks to "membership and fellowship in the world movement for economic emancipation. . ."[26] Debs admitted before a Fort Worth, Texas, audience that the Socialist party had not yet made "progress enough to make a decision on the race question," by which he meant recognition of social equality. He insisted, however, that Socialists believed in "absolute economic equality regardless of all previous conditions."[27]

In another address before a crowd in Butte, Montana, Debs declared that he had been opposed to discrimination all of his life and that the Socialist party was entirely free from race prejudice.[28] Debs had no qualms about attacking Negroes who he thought supported the white establishment. He singled out as an example Booker T. Washington, one of the most popular Negro heroes. "Mr. Washington is backed by the plutocrats of the country clear up or down to Grover Cleveland," he declared before this Montana audience. "They support his Institute. What fraction of one per cent of the eleven million Negroes in the United States will get the benefit of his industrial education?" He usually concluded his attack upon Washington with these rhetorical questions: "When did he ever advise his race to stand together as one? Why doesn't he tell the Negro that depending on charity is degrading?"[29] Debs' remarks befriending Negroes created controversy, but Debs welcomed the discussion on this important issue. In November 1903, Debs thought he could further this important cause by writing an article, "The Negro in the Class Struggle," to explicate his views on the subject.[30] He asked the editor of the *International Socialist Review* to print it.

This essay provoked a series of letters to the editor and prompted Debs to write another article defending his views. In this second article, "The Negro and His Nemesis," Debs angrily replied to those writers, especially one anonymous individual from Elgin, Illinois, who told Debs that he would "jeopardize the best interests of the Socialist party" if he insisted upon political equality for the Negro.[31] "Of course the Negro will not be satisfied with equality with reservations," Debs retorted. "Why should he be? Would you? Suppose you change places with the Negro just a year, then let us hear from you—with reservations." Other readers wrote and tried to dismiss Debs' charges by implying that he thought like a northerner and condemned the South while ignoring prejudice in the North. He countered these accusations by asserting that discrimination was reprehensible wherever it existed. Debs staunchly maintained that the Socialist movement sought to unite all workers regardless of race, nationality, creed, sex, or section of the country, and that anyone who did not subscribe to that philosophy was not a Socialist. If any member misunderstood this philosophy, Debs advised him to quickly return to "the capitalistic parties with their social and economic strata from the 'white trash' and 'buck nigger' down to the syphilitic snob and harlot heiress who barters virtue for title in the matrimonial market."[32] Debs' strong language indicated how vexed he became with opponents on this issue. He believed that only through an organized struggle in the labor and socialist movements "would the Negro win equality."[33] His active support of this issue and others resulted in continued demands for him to speak in all parts of the United States. Unfortunately, other labor and political leaders did not join Debs in urging equality for Blacks.

These speaking engagements supporting party unity, Negro rights, women's rights, workers' rights and other reform measures, required that Debs spend hours traveling by train. On many occasions he had to walk from the station to some remote town beyond the rail line. Often the trains ran behind schedule and Debs had to rush. When late he found his audiences weary from waiting. He soon discovered that his opponents had willing helpers in railroad managers who could deliberately make him late. Debs became furious on several occasions when he knew that the officials of the railroad had directed a "slow order," so that he would arrive too late to fill a speaking engagement. Whenever an engine developed trouble, Debs feared another "slow order" had been directed.[34] Since Debs required a fee, his speeches had to have publicity. Such publicity easily came to the attention of his adversaries, and whether they ran the railroads or organized a heckling chorus, they made Debs' tasks more difficult. Staunch supporters tried to make Debs' visits enjoyable, however. If time permitted, they planned elaborate dinners before the speeches and private conferences afterwards. Often they would keep Debs visiting until early morning or until the train arrived to take him to his next assignment. Because of this exhausting schedule, Debs had to take time to rest between tours. Debs met the inevitable problems in such a life with outward calm, but he and Theodore, who frequently accompanied him, often privately cursed those who inconvenienced them.

Sometimes incidents amused them. Arriving one evening an hour late for a speech, Debs and his host hurried down a darkened alley toward a back door that led to the stage. Debs felt a tug at his trousers and heard something tear. Upon entering the theatre, he realized that a piece of barb wire, frozen in the ground, had torn the front of his trousers. Theodore related that the "flap hung down like the ear of a Missouri hound pup with the damage plainly visible even to a man with a glass eye."[35] While Eugene made a hasty collection of pins, Theodore ordered the footlights extinguished, house lights dimmed, and while introducing his brother lowered the cloth on the speaker's stand. Although Eugene usually paced about the stage while lecturing, he remained behind the stand on this occasion and made a quick exit at the end.

During these tours Debs enjoyed visiting with the workers, ministers, businessmen, and professors who attended his talks. He had a remarkable memory for names and faces. The following typified these encounters. In New Orleans an old man came forward and asked Eugene if he knew him. "Surely," remarked Debs, who then proceeded to say the man's name. "You and I served together on an Illinois Central grievance committee for the Locomotive Fireman on that road; that was twenty-five years ago. You represented Lodge No. 40 and I the Grand Lodge. . . At that time you were firing a locomotive on the Central out of Bloomington, Illinois, and lived in that city."[36] Many similar accounts have been verified; however, Debs fooled some handshakers. On another evening Debs spoke on the East Side of New York City. He had spoken the previous year in that section of the city to striking garment workers. After the second address, many of the men in charge of the strike who had consulted with Debs about strategy, rushed forward to renew acquaintance. Theodore observed them and overheard one worker say, "He met us on one occasion and yet he remembered us all by name!" When Debs returned to his hotel room, Theodore asked him if he actually knew these men. "No, not all of them," Debs replied with a wry smile on his face. "You saw many Russian Jews among those I greeted. By mumbling the first syllable of their names and emphasizing the last, with a rising inflection of the voice, there was not much danger of going wrong. Their names all end with s-k-y!"[37] Thereafter when Eugene told a story that Theodore doubted, he would ask if this was another "s-k-y tale!"

During these years, 1901-1904, Debs enjoyed excellent health. With three or four hours rest, he could resume his rapid pace and continue the arduous speaking schedule. Even when home in Terre Haute, he would get up at five o'clock, shave, carefully read the papers, and attend to household chores or do some writing before breakfast. After breakfast he took a long walk and planned to open the office at eight. Tenants in the building referred to him as the "man who never sleeps."[38] Although he fought for the eight hour day, he never limited himself to such a day. After 1900, he never had enough time to keep ahead of all the letters that required answers or to fulfill requests for articles in newspapers and magazines. Debs zealously guarded his time but his enjoyment of argument and people made it difficult for him to limit visitors. When he had to go into local businesses, he frequently chose the alleys to avoid friends who might delay his work. In their home, Katherine never understood why Eugene visited so long with people and would usually busy herself with household chores rather than sit and listen to his guests.

Debs maintained his office at his own expense. He furnished it simply and took pride in keeping everything from the broom to twine in its proper place. On the walls Debs hung pictures of Victor Hugo, Robert Ingersoll, Rodin's "The Thinker," a red Socialist pennant, a colored plaster emblem of the Socialist Party, and a map of the United States. To speed up their office work, Eugene had Theodore place his desk next to his own. Together they attempted to answer the ever increasing piles of mail. Debs believed that if anyone took the trouble to write him, he deserved the courtesy of a reply. Into each of these letters Debs would place a reprint of one of his speeches or some article he had written. His walnut desk had a high cabinet top with numerous compartments which he filled each week with various leaflets. In the evening he would take several additional hours of work home with him. After supper he would retire to his small workroom upstairs and continue his work. As he read newspapers and magazines, he underscored heavily with a blue pencil those ideas that intrigued him. After finishing his reading he would clip out these writings. Many he saved and had Katherine or Theodore paste in his scrapbook; others he took to the office and mailed to workers he thought might be influenced. Debs wanted some propaganda material to go into the mails each day! He insisted that "if the feet of one workingman out of fifty" turned into "the right path" the time and money spent on letters was worth it.

While on tour Debs tried to keep up with his correspondence. After his speeches, he collected the names and addresses of non-Socialists who seemed interested. He mailed these names to his home office with instructions as to which leaflets Theodore should send to each. He also attempted to get a copy of any newspaper articles that appeared before and after his addresses. These he sent to Theodore for filing.[39]

To carry out his agitation on behalf of labor and socialism, Debs continued to write many pamphlets, but he still lacked the money to buy a press. In 1901, Debs had changed the name of his publishing outlet from his own name to Standard Publishing Company. Evidently he hoped to sell more books and pamphlets that aided unity and spread socialism with this less easily identifiable name. When Tom Woodburn and Bert Viquesney left Moore-Langen Printing Company and started their own presses, Debs divided his business between these printers who had been helping him.[40] Ray J. Owen, who worked for Bert Viquesney, said that the linotype setting for Debs' many pamphlets was done at the *Terre Haute Star,* and that he and Frank Simpson, foreman at the *Star,* read the proof. On one occasion when delivering galley proofs to Debs, Owen inquired if Debs would explain what he meant in certain paragraphs. He took an hour to interpret what he meant. Although usually very busy, Debs was the kind of man who would take time to explain his ideas. This led to a lifelong friendship, and thereafter Debs answered many questions that Owen and Simpson asked.[41]

In addition to adopting the Negro resolution at the 1903 St. Louis convention, the delegates endorsed a rule excluding from the party any member who actively supported any other party. If Socialists held offices in other political organizations, they had to resign. Debs agreed with this procedure because he thought that the party had sufficient strength to assert itself. This became a source of disunity because some leaders, especially Job Harriman, disagreed. Harriman, former running mate of Debs, had formed a coalition of labor unions in California. He had left New York to live on the desert near Indio, California, in order to cure himself of tuberculosis. In spite of severe attacks from this disease which curtailed his activities for weeks at a time, he succeeded in making many contacts with dissident labor groups in the state. As he was unable to work as a lawyer much of the time, his old New York Eastside friend and party ally, Morris Hillquit, sent him money whenever he requested.[42] At the St. Louis meeting, Hillquit reversed his former stand on this issue and agreed with Debs. This offended Harriman. After receiving the convention proceedings from Hillquit, Harriman replied: "I have not seen nor read of a more unsocialistic or unconstitutional proceedings than this body was guilty of. It is a shame and outrage. . ."[43] Harriman staunchly maintained that nothing short of joining with labor organizations could ever hold the Socialist movement from "the grasp of the middleclass."[44] He chastised Hillquist for not agreeing with him that workers first had to be organized into unions for economic reasons before they could be organized into a political party of any power. Although this incident resulted in Hillquit losing Harriman's support, it represented a closing of the differences that Debs had with Hillquit. Greenbaum, the national secretary, disagreed with this hard-line approach and resigned. The delegates selected William Mailly and decided to move headquarters to Omaha. At this 1903 convention Hillquit worked with Berger on several committees and became increasingly disenchanted with his dominating manner. In a letter to his wife, he confided that he disliked Berger and suspected his being "very sweet" to him.[45] Debs had already had his differences with Harriman and Berger; now Hillquit seemed to be forming the same opinions. Unity within the Socialist Party was always tenuous because the alliances shifted, but the combination of Debs supporters with Hillquit's would make a formidable and important block of votes, if needed.

Hillquit could not always attend the periodic national executive committee meetings, but he had a faithful reporter in Mailly, the new secretary. In a meeting in June, he said that he had a talk with Berger about whether Debs would run for president. He asked Berger to speak with Debs about the matter. Mailly added that Berger "seemed pleased when I told him you Eastern fellows were satisfied to have Debs."[46] If Debs refused to run, Berger suggested Max S. Hayes or J. Mahlon Barnes. "Didn't seem favorably impressed with Ben Hanford," Mailly reported.[47] Evidently Hillquit had suggested that Hanford be considered if Debs declined, and that Hanford make a speaking tour to become better known. Berger agreed to this proposal and invited him to Milwaukee. In a later meeting Mailly informed Hillquit of his fight with Berger over moving the party headquarters to Chicago. "We would be in hell all the time. There are too many different factions and meddlers there and we would have no peace," Mailly declared.[48] He added that Berger was displaying "old signs of the big head again and the quorum meetings would not last over a day and a half if it were not for his actions."[49] After describing Berger as the "most aggravating man I ever dealt with," he mentioned that Debs attended the meeting "toward the close of it." After the session Debs visited with members of the committee and reported upon his activities.

While Hillquit took time to write a book, *The History of Socialism in the United States,*[50] Debs continued to work to unify the party and collect support for the forthcoming 1904 presidential campaign. When finished with his book, Hillquit sent Debs an inscribed copy. Debs thanked Hillquit and stated that he had written the "very book needed at this time."[51] Debs liked the long historical introduction that traced the European roots of American socialism and the fact that in the chapters discussing the development of the party in this country, Hillquit had written only about the official actions taken by the party and left out all of the details about the inner-party strife. Although unfortunate, a history that elaborated upon the party battles would have alienated the very leaders within the party that Debs had worked so diligently to unite.

Chapter VII
A Willing Candidate

In planning ahead for the 1904 campaign and the years after it, Debs realized that he had to play a more active role in his party if he expected unity to continue and the party's socialistic goals to be achieved. Between 1904 and 1908, Debs became discouraged with the slow progress that workers made at the bargaining table and joined the militant Industrial Workers of the World. This move by Debs alienated more conservative Socialists and caused disunity within the party. Debs volunteered to help edit the popular *Appeal to Reason,* because he wanted the opportunity to explain his views and convince readers that a more aggressive approach would bring about necessary changes in society. Debs began his more overt role in party machinations with the 1904 campaign.

Prior to the 1904 convention, planned for Chicago, Debs informed key men on the central committee that he would accept the nomination. Enthusiastic over the growing party, he had cast aside his previous reluctance to seek any office. Just when party officials had become accustomed to Debs not attending conventions, he cleverly changed his strategy and surprised delegates by appearing at this meeting.

In the preliminary reports before the nomination, William Mailly proudly announced that in the past fifteen months membership had increased from ten to twenty-two thousand members.[1] Some facts about the one hundred and eighty-three delegates indicate the variety of leaders in the party that Debs actively sought to lead. The oldest delegate was seventy, and the two youngest were twenty. The average age was thirty-nine; one hundred and twenty were born in the United States; seventy-eight delegates held membership in trade unions. The party representatives listed sixty-five different occupations with twenty classifying themselves as editors, sixteen as printers, fifteen as lawyers, eight as teachers, seven as lecturers, six as cigar makers, five as organizers and agitators, five as physicians, five as farmers, and four as journalists. The other 92 delegates represented by four or fewer members listed the following occupations: architect, brewery worker, butcher, clergy, porter, tinner, janitor, machinists, sawmill operator, iron worker, plumber, etc. Certainly the delegates represented a variety of incomes, education, and social classes, but at least seventy-five of the one hundred and eighty-three delegates could be considered professional men.[2]

At the convention the delegates quickly chose Debs to run a second time. They selected for his running mate, Benjamin Hanford, a popular New York typographer. Hanford had attracted national attention with his mythical "Jimmie Higgins," a whimsical cartoon character who represented the rank and file Socialist who did all the work while party leaders took all the credit.[3]

At this convention no one had to read an acceptance telegram from Debs because he came prepared with an address for the occasion. In accepting the nomination on May 6, 1904, in Brand's Hall in Chicago, Debs told the delegates, "Personally I could have wished to remain in the ranks, to make my record, humble though it might be, fighting unnamed." Debs further stated that he hoped to fulfill the party's expectations; to carry proudly in the coming contest the banner of the working class; and to make his utterances and acts prove his worthiness to bear the standard of the only party that proposed to emancipate workers from "the thralldom of the ages."[4]

The 1904 platform continued to represent a compromise between the "Rights" in the party who believed in evolutionary socialism and the "Lefts" who favored revolutionary socialism. The platform contained essentially the same planks as those adopted at the 1901 unity convention. Debs and A. M. Simons, editor of the *International Socialist Review,* urged the delegates to censure the AFL for supporting craft unionism and conservative political measures, and to declare themselves in favor of industrial unionism. They failed in this attempt. Debs was disappointed that the official Socialist position permitted workers to join the AFL.[5] The platform, however, warned that "such measures of relief as we may be able to force from capitalism are but a preparation of the workers to seize the whole powers of government, in order that they may thereby lay hold of the whole system of industry, and thus come into their rightful inheritance."[6]

After the convention Debs held several meetings with the campaign committee to plan the activities for the following months. In 1900, the committee had delayed the opening of the campaign until September 29, but in 1904 they advanced the date to September 1. Debs delivered the opening speech in Indianapolis. In this address he presented a series of arguments that he repeatedly used in the numerous campaign talks that followed. In his introduction Debs asserted that America's twenty-five million wage-workers had become twentieth century slaves. He called the term "labor market" the most barbarous description in all Christendom, for it expressed to him the "animalism of commercial civilization." "The workers have but one issue in this campaign," Debs announced, "the overthrow of the capitalist system." Such a strategy of centering his objections to the opposing political parties around one militant issue differed from his approach in the 1900 campaign. In the previous campaign, Debs usually first attacked the Republicans on an issue and then the Democrats on the same issue. He had consistently pointed out that the Republicans represented the large investment holders, and the Democrats the middle class and small business owners. But in opening the 1904 campaign, Debs declared that he no longer intended to discuss the opposition's issues on an individual party basis—a promise that he did not keep. "The Republican-Democratic parties, or, to be more exact, the Republican-Democratic party, represent the capitalist class in the class struggle," he announced, "and such differences as arise between them relate to spoils and not to principles." With either of these parties in power Debs guaranteed that capitalists would remain "in the saddle and the workers under the saddle." He declared that his opponents could have the tariff, finance, imperialism, and "other dust-covered and moth-eaten issues" because Socialists knew that if they endorsed these issues, capitalist rule and wage-slavery would continue.[7] In Debs' judgment the other parties' weak labor platforms evaded issues by stating "justice to capital and justice to labor." Vexed, Debs shouted, "This hoary old platitude is worse than meaningless."[8]

In this speech Debs made a detailed analysis of the past attacks upon labor by both the Republican candidates, Theodore Roosevelt and Charles Fairbanks, and the Democratic hopefuls, Judge Alton Parker and Henry G. Davis. He charged that each of these four candidates had at various times worked for business interests, or otherwise made decisions against labor. For example, Debs informed his listeners that Parker had served as one of the New York Supreme Court judges that declared the eight-hour law unconstitutional. Mr. Davis had been instrumental in calling an injunction against Debs and the miners of West Virginia in 1897. Later Debs completed his attack upon the vice-presidential candidates by predicting that wageworkers would have no trouble in making their choice between "that precious pair of plutocrats" in order to cast their votes for Ben Hanford, a calloused handed worker.[9]

Before ending his address Debs called attention to the striking Colorado miners and their fight for union recognition which had resulted in bloodshed and numerous imprisonments. In summary Debs restated his contentions and exhorted his listeners to work for a November victory: "We know our cause is just and that it must prevail. . . We hold our heads erect and with dauntless spirit marshal the working class for the march from Capitalism to Socialism, from Slavery to Freedom, from Barbarism to Civilization."[10]

After formally opening the campaign on September 1, Debs left Indianapolis and for the next two months spoke in every state in the union. The national chairman first sent him to New York, then to California, and back across the country to Maine, speaking every day in several different towns. Stephen Reynolds, flamboyant Terre Haute lawyer and friend of Clarence Darrow, joined Debs and his brother in Chicago on October 17 and helped with the campaigning from there to Portland, Maine, and back to Terre Haute on November 8. Reynolds later wrote that Debs never missed an appointment and spoke from two to four times daily giving speeches which were seldom under two hours in length.[11] The party met campaign expenses by charging twenty-five cents admission to the speeches. This practice, unusual for a political speaker, did not decrease the size of Debs' audiences. At the end of the campaign, Upton Sinclair, an avid supporter of Debs, estimated that Debs had spoken to approximately two hundred fifty thousand people.[12] Active state organizations sponsored many other rallies. In Illinois forty-five volunteer speakers made speeches and distributed over half a million Socialist pamphlets.[13] On election eve Debs addressed the largest crowd ever assembled in the Terre Haute Coliseum. "There will be no change in conditions," the candidate declared, "until you workers become the master of the tools. . ." "If we got along without King George," he continued, "we can get along without King John—Rockefeller or King Andrew—Carnegie." Debs praised workers for learning how to strike together, to unite against injunctions, even to die together, but he asked when they would vote together. After announcing that everything he wore carried a union label, he asked in return that each worker "place the union label" on the ballot the next day. "I'm not absolutely certain that I will be the next president," Debs quipped. "If I am not, it won't be my fault."[14]

The November election results revealed that Debs and the Socialists had quadrupled their voting strength over 1900. Debs received 402,321 votes. Newspapers commented chiefly upon Roosevelt's two million majority, but they also noted with alarm the great increase in the Socialist vote.[15] During a speaking tour after the election, Cardinal Gibbons of St. Louis urged his Catholic followers to help curb the progress of this movement by explaining to their friends the inevitability of inequality of rank, station, and wealth. In his view Socialists lacked "the capacity to discern that this condition must result from a law of life established by an overruling Providence."[16] Theodore Roosevelt frankly admitted that this third party represented a threatening political force "far more ominous than any Populist or similar movement in time past."[17] Roosevelt suggested reforms in capitalism before the Socialists took more drastic action, but this advice created opposition. In a letter to William Allen White he complained, "As you know, I have incurred the bitterest attacks, not merely from the Socialist and anarchist crowd, but from men of predatory wealth who prefer Socialists and anarchists to my style of conservatism."[18] All of this controversy pleased Debs, for he believed that it called socialism to the attention of many who otherwise might have ignored it. Debs was further gratified that the factions within the party had cooperated throughout the campaign and had given him strong support. While resting after the campaign, he wrote to thank Morris Hillquit. "There was a time, I confess, when I did not like Morris Hillquit," Debs admitted. "I did not know him. I do know him now and am trying to make up for past remissness."[19] Such political fence-mending by Debs helped to continue a brief period of harmony within the volatile party.

The arduous campaign had taken Debs away from his Terre Haute office, and he quickly returned to his routine of writing and speaking on behalf of labor and socialism. He had become increasingly aware of the limitations of craft unionism. Because of the controversy in the last national convention over Socialists joining AFL unions, Debs did not attack craft unions during the campaign. Now he felt free of his restriction and began to write and speak against them.

To counter the strength of the AFL organization, Debs attended a secretly planned meeting in Chicago on January 3, 1905, at which a new National Trades Union was established. It later became known as the IWW. Approximately thirty other Socialists and radicals met to establish a new industrial union. Charles Moyer, Bill Haywood, and John O'Neil, all members of the Western Federation of Miners, had initiated plans for the session. Others present included A. M. Simons and Ernest Untermann representing the Socialist Party; Clarence Smith and Daniel McDonald from the AFL; Frank Bohn, representing DeLeon, from the Socialist Labor Party, Lucy Parsons, widow of Albert Parsons—martyr of the Haymarket tragedy; and Fr. Thomas Hagerty, a Catholic priest who served as editor of the *Voice of Labor*, the journal of the American Labor Union. The delegates signed a Manifesto which included a list of labor grievances, a demand for the end of capitalism and an end to all craft unions. After the convention, they agreed to circulate the Manifesto to all unions in the United States and invite any interested members to a national conference in June.[20] Fr. Hagerty has been given credit for playing the major role in writing the Manifesto.[21] A careful reading, however, revealed no new ideas that Debs had not written or spoken about in previous years. In fact many of the arguments, especially those on craft unions, closely paralleled Debs' remarks on behalf of the ARU. Hagerty knew Debs well. In fact in 1902, Hagerty had accepted Debs' invitation to join him on a speaking tour of Colorado mining camps.[22] Debs admired Hagerty's speaking style: "On the rostrum Hagerty is a striking figure, and when aroused is like a wounded lion at bay," Debs declared. "He has ready language, logic, wit, sarcasm, and at times they roll like a torrent and thrill the multitude like a bugle call to charge."[23] The Catholic Church excommunicated Hagerty.[24] He continued as a party lecturer, and Debs saw him between tours at the *Appeal* office. Thus it was not surprising that Debs and Hagerty shared many of the same ideas.

Debs declined to accept any position with the new organization because he felt he had too many other unfinished assignments. William Trautman, editor of the *Brewery Workers Journal*, became secretary of this group. Victor Berger suspected that Trautman would lead the group into the Socialist Labor Party. He wrote Hillquit to indicate his concern over Debs associating with the IWW planning group. "I will go and see Debs personally next week," he stated. "Debs must come out immediately and come out in a decided and unequivocal manner or there will be war. If Debs stays with that crowd, he will lend some prestige for a little while, but I am sure that would be the end of Eugene V. Debs," he concluded.[25] Debs did stay with "that crowd" and tried to assure Berger that their party could gain from the alliance and that at future conventions, safeguards could be instituted to prevent Trautman or DeLeon from controlling the organization. Others within the NEB must have been concerned, because Berger later wrote Hillquit that "the danger of a split on the industrial question is far more serious than you imagine, judging from letters from Debs and others."[26] In spite of the controversy, Debs again conducted the same type of avid campaign for industrial unionism that he had as leader of the American Railway Union.

When the Industrial Workers of the World organized on June 27, 1905, Debs gave one of the key addresses. His presence at this meeting indicated a shift in his labor views to a more aggressive position. When he addressed forty-three unions representing sixty thousand workers at this convention, Debs called for a new union party based upon the economic problems faced by the working class.[27] Although Debs had previously disagreed with Daniel DeLeon on militancy in labor, he assured the audience that the "whirligig of time" united them on this plan to organize the workers as a class.[28]

In this IWW meeting, delegates who represented diverse left wing political groups overlooked their differences because they agreed that the American Federation of Labor's support of craft unionism hindered the growth of industrial unions. Delegates repeatedly condemned Samuel Gompers' conservative leadership. They formed a new organization for all laborers based on the principles Debs followed in establishing the ARU for railroaders. Delegates quickly added the additional goal that the new union should be revolutionary and eventually overthrow the capitalist system.[29] Some delegates, however, refused to support the new organization and left before the final gavel ended the twelve day convention. Ernest Untermann, translator of *Das Kapital* from German into English, and Adolph Germer disappointed Debs with their withdrawal. "It was a mixture of conflicting personalities and ideologies, including a number of screwballs and more than its share of detectives," Germer later wrote a friend.[30]

Debs delivered many speeches on behalf of the IWW, especially in the Chicago area. In his speech, "Craft Unionism," he announced, "there is but one hope, and that is in the economic and political solidarity of the working class; one revolutionary union, and one revolutionary party. It is for this reason that the Industrial Workers, an economic organization, has been launched and now makes its appeal to you as wage-slaves aspiring to be free."[31] In other addresses he emphasized the argument that laborers had no control over their welfare. "You have all these marvelous machines and now your employment depends upon you having access to them," he asserted, but when the capitalist "orders his tool houses locked up, and you workingmen locked out, you have not a word to say."[32] To solve this problem Debs recommended that workers own and operate the factories and divide the profits. He told his audiences that the workers must prepare for this great change through organization and education. "Were it to come today, it would result in collapse," Debs admitted, "because if, for example, the Illinois Steel Works were turned over to the workers today they would not be fitted, trained, drilled, equipped for the operation of this mammoth industrial enterprise."[33] In other speeches he called upon workers to join the OBU, short for "one big union," and demand their rights. For these rallies, Joe Hill and other IWW members, wrote special songs—

some of the most colorful and vituperative ever found in political song-books. The Socialists had been noted for their flamboyant rallies, but the IWW outdid them with songs and poems.

To the tune of "Marching Through Georgia," the IWW crowd would sing, "Bring the good old red book, boys, we'll sing another song. Sing it to the wage slaves who have not yet joined the throng of the revolution that will sweep the world along to One Big Industrial Union."[34] If this song lagged, the IWW song leader would switch to another equally strong and emotional. Sometimes workers' poetry would be recited. Debs stood in the back of the auditorium while the crowd sang the warm-up songs and then the local IWW officers would escort him through the audience to the plat-form. With preliminaries such as these, Debs easily gained an emphatic re-sponse, and some of his remarks paralleled the ideas found in the songs.

Repeatedly Debs stressed, as he did in his speech titled "Industrial Union-ism" which he originally delivered in Grand Central Palace in New York City in 1905, that laborers could not advance as long as the "capitalists owned the tools they do not use, and the workers use the tools they do not own." Debs also repeated ideas found in the "Preamble" adopted at the first IWW convention, especially the charge that trade unions fostered conditions which allowed one set of workers to be pitted against another group of work-ers in the same industry, and thus defeated workers in "wage wars." By organizing industrially Debs felt workers would form a basic organization to structure a new socialist society.

In his earlier labor speaking, Debs had pointed out ways workers could gain their rights by commanding respect and convincing the management that happy workers made money for the company. Speaking for the IWW Debs used an angrier tone in saying to a New York audience, "The Indus-trial Workers is organized not to conciliate, but fight the capitalist class. We have no object in concealing any part of our mission."[35] The increasing number of legal charges against IWW leaders prompted part of this mil-itancy in Debs.

Debs vigorously protested when Bill Haywood, Charles Moyer, and George Pettibone were imprisoned for the alleged murder of ex-Governor Frank Steunenberg of Idaho on December 30, 1905. All of the accused had been active in the organization of the Western Federation of Miners. Steunenberg had been especially critical of Haywood's militant strike lead-ership. The Supreme Court denied the defendants a petition for a writ of habeas corpus in December 1906. Debs charged that justice had been cir-cumvented. He felt that more agitation would help free these men. His own speaking and writing on their behalf in 1906 had reached only a small segment of the total population. When he decided to help edit the popular *Appeal to Reason,* he saw a chance to do more for this cause.

With the editor, J. A. Wayland, he wrote a special edition at each cru-cial time during the trial in 1907. In addition to the three hundred thousand regular subscribers, each special edition sold between three and four million copies. Since the imprisoned men had been "kidnapped" from Colorado without proper extradition proceedings, and prosecuted in Idaho, Debs claimed that here was another example of collusion between government and capital. In an editorial Debs charged that, ". . . it is not only an infamous outrage upon law abiding citizens, but the sole cause of the brutal persecution of these men is their official connection with a labor union."[36]

With this new writing assignment, Debs left the IWW speaking platform in 1907 and moved to Girard, Kansas, where Mr. Wayland privately published his paper. Katherine Debs decided to remain in Terre Haute, for she knew Eugene would continue to travel, and she had no intention of being left alone among strangers in a small Kansas town. She never acquired the outgoing personality of her husband and felt secure only with members of her family or a few close friends. Debs also stated at this time that he would never sell his Terre Haute home, even if his work would not permit him to stay in town as much as he liked. Since Katherine took pride in the big house and constantly cleaned and improved it, she preferred to remain in it and not close the house for an indefinite stay in Kansas. At this time she did help Theodore in the office and answered some correspondence. Debs hoped to be able to come home every month. Before leaving he canceled his engagements for the next year with Central Lyceum Bureau in Chicago, the Midland Lyceum Bureau in Des Moines, and the Columbian Lyceum Bureau in St. Paul.[37] These engagements would have been most profitable and would have enabled Debs to accumulate some savings, but he chose otherwise.

Since Debs had admired Wayland for a long time, he enjoyed his work on the *Appeal*. Wayland's socialist colony ideas had once impressed Debs but now he found his press and propaganda work more impressive. In addition to the *Appeal* the press published many pamphlets on a variety of subjects including socialism and sold them by the thousands. Debs had another friend in Girard, Fred Warren, who influenced his decision to join the staff. Warren, managing editor and chief assistant to Wayland, had great skill in editing and selling papers. He made an ideal associate for Wayland who was known in the Socialist movement as the "One Hoss Philosopher." Although Wayland wrote more editorials, both men were competent propagandists. Interestingly Wayland had continued to accumulate a modest fortune in Kansas in business and land speculation. Sometimes Debs had to explain Wayland's financial holdings to other Socialists. In such situations Debs readily admitted that Wayland had made money and "that this has always been a skill of Wayland's but he uses every dollar to fight capitalism." Debs took a room at Kloeb's Hotel in Girard, but frequently visited in the homes of Warren and Wayland, especially enjoying their children.[38]

After Debs joined the *Appeal* staff, he continued to publish articles supporting the IWW in other journals. Between newspaper assignments he went on long speaking tours for the organization. Katherine seldom saw Eugene during these years, for he had to spend his time between tours at his desk in Girard. Once a week Debs sent a note to his druggist brother-in-law asking him to send Katherine a box of chocolates. Grace Brewer, Debs' secretary in Girard, noticed that Debs, no matter how busy, took time at the end of each day to write Katherine a letter. He always addressed them to his "Dearest Ducky." Although separated, Debs remained devoted. Katherine preferred a quiet life and so he never insisted she join him.

Grace Brewer had the job of coordinating Debs' multiple activities. She found Debs a considerate employer who insisted upon accepting responsibility for any errors. He liked to have her type while he dictated. When he was out lecturing, he wrote his letters in longhand. No other member of the *Appeal* staff could read his handwriting. Her husband, George Brewer, accompanied Debs to take care of reservations, box office management, committee meetings, and introductory speeches. When possible, Mrs. Brewer scheduled Debs for three weeks of speaking followed by three weeks of writing in Girard.[39] In order to book Debs for a lecture, the local committee had to guarantee the purchase of one thousand tickets at twenty-five cents each. For each additional ticket over the guarantee, the *Appeal* received fifteen cents and the local group ten cents. Each ticket buyer also received a forty week subscription to the *Appeal*. For each Debs address the *Appeal* furnished window displays, bills for advertising and $25.00 for hall rent.[40] With these arrangements, Debs secured for the *Appeal* approximately $225.00 as a minimum for each speech, plus all of the additional readers.

Through the *Appeal to Reason* columns and in his speaking, Debs frequently attacked statements of William Jennings Bryan and Theodore Roosevelt. Both Bryan and Roosevelt had sought the votes of labor in the past. Bryan remained silent on the controversial Haywood-Moyer-Pettibone case, and Debs never forgave him for not speaking out. "It has been hinted that Mr. Bryan dare not open his mouth against the criminal mine owners, who are at the bottom of this conspiracy, for the reason that they subscribed liberally to his campaign funds," Debs asserted. "What a spectacle for the peerless leader of the 'common people.' Let it be remembered that he whose lips are sealed while labor is being murdered can never again pose as friend of toil."[41] Debs suggested massive labor violence could follow in retaliation if Haywood *et al.* were found guilty. President Theodore Roosevelt made the mistake of prejudging the confined men in Idaho. Debs had detested Roosevelt for several years and referred to him in speeches as early as 1900 as the tool of capital.[42] Debs thought that Roosevelt's remark prejudiced any jury that might serve in this case, and stated that when the President denounced Moyer, Haywood, and Pettibone as murderers, "he uttered a lie as black and damnable, a calumny as foul and atrocious as ever issued from a human throat."[43] Debs' reprimand provoked wide comment. The *New York Evening Post* reported, "It is about time for President Roosevelt to do something for organized labor. We look any day for some letter or speech to pacify the unions. . . Not in years have the unions been so excited over anything as this Idaho trial and the President's comment." "We have before us," the editor related, "a comment of Debs' attack on the President, which Mr. Roosevelt will doubtless welcome—he is always fortunate in his enemies—but which nonetheless represents union feeling in the matter today, and is widely printed in the Socialist and labor newspapers."[44]

Debs had packed his suitcase to go to Boise for the trial. When Clarence Darrow, counsel for the defense heard this, he sent Debs a letter requesting that he not come because he feared his presence would inflame the public, prejudice the jury, and jeopardize the lives of the defendants. Although disappointed, Debs realized that Darrow knew the situation best.[45] Debs contented himself by writing more protest articles in the *Appeal;* by collecting funds to pay the expenses of the trial; and by making more speeches on behalf of the imprisoned men.

After several delays Haywood's case finally reached the jury. Darrow gave this rousing peroration: "The eyes of the world are on you twelve men of Idaho tonight. . . If you decree his death, the spiders and vultures of Wall Street will send up paeans of joy, but if you acquit this man there are millions of men—out on the broad prairie, on the wide ocean, in the mills and factories and down deep in the earth, plus their women and children, who will pray for you."[46] After twenty-one hours the jury returned a "Not Guilty" verdict. The court also released Moyer and Pettibone. Debs admired Darrow's speech and sent a note of congratulations. A decade later Debs made quite similar remarks before a jury on his own behalf.

In addition to his efforts in this sensational case and in various other strike cases, Debs continued his campaign against women and children working in factories. In special *Appeal* articles and speeches he reiterated that he abhorred child labor and blamed the capitalistic system for such conditions. Occasionally he addressed women's groups on this topic, but more frequently he included near the end of his speeches a special appeal on this subject for women in the audience. He dramatically narrated for the Women's Club of New Orleans a description of the working conditions in the sweat shops of Chicago where little girls and women worked "under the most wretched conditions that would repel an animal."[47] A Detroit newspaper stated that when Debs discussed the child labor evil, the women in his audience brought out their handkerchiefs, and mothers put their arms around their little ones to protect them.[48] Debs often spoke about women achieving equal rights faster through the socialistic system. This remark from a speech in South Chicago indicated that belief: "In that new democracy, there will be no labor of little children, no weary women wearing out their vitality in factory and in mill. The daughters of poverty will no longer marry for shelter and exchange their chastity for a pallet of straw."[49] Debs frequently insisted that girls who worked in factories ruined themselves for motherhood. "Their nerves are worn out, their tissue is exhausted. They have been fed to industry. Their offspring are born tired. That is why there are so many failures in our modern life," he asserted.[50]

Although Debs now devoted full time to lecturing and writing, he always considered himself a laborer. In lectures he often repeated this line: "As long as there is a laboring class I am a part of it." When delegations met him at the train and asked him to ride in a carriage to the platform, he refused and walked with the workers. In another statement frequently found in Debs' spoken and written rhetoric, he avowed that when he rose it would be with the ranks and not from the ranks. The spokesman never led the workers to believe that he or some other labor leader could bring about changes. In his remarks, especially in this crucial period for labor and socialism, Debs, the blue-denim leader, carefully pointed out that workers must rely upon themselves because they had waited too long for a Moses to lead them out of bondage. "I would not lead you out if I could," Debs declared, "for if I could lead you out of bondage, someone else could lead you back in again."[51]

When the Haywood trial ended, Debs deliberated whether to remain with the newspaper or to return to Terre Haute and possibly lead a quieter life. Life for Debs since the Pullman strike had been very hectic. He certainly had had little time for reflection or study of either his accomplishments or failures. After the "Liberty" speech which Debs delivered following his prison sentence in 1895, he could have retired into oblivion. He had been legally defeated and his ARU financially destroyed. In the decade that followed Debs refused to admit defeat and worked to repay the $40,000 debt. In the same period he changed many of his ideas. He counseled "no strikes" in the 1880's and again after the Pullman failure in the 1890's. After 1900, as a labor leader, Debs readily advocated strikes whenever labor-management seriously disagreed. If a strike failed, Debs asserted that "no strike had ever been lost and that there could be no defeat for the labor movement."[52] Debs early championed arbitration, but lost faith in it. In the beginning he spoke for a "fair share" for workers but after joining the Socialist Party orated that workers should control the sharing. His joining the IWW movement signified his growing disillusionment with the status quo in American labor and politics. He started as a cautious editor for the *Fireman's Magazine*,[53] but by 1908 he had a reputation as a radical writer for a newspaper which many conservatives called the "Appeal to Treason." Spokesman Debs made less change over these same years in his support of justice, women's rights, and equality of Blacks. He knew that his remarks created turmoil. "You railroad men are told that I am too radical, that I am dangerous, but the time will come when you will know that I was true to you," Debs declared. "Mark it! Make note of it! Ask your grand officer why trade unions fold first in depressions and make a note of his answer. Don't allow him to dodge by calling me a *Calamity Howler*."[54] Whether conservatives viewed Debs as a calamity howler, or liberals hailed him as the Wendell Phillips of the labor movement, he became known to masses of blue-denim men with dinner pails as a friend and spokesman.[55] William J. Pinkerton, director of the famous detective agency, certainly had a different view. Debs' writings in the *Appeal* and his other activities prompted Pinkerton to write a special pamphlet to workers titled, "Deb's Treachery to the Working Class." Pinkerton informed Debs that it took only a "portion of a gnat's brain to see through you and the rotten sheet you represent, *The Appeal to Reason,* known to genuine industrial workers whom you betrayed by another name, *The Appeal to Treason.*"[56] He decided to remain with the newspaper and build support for the party in the 1908 campaign. Debs' two early campaigns for president had attracted wide attention. These past election contests gave Debs and his supporters experience in campaigning and ideas for the biggest Socialist campaign of all—the 1908 Red Special campaign.

Chapter VIII
The 1908 Red Special Campaign

When the Socialists convened in Chicago on May 10, 1908, Debs decided to remain in Girard writing articles for the *Appeal to Reason* and avoid direct participation in any possible convention feuds. He rationalized his nonattendance by insisting that the delegates already had heard his views. Debs knew in advance that the "Left" faction, which he endorsed at this time, would demand a plank on industrial unionism that included recognition of the IWW.

Soon after the convention opened the delegates became embroiled in a squabble over the platform. The "Rights," led by Victor Berger and James F. Carey, insisted upon a moderate program so they could win more city elections and increase support for progressive legislation on the state and national levels. The "Lefts" reiterated Debs' argument that the party should oppose any measures which left the capitalists in control of the government. The "Center" faction eventually worked out a compromise that essentially followed the 1904 platform. The delegates avoided endorsement of the IWW, but they included stronger planks demanding abolition of the Senate, a graduated income tax, and short term election of judges with limited injunction powers.[1]

The delegates expressed their concern about the sincerity of the reform efforts of the opposing parties by including in the platform this statement: "The various reform movements and parties which have sprung up within recent years are but the clumsy expression of widespread popular discontent. They are not based on an intelligent understanding of the historical development of civilization and of the economic and political needs of our times. They are bound to perish as the numerous middle class reform movements of the past have perished."[2]

In 1908, the fight over the platform continued into the nominating session. After Debs' name had been placed in nomination, "Right" and "Center" leaders protested that Debs had lost their respect because of his support of the IWW.[3] Others believed that the Socialists should avoid the stigma in the label—a one man party. Seymour Stedman of Chicago led the opposition against Debs. Rather than attack Debs' candidacy directly, he claimed that Debs' recent throat operation left him unable to conduct a speaking campaign.[4] He nominated A. M. Simons, a former editor of *International Socialist Review*, writer of books on socialism, and a popular speaker, to replace Debs. Ben Hanford jumped up and read parts of a letter from Debs: "As to my throat and general health, I have improved considerably since I have had a chance to lead something like a regular life. . . . In the coming campaign, I would prefer, if I had my choice, to see what I could do with my pen and give my tongue a rest. . . . I have never refused to do, as far as I could, anything the party commanded me to do, and never shall. You need have no fear that I shall not be in condition, and I hope there will be no good ground for complaint when the fight is over."[5] This letter did not stop nominations, but Debs won over three other rivals by a large majority.[6]

On May 23, 1908, Debs unexpectedly gave the opening speech of the 1908 campaign in the town square of Girard, Kansas. Fred Warren, another editor on the *Appeal* staff, came into Debs' office and invited him for a walk. Warren led the presidential candidate to a pre-arranged rally. The occasion called for a speech, and Debs proved in a two hour extemporaneous address that his throat had healed. After attacking the Goulds and Rockefellers because he felt they kept the workers from realizing "the vision of a better life," Debs asked the townspeople to stand on a mountain with him and look down into the future: "When we are in partnership and have stopped clutching each other's throats, when we have stopped enslaving each other. . . we will be comrades. . . we will begin the march to the grandest civilization the human race has ever known."[7] Warren had employed a stenographer to copy the speech. The full text appeared in the *Appeal to Reason* and the "Jimmie Higginses," the faithful dues-paying members, went to work and sold one million copies of this issue. The editor estimated that four million people read the issue, or one-fourth of the voting population of America. Although Debs had intended to conduct much of the campaign from behind a desk in Girard, on June 1, he accepted a week of speaking engagements in the New York City area.[8] Debs planned a series of meetings in New York City in which he hoped to convince listeners to work harder for him and to increase the Socialist vote.

In one meeting arranged for a large group of ministers at Carnegie Hall, Debs' friend, Edwin Markham, the poet, spoke on his behalf. Reverend Ellis Carr, editor of the *Christian Socialist,* introduced Debs as a prophet who could not be intimidated. In his address, Debs called Moses a strike leader, and compared the persecution of Christ to the treatment strikers had received. He condemned the courts as tools of the capitalists. Shortly after he started speaking a woman leaped up in the audience and proclaimed loudly: "There he is, there he is! Gene Debs, not the missing link but the living link between God and man. . . . Here is the God consciousness, come down to earth."[9] Reports of this incident, which Debs modestly ignored, appeared in major newspapers and many Socialist publications. It became a part of the Debs legend.

After the New York speeches, Debs returned briefly to Terre Haute to make plans for a speaking tour throughout the West and Southwest at Socialist summer camps.[10] The national party, particularly in this election year, encouraged Socialist family summer camps. They were quite popular in 1908. Miners, farmers, and ranchers drove many miles to some central camp to hear leading Socialist orators. Mother Jones, Kate Richards O'Hare, George Creel, George Herron, Ben Hanford, George Goebel and Debs were popular keynoters.

92

Debs received $100 for the campaign fund for each camp visited. On July 18, he wrote the *Appeal to Reason*, "Haven't had a chance to write—am constantly besieged and surrounded, early and late on the trains, everywhere. Had the greatest meeting at Coalgate, Oklahoma. Thousands and thousands. One newspaper said '5000—woods full of 'em, all blazing with zeal for socialism.' Great meeting at Oklahoma City and two at Fort Smith. Spoke four hours and a half, afternoon and evening, yesterday."[11]

The excerpts that follow indicate the kind of persuasion that Debs used before these summer camp audiences. "It is a choice between agitation and stagnation," Debs informed these listeners. Rhetorically questioning the audience, he continued, "Are the capitalists trying to educate you working men? . . . You are satisfied with too little. I am doing what I can to incite you to discontent. Intelligent discontent is the torchbearer of civilization. Jefferson, Paine, Otis, Franklin, Adams, all of these revolutionists whose memories you revere, yesterday were agitators."[12] Debs accused both Taft and Bryan of accepting "corruption fund" campaign money, citing contributions to both parties that represented large commercial interests. After illustrating historically how labor had made few gains under either party's administrations, he emphasized that "William Howard Taft issued one of the first injunctions that paralyzed organized labor."[13] Before these audiences of women dressed in bright calico prints and men in clean but faded denims or black wool pants usually reserved for church, Debs chided Taft for running on an anti-injunction platform that appealed to working men for support. Wittily, Debs remarked, "But for the injunctions Taft issued, I would not be the candidate for the presidency on the Socialist ticket." With an appeal for a Socialist society to rule instead of the trust, Debs concluded with this remark, "As soon as we have socialized these trusts, we will give work to all. Then the working day need not be more than four or five hours long." He lamented, however, that society could not be given at this time the perfect machine.[14] A month later, he repeated some of these same views when he delivered his "Unity and Victory" speech to the state convention of the American Federation of Labor that met in Pittsburg, Kansas.[15]

While Debs delivered speeches at summer camps, the central committee of the Socialist party planned for the final two months of the campaign. Hesitatingly, J. Mahlon Barnes, party secretary, suggested the idea of a "Red Special" train. He knew the party lacked the $20,000 for such a venture, but the idea of sending Debs around the country in a special train loaded with party literature and additional speakers fascinated him.[16] Before election time Comrade Debs could make only sixty major speeches, Barnes argued, but with the train he could make ten times that many. After the initial shock of the cost and magnitude of the idea had subsided, the committee decided to seek ways of raising the needed funds. On August 1, the *Appeal* announced that $15,000 out of the required $20,000 must be raised within the next two to three weeks. "An average of fifty cents each dues paying member will make it go," Editor Wayland pleaded, "and such a plan is sure to attract wide attention. It will advertise Socialism as it has never been done before."[17] All possible Socialist speakers went into action, including many who were Debs' opponents at nomination time. Rallies took place wherever a sponsoring group could be located. During August, William Haywood of labor-striking fame spoke repeatedly for the Red Special in the Pennsylvania, Kentucky, and West Virginia mining areas. When he asked for donations, the "Jimmie Higginses" turned their pockets inside out to give him their last nickels and dimes for the chance to see Debs on the Red Special. Debs continued to speak in the Southwest and Midwest while his running mate, Ben Hanford, spoke in the East. When $6,000 reached party headquarters in Chicago, the officers signed the train contract. Five hundred speeches had been booked and plans called for the train to cross the United States twice.[18]

On August 31, Debs boarded the Red Special in Chicago's Union Station. His crew consisted of Theodore Debs and Stephen Reynolds, "companions and secretaries;" Harry C. Parker, manager of the train; Otto McFeely, publicity agent; Charles Lapworth, Sheffield, England, assistant and correspondent; A. H. Fleaten, manager of the literature department; John C. Chase and Algie M. Simons, speakers; W. W. Buchanon, John Hansen, Lewis Kewman, "assistants wherever needed;" and a band of fifteen members from seven different states.[19] A combination sleeper-diner-observation car with platform for speaking, a day coach, baggage car, and engine made up the Red Special.[20] A crowd estimated at one thousand helped send the train and crew on its way. At nearby Lemont Park Debs addressed the crowd, but he encountered great difficulty in delivering what the *Chicago Record Herald* called his "opening gun" speech. When enthusiastic listeners climbed on the roof of a pavilion fifty feet from the speaker's stand, the park owner protested. No sooner had Debs made his first verbal attack upon the Republican and Democratic parties than the owner complained again. When Debs emphasized a point, his supporters responded with a vigorous pounding of heels upon the tin roof of the structure. The owner, wearing a special policeman's star, crawled upon the roof and attempted to clear it. Debs called out, "Let the boys alone, the roof has not broken through yet." Several of the hefty "kickers" started to throw the owner to the crowd below. The crowd shouted, "Keep him up there." Debs calmed the audience, but thirty minutes later when he spoke disparagingly of Samuel Gompers, who on the preceding day had accused Debs of receiving aid from the Republican party, the crowd, especially those on the roof, cheered, hissed and stomped. The owner bellowed, "Get off my roof." This started another chase over the roof top. This last interruption terminated the speech, but Debs had been given a "continuous ovation" from the time of his appearance until his departure on the Red Special.[21]

By late afternoon the crimson flyer reached Davenport, Iowa, where a large rally occurred. Then the train headed toward Des Moines. "Debs is a keen speaker," wrote Faith McAllister, special correspondent. She described this as a typical Red Special scene: "With band playing and colors flying the train comes to a stop. Most of the crowd is there for curiosity. He begins to speak. 'You have heard of these monkey dinners the swell sets give. You help furnish the money for those dinners. And those people wouldn't even give you an introduction to one of the monkeys. When society gets in such a state that it cares more for the rich woman's poodle dog than it does for the poor man's child, it is time some of you were taken a tumble.' "[22] At Creston, Iowa, Debs overheard a farm woman say, "Why only one of them has whiskers and none of them have long hair." In reply the balding Debs quipped, "We have long hair—my brother Theodore and I. We have just three of them between us."[23]

From Iowa the train moved into Missouri with Kansas City scheduled for the state's big rally. Ten thousand paid to hear Debs claim that the trusts owned the upper branch of Congress and the lower branch belonged "unequivocally to Joe Cannon,"[24] the arbitrary speaker of the House who consistently fought progressive legislation. In a twenty minute speech in St. Joseph, Missouri, Debs called attention to "the ridiculous and hypocritical attitude of the Democratic party toward labor." He questioned Mr. Bryan's sympathy toward labor when he had been silent during the Haywood and other strike cases.[25] When the Red Special arrived at the Omaha station, eager Socialists tied red banners and bunting from one end of the train to the other. The Omaha News commented that the three thousand people in the audience showed great enthusiasm for Debs' "sarcastic and dramatic address." The audience demanded via cheers and shouts to hear more about Gompers, but Debs countered this by saying that he wished "to pass up all the dead issues, and devote his time to an analysis of the capitalist parties and the leaders of both who masquerade for purposes of vote-getting as the champion of the man who works."[26]

As the Red Special traveled from one town to the next, local Socialists boarded the train and rode as far as they liked. They paid two cents a mile and fifty cents for each meal. All of the special train party, including Debs, had their meals with the guest riders. Socialists packed into all the available space "absorbing inspiration from the great propaganda enterprise."[27] Carrying these special passengers caused frequent stops, but whenever possible, the train's management preferred stopping only in the larger towns, not at every prairie crossroad. As these riders left the train at the next stop, they made an animated claque in getting the new rally under way. In many cases, farmers had driven as much as fifty miles to see the Red Special. Travelers on passing trains waved handkerchiefs and shouted greetings. Farmers in nearby fields threw their straw hats into the air. This enthusiasm continued: "All through the mountains on the way from Denver west, ranchers and miners would spring to their feet waving and cheering as they realized the identity of the train from its decorations."[28] Crowds gathered at rail stations along the way at all hours, day and night. Even when Debs attempted to catch some sleep and rest for his sore throat, they would yell for a speech from him. Socialist locals all over the country had responded to an *Appeal* suggestion to collect dinner pails that once had been used in their localities. "Get all you can together and exhibit them at every Socialist meeting. They would make excellent decorations for the Red Special, as it whizzes its way twice across the continent." The depression of 1907 had caused more unused dinner pails than usual. The Socialist estimated that "the steel trust alone left one hundred thousand empty."[29]

After the Denver speech, Debs elatedly wrote of the cheering crowd and concluded: "The miracle is working all around us and before our very eyes. . . These grand old mountains all about us are smiling their benediction upon us and the green plumed pines along our iron highway seem to sway in gladness and join in the applause."[30] Three different Denver newspapers had other views. One accused Debs of trading adjectives for train money. Another disagreed when Debs classified Americans into either of two classes: one which owned tools it did not use, and the other used tools it did not own. The third strenuously objected to the band playing the "Marseillaise" while Debs mounted the platform, and quipped that all speeches belonged to the "red flaggiest order."[31] In this Denver speech, Debs called the Republican platform a political omelet made of stale eggs; Mr. Bryan a political tightrope walker, Roosevelt's election the biggest debauchery found in political history; and the U.S. courts the bulwarks of capitalism.[32] From Denver the train moved to Colorado Springs, Leadville, Salada, Glenwood Springs, and Grand Junction, where Buffalo Bill joined the train for a visit and ride.[33] In all of these towns and others, Debs met an eager audience composed largely of miners. Many miners renewed their acquaintance because in previous years Debs had spoken in the area during crucial strikes.

"Five minutes after arrival at any station the Red Special has a crowd," Debs wrote the *Appeal* from Colorado Springs, and, "We are thoroughly organized and take full advantage of every minute. We are ready to drop off at a minute's notice and make a speech of half a minute to a hundred people, or of two hours to twenty thousand people.[34] Describing the procedure followed at each stop, Theodore Debs stated that Simons opened "the ball with a short and telling speech that carried the crowd. McKee's talks had the same effect." Several short speeches preceded Debs' talk. Theodore continued, "The speaking battery of the Red Special is of the rapid-fire kind, and when a crowd has been bombarded at a station, it is a safe guess that Socialism will be the theme in that community for the rest of the day if not longer."[35] Before, during, and after the speaking, the entire crew sold pamphlets, watch fobs with Debs' picture, buttons, and red flags. In large cities, extra supplies had been shipped ahead. Thousands of leaflets were handed out free. Stephen Reynolds had just published his book, *Debs: His Life, Writings and Speeches,* so he sold and autographed these. Even with all of these commercial activities, plus admission prices for the speeches ranging from ten to twenty-five cents, the Red Special ran out of funds by the time it reached California. At first, the party officials decided to cancel the Eastern tour, but several pamphlet salesmen signed notes for quantities of Socialist literature, and this enabled the train to proceed into the Northwest. Also emergency appeals in all of the Socialist publications began to bring in money.

In California Debs addressed some of the largest audiences of the entire tour. He also encountered in this state some of the strongest opposition in the form of heckling and unfavorable press reviews. Fifteen thousand heard the candidate speak in San Diego. In Los Angeles' Springer Auditorium, the crowd overflowed into the street. The Democrats rushed Theodore Bell, chairman of their national convention, to "the scene of these demonstrations to see what effect they had" on the voters.[36] In San Bernardino, according to the *Daily Sun*, "The Socialist nominee for president gave the most concise and clearcut statement of the elementary principles of Socialism that was ever given in this city." After the speech the reporter interviewed some of the listeners. An emphatic voter "of the old school" commented, "Yes, Debs is a pleasing speaker all right but what in the hell was there to it?" A group of railway men on the street corner "disposed of the orator and his speech by declaring, 'Debs put more men on the bum tonight than any other man in America.'" They were referring to the ARU strike failure in 1894 that they claimed put thousands of railroad men permanently out of employment. "Socialism means revolution," the reporter continued, "but under the skillful hands of Debs the suggestions that jar are masked, and with the flow of words that are eloquent themselves, a ready wit, and a never failing fund of illustrations, he made a talk which held his audience with rare skill and made socialism a most alluring prospect."[37]

J. Aubrey Jones, a Democrat in a Berkeley crowd, arose in the middle of Debs' speech there, and asked if the Socialist leader could prove his statements about Peter S. Grosscup, the judge who had reversed Judge Kenesaw Landis' $29,240,000 fine against Standard Oil of Indiana for accepting rebates. "Absolutely," declared Debs, "furthermore, I wish you would take an exact copy of this speech and send it to Grosscup." "If Socialism went into effect," replied Debs, "we would not be ruled by a Constitution a hundred and twenty years old, or governed by the dead." Jones demanded answers to other questions until the audience shouted for him to sit down. Debs asked him to proceed. Since Debs frequently encountered hecklers, he did not become irriated at men like Jones. He quickly and aggressively answered him in an authoritative voice. Debs' assured manner enabled him to evade a demand for specific facts and to respond with another generalization. After the interrogation ended, Debs discussed child labor, the necessity of the strike, and the lack of health and insurance benefits for laborers.[38]

One of the final California speeches Debs delivered at the University of California in their outdoor Greek Theatre. He gave "a speech that was strong: one that burned and soothed." The university newspaper reported that "Comrade Debs discussed without reserve from the working man's point of view the vital issues of the day. Some in the audience were shocked, others touched to the heart-strings, all ennobled and enlightened."[39] After the University of California address the administration at Stanford University refused Debs' request to speak in its chapel.[40]

From California the Red Special moved into Oregon. It followed its iron road back across the northern tier of states and into Chicago before proceeding to the East Coast. In this return trip, party headquarters scheduled a major address in St. Paul. In this speech Debs blamed the Republican party for the recession that led to the large number of unemployed. Early in the campaign, labor leaders had asked Mr. Taft how he would aid the unemployed. Debs pointed out to this audience, as he had to many others, Taft's answer—"I do not know." Debs poked fun at this answer and concluded that Taft had "his nerve" to ask for labor's vote. He followed this point with a bitter attack upon laborers who voted Democratic. "You are even worse than the fellow who votes Republican. The only reason you vote the Democratic ticket is because your grandfather did. Times are different now. . . . Everything has changed since the days of your grandfather except for one thing—his grandson—the one who votes the Democratic ticket." Cynically referring to the Democratic plank guaranteeing bank deposits, he asked if any laborers had anything in a bank. He concluded by inviting the women present to attend his inauguration, and to remember that the Socialist party first recognized women as having any political rights.[41]

When the Red Special reached Chicago on September 15, Debs and crew had traveled 9,000 miles and made 187 speeches in twenty-five days before an estimated 275,000 people.[42] Without even a day's rest after the completion of this Western tour, the crimson express headed into a series of rallies in Wisconsin, Indiana and Ohio. Although Debs was weary from his day and night existence on the train, and his throat sore from the numerous talks, he did not complain. On several occasions when his voice failed or he was too exhausted to make a talk, he would greet the crowd and ask Theodore to speak.

Debs particularly enjoyed the Red Special campaign in Wisconsin because a young energetic Carl Sandburg met the train on September 23 at Green Bay and stayed throughout the tour until September 28. Sandburg had admired Debs for several years and in 1907 had become an organizer for the party. In Wisconsin he had continued his organizing activities and spoke for the Socialists at Chautauqua meetings. Sandburg wrote his daughter, Paula, from aboard the Red Special; "All tumbled and hurried and dusty, here we are. The success of the train has been understated, if anything. Debs is superb. Crowded house, all kinds of enthusiasm. . . . Will sleep on the train tonight—not very restfully, but hell the revolution tingles and whirls around here." In another letter three days later to Paula, Sandburg described Debs as a "lover of humanity." "Such a light as shines from him—and such a fire as burns in him—he is of a poet breed, hardened for war. . . . I will see more of Debs," Sandburg declared.[43] From Wisconsin the train moved across Indiana making several short stops and headed for a big rally in Toledo, Ohio.

On September 29, in Toledo, Ohio, Debs called Roosevelt an arch-hypocrite. Although Roosevelt had declined to run again, Debs often spent more time attacking him than Taft. Since Taft represented Roosevelt's choice, Debs wanted the people to know Roosevelt's record on labor issues, and then he implied that Taft endorsed Roosevelt's actions. "You applaud Roosevelt. You look to him as one who has done a great deal for you. But as a matter of fact he has never done anything for the working class. He is a capitalist and serves that class efficiently."[44] According to one reporter this "famous undesirable citizen minced no words in discussing campaign issues before the muscle, sinew and bronze of Toledo."[44]

Charles Evans Hughes, then Republican governor of New York, refused Debs' offer to debate in Cleveland on September 30. Both candidates had scheduled addresses at the same time. On that date each attracted an audience of between six and seven thousand. Governor Hughes spoke as a lawyer, his arguments and principles following and amplifying each other in legal and logical fashion. Candidate Debs addressed his audience like the founder of a new religion, hurling impassioned appeals, reverting to moral principles, and demanding the destruction of the industrial system which Governor Hughes represented.[46]

Whether from curiosity to see Debs, or to learn more about socialism from an authority on the subject, two thousand Erie, Pennsylvania, citizens packed the largest auditorium in town. Before this audience Debs hypothesized that "hereafter it is Socialism and anti-Socialism in this country." Declaring that the day of vague issues, such as rate regulation, tariff and similar "befogging proposals" had passed, Debs exclaimed, "What the producers on the farm and in the cities want to know is how they are to get the full benefit of their labor when it is applied to the marvelous machinery invented and put into use in the last seventy-five years." Debs maintained before this cheering crowd that the problem of production in America had been solved, but because the capitalists owned the machines the product was wasted in competition or "gobbled by the few."[47] An editor in Rochester, New York, the next major stop on the Special's itinerary, prepared for Debs' arrival with an editorial in the leading paper asking the citizens to extend their hospitality and sense of fair play to Debs. ". . . If he has something of real value to offer, the country needs it. And if not, the best way to learn wherein he is wrong is to learn it at first-hand."[48]

The New York City visit of the Red Special had received much advance publicity and the city's large number of Socialists had made elaborate plans. New York had Socialist candidates for office in each of the districts. These candidates hoped that Debs' speaking would help them in their districts, especially if they could get Debs to appear in their area. When the train arrived in Grand Central Station, the police called for reserves because they could not contain the wild enthusiasm of the four thousand spectators who pushed, as one journalist stated, "to touch even so much as the hem of his coat."[49] At the same time seven thousand people awaited Debs in the

Hippodrome and 2,500 in the American Theatre. The demand for the fifteen to fifty-cent tickets to hear Debs had been so great that this second auditorium had been rented and filled ten days before Debs' arrival. Ticket speculators sold extras at three and four times purchase price on the day of the speeches. The station mob broke through the iron gates at the sight of Debs and swept him away from the police guards. According to one reporter, "They jammed him against the Vanderbilt Avenue entrance. He was battered and shoved and clawed as they carried him down Vanderbilt Avenue to Forty-fourth, over to Forty-second. Now and then he was lifted from his feet, and you could see his bald head bobbing like a cork above waves of black and brown derbies." He appealed huskily for release, but his voice provoked "tornadoes of yelling."[50] Finally the police drove a phalanx into the heart of Debs' captors and quickly guided him to his hotel for a short rest.

To occupy the waiting audiences in both of the auditoriums, Socialist organizers planned a series of prefatory speeches by leading party members. These speeches began at two o'clock and continued until Debs' arrival. Morris Hillquit, candidate for Congress and best known New York Socialist, ended his speech at the Hippodrome by stating that as far as the working men in America could judge, the only difference between Bryan and Taft "was one of avoirdupois." Upton Sinclair came forward as a volunteer speaker at the same rally and entertained the crowd with his monologue, "How I Tamed Teddy Roosevelt."[51] He also spoke about writing his book, *The Jungle*. Finally at four o'clock Debs arrived at the American Theatre where he spoke for one half hour. At each major point in his speech, the Socialist crowd would jump to their feet and twirl red flags around their heads. Prior to the address bolts of bright red cotton had been sold in five cent squares. The *Times* admired this bit of strategy: "The red flag idea was a flash of genius. When the audience became enthusiastic, the interior of the halls became a sea of waving red, out of which came thunderous applause."[52]

At five o'clock Debs reached the Hippodrome, where the audience had grown weary of the preliminaries. Many had been in their seats since noon, but when Debs appeared they started cheering and wildly lashing their little red flags into a fiery fury.

The speech that lasted an hour represented a compilation of arguments that Debs had often used before, but the language differed. His word choice, heightened perhaps by the excitement in the audience, indicated that Debs became vitriolic. Although Debs had previously made personal attacks upon his political rivals, those that he made in the Hippodrome speech represented some of the strongest that he uttered in his political career. Debs paid little attention in his remarks to Taft except to describe him as Roosevelt's echo and label him "that creature Roosevelt has nominated as his successor." "Roosevelt," Debs emphatically stated, "is the arch enemy of the laborer, and when he leaves the White House and goes to Africa, where he properly belongs, he will have rendered his first service to the working class."

Next Debs reminded his animated hearers of the alleged $100,000 gift that Standard Oil had given Roosevelt in the last campaign. He asserted that "Teddy" only pretended that he did not know about the fund when he denounced it. Poking fun at Roosevelt's denial of Edward H. Harriman's assistance, Debs paraphrased one of the former president's letters to Harriman: "My dear Harriman, come around to the White House in the dark of the moon and help me write my message to Congress." From these illustrations, Debs assured his audience that Theodore Roosevelt "always kicks a man when he is down. If he has any brave act to his credit save shooting a Spaniard in the back, I never heard of it!"[53]

Debs associated Bryan's name with Tammany—"a political leprosy." When Bryan for political reasons had denounced his former friend, Roger Sullivan of Illinois, he revealed himself in Debs' opinion as a self-seeking hypocrite. "The words coward and traitor," Debs shouted, "are too mild to use on Bryan."[54] Debs excoriated the Democratic party as a mass of crawling parasites. He resented the fact that some workers supported the Democrats. "Hands—mill hands, factory hands, farm hands—hands, hands,—that's what they call you," Debs thundered, "but not brains." This lack of recognition of workers in either party as being important, especially when the workers in America constituted a majority of the voters' Debs deplored. He closed with this ringing peroration: ". . . You have an overwhelming majority. Unite, stand together, and this country is yours. Knock down this capitalistic system, raise up the socialistic system, and labor will be a brand of nobility."[55] Marie Trommer who heard this speech stated, "I can still see him on the platform of the Hippodrome. When he concluded with outstretched arms and finger pointing at the audience, it set all the banners waving." As Debs departed, the *Times* stated, "A cyclone of applause tore through the building."

That evening New York party leaders arranged a special banquet honoring Debs, but the orator regretfully declined to attend. Nearly exhausted from the day's activities Debs was persuaded by his brother, Theodore, to rest before going on to Boston the next day. Fund raising continued at the banquet. Rose Pastor Stokes, a cigar factory worker in her youth, climbed on top of her table and dramatically took off her jewels and tossed them in the contribution box. From her rostrum, she pleaded with other women to do the same. Soon other ladies leaped upon their tables and gave their baubles to the cause.[56]

Boston Socialists scheduled Debs' major address in their city for 8:00 p.m. in Faneuil Hall. Debs had spoken in this famous hall on two previous occasions; once as a young labor organizer, and in the campaign of 1900. At 7:30 the doors closed and over six thousand stood outside waiting for a glimpse of Debs. Three thousand admirers and three bands awaited Debs' arrival at the downtown station. Railroad officials decided to shift the Red Special to the North Station, and jostled Debs and crew around for two hours in the railroad yards. Finally at ten o'clock Debs reached Faneuil Hall. Although hoarse in the beginning, Debs' voice improved as he spoke.

He noticed the many women in the audience, and quickly made an impassioned appeal to end political discrimination against women. He proceeded to denounce the two parties and to repeat many of his New York statements.[57] The Boston *Journal* reporter praised the enthusiasm in the audience and claimed that "the Reds have both big parties rolled into one and beaten by fourteen miles on this score." He attributed part of the enthusiasm during the speech to Debs' smile and said "that smile is an important part of his oratorical equipment."[58]

When Debs emerged from Faneuil Hall at eleven fifteen, he heard a deafening outcry. The crowd burst forth with "We Won't Go Home Until Morning." Several eager Socialists lifted Debs off his feet and carried him to a speaker's stand set up in the center of Faneuil Hall Square. Here he delivered a short address stressing the growth of the party, proclaiming that the echo of Socialist progress in America would be heard around the world. The brevity of this outdoor speech took the crowd by surprise, and before the audience realized what had happened, Debs darted into a carriage and headed for North Station and a night's sleep on the railroad siding.[59]

From Boston the Red Special moved into Rhode Island and Connecticut. In Pawtucket, Rhode Island, he addressed a crowd at the station, and another in Infantry Hall that evening. The audience "was the most cosmopolitan ever seen in the city and several city clergymen sat on the platform."[60] At Hartford, Connecticut, Debs' political efforts consisted of a brief speech in connection with a bridge dedication. In New Haven that evening, Debs spoke for two hours "on his hobby and successfully held them spellbound."[61] In this political speech he set out to prove that Bryan was not the champion of the people. The reporter assigned to review Debs' speech in Bridgeport decided to listen rather than follow the rapid utterances of the apostle of Socialism because his speech "outran the speed of my pencil."[62]

The final leg of the tour for the Red Special started with Debs' arrival in Philadelphia on October 12. Twenty campaigning days remained before the election, but the Red Special had already visited most of the major cities in the country, especially those above the Mason-Dixon line. In these remaining days the train made numerous short stops as it chugged through Pennsylvania, Ohio, Illinois, and Wisconsin. Appropriately, Terre Haute had been selected as the site for the official farewell to the Red Special.

By this date on the tour schedule, Debs had learned to avoid his overenthusiastic admirers at the previously announced stops at main railroad stations. For example, before Debs arrived in Philadelphia, his managers contacted George Caylor who served as chairman of the rally, and arranged for him to meet the candidate at the Spring Garden Street station in the suburbs. The Red Special continued on its way to the station where the crew apologized for Debs' absence, but promised that after some rest he would appear to give the scheduled lecture. This scheme helped save Debs' energy and overstrained voice.[63] Philadelphia police disapproved of the

Debs meeting, and irritated the huge crowd before Debs arrived by arresting two speakers who had attacked the city's Republican administration and claimed that policemen in the city had been forced to contribute fifteen dollars to the party.[64]

Debs used a different idea for content in his Philadelphia speech. He did not start out with the usual discussion of the Republican and Democratic parties and then proceed to point out his views on the inadequacies of each of the party's candidates. Building this speech around the thesis that a third revolution rapidly approached, he pointed out that the first revolution destroyed the divine right of kings and gave the colonies their independence, and that the second had abolished chattel slavery and destroyed the right of property in human flesh. The third, Debs asserted, would emancipate the workers from the control of the capitalist. This third revolution, he proclaimed, would come about by evolutionary social processes unless the capitalists thwarted it.

Using Philadelphia as an example of a typical city controlled by corrupt politicians, Debs illustrated how he believed these vested interests stayed in power. (Perhaps by leaving the train earlier, Debs had more time to meet with Caylor and become better informed about Philadelphia politics.) He lashed out at Philadelphia employers who invited some of their workers to dinner before elections. Digressing from the point that these invitations constituted vote bribery, he described high society: "Men are dressed up in clawhammer-coats, and yet all that is divine in man is extinct in them. In that atmosphere they have become moral perverts. There is as much immorality there as in the slums. The only difference is that the fallen ones do not have to go on to the red light district."[65] Returning from this digression, Debs continued to extoll the virtues of socialism and the necessity of the thirty million workers voting the Socialist ticket so that the third revolution would come about. He warned his listeners about Roosevelt and characterized Teddy as the "Don Quixote of American politics." In closing he mentioned that on November 4, the Socialist Party would open its 1912 presidential campaign, and by so doing indirectly indicated that the Socialists had little hope for winning the present one. This remark partially substantiated the opinion that Debs undertook these lengthy presidential campaigns just to instruct the workers and prepare them for some eventual victory. Following this speech before three thousand at the Kensington Labor Lyceum, Debs repeated many of the same ideas in another packed hall, the Old Labor Lyceum.

After the Philadelphia speeches Debs journeyed to Camden, New Jersey, where he spoke at the Temple Theatre. Debs had a special interest in this town because his admired friend, Walt Whitman, had lived and died there. Several times on the Red Special tour of the West, while viewing scenic sights out the moving train window, Reynolds and Debs recited passages from Whitman's poetry.[66] During the speech Debs praised Whitman and elaborated upon his view of freedom. While Debs extemporized in the Temple Theatre, Camden policemen arrested several Socialists for selling pamphlets in front of the theatre.[67]

Debs attracted huge crowds in Pittsburgh, Cincinnati, Evansville, and other cities as he campaigned day and night for the presidential office he never expected to fill. In an interview Debs surprised Lincoln Steffens by admitting that when the Socialists got close to electing a candidate he would decline to run. "I am not fitted either by temperament or by taste for the office," he admitted to Steffens.[68] Perhaps the October publication of Steffens' interview in *Everybody's Magazine* attracted part of these Mid-western crowds.[69] Taft had difficulty in filling the Music Hall in his home town, Cincinnati, but Debs' ticket sellers had to turn many listeners away. In Evansville, Taft and Debs spoke on the same night, October 22. Debs diligently tried to arrange a joint debate, but Taft declined. Debs suggested that they switch audiences and each address for twenty minutes the other's rally, but to no avail. While crossing Illinois on October 23, Debs delivered seventeen short speeches. In Woodstock he used the front steps of the jail in which he had been imprisoned for six months for a stage.

When Debs reached Milwaukee on October 31, he had to speak in three different halls to accommodate the seven thousand successful ticket holders.[70] Other thousands stood outside. Such crowds in Milwaukee did not surprise Debs, for this city, under the leadership of Victor Berger, had elected in the past years more Socialists to office than any other city of its size in America. Debs started the first of his three speeches at eight and finished with the third at twelve o'clock. A reporter who heard each of the addresses was amazed at the physical energy Debs exerted as he clenched his fists, waved his long arms and body to and fro with great streams of perspiration running from his face. Before the Westside Turner Hall audience he predicted that, "This year will be historic. It will mark the entrance of Socialism into the arena of national politics."[71]

On November 2, the three presidential candidates headed for their homes and final speeches. Before a welcoming Lincoln, Nebraska, crowd, Bryan declared that, "I am going to be elected by more than a bare victory." Taft gave the last speech of his campaign in Youngstown, Ohio, before heading to Cincinnati to vote. In this address Taft advised his followers to "Vote the Republican ticket and preserve prosperity, protection to American industries, business integrity and the right of labor." After stepping from the rear platform of the Red Special for the last time, Debs repeated before two audiences in Terre Haute his key ideas that the Socialist party stood for the emancipation of wage slaves, and that laborers in the party stood for more than hands. Debs evoked great applause when he announced that he did not appeal to the voters to cast their ballots for him, as the other candidates did, but that he wanted them to read the Socialist literature, especially the young men that had to solve "the problems that the rising generation faced." He thanked his home town friends, including the members of seven different small bands, for turning out, and said, "this same enthusiasm greeted the 'Red Flyer' everywhere it went."[72] Bill Haywood introduced Debs at both rallies: one in the Coliseum; the other in the Armory. Haywood asked working men either to vote for Debs or

Debs would have to start the next campaign on November 4. Haywood quipped that he would rather go to Washington on March 4 and paint the White House red.

The Terre Haute speeches marked the end of one of the most aggressive speaking campaigns ever undertaken by a presidential candidate. The Red Special crossed the country twice and covered 20,000 miles in 33 states. The trip had cost $35,000.[73] Of this amount $14,000 had been dropped into the ticket boxes. The balance arrived in the mail at the national headquarters. Samuel Gompers, who persuaded the AFL to back Bryan, accused the Republican party of financing Debs' Red Special. In reply the Socialists published their 15,000 contributors' names and donations in the *Bulletin*.[74] In this speaking marathon Debs had campaigned continuously for 65 days. His voice became hoarse after the first week and remained that way. During the last half of the tour numerous newspapers commented upon his pale appearance and weakened condition. He had delivered on the average two major addresses each day and countless five to ten minute speeches at whistle stops along the Red Flyer's way.

Although Debs did not expect to win, the election results must have disappointed him, for he had predicted the returns would mark the entrance of socialism into national politics. Several leading newspapers in pre-election forecast predicted that Debs would receive a million votes. The 420,793 votes he did receive represented only 18,472 more votes than in 1904.[75] Several factors partially explain this result. A sudden upturn in prosperity the last three months of the campaign helped the Republicans and caused many voters to forget the recession of 1907. Debs' support of the IWW alienated some potential voters. Gompers called Debs an apostle of failure and led his AFL workers into the Democratic camp.[76] The AFL leader vigorously campaigned for Bryan both in the union meeting halls and on the campaign circuit. The Socialists had picked up votes in 1904 when the Democrats nominated Alton Parker, an enemy to laborers; they failed to realize that when Bryan returned as candidate, many of these voters returned to the Democratic Party. Also, Bryan had support in the same western states where Debs had worked hard as a union organizer. The large Taft vote indicated that many voters thought him capable of carrying out Roosevelt's progressivism.

The prospect of both parties granting reforms demanded by agriculture, small businessmen, and laborers cannot be discounted. Voters who might have abandoned the older parties at this time heard speakers from these parties promise reforms and saw planks in their platforms that expressed the same. Why, they reasoned, should they support the Socialist Party when the present parties could accommodate their demands? In this campaign Debs knew the effectiveness of these promises and repeatedly informed his listeners of the insufficiency of such measures and asserted these changes would not solve capitalism's basic problems. From the beginning of the campaign, the Socialists had recognized the threat of reforms by other parties by including in their platform statements opposing such efforts by any party other than their own. Whether Debs influenced Morris Hillquit, respected party theoretician, on this point or vice-versa cannot be ascertained, but both men held the view that Socialist reform must be in the nature of a working-class conquest. In Hillquit's book, *Socialism in Theory and Practice,* which he finished during the campaign year, he stated that the aim of Socialist reforms was to strengthen the working class economically and politically and to pave the way for the introduction of the socialist state.[77] Hillquit referred to these reformers as "kindhearted but shortsighted gentlemen" who saw evils in the social system but failed to see the connections between the evils and the system. Like Debs, Hillquit asserted that the Socialists regarded all problems of trusts, unemployment, poverty, etc., as "symptoms of one deep-rooted disease of our social organism" and that the symptoms could be cured only by "attacking the real disease."[78]

One Debs admirer explained the election defeats as follows: "The publicity accorded the Red Special was magnificent, and crowds were tremendous, but the Socialist vote was only fair, because the voters followed after an abdominous Pied Piper, named Taft, who carried a slogan, 'the full Dinner Pail.' "[79] Two months before election clerks throughout the country counted the votes, Debs explained his philosophy in running in 1908 to Lincoln Steffens. "We aren't playing to win—not yet. We want a majority of Socialists, not of votes. There would be no use getting into power with a people that did not understand; with a lot of officeholders undisciplined by service in the party. . . . I am running for president to serve a very humble purpose: to teach social consciousness and to ask men to sacrifice the present for the future, to throw away their votes to mark the rising tide of protest. . ."[80] With this philosophy or rationalization Debs could not have been disappointed long.

List of Illustrations

	Page
Debs' Home and Parents	108
Family Grocery and Debs' First Job Picture	109
Wedding Pictures and New Home	110
Debs as Young Organizer and Writer	111
Pullman Strike 1894: Federal Troops and Cartoon	112
Examples of Debs' Writings	113
Official 1908 Campaign Photo of Debs	114
Red Special Train Tour in 1908	115
Itinerary of Red Special Train for Eastern USA	116
Debs' Popular Anti-War Leaflet "Never Be A Soldier"	117
Debs Enters Prison; Pamphlet to Aid Alabama Strikers	118
1920 Socialist Platform; Debs Notified of Nomination	119
1920 Campaign Message from Debs	120
Debs in Prison; Excerpts from Canton Speech	121
Rally Poster of Meeting to Free Debs	122
Special Magazine and Pamphlet by Debs to Help Rebuild Party	123
Debs Released from Atlanta Prison	124
Tickets for Debs' Speeches; Debs in Action	125
Notices of Debs' Death	126

Debs' Mother, Marguerite or "Daisy" to her children. Neighbors described her as a small quiet woman who showed great love to her children.

Eugene V. Debs' birthplace—a simple four room house at 447 N. 4th Street in Terre Haute, Indiana. Later the front room became the grocery store.

Debs' father, Jean Daniel or "Dandy" to his children. Neighbors found him stern and direct, but honest as a businessman.

When the grocery business increased, the Debs family moved into this building at 11th and Wabash in Terre Haute. The Debs family of eight lived upstairs.

Young Debs, first on the left of the front row, began working at 14 as a painter in the local railroad yards of the Terre Haute, Indianapolis and Richmond Railroad.

Wedding portraits of Katherine Metzel and Eugene V. Debs. To symbolize their new life together, they married at dawn on June 5, 1885, in the Episcopal Church in Terre Haute.

The Debs' home at 451 North Eighth Street which they had built to their specifications. It became Kate's refuge from the outside world.

Debs as a young union organizer quickly attracted attention when he formed the ARU and succeeded in securing many new locals.

One of Debs' first pamphlets. In this essay he explained why craft unions had failed and encouraged workers to join the ARU—an industry wide union.

Federal troops set up camp on the Lakefront during the Pullman Strike in 1894. (Courtesy Chicago Historical Society.)

Cartoon appeared during the Pullman Strike July 21, 1894. Notice that Governor Waite of Colorado (on the left) and Governor Altgeld of Illinois preceed Debs.

THE VANGUARD OF ANARCHY.

The Socialist Party and The Working Class

By EUGENE V. DEBS.

Opening address delivered by Eugene V. Debs, candidate of the Socialist Party for President, Indianapolis, Ind., September 1, 1904.

Mr. Chairman, Citizens and Comrades:

There has never been a free people, a civilized nation, a real republic on this earth. Human society has always consisted of masters and slaves, and the slaves have always been and are today, the foundation stones of the social fabric.

Wage-labor is but a name; wage-slavery is the fact.

The twenty-five millions of wage-workers in the United States are twenty-five millions of twentieth century slaves.

This is the plain meaning of what is known as

THE LABOR MARKET.

And the labor market follows the capitalist flag.

The most barbarous fact in all christendom is the labor market. The mere term sufficiently expresses the animalism of commercial civilizati~

~They who h~

Sample headlines from the famous Appeal to Reason *newspaper. The Debs editorial "Arouse Ye Slaves!" later appeared in a widely circulated pamphlet. In this article he challenged workers to rebel and not become the slaves of capitalist factory owners. "The Socialist Party and the Working Class", another popular Debs' pamphlet, explained reasons why workers should immediately join the party.*

FOR PRESIDENT

EUGENE V. DEBS

Debs' official campaign poster picture. (Original in Becker Collection at Smithsonian Institution.)

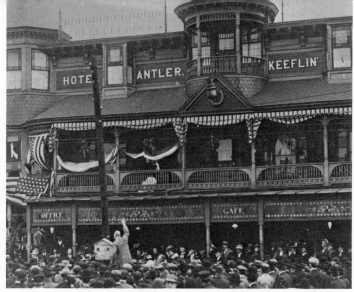

Typical crowd picture of Debs speaking to an audience in 1908.

The Red Special train with its official crew and band.

Debs and his brother Theodore aboard the Red Special trying to keep up with the correspondence sent to them. Eugene often dictated letters and articles while Theodore typed them.

SOCIALIST SPECIAL TRAIN

Trans-Continental Campaign Tour

EASTERN TRIP

SPEECHES AND BAND CONCERTS

Time and Place of all stops of flyer sent out by the Working-Class
in its record-breaking educational effort

EUGENE V. DEBS

CANDIDATE FOR PRESIDENT and OTHER SPEAKERS
and the Famous Socialist Volunteer Band will be aboard

STOPS AND EXACT TIME

This detailed schedule represents the last half of the Red Special tour. A western tour, even longer with fewer stops had preceded this windup tour before election day. Notice that the party billed it as an educational effort.

Never Be a Soldier

BY EUGENE V. DEBS

67A

Working men are forced into war as working women are into prostitution.

Let us think for a moment!

The working man who turns soldier today becomes the hired assassin of his capitalist master. He goes on the murderers' pay roll at fifty cents a day, under orders to kill anybody, anywhere, at any time.

To refuse to brain his own mother in a hunger strike is treason to his pot-ellied master.

This is the vile and abject thing we call a soldier. Lower than the slimy, ripping depths in which this craven creature crawls, neither man nor beast can er sink in time or eternity.

Let us think another moment!

War is the crimson carnival where the drunken devils are unchained and the snarling dogs are "sicked" upon one another by their brutal masters; where they shoot off one another's heads, rip open one another's bellies and receive their baptism of patriotic devotion to their masters' anointed moneybags in a thousand spurting geysers of their own blood and brains and guts.

Working men and working women of America! Let us swear by all that is dear to us and all that is sacred to our cause, **never to become a soldier and never to go to war!**

If the pot-bellied masters insist upon the Crimson Carnival, the Devil's Bloody Debauch, they will henceforth rip out their own loins and livers, riot in their own blood and entrails and offer up their own mangled and putrescent carcasses on the blood-drenched altar of Mars and Mammon.

The dastard jingoes even now are plotting to force the United States into the seething maelstrom of fire and slaughter, pestilence and famine, misery and hell. Every subtle agency known to their infernal ingenuity is being employed to accomplish their satanic design.

The working men of America have it in their power to foil this monstrous piracy; to slay the demon of destruction and put an end to war here and erywhere, now and forevermore.

They have but to stand up like men and in the commanding voice of their ass and the eternal glory of their cause proclaim the fiat of civilization and humanity:

LET THERE BE PEACE!!

Aug 1915 appeal

One of numerous leaflets Debs wrote opposing World War 1. Opponents sent copies of this and other antiwar statements by Debs to the Attorney General's office.

"Whoever would overturn the liberty of the nation must begin by subduing freedom of speech."

"Workers of the world, unite! You have nothing to lose but your chains and a world to gain."

The New York Call

TWELFTH YEAR. NO 104.   TEN PAGES.   NEW YORK, MONDAY, APRIL 14, 1919.   **   PRICE, THREE CENTS.

DEBS ENTERS U. S. PRISON;
'UNCONQUERED,' HIS LAST WORD

ESSEN STRIKERS, SEEKING LABOR REPUBLIC, SLAIN BY GOV'T TROOPS

RADICALS RISE IN DANZIG
—CITIES DECLARED TO
BE IN A STATE OF SIEGE
BY GENERAL.

SPARTACANS REINFORCED
IN DUSSELDORF REVOLT
—SEIZE R. R. STATION
AND BUILD BARRICADES

BASLE, April 13—General
von Below, German military
governor of Danzig, has declared

Australian Trades Unions Aim to Get Week of 40 Hours

MELBOURNE, Australia, April
13.—The Trades Hall Council of
this city today began a movement
for the establishment of a 40-hour
week in all Australian industries.
In a circular it is pointed out
that the increase of productivity
during the war, the cessation of
remunerative work since the sign-
ing of the armistice, and the de-
mobilization of soldiers tend to
increase the unemployment problem.

CITY MILITARY GUARD TO DOWN LABOR BY FORCE SOUGHT IN BILL

BILL CREATING FORCE
FOR WAR "OVER HERE"
UP IN ASSEMBLY, AFTER
PASSING SENATE.

GETS CONVICT'S NUMBER IN EXCHANGE FOR NAME, BUT SAYS "MY HEAD'S ERECT"

Kidnapped From Cleveland by U. S. Marshals—15,000 Workers March to Federal Building, Singing "Marseillaise," as
Protest When Debs' Train Pulls Out—Sends Last Message
to New York Socialists.

BULLETIN.
By DAVID KARSNER.

Debs Shows U. S. is Controlled by Bosses

Alabama Operators Refuse Submission to the Decision of Department of Justice, and were Not Indicted, Ordered Clubbed or Shot.

The issue, a concrete case of capitalism, is here presented as a campaign issue to the working people of the United States. The coal operators of Alabama refused to abide by the decision of the Department of Justice, rendered under the Lever act, in their controversy with the miners. They not only treated the decision with contempt, but defied the government, and got away with it.

The Attorney General and the capitalist government he represents abjectly surrendered to their master, the robber coal trust.

Meanwhile the miners remonstrated with the operators, and appealed to the government to enforce its decision. All in vain.

The operators spurned the decision, refused to recognize the union of the miners, and told the government to go to h——

Was any operator indicted or arrested? Any injunction is-
sued? Any mandatory orders? Any policemen ordered to club the lawless operators? Any soldiers ordered to shoot them?

Certainly not; they are the capitalists, the master class under capitalism. They don't obey the law, they are the gover——

Can you not see it, Mr. Wage-Slave? They don't submit to government, they are the gove——

totally blind. It is so crystal clear.

if you ha—

No——

In his 1919 press statement Debs declared, "I enter the prison doors a Flaming Revolutionist" and promised "Everything will come out all right."

Debs wrote this leaflet on behalf of striking coal miners in Alabama. Whenever strikers needed a leaflet or broadside, Debs tried to oblige.

National Platform
OF THE
Socialist Party
1920

IN the national campaign of 1920 the Socialist Party calls upon all American workers of hand and brain, and upon all citizens who believe in political liberty and social justice, to free the country from the oppressive misrule of the old political parties, and to take the government into their own hands under the banner and upon the program of the Socialist Party.

The outgoing administration, like Democratic and Republican administrations of the past, leaves behind it a disgraceful record of solemn pledges unscrupulously broken and public confidence ruthlessly betrayed.

It obtained the suffrage of the people on a platform of peace, liberalism and social betterment, but drew the country into a devastating war, and inaugurated a regime of despotism, reaction and oppression unsurpassed in the annals of the republic.

It promised to the American people a treaty which would assure to the world a reign of international right and true democracy. It gave its sanction and support to an infamous pact formulated behind closed doors by predatory elder statesmen of European and Asiatic Imperialism. Under this pact territories have been annexed against the will of their populations and cut off from their nations seeking their freedom in the exercise of the m... have been brutally fought with arm...

To...
tle, to th...
erty to...
ideal o...
peace ...
actiona...
nation...

abroad...
and...

pub...
tat...
ac...

Interesting platform the party adopted when Debs ran for the presidency from behind the bars of Atlanta Prison in 1920.   **119**

The insert shows Debs receiving the 1920 presidential nomination from an official delegation from the Socialist Party Seymour Stedman, vice presidential candidate and a Chicago lawyer is on Debs' left.

A Word To The Workers

By EUGENE V. DEBS

As I may not meet you face to face in this campaign I address this brief message to you from my prison cell.

I am, as you know, the candidate of the Socialist party for president of the United States. The nomination came to me unsought, contrary to my personal wishes, by a unanimous vote of the convention.

The election takes place November 2nd. On that day the workers will register the degree of their intelligence or their ingnorance, according as they cast their votes for themselves and their families or for their exploiting masters and their families. They will decide for four years more the political and industrial destiny of the nation.

The workers have a majority of votes. They outnumber their masters and bosses overwhelmingly at the polls. There they are masters, if they only will.

DEBS IMPRISONMENT CHALLENGES POWER OF SOCIALIST PARTY

Unspoken Words of Champion of Oppressed Call From Prison to Workers Everywhere to Drop All Bickerings and Unite Against Common Foe

By DAVID KARSNER,
Staff Correspondent.

MOUNDSVILLE, West Va., April 28 (By mail) — On . . .
'· international h-l·'·

:ial from
United

:e in this

ected to
:al rulers
es of the
sible for

:e House
of Wall
:he same
voters to
iced him
iponsible

of race
float or
destined

In this 1920 campaign leaflet, "A Word to the Workers" Debs stressed that the workers of the country controlled the majority of the votes and that they outnumbered their masters if they would only vote correctly.

Debs at the Atlanta Prison.

Excerpts from the Canton, Ohio, antiwar speech that sent Debs to prison.

"I would rather a thousand times be a free soul in jail than to be a sycophant and coward in the streets."

* * *

"They may put those boys in jail—and some of the rest of us in jail—but they can not put the Socialist Movement in jail."

* * *

"I would be ashamed to admit that I had risen from the ranks. When I rise it will be with the ranks, and not from the ranks."

* * *

"I hate; I loathe; I despise Junkerdom. I have no earthly use for the Junkers of Germany, and not one particle more for the Junkers in the United States.

* * *

"If war is right, let it be declared by the people—you, who have your lives to lose; you certainly ought to have the right to declare war, if you consider a war necessary."

* * *

"The little that I am, the little that I am hoping to be, is due wholly to the Socialist Movement. It gave me my ideas and my ideals; and I would not exchange them for all of Rockefeller's blood-stained dollars."

* * *

"Do not worry over the charge of treason to your masters; but be concerned about the treason that concerns yourselves. Be true to yourself, and you can not be a traitor to any good cause on earth."

* * *

"We Socialists are the builders of the world that is to

ATTEND THE
MASS
MEETING
FOR THE
RELEASE OF
DEBS

"CONVICT No. 9653"

AND ALL POLITICAL PRISONERS
FRIDAY, JAN. 14, '21, 8 P. M.
AT THE
INDUSTRIAL HALL, ROCK ISLAND, ILL.
Auspices Tri-City Federation of Labor

Speakers: Wm. F. Kruse and Mrs. Rodriguez from Chicago

Why is he in jail? Because he made a speech in 1918 telling the truth about the World War and its Profiteers. His devotion to the workers got him into jail; the workers devotion to him must get him out.—DEBS FREEDOM CONFERENCE.

Typical rally posters of mass meetings held to create public pressure to free Debs.

For a United Working Class on Every Front

(Debs is not financially interested in this Magazine. He is responsible only for articles appearing over his own name.)

DEBS MAGAZINE

A Magazine of Militant Socialism

| Vol. I | CHICAGO, ILL., MARCH, 1922 | No. 7 |

Give Account, Mr. Hoover!

Eight millions of people disappeared from Russia between the years 1916 and 1920, says the census just published. Plague, pestilence and famine swept them away. Starvation has destroyed its victims by multitudes in the fertile valley of Mother Volga. Horrors beyond the power of pen to paint; misery surpassing conception, agonies multiplied beyond imagination; have swept over Russia in a steady stream.

In America the farmers have been bur... their corn by carloads be... sell it...

and destroy that movement and to make it of none effect.

Hoover's efforts have not succeeded entirely. In direct answer to his attack, Gov. Blaine of Wisconsin has proclaimed a Famine Relief Week, and every citizen of the state is officially asked to give what they can to save the dying babes and women of Russia. All hon... nors and s...

The Day of the People

By Eugene V. Debs.

Upon his release from the Kaiser's bastile — the doors of which were torn from their hinges by the proletarian revolution — Karl Liebknecht, heroic leader of the rising hosts, exclaimed: "The Day of the People has arrived!" It was a magnificent challenge to the Junkers and an inspiring battle-cry to the aroused workers.

From that day to this Liebknecht, Rosa Luxemburg and other true leaders of the German proletariat have stood bravely at the front, appealing to the workers to join the revolution and make it complete by destroing what remained of the criminal and corrupt old regime and ushering in the day of the people. Then arose the cry that the people were not yet ready for their day, and Ebert and Scheidemann and their crowd of white - liver-ed reactionaries, with the sanction and support of the fugitive Kaiser, the infamous Junkers and all the allied powers, now in beautiful alliance, proceeded to prove that the people were not yet ready to rule themselves, by setting up a bourgeois government under which the working class should remain in substantial-ly the same state of slavish subjection they were in the beginning of the war.

...issue—as to wheather the terrible war has ...ther its appalling sacrifices

Debs regularly contributed articles to this magazine to help rebuild the diminishing Socialist Party in 1922. Irwin St. John Tucker served as editor.

123

The Socialist Party circulated "The Day of the People", a 4-page pamphlet in which Debs praised the workers in Germany and Russia for rebelling against their rulers.

Headline on day Debs left prison.

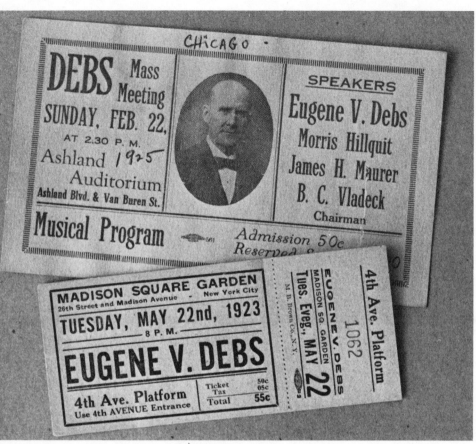

CHICAGO -

DEBS Mass Meeting
SUNDAY, FEB. 22,
AT 2.30 P. M.
Ashland *1925*
Auditorium
Ashland Blvd. & Van Buren St.
Musical Program
Admission 50c
Reserved

SPEAKERS
Eugene V. Debs
Morris Hillquit
James H. Maurer
B. C. Vladeck
Chairman

MADISON SQUARE GARDEN
26th Street and Madison Avenue — New York City
TUESDAY, MAY 22nd, 1923
8 P. M.
EUGENE V. DEBS
4th Ave. Platform
Use 4th AVENUE Entrance

Ticket	50c
Tax	05c
Total	**55c**

4th Ave. Platform
1062
EUGENE V. DEBS
MADISON SQ. GARDEN
M. B. Brown Co., N. Y.
Tues. Eve., MAY 22

After Debs' release from prison, he once again gave numerous speeches to raise funds to keep open the Socialist Party headquarters.

At time of Debs' death, long articles appeared praising Debs for his leadership as a spokesman for the blue denim masses in America.

Chapter IX
A Limited Success

In the final month of the 1908 campaign, Debs began to promise his supporters that the next campaign would start the day after the election. Although he did not say that he would run, he certainly made it clear that he planned to spend the next four years preparing for this contest. The euphoria from the publicity and success of the Red Special encouraged him to think that with renewed efforts socialism might become a reality in America.

On January 17, 1909, Debs went to Washington, where he presented to congressmen ideas for legislation that would prevent federal intervention and use of troops during strikes. He also pressured any legislators who would listen to ask the president why he would not publicly release the contents of his special appointed committee's report on the Goldfield, Nevada, strike. He met with little success on either count. This strike, which started when the miners refused to accept their pay half in gold and half in scrip, with no redemption date, occupied much of Debs' time in 1909. When Governor Denver S. Dickinson called for federal troops, Debs claimed that this action caused further rioting and delayed settlement.

In this post-campaign period Debs sometimes spent a great amount of time in his speeches and his writings reflecting about famous people he had known and what he had learned through his efforts on behalf of labor. Now fifty-four years old, Debs had reached that point in life when he enjoyed reviewing his past and pointing out that the public failed to recognize the merits of the crusaders in their midst. His article on Susan B. Anthony typified this kind of nostalgia." Her face fairly glowed with the spirit of her message," he said, "and her soul was in her speech." The "superb quality" and the "crowning virtue" she possessed Debs called "moral heroism." He recalled that "she fearlessly faced the ignorant multitude and walked unafraid of those who scorned her." As a youth Debs had met Susan B. Anthony and declared that she influenced his suffrage views. He met her again shortly before her death in 1906 and described her as the same "magnificent woman."[2]

Publicly Debs gave this relaxed, retiring image of himself but privately he participated actively in the inner party disputes. Although he continued to avoid conventions, he made sure that all of the leaders of the various factions in the party knew where he stood on key issues. Debs worried about the rapidly increasing party membership. He wanted more members, but he feared that many joined the party without accepting the revolutionary premise. Debs wrote to the Socialist writer, William Walling, "The revolutionary character of our party and our movement must be preserved in all of its integrity, *at all costs,* [underlined by Debs] for if that be compromised it had better cease to exist."[3] The evolutionary vs. the revolutionary argument had been an issue periodically in the past campaigns, but it now became a divisive force. Berger, Simons, Hillquit, Spargo, and other "Slowcialists" encouraged members to join and help work out compromises. Debs disagreed, for "If the trimmers had their way we'd degenerate into bourgeois reformers."[4] If the attention of the "rank and file" Socialists could be focused upon these compromises, Debs believed such "cowardly tendencies" would end.[5] Berger particularly irked Debs because he would not support his views. At this time Walling and Charles Kerr also led a drive to oust Berger, Spargo, Hunter, Simons and Hillquit from the executive committee. Walling asked Debs and Fred Warren to run for two of these positions, but they declined. Berger knew of this campaign and complained to Hillquit about this latest move of the "impossibilists," the name he gave to Debs' supporters.[6]

Morris Hillquit of New York City played an important intermediary role between Debs and Berger. The conflict between these two men became more than the issue of whether capitalism should be modified a step at a time or replaced immediately by socialism. When Hillquit asked Debs if he would accept the nomination as an additional party representative on the International Socialist Bureau, Debs declined. Since the Socialist Party had refused to recognize the Socialist Labor Party, Hillquit proposed that Debs take their representative's seat on this international board. Debs disapproved of "that method of extinguishing a rival party."[7] Alhough Debs agreed with Hillquit that the Socialist Labor Party "ought to be out of the way," he replied that the SLP had not been fairly treated. He called the move that Berger led which prevented the SLP unity proposition from going to a referendum vote of the whole party a "tactical blunder." If the vote had been taken, Debs predicted that "unity would have resulted and the decent element would have been assimilated into the united party. The few troublemakers would have slunk away or had their fangs extracted."[8] Debs attributed the increased SLP membership to a direct result of this error. "These who declared, like the oracular Berger, that there was no SLP to unite with, are not evidently haunted by its ghost," Debs wrote. "At any rate I am opposed to striking even the ghost of a dead rival below the belt."[9] Hillquit further informed Debs that he ought to accept this position because he needed closer contact with the international movement. Debs agreed that he had long needed this opportunity but lamented that "somehow I am always held in leash by the hand of fate."[10]

In a second letter Hillquit pressed the matter, but Debs remained adamant. "Evidently the National Committee did not want the rank and file to determine the question," Debs surmised, but in so doing he thought they created "a good deal of dissatisfaction among our own members." Debs added this advice: "This question has finally got to be met and disposed of on its merits and our party will find all effort to evade it. . . . to be vain. . ."[11] Obviously Debs knew that he had a greater chance of proving his point on this matter and others with the "rank and file" than with the National Committee. In the final paragraph of this same letter, he praised Hillquit for "crowding DeLeon from the ticket when you had the chance." "That is my idea of winning tactics," Debs concluded.[12] Evidently Debs regarded this move by Hillquit as within the jurisdiction of the N.E.B.

Unknown to Debs, Berger actively campaigned for the position on the International Socialist Bureau. He wrote Morris Hillquit: "Now you boys owe me active support to elect me as one of the delegates to the next International Congress. My election would be the logical thing, for the reason that if we want the second seat in the International Socialist Bureau there are probably not many American Comrades who can do more to secure this than I. Besides, I have begun this work, and I ought to be put in a position where I can hope to finish it. You, Morris, might use your good services with the *Call*, the *Volkszeitung* and the *Jewish Forward*."[13] Hillquit preferred Debs for this position and refused to aid Berger, since he knew Debs' views on the matter.

During this period Debs created further dissension within the executive ranks of the party when he insisted upon advocating the general strike. Berger, Hunter and other prominent Socialists disagreed. Hunter, a former Terre Haute childhood friend of Debs, stated that he failed to dissuade Debs on this issue. A sociologist, Hunter was recognized as an authority on poverty and working conditions in America. He told Debs that these strikes usually failed and created too much adverse public opinion against unions and their party.[14] Hunter argued that a successful general strike demanded superb leadership, perfect solidarity, a grievance of most serious and definite character, and a state of popular mind bordering upon insurrection.

In addition to paying attention to these inner-party problems, Debs continued to help strikers whenever he could. In 1909, when the city authorities in Philadelphia called out the state militia to end the trolley strike, the Central Labor Union responded by calling a general strike, and by asking Debs to speak. Prior to Debs' arrival the unions planned a mass meeting at two o'clock in the Philadelphia Baseball Park, but state troopers on horseback stopped the affair. Quickly the unionists in charge prepared for Debs' evening address in the Labor Lyceum by going to athletic clubs in town and rounding up their members to attend. These athletes, plus the sturdiest of the workers, escorted Debs into the hall. Inside the auditorium, Debs faced "200 uniformed policemen." He told these officers that they, too, represented working people and should have been ashamed of interrupting the afternoon meeting.[15] The night meeting continued without interruption. Debs remained in Philadelphia several days after the speech and helped organize the strikers.

At the same time the textile workers struck in Minersville, Pennsylvania. When these strikers heard that Debs had appeared in Philadelphia, they insisted that he conduct a rally for them. On this occasion Debs met another colorful agitator, Elizabeth Gurley Flynn, who years later left the Socialist Party and eventually became a leader of the Communist Party. At this time Elizabeth was one of several aggressive feminists who participated in organizing and directing strikes. In style and manner she followed closely her older Socialist sister colleagues, Mother Jones and Kate Richards O'Hare. Debs joined Flynn on the back of an old wagon and addressed the strikers. According to Flynn, Debs spoke directly to each individual and "smiled encouragement to those young girl strikers."[16]

In 1910 Debs opened the Cook County Socialist campaign with a speech in Chicago in which he asserted again that the primary need of the workers remained industrial unity. Such unity would lead to economic unity and then to political unity.[17] Such comments as this allied Debs with the IWW group, an organization that Berger's faction thought Debs should ignore if the Socialist Party planned to win any elections. The party consisted of 3,200 local organizations and an estimated 50,000 dues paying members.[18] Debs appreciated more members but cautioned that some joined without accepting the premise that socialism must totally replace capitalism.

In the 1910 election, Socialists won numerous political offices in various states, which caused great rejoicing at national party headquarters. Since some individuals on the Socialist ticket ran far ahead of the party, Debs cautioned his followers that "in the light of some personal observations during the campaign, this is not entirely a matter of jubilation. Some of the votes to our credit this year were obtained by methods not consistent with the principles of a revolutionary party, and in the long run will do us more harm than good."[19] Significantly, Debs did not mention Berger's election to the House of Representatives in 1910. Debs predicted that the party would attract elements which it could not assimilate and asked his supporters to keep out of the party those who would not endorse socialism as a working class revolutionary enterprise.[20] Although official party membership totaled only 50,000, California, Illinois, Pennsylvania, Ohio and New York each had an official vote of approximately 50,000 in 1910, but Wisconsin with an official vote of 39,515 had the largest number of Socialist office holders.[21] More than 100 Socialists held various offices in Wisconsin, with Milwaukee the party stronghold.[22] Certainly Berger's leadership aided this success, even if Debs opposed his strategy. Berger became the first Socialist in Congress. In order to win a seat in the House of Representatives, Berger had carefully built a political base among Wisconsin Socialists. He edited the Milwaukee *Daily Vorwaerts* from 1892-1898; later called the *Social Democratic Herald* and after 1911 the daily *Milwaukee Leader*. (His supporters elected him a member of the National Executive Committee of the Socialist Party from 1898-1923.)

An important factor in the spread of Socialist ideology in this period was the increase in the number of Socialist newspapers, pamphlets, and books. Some sixty newspapers supported the party at this time. Thirty of these papers appeared in foreign languages. Several of the weeklies and dailies such as the *Chicago Daily Socialist, New York Daily Call, Jewish Daily Forward,* and the *Appeal to Reason* had large circulations. *Wilshire's Magazine* and the *Appeal to Reason,* which Debs continued to help edit, each had a subscription list of a quarter of a million.[23] Significantly, these newspapers and magazines, including *Progressive Woman*, *International Socialist Review*, *The Progressive Journal of Education*, and *The Little Socialist* (last two aimed at youth), supported Debs.

The same cannot be said about books on socialism published by prominent party members. Although none of these party authors openly attacked Debs, they either mentioned Debs briefly or ignored him completely in their discussions of the Socialist Party in America. When Hillquit discussed the Socialist movement in America in a chapter of his 1909 book, *Socialism in Theory and Practice*, he never mentioned Debs in that chapter—or, for that matter, in any other.[24] In the 1903 and later 1910 revised editions of *History of Socialism in the United States*, Hillquit mentioned Debs briefly and praised him for his part in the Pullman strike. Hillquit's only reservation had to do with a secret meeting that planned the first IWW convention, a group which included "persons well known in the radical labor movement of the country including the late presidential candidate for the Socialist party, Eugene V. Debs."[25] Debs is hardly mentioned in John Spargo's books, *Socialism* (1906), *The Substance of Socialism* (1909), *Sidelights on Contemporary Socialism* (1911), and *Americanism and Social Democracy* (1918).[26] Spargo does, however, explore controversies in the party in *Sidelights on Contemporary Socialism* which he dedicated to Victor Berger. "Sometimes the anti-intellectualism assumes the dimensions of a crisis," Spargo wrote. "Important elections in the party are fought upon the issue. At such times the life of the movement is jeopardized, for if the demagogic element should succeed the intellectuals would either be forced to submit to rule by demagogues or leave the party and establish a new saner one. . ."[27] Spargo, more than any other writer of the time, insisted that the Socialist Party needed intellectuals and needed to return to Marx.[28] Not very much is said about Debs, either, in W. J. Ghent's book, *Socialism and Success*. Interestingly, in the same year as the book was published, Ghent became Berger's secretary in Washington.[29] Debs read and owned copies of all of these books. He made little direct use of these books but he did underline parts of some books. Frequently he underscored statements or facts about party history that he evidently wanted to remember. With a heavy blue marking pencil which he always used, he also underlined ideas that he had advocated. Two writers did avidly endorse Debs during this period however: Stephen Reynolds in *Debs: His Life, Writings and Speeches*, and William Walling in *Socialism As It Is*.[30] Walling attacked Berger especially for not adequately representing socialism in Washington. Walling criticized Berger's second speech in Congress proposing an old age pension bill as an accommodation to the old parties to avoid an overthrow by socialism. "Its common adoption by progressive capitalists," he wrote, "would seem to indicate that they consider it as being either directly or indirectly to their own interests."[31]

The establishment of the Rand School of Social Science in New York City also aided Debs and the spread of socialism. Mrs. Carrie Rand gave the income from a $200,000 trust for a school to train young Socialists for agitation. Her son-in-law, George Herron, former popular professor at Grinnell College in Iowa and a prominent Socialist writer and propagandist, taught in the school along with several other former college instructors.[32] Debs, at this time a close friend of Herron's, actively supported the school. Students read Debs' writings as well as those from authors who philosophically aligned themselves with Berger. The school offered no course on Debs' theories of socialism but did include a course titled "Public Speaking by Debs"![33] School officials advertised this course by correspondence for those who could not come to New York City to study.

With all of these activities, and in spite of party cross-currents, Debs maintained his popularity as the leading figure in the party. The right wing of the party had a majority on the National Executive Board but were not as popular as Debs was with the Jimmy Higginses who paid the dues. None of the factional leaders, including Berger, could gain control of the party as long as Debs remained active on the stump and in the press. He continued to write, especially articles for the *Appeal to Reason,* which detractors both within and outside the party dubbed the "Appeal to Treason", the "Appeal to Unreason", or the "Squeal of Treason."

Although Debs privately participated in the inner struggles of the party, he publicly tried to serve as arbitrator, especially as the election of 1912 approached. He saw this as his mission at that time, but he overstated when he wrote that Socialists agreed on fundamental principles but disagreed on tactics. "The matter of tactical differences should be approached with open mind and in the spirit of tolerance," he counseled.[34] Before pleading for less rancor and more toleration in the discussion of differences, Debs admitted that perhaps he did not have "the right idea about tactics" but he was "open to correction" and "ready to change" whenever he found himself wrong. Although the early part of this essay may have encouraged his opponents to compromise, Debs' request near the end of the article for understanding a controversial statement by William Haywood and Frank Bohn heightened the conflict. Bohn and Haywood had written that when the worker, either through experience or through study of socialism, "knew the truth," he should act accordingly which meant disregarding laws regarding property and using any weapon that would win.[35] Although Debs admitted that "a number of comrades of ability and prominence disagreed" with this advice, he believed it "entirely sound." Such open support of Haywood irked Debs' friends, but he remained loyal to the IWW and let its leaders do part of his thinking. His active support of the IWW definitely limited his effectiveness as an arbitrator and certainly added to the conflicts at party conventions.

When the Socialist convention opened on May 12, 1912, in Tomlinson Hall in Indianapolis, two controversial issues forced the delegates to divide quickly into two factions. Both issues involved the energetic IWW backing of the violent Lawrence, Massachusetts, strike case and the San Diego free speech fight. The "Slowcialists" group's success in the 1910 elections made them more aggressive in this convention. They hoped to rid the party of the IWW ties at this meeting. The past conventions had never been free of factional fights, but the 1912 conclave produced more than usual.

Debs stayed in Girard, Kansas, and ignored all pressures to attend. He probably wanted this nomination more than any other, for he realized that the Berger-Hillquit-Spargo forces would change the Socialist Party into a more conservative political body and remove his supporters from roles of influence. He knew that his opposition had never been stronger and that, unfortunately, his faction lacked a leader to replace him and challenge these opponents. To lose to these forces within the party would have been a bitter defeat, and Debs assumed from the reports Theodore collected on who planned to attend the convention that he had sufficient delegate support. He asserted that on both issues under contention—the Lawrence strike and the San Diego boycott against certain speakers—the delegates knew his opinions. In *Appeal* articles Debs had clearly aligned himself with the "Lefts" who supported the IWW in these encounters.

The conflict began when the convention finance committee received a request for funds to aid these two causes.[36] When the conservative delegate, John Spargo, declared that the free speech fighters belonged to a "vicious element with criminal faces" in the party, a debate ensued.[37] Eventually the "Lefts" won a partial victory with a motion to send the San Diego comrades $250, a much smaller amount than requested. Before the convention ended the delegates heard that Emma Goldman, "queen of the anarchists," had been escorted out of San Diego after she gave a speech. Her manager, Ben Reitman, received a tar and feather treatment and the brand IWW on his back from the same local vigilante group.[38]

During the Lawrence strike, Arturo Giovannitti and Joseph Ettor had been arrested for the murder of a striking girl picket. These workers claimed that, at the time of the murder, they were in another town several miles away. Debs was convinced of their innocence and hoped the delegates would provide funds to defend these men. Partially because of this strike and reported violence by the IWW in other strikes, Berger and other conservatives skillfully maneuvered a constitutional amendment through the convention. "I can see anarchy under the guise of the IWW eating at the vitals of the party," Berger shouted.[39] The amendment called for expulsion from the party of anyone who advocated sabotage in any strike.[40] The "Lefts" failed to block this action. They still hoped to secure the nomination for Debs.

When nominations opened, Dan Hogan of Arkansas immediately demanded the floor and quickly nominated Debs. Immediately Hogan and other Debs supporters launched a long colorful floor rally.[41] When the noise subsided, Berger feebly inquired if Debs could stand the rigors of another campaign. The chairman, George Goebel, replied that those "in the know" had assured him that Debs could. The Berger and Hillquit groups nominated two other candidates. For the first time, Hillquit had been particularly active in the opening days of the convention trying to secure sufficient delegates to nominate someone other than Debs. Spargo also circulated a report to delegates in which he stated that during his travels for the party he found little "Debs sentiment" and "not much demand for his nomination."[42] Since the conservative wing divided over Emil Seidel, former mayor of Milwaukee, and Charles Russell of New York, Debs won on the first ballot. Seidel's selection as vice president marked a consolation victory for the conservative wing.[43] Rumors circulated that Debs would come to the convention to deliver his acceptance speech, but these failed to materialize. Instead he sent this telegram: "It is written in our stars that socialism is to be the only issue in the coming campaign." J. Mahlon Barnes, according to Hillquit, deserved the nomination for campaign manager again, and the committee concurred. They scheduled June 16 for a big campaign rally in Chicago.[44]

Once the campaign began, Debs wrote a friend that had the delegates any doubts about his fitness for an all out campaign, they might have forced the campaign committee to curtail his tours. However, this committee, Debs reported, ". . . planned a speaking tour for me the like of which no presidential candidate had ever made in the history of the United States."[45] Plans called for sixty-eight days of speechmaking with five and six appearances a day scheduled in large cities—all without the aid of the "Red Special." "There were times when I thought I would drop in my tracks," Debs later said, "but I kept on determined to fulfill the expectations of the comrades throughout the country."[46] Although the central committee arranged another coast to coast tour, the 1912 campaign tour lacked the color and fanfare of the Red Special. As in 1908, newspaper accounts described huge audiences, but they reported less enthusiasm and fewer cases of physical mauling of Debs.

A cartoon appearing in *Harper's Weekly* in the fall of 1912 cleverly depicted the political enigma that Debs faced in his fourth presidential campaign. The cartoon pictured a naked Debs in the old swimming hole. In the bushes near the edge of the water, William Jennings Bryan, also unclothed, calls out to Debs: "Say, Debs, he hooked everything that belonged to me, and now he's gone off with yours." Teddy Roosevelt, with a big-toothed grin, appeared to be running over a hill with clothes slung over his shoulder labeled "socialism."[47]

This campaign can best be described by focusing upon six key speeches. Rather than refute the varied reform planks in the opposing parties' platforms, Debs argued that socialism provided the only answer to permanent reform. These six speeches by the fourth-time Socialist candidate illustrate this thesis: "Address of Acceptance" in May; "This Is Our Year" campaign "opener" in June; Milwaukee "Fight for Freedom" speech in July; Fergus Falls, Minnesota, "Capitalism and Socialism" oration in late August; Madison Square Avenue address in September; and Terre Haute closing speech in November.

In his "Address of Acceptance" Debs told his listeners of the recent rapid gains in the Socialist Party membership and concluded that the

134

"world's workers are aroused at last."[48] In the first third of this address, he carefully attempted to delineate the differences between the Socialist Party and the three capitalist parties. "The infallible test of a political party is the private ownership of the sources of wealth and the means of life," he declared. "Apply this test to the Republican, Democratic and Progressive parties and upon that basic fundamental issue you will find them essentially one and the same." In Debs' estimation, Socialists did not plead for votes because the workers gave them freely when they understood. He emphatically advised his listeners not to consider Roosevelt's new party until they received assurance that the trust owners financed the Progressives in order to put themselves out of business.[49]

This speech differed from most that Debs gave. Rather than the usual extended illustrations and personal attacks upon specific political rivals, Debs concentrated upon an expository analysis of what he thought socialism had to offer Americans in 1912. He spoke briefly of unemployment, child labor, poverty, and prostitution without digressing into examples of each among the working class. The organization of this speech built to a climax, where most of Debs' orations ended after some final pointed illustration. He structured his arguments into a final appeal for the emancipation of workers. "Capitalism is rushing blindly to its impending doom. The Socialist Party makes its appeal to the intelligence and conscience of the people," he asserted. This party stood for equal rights and opportunities for all men and women, Debs promised, and signalized "the birth of a new civilization and the dawn of a happier day for all humanity."[50]

On June 14, Debs hurriedly sent a half page letter to his friend, Ryan Walker, cartoonist for the campaign. He thanked Ryan for his drawings and letters, but said that he would have to wait to study them on the train. "They are crowding me for my speech in manuscript and it is taking all my wits to meet the demands," he protested as he prepared his opening campaign speech.[51] The Socialist campaign committee had chosen a strategic time and place for Debs' address. In Chicago on this same Sunday, June 16, Republican party delegates gathered for one of their most bitterly contested conventions. Both Taft and Roosevelt had made extensive speaking tours prior to the convention, trying to convince the various state delegations that they deserved the nomination. Roosevelt had arrived on Friday and worked feverishly to secure delegates to support him. News media covered every move he made. Taft remained in Washington, but had a special wire connected to the convention floor. To compete with the convention the Socialists held a gigantic picnic for Debs at Riverview Park.

Before Debs delivered his written remarks, he praised his audience. "This vast outpouring of the workers, this tremendous and inspiring demonstration of the working class is far greater than I had expected," he announced to the red flag waving crowd. Evidently the crowd encouraged him, for he continued, "I never stand in the presence of such an enthusiastic multitude as this but I grow stronger and feel as if I had received a fresh consecration to the cause of liberty." Briefly he recalled his visit to Chicago during the

Pullman strike eighteen years earlier. He drew an analogy to the Chicago Pressmen's strike under way at that time. Turning to his script, Debs made this explanation: "It is only on rare occasions in delivering public speeches that I use manuscript, but having been told that this would be the opening of the campaign, I concluded for obvious reasons to reduce it to writing, in order to prevent my remarks from being garbled or misrepresented by the capitalist papers." Titling the speech, "This Is Our Year," Debs focused his arguments around this contention: "In this campaign there are but two parties and but one issue." Midway in the speech he restated that "there is but one issue that appeals to this conquering army—the unconditional surrender of the capitalistic class."[52] This remark indicated the more militant stand that Debs took on all issues during this campaign.

Several factors accounted for the change of tactics obvious in this speech. Debs had been disappointed that the 1908 Red Special campaign yielded so few votes. During the four years between campaigns Debs had fought some of his bitterest battles within the party via the press and stump. Nearly fifty-seven years of age in 1912, he realized that his old methods had not always succeeded, and he became impatient. The facts that every state in 1912 had an active organization sponsoring candidates, that the national party treasury had funds for the campaign and additional speakers, and that numerous cities had elected Socialist candidates in 1910, spurred Debs to lash out aggressively at all capitalists. In 1912 when his Indiana comrade, James Oneal, published a pamphlet, "Militant Socialism," Debs endorsed it. Oneal concluded his booklet with a remark that Debs often used in the campaign, "The Socialist party may not win in the coming election, but it can raise working men to power. A Socialist elected to a law-making body is so much power to be used in defense of the working class. We must have this power to overthrow capitalist rule."[53]

Debs reflected militancy in the loaded terms that he selected to portray conditions in 1912. In a high voice he shouted to the cheering picnic guests that on the one hand are the trusts, ". . . the plutocrats, the politicians, the bribe-givers, the ballot-box stuffers, the repeaters, the parasites, retainers and job-hunters of all descriptions; the corruption funds, the filth, slime and debauchery of ruling class politicians, the press and pulpit and college, all fearing capitalist collars, . . . glorifying its plundering and profligate regime." The word choice in other statements he uttered further illustrated his increased militancy: "against industrial robbery and political rottenness"; "the filthy game of capitalist politics"; "parasites in palaces and automobiles and honest workers in hovels and tramping the ties"; "corporations dripping with corruption and putridity"; and shouting "THIS IS ENOUGH! THERE MUST BE A CHANGE."[54]

In this address Debs skillfully wove into the oration each of the controversial issues that had divided the past convention. He ignored the majority "Slowcialist" decisions on these issues by praising the free speech fighters in San Diego and the mill workers in Lawrence, Massachusetts, and by vigorously proclaiming the innocence of Ettor and Giovannitti. He also lauded the striking press workers in Chicago. After discussing each of these cases, Debs summarized: "Whether it be in the textile mills of Lawrence . . .; or in conflict with the savages in San Diego where men who dare to be known as members of the Industrial Workers of the world are kidnapped. . .; or in Chicago where that gorgon of capitalism, the newspaper trust, is bent upon crushing and exterminating the Pressmen's Union; . . . the Socialist Party . . . is freely pledged to render them all the assistance in its power." This last statement proved that Debs had paid little heed to the edicts of the convention, for such a pledge could not have been secured in the 1912 conclave! Referring to Ettor and Giovannitti, Debs declared, "They were staunch and true; their leadership made for industrial unity and victory and for this reason alone the enraged and defeated millowners are bent on sending them to the electric chair."[55]

Debs capitalized upon the bitter struggle between Taft and Roosevelt. "We have before us in this city an exhibition of capitalist machine politics," Debs asserted, for "Taft and Roosevelt in the exploitation of their boasted individualism and their mad fight for official spoils have been forced to expose the whole game of capitalist class politics."[56] Debs' conclusion closely followed the peroration in his acceptance address, except for its greater length and more militant tone. He appealed for unity among the masses, saying, "They have been deceived, misled and betrayed, and are now hungering for the true gospel of relief and the true message of emancipation." In a second short speech to reporters that followed, Debs thanked Taft and Roosevelt for doing some excellent campaigning for him. "They are telling the truth about each other and are verifying what the Socialists have been saying about them and their kind for a long time," quipped Debs. "Roosevelt never had a principle. He will subscribe to anything to get into office. He has the air of a braggert and a loafer." Referring to the fact that Roosevelt had been labeled socialistic by Taft backers, Debs snapped, "I resent the imputation. We would not take him into the party."[57] After these two speeches Debs returned to his hotel and awaited a hectic meeting the next day with the Socialist campaign committee and Barnes.

In 1912, the Democratic Party discarded Bryan in favor of Woodrow Wilson. When Taft won the Republican Party nomination, Roosevelt carried out his threatened exit. Now, instead of the usual two opponents, in this campaign Debs faced a third opponent, the Progressive or Bull Moose candidate. In his third campaign, Debs had warned audiences of what he called pseudo reform efforts of the two major parties. In 1912, all three opponents' platforms contained planks that were much like part of the 1900 and 1904 Socialist Party demands. Roosevelt's adoption of Populist-Socialist Party planks annoyed Debs. He found some of his favorite planks included in the Bull Moose Party platform: woman suffrage, direct primaries, direct election of senators, corrupt practices acts, a department of labor, and the extension of the eight hour day to all industries.[58]

J. Mahlon Barnes' appointment as campaign manager had caused considerable protest from the Christian Socialists and from many of Debs' left wing supporters. These men thought that Debs should dismiss Barnes. Barnes had had an affair with Jane Keep, a secretary in the national office, and had participated frequently with some comrades in drunken parties. In August of 1911 a special party committee had investigated the Barnes affair after Miss Keep ended the relationship. The committee reported that Barnes had forced Miss Keep to have an abortion to end an earlier pregnancy; declared further that Manet Keep was Barnes' son; claimed that Miss Keep did not know Barnes had a wife; and produced for the National Executive Board's study and circulation a series of love letters from Barnes that documented their relationship. When Miss Keep worked as a secretary in the national office, she used the assumed name of Jean Sipple. While working she discovered that Barnes, who had given her the job, had recorded her salary at $14 a week but paid her only $9. The pay discrepancy alone did not prompt her actions, for she soon learned that Mrs. Mabel Hudson and a Miss Annie Flaherty, co-workers in the office, also had more than an employee-employer relationship with Barnes.[59] Because of the continuing controversy, Barnes came to Terre Haute in late May and informed Debs that the Berger-Hillquit majority forced him to accept the managership.

After Barnes' visit, Debs explained his attitude toward Barnes' appointment in a letter to Fred Warren, the *Appeal to Reason* editor. "I would have no more right to ask him to resign than he would have to ask me to resign. The question of his past relations with the party and difficulties in connection with his office were all known to the convention, and in face of all this the convention, acting for the party, elected him to manage the campaign."[60] Warren disagreed with Debs and commented in several editorials in his paper during August on the Barnes' matter. Other Socialist papers such as the *National Socialist, St. Louis Labor* and *Chicago World* supported Barnes. All of this publicity resulted in hundreds of letters of protest—overwhelmingly against Barnes. Warren had encouraged this response in his paper by adding a last line to his editorials: "Write Debs your views." When Debs read Berger's letter upholding Barnes in the *National Socialist*, he wrote him a letter of protest. In this letter Debs questioned Hillquit's wisdom in selecting Barnes and asked for Berger's support in settling the issue before it created further disharmony in the party and had an adverse effect upon the campaign.[61] Debs also accused Hillquit of "bossism" and informed Berger that he would oppose Hillquit when he ran for another term on the national committee. Obviously Debs was changing tactics and retaliating against Hillquit's open opposition to him in the past convention, and his foisting of Barnes into the campaign manager's role.

As pressure to oust Barnes mounted, Debs decided that he had to ask the campaign committee to meet in Chicago in mid-June to reconsider the appointment. The committee refused, and throughout the rest of the campaign little harmony existed between the candidate and the national office. Insight into this committee meeting that supposedly met for the expressed purpose of scheduling the rest of Debs' speaking dates, can be gained from a letter from Debs to Warren which was recently found. "The whole official machine and all who depend upon it for a job are against me . . . all for Barnes," Debs wrote. "Berger who has never been out of office since he has been in the Socialist Party, who is a chronic office seeker . . . says I think I own the nomination and . . . charges that I am swelled up with self-conceit. In his heart he knows that he never uttered a more deliberate falsehood. Spargo used to be a preacher . . . This may account for his weeping great weeps over my cruelty to Barnes while he puts both his heels on the neck of the woman whose life was wrecked and damns her . . . to paint white as a lily the man, his official confederate (Barnes) who was responsible for her ruin."[62] Although Debs disagreed with the National Executive Committee's decision, he wrote to Ryan Walker that he would "bear it all without attempting to answer a single falsehood, or a single slander, at least until the campaign was over." Debs further confided to Walker that the trouble started years earlier when he gave Berger to understand that he did his own thinking. "But it (the NEB) could and did get control of my campaign," Debs admitted, "as it did four years ago."[63]

Debs did not state to Walker the argument that George Goebel had presented to Debs at this meeting. Goebel reasoned that Debs should have been willing to overlook Barnes' affairs since the committee had tolerated his drinking in earlier years. After the session Goebel reiterated this view to Debs: "It should be needless to say I have loved you, been for you, even lied for you, to conceal your failing, instead of shouting it from the housetop, as you would have Barnes."[64]

In spite of the conflict, Debs accepted the committee's request to speak on July 21, in Pabst Park in Milwaukee—Berger's bailiwick. Near the end of the speech, Debs lauded Milwaukee for electing a Socialist mayor and sending the first Socialist to Congress. "Victor Berger has made good at Washington," he stated, and "for the first time the voice of labor has been distinctly heard on the floors of Congress. . ."[65] Debs could be charged with being double tongued, but he was in another sense consistent in that he refrained from discussing party troubles in public speeches. In this major address, Debs reiterated his contention that politics in America had been reduced to a contest between two parties, the capitalist and the Socialist. Accusing all capitalists of being conservatives and standpatters, he singled out Roosevelt for special attack. Vexed with Roosevelt's brand of progressivism, Debs called it "sheer buncomb."[66] For proof he charged that when Roosevelt "was in office and had the power, he did none of the things, nor attempted to do any of the things he is now talking about so wildly. On the contrary, a more servile functionary to the trusts than Theodore Roosevelt never sat in the presidential chair."[67]

Before this huge Wisconsin crowd, Debs took the opportunity to discuss the inconsistencies in LaFollette's support of Roosevelt. He chided LaFollette for not discovering that Roosevelt's presidential record was a trust record until "after Roosevelt threw him down in the progressive scramble for the Republican nomination." When LaFollette challenged Roosevelt to list his campaign contributors, Debs told his audience, the Senator asked too simple a question. Debs then proceeded to name the principal financial backers of Roosevelt, Taft, and Wilson. Debs usually said little about Wilson, but in this speech he elaborated upon Wilson's background and cited his anti-strike edicts at Perth Amboy and other industrial centers in New Jersey. After the Milwaukee address, Debs started a five-week speaking tour of the Midwest.

On August 27, 1912, Debs spoke to a packed audience in the Lyceum Theatre in Fergus Falls, Minnesota, a town in which Debs had a large following ever since the days of the Great Northern strike. He titled his speech "Capitalism and Socialism"—a label he had used for addresses in other campaigns. Early in the address he promised his listeners in this rural community that a new order was struggling into existence.[68] Like a scholar of social movements, he stated that social changes are preceded by agitation and unrest among the masses. He followed this point with a Marxist interpretation of the economic motivation back of his opponent's parties. Later, discussing the inadequacies of worker's wages, he quoted Professor Scott Nearing's research: ". . . half of the adult males of the United States are earning less than $500; three quarters of them are earning less than $600; nine-tenths of them are receiving less than $900 a year, while ten per cent receive more."[69] Throughout this speech Debs used figures compiled by Scott Nearing—the Socialist economist that University of Pennsylvania fired.[70] At the end of this address Debs confronted his audience in sharp, succinct phrases with this series of specific demands for the workers: The machinery of production; control of society; enfranchisement of women; equality for all races, colors, and creeds; end of child labor and equal educational opportunity for children.[71]

The party strategists saved the last two months before the election for a tour of the Eastern States. New York City Socialists made their usual elaborate plans for campaign rallies. Thirteen thousand persons paid from a quarter to a dollar to hear Debs in Madison Square Garden. Two hundred girls wearing white dresses with red sashes moved through the audience selling Debs' buttons and pamphlets. In his speech Debs lauded the workers and flailed the capitalists. Receipts for this speech, according to the *New York World,* totaled $10,000.[72]

John Haynes Holmes, editor of *Unity* magazine, heard Debs speak for the first time in another New York address at Carnegie Hall: "It was not even a good speech," Holmes wrote, for "I saw at once that he had given this speech fifty or a hundred times before. I know enough about public speaking to know that the quick, jerky gestures meant taut muscles in a man too tired to talk, almost too tired to stand." But Holmes changed his views as the address progressed: "Every now and then . . . there came great moments. The muscles relaxed just for an instant, the voice took on a tone of freshness and vigor . . . These were the moments when Debs spoke of the children toiling in the factories; women slaving in the slums; of the poor whose destruction was their poverty. In an instant, under the influence of such thoughts, he was a man reborn, and I knew, for the first time why people loved him."[73] After the New York speeches, Debs made a tour back across the country.

On the final day of campaigning in St. Louis, Debs addressed four audiences. Then he caught the late train for Terre Haute, and slept most of the next day. That evening, with the aid of five bands, he led the biggest parade that old timers could remember. He had to deliver two speeches before separate overflow audiences in the Opera House and Boys' Club.[74] After commenting on the bitter battle taking place in Terre Haute politics over charges of corruption by incumbents in city offices, Debs proclaimed to the Opera House listeners that the Socialists had the only living issue in the campaign—the emancipation of the working class. Stressing the importance of knowing your candidates, Debs argued: "We are profuse in our literature explaining things. The other three parties give you no literature. Their salvation depends upon your ignorance."[75] Local suffragists filled the boxes nearest the Opera House stage, and waved banners bearing the inscription "Vote for Women." Turning toward the ladies, Debs praised their suffrage efforts, and quipped that even Roosevelt had "progressed" in spite of himself on this issue.[76] Predicting great gains for socialism in the election, he concluded with the promise that socialism would eventually sweep Terre Haute.

On election day, Debs celebrated his fifty-seventh birthday. The election returns, telegraphed to him by "Jimmie Higginses" throughout the country, soon indicated that the 1912 campaign had been his most successful when measured at the ballot box. In spite of Roosevelt's and Wilson's liberal promises and the dissension within the party, final returns showed that Debs received 897,011 votes or six per cent of the total.[77] In Indiana, the Socialist vote of 36,000 represented a gain of 270 per cent over 1908.[78] However, little did Debs realize that socialism had reached its electoral peak in America in 1912.

With the election scarcely over, Debs became embroiled in a law suit. The federal government charged associate editor Debs, Fred D. Warren, editor of the *Appeal,* and J. I. Sheppard, Warren's attorney, with obstructing justice by inducing a witness to leave the country so that he could not be found to testify against these three members of the *Appeal* staff. The government charged that the *Appeal* had misused the mails in posting articles concerning conditions in the federal prison at Leavenworth, Kansas. Although the federal court in Topeka had dismissed the case three months previously, the government reopened it. J. P. McConough, formerly a prisoner in Leavenworth, testified that the defendants paid him $200 to go to California. Supposedly the defendants admitted payment, but said it was to discharge a debt. Debs retorted that the "charge was hatched by those who openly boasted they would see us in the penitentiary and bankrupt and destroy the *Appeal* for printing the prison article."[79] One source claimed Debs listened to a "hard luck" story from the convict and gave him all the money he had to start life anew.[80] To complicate matters, J. A. Wayland, owner of the *Appeal*, committed suicide. Debs greatly admired Wayland and grieved over his death, which he attributed to continued government harassment.[81] Warren and Sheppard posted $1,000 bonds for their release. Two months later two deputy marshals from Indianapolis arrested Debs in Terre Haute—a visit he had long anticipated. Theodore and his brother-in-law, Arthur Baur, posted bond which stipulated that Debs would appear for the May term of the federal court in Kansas.[82]

While waiting for trial, Debs turned his attention to another miners' strike in West Virginia. The National Executive Committee [formerly called Board, or NEB] of the Socialist Party met in Briggs House in Chicago and voted to send Victor Berger, Adolph Germer, and Debs to Charleston to conduct an investigation. Officials of the United Mine Workers brought a parade of witnesses before the group. These witnesses accused the mine owners of intimidation, gunfire, and unjust arrests in the New River, Paint, and Cabin Creek districts. Several men had been killed and martial law had been invoked. Word came from Governor Henry D. Hatfield that he would rather lock up the committee than talk to them. Tom Haggerty, respected member of the International Miners' Board, ignored the remark and prevailed upon the governor to meet Debs. Debs refused to go until the other two "investigators" could accompany him. Germer, a former Illinois miner and organizer for the UMW, stated that Debs calmly argued with a belligerent Hatfield for several hours.[83] Debs asked that Hatfield free fourteen men who had unfair trials; that hired "gunmen of the coal companies" stop breaking up public meetings; that the *Huntington Star*, a labor paper, receive payment for damages done by raiding state troopers; and that he recognize the miners had a justifiable cause in striking. Hatfield promised to make an investigation and, if he found Debs truthful, to help settle the strike. On April 28, 1913, the strike ended, and Hatfield kept his word, which included the release of Debs' crony on the agitation stump, Mother Jones, who was then past eighty.[84] Debs hurried to Girard, Kansas, for his own trial. After a brief investigation, Debs rejoiced, for the court dismissed all charges for lack of evidence.[85]

After his return from Girard, Kansas, Debs took several short lecture tours. He joyously announced in October that after nineteen years he had paid off the last of the $40,000 debt of the American Railway Union.[86] Debs also continued to play a part in Terre Haute politics. He wrote numerous letters to the editors of the local papers and gave his views on an investigation into voting irregularities in the last election, including the fact there were no recorded Socialist votes in his own precinct. He wondered how many more precincts in the country also had refused to count Socialist votes. These letters, however, did not create the local furor that his taking custody of Helen Cox caused. Miss Cox, daughter of a Methodist minister, had been arrested for prostitution. Her family had disowned her and her former husband, the son of a wealthy family, had divorced her and been granted custody of their child. Debs asked Judge Batt to permit the young woman to leave the jail and live in his home. "This case is a challenge to the Christianity of Terre Haute," Debs declared. "Will Terre Haute now help her or will its organized forces drive her to destruction? Let Terre Haute ask, what would Christ do?"[87] The police had warned Miss Cox to either keep off the streets or go to the red light district. Debs denounced this attitude and suggested that they tell all immoral men to also stay in the same district. Kate refused to talk with reporters. She fixed the little back bedroom upstairs for Miss Cox—the room she had intended for the maid Gene never hired. They treated Miss Cox as a member of the family. She remained with them for several months until she left to find work in another state.[88]

In September Debs fled to a ranch near Estes Park, Colorado, for a planned two month vacation. Kate Debs remained in Terre Haute. Debs put on overalls and worked on nearby ranches and on road construction. He was too restless and claimed the "lounging, lying around process" had not helped him.[89] For years he had talked of relaxing and doing again some hunting and fishing as he had done as a boy, but now these activities gave him little satisfaction. He had often discussed with his close friend, James W. Riley, his desire to live close to nature. When Riley came to Terre Haute, he used to stay several days. The two men would leave every evening after supper and visit the taverns between North 8th Street and the Wabash River. Debs had enjoyed introducing the poet to his blue collar friends, though on most "tours" both men drank too much. Now, if Riley had been able to join him for this vacation in Colorado, Debs might have enjoyed himself. As it was, his visit to the ailing Riley, who had suffered a stroke at Indianapolis before he left, had depressed him.[90]

During his stay at the Estes Park ranch, Debs spoke to striking Colorado miners, for, as he explained in a letter to Hillquit, he found it impossible "to be near enough the battle to hear the roar of guns and not have a part in it." His life, he told Hillquit, would be reduced to a few days "if it were not for socialism and for the little use" he might be to the movement.[91] After only three weeks Debs ended his vacation.

Debs quickly forgot the troubles over Barnes and also changed his views on the IWW. This shift of attitude on these two inner party issues helped to mend his differences with Hillquit and Berger. Gradually Debs came to realize that Haywood and his supporters could never be assimilated into the Socialist Party. When Haywood was ousted from the party in 1913, for advocating the use of sabotage in violation of section six of the Socialist Party constitution that had been added at the last convention, Debs did not protest. Although Debs saw some merits in the general strike, Debs disagreed with Haywood, Vincent St. John, Joe Hill and other "Wobblies" on tactics to use during such strikes. In 1912, the pamphlets, songs, cartoons and other IWW propaganda often contained the sabotage symbol of a black cat and a wooden shoe, borrowed from the days when European peasant strikers would destroy equipment by throwing their shoes into the machines. The words "sab cat," "Hoosier up," "kitten," and "Fix the job," were used by IWW advocates to suggest striking on the job, slow-downs and sabotage. Debs argued with Haywood and other IWW leaders that such advice created unnecessary problems. Although Haywood, St. John and other Wobbly speakers openly advocated the workers' right to use any tactics to gain better wages and working conditions, Debs did not. In a careful study of Debs' speeches, no remarks indicate he supported such tactics without reservations. Debs best explained his reasons why he could no longer support the IWW in a letter to William English Walling. "The IWW for which Haywood stands and speaks is an anarchist organization in all except name and this is the cause of all the trouble," he wrote. "The IWW has treated the Socialist Party most indecently," he continued. "When it gets into trouble it frantically appeals to the Socialist Party for aid, which has always been freely rendered, and after it is all over the IWW kicks the Socialist Party in the face."[92] Walling had written to Debs to ask his views on sabotage and law breaking. "I think you know that there is a very wide difference between the kind of political action Haywood advocates and the kind I advocate, even if we do happen to use identical words," Debs replied.[93] Before Debs would advocate breaking any laws, he assured Walling that he would have to know the exact circumstances.

Once Debs decided that the IWW harmed the Socialist Party, he had no hesitation in counseling others to denounce the IWW. He advised W. H. Thompson, a prominent leader among the mine workers in West Virginia, to take a stand against the IWW, telling him, "The very hour they find that they cannot dominate you and use you for their purposes they will denounce you as a traitor, according to their code."[94] When E. W. Richter, stalwart in the Detroit IWW group, challenged Debs' change of attitude, Debs replied that the "very name of IWW was offensive to the great mass of workers in this country" and that these workers justly should avoid anarchistic methods. Further, Debs stated that the IWW had made too many mistakes ever to restore the confidence of workers. He compared the reputation of the IWW to that of the Socialist Labor Party and claimed that neither had any future as great worker parties.[95]

Debs agreed with the principles of the IWW—its devotion to working class solidarity and its advocacy of industrial unionism. However, he did not support the tactics that were characterized as anarchist in the rhetoric of the time. While sabotage and violence were widely propagated as IWW tactics by the press, including the socialist press, they were not the policy of the IWW but were among matters discussed by speakers and pamphleteers of that organization. The effect was the same as if the IWW had actually had such policys. In fact, IWW strikes were generally non-violent except where violence was used against workers.

Berger and others on the party executive committee were relieved when Debs made this break with the IWW. They also had a right to be irritated that it had taken Debs so long to sever his ties. Debs became caught up, particularly between 1908 and 1912, in having to defend the rights of IWW members to due process regardless of their actions. Comments in several of Theodore's letters indicate that Debs had serious reservations about the character of several men he supported, especially Haywood.[96] However, Debs continued to advocate industrial unionism. "I am an industrial unionist but I am not an industrial anarchist," Debs wrote another mineworker.[97] "The spirit of Chicago IWWism is getting its deadly work done in the name of socialism, and if it is permitted to continue," he warned, it would destroy the Socialist Party.[98]

All was not complete harmony within the party, however, because the struggle over representation to the International Board continued. In the final voting for this honor, Debs' supporter, Kate O'Hare, won. Berger angrily wrote Hillquit: ". . . She will make the party ridiculous. But by so doing she will just represent the exact state of our American movement. I can't see what you or I can do about it at this time."[99] Although Berger and Debs could cooperate in such cases as the public strike investigation, they privately worked against one another. Berger's failure to gain reelection to Congress in 1914 increased his bitterness. Debs pressed even harder for industrial unionism and an aggressive stand against management. He suggested a Gunmen Defense Fund for the mine workers—another project Berger deplored. "The Rockefellers have not one particle more lawful right to maintain a private army to murder you union men than you have to maintain a private army to murder the Rockefellers," he announced.[100] Debs also became very concerned with the use of guns for another purpose, for he sensed a new issue in the gathering war clouds. He feared that while the industrialists in the United States would favor war, the workers would have to fight it.[101]

Chapter X
Militant Pacifist

Eugene V. Debs' hatred of war began as a child in Terre Haute, Indiana, when he saw Civil War widows claiming bodies at the depot near his home. He also observed the crippled and sick veterans in the local hospital. The location of Terre Haute, plus its transportation advantages, made the city a center of Civil War activity. As early as 1898, he had protested against Spanish-American intervention in Philippine politics, and pledged that a Socialist victory would hasten the day when war "shall curse this earth no more." "If there were no gold in the Transvaal," he declared at the time of the Boer War "there would be no British soldiers there."[1] In the opening speech of his first Socialist presidential campaign in 1900, Debs had presented himself as an ambassador of peace, a role he found congenial throughout his life.

As American involvement in world affairs increased between 1912 and 1915, Debs' anti-war remarks irritated patriotic citizens but pleased his supporters. When President Woodrow Wilson urged Congress to consider military preparedness in 1915, Debs warned workers against letting "the capitalists make cannon fodder" of them.[2] "It is the ruling class that declares war," he insisted, "and the working class that gives its life on the battlefield."[3] He refused to sign Upton Sinclair's statement supporting Wilson's preparedness program with the blunt assertion: "The workers have no country to fight for. It belongs to the capitalists and plutocrats. Let them worry over its defense. . ."[4] In caustic editorials for the *Appeal to Reason,* he repeated the same views that he presented to his lecture audiences.[5] Under the heading "Never Be a Soldier," he denounced war as a "crimson carnival where the drunken devils are unchained and the snarling dogs are 'sicked' upon one another by their brutal masters. . ."[6]

Since the threat of war occupied his thoughts, Debs declined to stand for a fifth Socialist Party nomination for the presidency in 1916. He accepted instead the editorship of the *Rip-Saw* in order to write more articles against war. At this time Debs also recognized that the party needed to develop some new leaders, and that he could best answer the charges that it was a one man party by stepping aside. But friends in Terre Haute insisted that he run for Congress, and he accepted the invitation as a means of opposing Wilson's military preparations.[7]

In a campaign which attracted national attention, he argued that the profits of the munitions industries never justified the human suffering caused by war.[8] Opposing the right wing of the Socialist Party, he censured Daniel W. Hoan, Socialist Mayor of Milwaukee, for participating in a patriotic preparedness parade. "Socialists are not required to demonstrate their patriotism," he scolded, dismissing "this perversion of principle" as a "vote catching" insult to militant Socialists.[9] Delivering an average of more than three speeches a day from September to November, he conducted a marathon campaign with the outside assistance of several prominent Socialists, including James Larkin of Ireland and Madame Alexandra Kollontai of Russia.[10] Noble Wilson of Terre Haute served as Debs' local campaign manager. Schubert Sebree, another local friend, assisted Wilson and drove Debs throughout the district in his Model T Ford.

The national Socialist Party officers had heard accounts that Debs had been drinking excessively. They appointed Maynard Shipley of California as manager of his campaign. Wilson and Shipley frequently disagreed on how to conduct the Fifth District campaign. Wilson and Debs resented the national party sending Shipley to Terre Haute, but Debs had known Shipley for a number of years and liked him.[11] During this campaign Debs' drinking presented no problem, for he concentrated his energies on trying to prevent war. Although he lost by a sizable margin to his Republican opponent, Debs nevertheless placed second and received three times as many votes in the Fifth District as he had in his most successful presidential campaign.[12] "Blessed are they who expect nothing," he concluded, "for they shall not be disappointed."[13]

After a brief rest following the strenuous campaign, Debs returned to writing and agitating. As he toured the Eastern states and as a declaration of war neared, his speeches became bitter, especially against Wilson. Pro-German sympathizers packed his lecture halls in the larger cities. When the United States entered the war on April 6, 1917, the Socialist Party, convening in emergency session in St. Louis, adopted Debs' suggestion that the party draft a strong proclamation opposing the war.[14] Using this document as a frequent text, Debs urged that workers oppose military conscription and the sale of war bonds; that "the masses" be enlightened on the "relationship between capitalism and war"; that vigorous resistance follow all measures curtailing freedom of speech.

As a result of Debs' increased and continuous agitation against war, many people wrote to him, asking for advice in forming organizations to oppose war; asking for materials to distribute at their meetings; asking him to give a lecture or suggest a replacement. No longer could Theodore keep up with the piles of correspondence. Mabel Dunlap Curry, wife of Professor Charles Curry at Indiana State Normal, began helping Theodore with the office work. In previous years she had worked in the office at campaign times, along with Gertrude Debs, Theodore's wife. In 1917-1918, when Theodore traveled with Eugene, Mrs. Curry ran the office. Mrs. Curry's work caused some embarrassment to her husband, a very popular English teacher who had even authored the college's alma mater song. His overwhelmingly conservative colleagues, including the college president, viewed with disfavor his wife's support of Debs' controversial stand on war and other issues. Since Professor Curry avoided all such activities, they could not condemn him, but thought that he should have better regulated his wife's activities.

In several letters to Rose Pastor Stokes between the years 1917 and 1921, Mrs. Curry discussed the college administration's attitude toward her work. In these nineteen letters from Mrs. Curry to Mrs. Stokes she also discussed her work for Debs and her feelings for him.

Mrs. Curry zealously supported the issues that Debs advocated. When Debs dictated letters to her, he discovered that she often had excellent advice for ideas that he should include. He found in Mrs. Curry a woman quite different from his wife. Mabel Curry unreservedly endorsed such controversial issues as birth control and opposition to the war. By contrast, Katherine Debs declined to comment publicly on such issues. As Debs' activities against the war increased, Mrs. Debs became increasingly fearful for his safety and refused to make appearances with him. Probably of all the controversies that he undertook, Mrs. Debs had the least sympathy for the war issue. Her family refused to support Debs in his anti-war crusade. Although Katherine Debs avoided discussion of the war, Mabel Curry sought ways to help Debs more effectively combat it. To lighten his load, Mrs. Curry accepted some speaking engagements in nearby cities. If Debs were in town, he would see her off to the train and present her with a box of candy and a newspaper. According to Mrs. Curry, Mr. Debs—always proper and dignified—made a statuesque figure at attention as the train pulled out.[15] Neither made any public display of their growing affection.

In time Debs and Mrs. Curry recognized that their relationship presented difficult decisions. Debs obviously had confided his feelings about Mrs. Curry to Rose Pastor Stokes, a militant feminist who championed the same causes as he did. Through an introduction from Debs, Mrs. Curry met Mrs. Stokes, the wife of wealthy J. Phelps Stokes. In letters to Mrs. Stokes, Mrs. Curry discussed at great length her fondness for Debs and the agony that tortured her because she had a good husband and family. She and Debs agreed that they had no right to destroy the lives of others to establish their own happiness. According to Mrs. Curry, her husband was unaware of her troubled emotions. She described him as a fine, clean, intellectual man who had carefully built an enviable reputation as an educator in the state upon old foundations.[16] In addition, she asserted that Mr. Curry had been an excellent father for their three daughters, and that until she had met Eugene their marriage had been one of peace and harmony. Now she asked Mrs. Stokes to somehow send her the strength and courage to break with the past and join what she called the new order. Certainly no one could accuse either Debs or Mrs. Curry of being immoderate youths, for at this time Debs was sixty-three and Mrs. Curry close to sixty. Little evidence ever indicated that, either before or after this time, Debs was fond of any woman except his wife. One other account has been recorded. While working in Girard, Kansas, he visited occasionally in the home of Elizabeth Vincent whose husband, Henry Vincent, also worked as a writer for the *Appeal to Reason*. Their daughter, Mary Vincent Cummings, published privately an essay before her death in February 1978 in which she recalled Debs' visits, always in the daytime when her father worked. In this essay, "The Memories of Girard, Kansas—Eugene V. Debs and me," Mrs. Cummings stated that she remembered the fondness of their embracing and thought Debs and her mother "were maybe a little more than close friends." Throughout his life Debs coresponded with the Vincents, especially sending notes to Mary, one of his favorites as a child in Girard.

Theodore knew of his brother's feelings for Mrs. Curry. He later told his wife, Gertrude, because Mrs. Curry often joined his family on mushroom hunting expeditions and visited frequently in their home.[17] Marguerite Debs, Theodore's daughter, remembered these visits and how Mabel Curry's vibrant, outgoing personality made any picnic a delight.[18] Rather than sever all associations, which neither seemed willing to do, Debs told Mrs. Curry that perhaps in time something would show the way.[19] The fact that Debs traveled constantly during these years made the waiting easier but reunions more difficult, especially since both Mrs. Curry and Debs worked in the same one room office with Theodore usually present answering another pile of mail. Debs had been unhappy at home for several years. Kate, a proud shy aloof woman, had less and less interest in Eugene's work. She never cared for the limelight and found public appearances painful. Debs' stand on the war added an additional strain to their relationship because she did not agree. Over the years the constant delegations and door bell ringers had irritated her. Frequently she refused to answer the door. Her home was a sanctuary to her but Eugene preferred an "open house." He learned to respect her wishes and took many guests to his brother's home where they were welcomed by Gertrude—Theodore's wife who wholeheartedly endorsed whatever the socialist cause might be at the time. Although Kate had grown weary of Debs' agitation activities, she maintained a poised front. In the few interviews she granted over the years, and one at this time, she publicly expressed her support of Debs.

Aside from the dilemma in Debs' private life, his public life included increasingly more anti-war activities which created controversy and comment. From the time of the adoption of the Manifesto by a party referendum, all roads that Debs traveled led to his eventual arrest and federal imprisonment. He refused to obey the Espionage Act which made it a crime to speak or act against the war. Later amendments made it illegal to obstruct the draft and to use the mails for propaganda, legal measures which ended some of Debs' most eloquent editorial appeals.[20] No magazine or newspaper could take the chance of losing its second-class mailing privileges by printing one of his essays. But he continued to speak. He defended Kate Richards O'Hare, Max Eastman, Rose Pastor Stokes, John M. Work, and other writers and speakers who had been arrested for anti-war activities. Claude Bowers, who heard Debs in Fort Wayne, Indiana, stated that "Debs did not utter a word to which the most supersensitive patriot could take exception. It seemed to me that he had prepared his speech with the realization that every word would be microscopically examined by secret agents."[21]

Ohio Socialists scheduled Debs as the keynote speaker at their state convention in Canton on June 16, 1918. Most of their leaders had been arrested for aggressive anti-war activities, and three officers, Alfred Wagenknecht, Charles Ruthenberg, and Charles Baker, were imprisoned in the Canton jail. George Goebel, an organizer from the Socialist headquarters, warned Debs about making remarks that might please overzealous federal agents. "I guessed his purpose," Goebel stated, "but Debs laid a hand on my shoulder and said, 'I cannot be free while my comrades and fellow workers are jailed for warning the people about this war'."[22]

In registering at the Courtland Hotel upon his arrival in Canton, Debs encountered Clyde Miller of the Cleveland *Plain Dealer,* who asked if he supported the St. Louis Manifesto. Debs responded affirmatively. "Surely you are not going to say that in your speech this afternoon," Miller replied. "I certainly am," Debs retorted.[23]

Leaving the Courtland Hotel, Debs went first to visit Ruthenberg, Baker, and other dissenters in the Stark County jail. While a crowd of 1,200 waited in the hot afternoon sun, federal agents circulated through the audience asking to see draft cards.[24] When crossing the street from the jail, Debs noticed that the speaker's stand in Nimisilla Park had been constructed so that his imprisoned friends could see and hear him from their first floor cells.

After a florid introduction by Mrs. Marguerite Prevey, a wealthy Ohio Socialist leader, Debs began the most controversial speech of his career.[25] "I have just returned from a visit over yonder," Debs remarked as he pointed to the workhouse jail. "They have come to realize, as many of us have, that it is extremely dangerous to exercise the constitutional right of free speech in a country fighting to make Democracy safe in the world."[26] When Debs stated that he must "be exceedingly careful and prudent" in what he said, the audience laughed.

Using sardonic humor throughout his two-hour speech, Debs kept his listeners laughing and applauding. "The Socialists in Ohio, it appears are very much alive this year," he remarked. "The party has been killed recently . . . nothing helps the Socialist Party so much as receiving an occasional death blow." After each sentence, the government-appointed reporter noted the audience reaction, labeling cheers, shouts, laughter, or applause. Evidently the reporter intended to prepare a document that would indicate to interested officials exactly what reaction followed Debs' words to an audience.

Midway in the address Debs asked his listeners if they opposed Prussian militarism. After shouts of "Yes! Yes!" he proceeded to recall "a little history" on the inconsistencies in the "official Washington attitude" toward Germany and war. He asserted that the American government supported the Kaiser in 1869 when Liebknecht, the German Socialist, opposed him. Debs reminded listeners that in 1910 "Teddy" Roosevelt visited Germany as guest of honor in the "Whitehouse of Kaiser Bill," while German Socialists languished in jail for speaking against him. Debs digressed into the background of the trials involving "labor and anti-war martyrs."[27] In recalling the cases of Rose Pastor Stokes, Bill Haywood, and one hundred twelve other members of the IWW in Chicago, he insinuated that "capitalist interests" had used the war hysteria to force the judges to order the arrests.

Listeners heard few inflammatory remarks; indeed, they heard only those that Debs had used repeatedly in other speeches. Some illustrations were borrowed from speeches he had given twenty years earlier. Much of what he said revealed an old man reminiscing about a career filled with losing struggles. He made six references to the war: 1. The master class has always declared war; the subject class had always fought the battles. 2. The working class furnishes the corpses but never has a voice in declaring war or in making peace. 3. If the war would end, Rose Pastor Stokes would be released. 4. Workers should know that they exist for something better than slavery and "cannon fodder." 5. The government maintains that workers should grow war gardens as a patriotic duty while an official report shows that fifty-two per cent of the tillable soil is held out of use by war "profiteers." 6. When the "war press says war," every pulpit in the land "will say war." These six statements later became the basis for a federal case against Debs. Public reaction to this speech followed immediately—aided by an eager reporter and an aggressive attorney.

In a news release to the *Plain Dealer*, Clyde Miller, the reporter Debs had met in the hotel, accused Debs of giving an address which "shocked the nation."[28] Miller also called his friend, District Attorney Edward Wertz in Cleveland, quoting several of Debs' remarks and asking if he would indict Debs for violation of the Espionage Act. Wertz agreed. Miller then telephoned this additional bit of information for page one. Four days later, Debs received an indictment charging him with "attempting to cause insubordination, mutiny, disloyalty, and refusal of duty within the military forces of the United States, and the utterance of words intended to procure and incite resistance to the United States, and to promote the cause of the Imperial German Government."[29] He was ordered to appear on September 9, 1918, for trial in the Federal Court in Cleveland.[30] Mrs. Prevey and A. W. Moskowitz of Cleveland posted $10,000 bond, freeing him to return to the stump.[31]

The indictment did little to deter Debs in his anti-war agitation. In speeches at Mishawaka, South Bend, and Terre Haute, Debs insisted that newspapers had distorted his remarks in Nimisilla Park.[32] He vigorously upheld his position by challenging anyone to show him a Socialist who sympathized with the German government; by declaring that the Russian Revolution culminated the Russian workers' struggle for their rights; by praising Wilson's peace plan; by condemning war profiteers; by insisting that the government retain control of the railroads after the war.[33] On each occasion government officials hired court reporters to make stenographic records of the agitator's discourse. "If a majority Socialist gives an honest opinion, he will probably be 'judged' by the minions of the Department of Justice," one editor sarcastically commented, "So comrades don't talk in public too much. Your tears for Debs and the IWW. . . . show you for the good German Socialists that you are. Why get into jail if you can keep out?"[34]

Debs reported for trial in Cleveland on September 8, 1918. The court room overflowed with curious spectators and loyal Socialists who had traveled great distances to support Eugene Debs. On the first day of the trial, Judge D. C. Westenhaver attempted to insure order by indicting several exuberant Socialists, including Rose Pastor Stokes, for contempt of court.

In the long court case, the government lawyers had several strategies in mind to prove that Debs represented a threat and danger to the security of the country. Before Debs spoke in his own defense, the government's two chief witnesses, Clyde Miller and Virgil Steiner, a stenographic clerk hired by federal officers to take notes during the Canton speech, took the stand. Miller eagerly told of his hotel interview with Debs and of his note taking during the speech.[35] Steiner even admitted that Debs spoke so rapidly that he had not kept up with him, even in shorthand. Other government witnesses followed; most of them were young men of draft age. It gradually became obvious that one of the key arguments in the government lawyers' case against Debs was to prove that young men in the Canton audience had heard Debs oppose the draft act.

When the government concluded its case, Debs surprised the court by taking the stand. No other witnesses appeared on his behalf. His lawyers reasoned that Debs would make his own best appeal. When Debs began speaking, most listeners failed to notice the heavy downpour outside. The dismal weather suited the somberness of his remarks in the darkened chamber. His two-hour speech lacked the fiery emotional appeals that characterized many of his earlier stump speeches.[36] Max Eastman, who attended the trial, reported that Debs indicated, both by his manner of delivery and by the words he used, that he would be unable to convince the jury.[37] "I have no disposition to deny anything that is true," Debs stated. "I would not, if I could, escape the results of an adverse verdict."[38] With this admitted, Debs proceeded to carefully present his arguments, for he recognized that now he faced his most difficult speaking assignment.

In his first contention, Debs maintained that history supported his stand against the social system. In his speech at Canton, he attacked the established social order in America, rather than our participation in the war. He contended that when great changes occur in history and when great principles are involved, "as a rule the majority are wrong. The minority are usually right." Citing the Revolutionary War as an example, he urged the jury to read George Bancroft or any other historian and to remember that the majority of the early colonists swore allegiance to the king, because they believed he had a divine right to rule over them. But Washington, Jefferson, Franklin, Paine, "and their compeers" did not believe this, Debs declared, and as a result Americans honor these patriots while "the great respectable majority of their day sleep in forgotten graves."[39]

By using a deductive approach to demonstrate that the Constitution guaranteed his right to free speech, Debs argued that America had had dissenters in every previous war; acknowledged that he had criticized the existing order; quoted the first amendment as evidence of his rights. He concluded these proofs with one of the most forceful statements in the annals of free speech: "I believe in the right of free speech. It is far more dangerous to attempt to gag the people than to allow them to speak freely what is in their hearts."

In closing, Debs stated that a verdict of conviction would not harm him but that a rash decision could damage America's basic freedoms. "There is an infinitely greater issue that is being tried in this court," he declared. "American institutions are on trial here before a court of American citizens."

Recognizing that Debs' speech might have had a positive influence on the jury, District Attorney Wertz began his summation with a long analogy filled with biting sarcasm. Wertz wanted to take up some time and not let the case end with Debs' strong appeals still fresh in the jurors' minds. He told about a farmer he had known who owned an old ewe. When the barn caught on fire, the farmer herded his flock out of the burning building into the yard. One old ewe bolted around the barn and led the whole flock back through another door. Then he abruptly turned, pointed his finger at Debs, and shouted, "If this old ewe wants to go to the penitentiary, I've got no objection, but I object to his taking a whole flock of people with him."

After six hours of deliberation, the jury found Debs guilty.[40] The judge denied a motion for a new trial but asked Debs if he had anything further to say. In this statement to the court before sentencing, Debs crowded memories of a lifetime spent advocating labor and socialistic causes.[41] Addressing the judge directly, he repeated his famous epigram about his kinship with all living beings: "While there is a lower class, I am in it, while there is a criminal element I am of it, and while there is a soul in prison, I am not free."[42] He recalled his youth in a railroad shop, his career as a freight-engine fireman, and his visits to workers in mines and factories. In closing, he reaffirmed his belief that Socialism would eventually solve America's economic and political problems and admonished his supporters to look to the future. "Let the people everywhere take heart and hope, for the cross is bending, the midnight is passing, and joy cometh with the morning."[43]

Judge Westenhaver replied with a brief speech summarizing his view of Debs: "I appreciate the defendant's sincerity; I may admire his courage but I cannot help wishing he might take better note of facts as they are in the world of the present time."[44] He then sentenced Debs to ten years imprisonment, but because of an appeal to the Supreme Court, Debs did not immediately enter prison.[45] After Theodore arranged bond, Debs returned to Terre Haute where he continued his attack against World War I.

Mrs. Curry had hoped to hear the trial but Theodore insisted that she remain in Terre Haute and occupy herself by running the office. After the trial, Mrs. Curry wrote to thank Rose Pastor Stokes for attending and helping Eugene make history. She lamented that above all other women she *should* have been present to console Gene, but that fate kept her elsewhere. She reiterated that if it had not been for her loving daughters and husband, she would have renounced her ties to home and joined Debs.[46]

Before Judge Westenhaver had released Debs he warned him against further anti-war speechmaking and restricted him to speaking in the northern district of Ohio or in cities close to Terre Haute. Ignoring Judge Westenhaver's edict, Debs asserted in numerous addresses that the Espionage Act was un-American; that deportations for some who had opposed the war was unconstitutional; and that "common people" gained nothing from war.[47] Federal authorities sent the Department of Justice a copy of his Toledo speech, delivered nineteen days after the Armistice. Toledo Socialists protested that since the war had ended, the lecture could not be construed as interfering with the military.[48] Federal officers replied that they had a right to investigate because the speech created the impression in foreign countries that the government did not have the united support of the people in its war program. Debs' speaking in this interim did little to allay the suspicion of Attorney General Palmer. The request for Debs' Toledo remarks represented another facet of what historian Charles A. Beard described as Palmer's "Hot war on the Reds" during this period.[49] Debs boldly returned to Canton, where in addition to denouncing the war, he proclaimed that Washington and Jefferson personified the real Bolsheviki in their time and that unions needed more men like Bill Haywood and fewer like Gompers.[50]

The Supreme Court denied Debs' appeal on March 10, 1919. Ordered to prison on April 13, 1919, seven months after World War I ended, Debs spent a busy month trying to write articles in advance. Since the U.S. Attorney General hoped to prevent any protest marches, he sent Debs, without any public announcement, to a state prison at Moundsville, West Virginia, an isolated small town on the Ohio River south of Wheeling. Evidently he feared that Debs' presence in a larger prison in a more populated city might stimulate demonstrations. Debs quickly adjusted to prison routine and took his turn at everything from cutting up rhubarb to washing clothes in the laundry.

Theodore, with the help of Mrs. Curry, immediately began to seek ways of securing release of Debs and other political prisoners. Mrs. Curry wrote Rose Pastor Stokes that both Eugene and Theodore had explicitly told her to keep out of the forefront of any campaigns to secure amnesty for anti-war prisoners. Bitterly she commented that the recent protest parade on behalf of Eugene had moved past Katherine Debs' house and that the flowers were left in Katherine's arms while she remained hidden in the office helping answer the mail—the only possible way for her to be of service.[51] Before he left, Eugene asked Mrs. Curry to call frequently upon his wife who had not been in robust health. He had told Katherine that what Mabel Curry called a "warm friendship" existed between them. Mrs. Curry found that Katherine resented these visits. Only an idealist such as Eugene, Mrs. Curry commented to her friend, Mrs. Stokes, would think that anyone, Katherine included, would like her.[52]

Anticipating that his letters would be censored, Debs had arranged a special code with Mrs. Curry so that they could correspond. They used special names to refer to themselves. In fact, it was a clever way to say, as Mrs. Curry later declared, some personal things in an impersonal way. She labeled herself Mr. Brewer; he labeled himself Mrs. Wilson![53] Gene arranged with the warden to send an extra letter each week to his secretary which he had designated as Mrs. Curry. He sent her many enclosures with penciled notes as to the response he thought best to each letter. He also included specific directions to Theodore as to which letters he should answer and other work he wanted him to do.

In mid-May Katherine visited Eugene at Moundsville. She only stayed several days. She decided that there was little she could do for Debs and that she would rather live in Terre Haute than take a room in Moundsville. The shortness of the visit pleased Mrs. Curry, for she had taken a speaking engagement for May 30 in Charleston, West Virginia, with the definite plan to visit Debs. The warden permitted Mrs. Curry to visit Debs for an hour and then he spoke with her for another hour and a half. Evidently Mrs. Curry charmed the warden, for he suggested that she stay another day and he would take her on a tour of the institution and let her visit Debs again.[54] During this second visit, the guard stayed outside the room. Mrs. Curry confided to Mrs. Stokes that Debs believed God had been with them in putting the suggestion into the warden's mind and that he would have gone mad if he had not seen her alone. After the visit, the warden loaned Mrs. Curry his chauffeur and car so that she could buy a rocker and a fan for Eugene. Later the warden's wife drove Mrs. Curry to catch her train in Wheeling.[55] The warden may just have been especially kind since Debs had been a model prisoner, or he may have hoped that his hospitality would prevent any adverse publicity about the prison in pacifist pamphlets advocating Debs' release.

In August, federal prison officers quietly and secretly moved Debs from Moundsville to the federal prison at Atlanta, Georgia. The officers moved Debs quickly to Atlanta to prevent any demonstrations from being organized. The move baffled Debs and his supporters. Reporters questioned the move but found no answers. Actually what had happened was that the warden at Moundsville had requested the federal prison officials to grant his institution additional funds for insuring the security of Debs. The warden had hoped to have the government pay the cost of several guards which he maintained were necessary in case a protesting group ever tried to free Debs. His attempt failed, because after several letters demanding such additional funds, he received notice to have Debs moved immediately to Atlanta.[56]

In Atlanta Debs spent his first year in reading and counseling other inmates concerning their personal problems. Soon he gained the respect of prison authorities by helping them to communicate with several incorrigible men.[57] Outside the prison numerous amnesty groups, led by Upton Sinclair,

Clarence Darrow, George Herron, Frank Harris, and others, besieged President Wilson with requests for Debs' release.[58] Wilson ignored their petitions. When Debs heard of Wilson's refusal to free him, he pointed out that he had never asked for a pardon since he had not committed a crime. He suggested, however, that Wilson sorely needed a pardon from the American people for his puritanical righteousness.[59] Wilson's adamant stand on freeing Debs annoyed many previously neutral writers such as Fred High, who announced in *Billboard*: "We have never aligned ourselves with the Socialist movement. . . but Debs has been unjustly imprisoned."[60] But Wilson had his supporters, including ex-President Taft, who thought Debs should remain behind bars.[61]

With Debs imprisoned many members of the Socialist Party saw merit in the idea of having Debs run again for president. These supporters, led by Karsner, thought no better way could be found to focus attention upon their amnesty campaign to free Debs and all other political prisoners. On May 13, 1920, delegates to the National Socialist Convention meeting in New York nominated for a fifth time Eugene V. Debs, Convict 9653, for President.[62] Edwin Henry of Indiana acclaimed Debs as the "Lincoln of the Wabash" in his nominating speech. Seymour Stedman, Debs' attorney in the Cleveland trial, received the nomination for vice-president.[63] The platform writers took a vigorous stand against incarceration of political prisoners and the deportation of aliens—the central campaign issues for the Socialists.

In his brief acceptance speech, before party leaders and press representatives in the warden's office, Convict 9653 chided delegates for not stressing the class struggle and Russia's revolutionary successes more prominently in their platform. He then declared that a platform meant little, however, because "we can breathe the breath of revolution" into it. In concluding Debs said: "I have never feared becoming too radical. I do fear becoming too conservative."[64] Morris Hillquit and other platform writers objected to Debs' remarks. Hillquit argued that since the war had ended, the platform needed to emphasize "the constructive side of the Socialist movement."[65] Debs replied that he agreed with their basic premises but he thought they should have stated them more "militantly and appealingly in the platform."[66]

During the campaign, the Attorney General allowed Debs to make one weekly five-hundred-word press release. Debs constructed each of these statements as a speech, and his brother Theodore arranged with party headquarters in Chicago for publication. In "A Word to the Workers," the imprisoned candidate began: "As I may not meet you face to face in this campaign, I address this brief message to you from my prison cell." After listing "a few direct questions" to candidates Harding and Cox, he cautioned the voters not to vote for either of them unless they wanted "wage-slavery" continued. The word limitation in the press releases forced Debs to be more precise, inventive, and discriminating in word choice than he had been in his speeches in four earlier campaigns.[67]

Evidently Debs read the newspapers carefully, for in these articles he challenged the remarks of his opponents: "Mr. Harding in his Omaha speech declared against amnesty for political prisoners on the ground that they were the same as yeggmen," a term used at that time for burglars or safebreakers. Thanking Harding for his candor, Debs sarcastically replied that "his flint face" had expressed this lack of compassion long ago.[68]

Predicting his election loss, Debs regretted only his inability to speak to the workers "as in other days." The returns showed 919,302 votes, or 3.5 per cent of the total, for Convict 9653. Socialist Party leaders wired Debs that he had helped the American people repudiate Wilson, Palmer, and Albert S. Burleson [Postmaster General who hated Socialists and denied second class mailing privileges to their newspapers and magazines throughout the war] and that although the party had lost, his "splendid statements" had at least contributed to the Republican landslide.[69]

Chapter XI
Delay and Disillusionment
After the Campaign

The campaign to free Debs temporarily ended with the campaign that elected Harding president. Debs' supporters knew that further pressures on Wilson would fail and suspended their activities anxiously waiting for Harding to take office. With fewer demands for articles, Debs relaxed and continued his regular prison routine. He worked a few hours each day in the laundry or hospital and spent many additional hours visiting with his fellow inmates. Both the guards and prisoners soon recognized Debs as an able counselor. In fact, Warden William Zerbst and his replacement, J. E. Dyche, encouraged Debs to help them with some of the more recalcitrant prisoners, including Sam Moore, a Black serving a twenty year sentence for assault.[1]

When Gene entered the Atlanta prison, the inmates had warned him of Sam's vicious temper and vile rhetoric. While imprisoned Sam and another Black had attacked a guard and briefly escaped. After recapture, Sam and his friend spent eighteen months in "the hole," a small cell without windows in the basement. At the end of this time the prison doctor sent Moore to the hospital because Moore had a nervous breakdown.[2] Debs, who sporadically had difficulty with his heart, happened to be in the hospital at the time and immediately went to Moore's room. He grasped Moore's hand and said, "Brother—Brother—Cheer up. I've heard so much talk about you." When Moore started to explain, Debs quickly cut him off with this remark: "I understand. Poor fellow. Is there anything I can do for you? What do you need? Would you like some fruit?"[3] When Moore replied, "Yes," Debs went to his room and brought some of the fruit that friends continually sent to him.

Each day thereafter Debs visited Moore. They talked for hours and Debs discovered that Sam had a keen mind. When Moore recovered, he had to return to solitary confinement in "the hole." Debs bent all his energies to getting Sam reassigned. A month later Sam received a job in the "duck mill," the prison clothing factory, and continued under Debs' influence and guidance.[4]

On one occasion, Sam, with slight provocation, broke forth with his choice profanity. Afterwards Eugene told him, "Sam, it isn't for me to pass judgment on your acts. You may feel yourself perfectly justified in using the language you did a few moments ago, but I wish that you would not use it in my presence."[5] Although Debs did swear when vexed, his ears could not tolerate Sam's stronger invective. According to Theodore Debs, Sam never swore again in Debs' presence.

Debs helped many other prisoners. He repeatedly asked the deputy warden to give some convict a second chance, especially if it meant saving him from "the hole." Father J. Byrne, the Catholic prison chaplain, praised Debs for his skill in counseling. When Debs went out into the yard for exercise, many convicts besieged him to write letters to judges or other officials; to get petitions for them; to suggest ways to solve personal and family problems. They kept Debs so busy answering questions that he seldom had a chance to enjoy a ball game or take part in any of the other physical activities. At times the prison doctor asked Debs to avoid the yard because the prisoners wore him out. When Debs failed to appear, some prisoners had the guards deliver notes requesting help or thanking him for his services. In one such note convict William Henson wrote: "I received the addresses which you sent me, and I want you to know that I riley appreciate them. . . I will never forget what you have did for me, and I am going to keep my promest that I have made you. . ."[6] Years later Sam stated, "If I had had a father or a friend like Debs when I was young and in the moulding—before I came to prison—I know I would have been somebody."[7]

After Harding's inauguration, Theodore Debs redoubled his efforts to secure his brother's release. Under his direction, Mrs. Curry wrote and answered thousands of letters to influence public opinion to favor Debs. At first Theodore and Mrs. Curry were encouraged because Upton Sinclair, Clarence Darrow, and others designated to carry petitions to Washington did receive courteous treatment and some assurances that Debs would be freed.[8] Debs rejoiced when the Supreme Court declared that Victor Berger had not received a fair trial in a 1918 Chicago federal court case. The case also involved William Kruse, Adolph Germer, I. Louis Engdahl, and Irwin St. John Tucker who had been sentenced at the same time as Berger for obstructing the draft and enlistment services. The Supreme Court released these men because of the legal technicality that Judge Kenesaw Mountain Landis had tried the case after Berger's counsel filed an affidavit of prejudice. Debs interpreted this decision as an indication of the government's changing attitude toward anti-war prisoners.[9]

In addition to his routine duties in the prison, Debs wrote news releases on a variety of subjects and sent these to Theodore for publication. Conservative readers were irked by articles in which Debs attacked former President Wilson, President Harding and those in which he asked for an understanding of Russia's revolution. "This lawbreaker turns his jail into a soapbox," the editor of the New York Times charged. "Free speech for convicts . . . it should end at once."[10]

In early March the Department of Justice took the matter of Debs' release into consideration. Attorney General Daugherty requested additional time for "personal investigation." On March 24 he arranged for Debs to make a secret visit to Washington. Without prison escort, Debs took the train to Washington and spent several hours visiting with Daugherty, who asked him to admit publicly that he had made a mistake in opposing the war and regretted his actions. Debs politely refused and told Daugherty that he had a right to dissent. Debs also informed Daugherty that he could not accept a pardon that did not include his fellow political prisoners. Obviously Daugherty wished to find some way to placate the veterans groups and yet release Debs to his supporters.[11] A disappointed Debs quietly returned to Atlanta Prison. He sent Theodore the official terse letter of introduction to Daugherty which stated: "Dear Mr. Gibbs: the bearer is Eugene V. Debs whom the Attorney General desires to see Thursday at 10:00 A.M. Signed T. G. Zerbst, Warden." Debs added this note, "Souvenir of a memorable interview March 24, 1921."[12] Unsubstantiated rumors spread that Daugherty and Harding had hoped Debs would escape and flee to Russia as Bill Haywood had done.[13]

Under Theodore's supervision, representatives of the Socialist Party planned their most highly organized amnesty campaign to climax with political pressure on both houses of Congress and petitions to President Harding on April 13, 1921, the second anniversary of Debs' imprisonment. Numerous other organizations joined the renewed campaign. Even Gompers and the AFL rallied to Debs' support and 110 unions set about gaining signatures on petitions. The Industrial Workers of the World, the Workers' Defense Union, the American Civil Liberties Union, the World War Veterans, the Private Soldiers and Sailors' Legion, and the Farmer-Labor Party all helped swell the tide of protest. Newspapers and magazines such as *The Call, The Oklahoma Leader, The Milwaukee Leader, The Seattle Union Record,* the *New York World, The Minnesota Star, The Freeman, The Nation, The Oakland World, St. Louis Star, Appeal to Reason,* and some twenty-five Scripps newspapers assisted with editorial comments. All of this agitation culminated in a huge demonstration in Washington and the presentation to Congress of a petition with 300,000 signatures. Committees of lawyers and humanitarians arranged visits with congressmen from each state, administrative officers, and President Harding. Morris Hillquit, organizer of the amnesty movement in New York City, headed the delegation that visited Harding. "The men and women whose cause we are pleading have committed no offense against the person or property of their fellow men," Hillquit told Harding. "They have been tried and convicted solely on the basis of their political convictions. . . They spoke and acted not in hostility to their country and their fellow citizens but in the courageous performance of what they deeply and sincerely felt to be their civic duty."[14] In Congress, Socialist Representative Meyer London from New York led the attack and introduced a resolution calling for the release of all political prisoners. Debs heard of all these events and optimistically wrote his brother, "I anticipate favorable action. I may be with you in the next week or two, and we will soon be booked up again and have things going our way."[15] All of these activities created considerable turmoil in Washington and stimulated the American Legion and other patriotic groups to intensify their efforts to keep the jail doors closed on dissenters. The administration worried about all of these protests and the effects they would have on the pending peace resolutions before Congress. Since no official treaty had been signed, Daugherty delayed taking any action regarding political prisoners.

In a news release on June 7, Daugherty stated that his department's recommendation on the question of granting a pardon to Debs might contain the department's views on general amnesty for all prisoners confined for violation of the espionage laws. He concluded by saying that it would be several weeks before he submitted his conclusions. Debs angrily cut this clipping out of the paper and wrote beneath it to Theodore: "There is no use to wait any longer. There is now not the slightest doubt that he is stringing us along. At first he said the case would have his precious attention and that action would not be delayed on account of pending peace resolutions. Several times since he has announced that the case required more time for 'personal investigation.' This is unadulterated bunk. He has heard 'his master's voice—the same master that Wilson heard. . ."[16]

Mrs. Curry and Theodore Debs sensed Eugene's increasing despondency and decided to organize a series of marches. Earlier that spring marches on the capitol had evoked widespread favorable and unfavorable comment from citizens. Oswald Garrison Villard, editor of *The Nation*, suggested in a letter to a friend of Debs that Harding be given a couple of weeks to gain the adoption of the peace resolution.[17] On July 21, a month later, he again wrote that he had visited President Harding the previous day. Harding stated to Villard that "no one in the administration had any feeling against Debs" but that a tremendous storm had broken out, coming from the American Legion and others, since Debs' visit to Washington.[18] Villard informed the President that he now feared that months would elapse before he would ever get the Versailles Treaty through Congress, and that he might have "trouble on his hands." "If there was any picketing done, it would be the very worst thing that could happen for Debs," Harding quickly replied. "If the friends of Debs wanted to keep him in jail, it would be the best that they could do." After urging Villard to prevent any picketing, he asked that he regard the President's comments as "absolutely confidential."[19] Villard also wrote Mrs. Curry and advised her to "call off the pickets" and not quote the President "under any circumstances."[20] Mrs. Curry replied that she reluctantly understood "the necessity of silence." She lamented that all the peaceful methods have been used and they are ignored.[21] J. Mahlon Barnes, the controversial party choice for campaign manager in 1908, tried to persuade George Bernard Shaw to come to America and speak on behalf of Debs and other political prisoners. Shaw refused. "If they put E. V. Debs in prison for ten years for an extraordinarially mild remark, what would they do to me, who never opens his mouth in public without sayings things that would shock Mr. Debs to the bottom of his all too tender heart? Electrocute me, perhaps." He concluded, "What a country! Afraid of Debs and proud of Dempsey! It's too silly."[21]

Intermittently throughout the summer and fall, Attorney General Daugherty gave out news releases stating that his department could not be rushed because an important policy was involved in the Debs' case.[23] In August, Theodore helped organize the Debs Minute Men, a national group devoted to agitating for the release of political prisoners. Obviously the idea of the minute men had been borrowed from Wilson's avid supporters who had conducted patriotic rallies and sold bonds, but the idea failed when modified by Debs' followers. From the beginning, the public misunderstood the intent of the group. Many assumed that the Debs Minute Men desired to create a new political party. Since this misconception threatened to divide the various organizations supporting the release of political prisoners, the Debs Minute Men disbanded in September. However, this group's publication, *Debs Freedom Monthly,* continued.[24]

Theodore continued to coordinate all of the activities pressuring for Gene's release. Again he permitted Mrs. Curry to be designated Eugene's secretary but certainly did not tell Katherine Debs. After Eugene went to Atlanta, Katherine evidently had insisted that his one letter a week should come to her. In time Gene made arrangements for the second letter to his secretary. Mrs. Curry insisted to Rose Pastor Stokes that Eugene's letters contained many messages between the lines. Mabel Curry wrote poetry to disguise and yet express her feelings to Eugene. She sent Mrs. Stokes samples of her writing. For example, one "sonnet" made references to anniversaries she shared with Eugene.[25]

In late August Theodore sent Harding a telegram protesting his reported decision to not free political prisoners until all peace negotiations had been completed. "It is not only silly and disgusting but cowardly," Theodore stated.[26] He intimated that Harding should have learned a lesson from the "unlamented Wilson" on delaying decisions. His concluding remark probably irritated Harding. "Lincoln said something about fooling the people which the politicians in Washington would do well to read and ponder."[27]

Theodore wrote the telegram to Harding after hearing from David Karsner about bickering in the New York group and confusion over whether Sam Castleton represented Eugene as his attorney and official spokesman. Theodore thought that his writing the telegram would indicate to federal officials that he served as his brother's chief advocate. Evidently Sam claimed he had been assigned such duties. Sam also planned to write an official biography of Debs—a fact that irked Karsner, who had already written a Debs biography. "Since going to prison," Theodore declared to Karsner, "Gene has had no occasion to employ a lawyer and has not been professionally represented by anyone." Theodore further asserted that if the reports about Sam's office that he had heard were true, "it was not only in bad shape but it was a hell of a place."[28] Theodore was indirectly making reference to Sam's efforts to form a coalition group of Socialists and former party members that had joined the Communists. Discouraged with the continued internal fighting within the party and the increasing frustration over finding some way to gain Gene's release, he concluded the letter with some of the exact remarks that he had sent to Harding.[29] Writing to close friends such as Karsner served as a catharsis for Theodore, and after such writings he renewed his efforts to secure the release of all anti-war prisoners. A month later he again wrote Karsner and optimistically announced "the fact is that Harding is skeered, damned badly skeered. The raid of the officers of the American Legion left him with his knees rattling like a 'Lizzie' coming over a corduroy road."[30] Theodore referred to a series of events in July in which Legion members raided newspapers offices, broke up peaceful gatherings, and abducted speakers considered too radical.[31]

In November 1921, Debs' supporters raised money to pay for the publishing and wide distribution of his Canton speech, the one that led to his prison sentence. "This emphasizes the fact," the *New York Times* editor wrote, "that Debs had never expressed any regrets for his efforts to interfere with his country's efforts in time of war." Later the editor indicated a change of earlier opinions when he remarked that "nobody has any fierce desire to have Debs serve his full sentence." If released, the writer predicted that Debs would resume the preaching of sedition and turn the United States into another Russia if he could.[32] Hanford MacNider, National Commander of the American Legion, continued his efforts by asking President Harding that "no leniency be shown those traitors who stabbed the Legionaires in the back while they were giving their all to their country."[33] MacNider's telegram just completed another cycle in the persuasive battle over releasing political prisoners. During November 1921, the Justice Department completed its recommendations and submitted them to the President who waited for an opportune time to reveal their contents.

On December 23, 1921, President Harding finally decided that the time had arrived for the release of Debs and twenty-three other political prisoners. In the euphoria of the Christmas season, Harding made his announcement—one that ended Debs' prison term at two years, eight months and ten days. Harding also did not explain his reasons for acting when he did. Debs' neighbors in Terre Haute believed that Harding's action came as a result of the petition with 30,000 local signatures that had been delivered to the President two days earlier. Members of Debs' family had no prior knowledge that he would be released, other than rumors, but such had circulated on several other occasions. After taking the Terre Haute petition to Washington, Theodore planned to spend Christmas with Eugene. He and Karsner arrived at the prison the evening before Debs' release. With the release announcement the Department of Justice issued a comment on each case. In Debs' case, they noted that although he was an old man with immense personal charm, he was dangerous and "mislead the unthinking and afforded excuse for those with criminal intent."[34] Although Harding freed Debs and the other men, he did not restore their voting rights.[35] Evidently Harding adopted this strategy to counter expected objections of patriotic groups. Harding also requested that Debs, and not any of the other released men from the prisons, visit him in Washington before he returned to Terre Haute. This was another act on Harding's part that showed his concern and ambivalence in the case.

Warden J. E. Dyche delivered the news to Debs in his small hospital room. After he thanked the warden, Debs just stared at the wall in disbelief. After a time he went out into the corridor, stretched out his arms and began to weep. Other prisoners quickly came to him and asked if he had been turned down again. "No, not this time," he stammered, "and "that's what is the matter with me." "There is no joy in my leaving when I know in my soul that many of you have loving wives and little children praying through the long nights that you will be returned to their arms." He continued by promising his fellow inmates that he would help them. "I live in Terre Haute, Indiana," he stated, "your letters will reach me if just addressed that way." Slowly he made his way through the group, embracing and shaking the hand of each.[36] After packing a few personal effects and remembrances that had been sent to him, he went to the warden's office, where he received the usual check given to released prisoners. He turned and gave it to Karsner and asked him to send it to the Sacco and Vanzetti defense fund.[37] As he left the prison, the inmates crowded to the outside windows and shouted farewells.[38] According to an *Indianapolis Star* reporter Debs turned back amid loud cheers from the 2,300 convicts, waved and started weeping again. Theodore took his brother's arm and led him to a car which took them to catch the train to Washington.[39]

At the White House, Debs spent two hours visiting with President Harding. When he left the conference, reporters begged for an account of their visit but Debs abided by the President's request for no publicity and remained silent.[40] He called himself a liberated citizen of the world and promised that after a rest he would again take an active part in politics. In a certain sense, Debs appreciated the President's action in releasing him, and he knew that too much notoriety would only make it more difficult for the 135 other political prisoners that Harding had not freed.[41] In later correspondence, Debs revealed some of the items they talked about. After the President asked Debs about his future plans, he explained to him his disenfranchisement. Debs closely questioned Harding's reasoning on this matter. "I now quote his exact words to me," Debs wrote to Morris Hillquit. " 'The restoration of your citizenship is a matter for after-consideration.' "[42]

Katherine Debs remained in Terre Haute and awaited the return of her husband.[43] She heard the news from a reporter and without tears stated, "This will be my happiest Christmas."[44] She had been suffering from heart trouble and spent a considerable part of each day in bed. Because of her health she had not been told of Eugene's release until after he left the prison. While fingering the coverlet on her bed, she told the reporter that she preferred a quiet Christmas celebration. "We are getting old, Gene and I," she said. "We have been married 36 years. We have no children and we need each other."[45]

Enroute to Terre Haute, Debs declined invitations for speeches and rallies in many cities and made only a few brief appearances in cities the train passed through, but he could not stop his fellow townsmen from planning a homecoming celebration. Percy Head, president of the local Central Labor Council, took charge of the arrangements. Hundreds of supporters came from Chicago and other cities to join in welcoming Debs home. Others boarded the train and rode with Debs back to Terre Haute. Debs rejoiced when his niece, Marguerite, and her mother, Gertrude, boarded the train at Richmond, Indiana. When the train arrived at the old red brick station in Terre Haute, a crowd of 50,000 greeted Debs.[46] Mabel Curry remained in the background and only came forward to shake Debs' hand.[47] With numerous bands and unionists carrying bright red placards imprinted with such messages as "Everybody Smiles Now," and "Prison and Presidents Can't Scare Me," the vast crowd followed Debs the short distance to his home. From the front porch, while Katherine waited inside, Debs made a few remarks. "You have secured my liberation but I am not free," he asserted. "My joy was not completed because I was compelled to leave behind me in prison at Atlanta others no more guilty than I, and I will not stop until every one of them is free." After assuring his listeners that he held no bitterness against anyone, he said, "I cannot make a speech tonight, but I can love you, and I do thank you from the depths of my heart."[48]

Chapter XII
Citizen of the World

For several months after his release Debs rested and enjoyed long visits with old friends, but he retained his active interest in political events. Although he planned to take life easier, he never seemed to miss an opportunity to make his views known. The increasing struggle in 1921-1922 between the leaders in the Socialist and Communist parties made it difficult for Debs to remain neutral. The Communists hoped that Debs' bitterness over his imprisonment and his failure to regain citizenship would prompt him to join their cause. When the IWW repudiated the new "Red Party," reporters sought Debs' views. Through his friend, James Oneal, a member of the National Executive Committee of the Socialist Party, Debs announced that he planned to remain with the Socialists because he continued to believe in legislative action and lawful means of changing the structure of the government.[1] Oneal, a former West Terre Haute coal miner who became a prominent writer on Socialist labor history, admitted that the new workers' party had made "desperate efforts to land Debs."[2]

While in Atlanta Debs had several visitors who had escaped from Russia and these men convinced Debs that the new regime had not created a workers' utopia.[3] He assured Theodore that several of his informants were old friends, quite reliable, and it grieved him to hear that the Russian workers suffered under the new regime. In spite of this information, Debs was reluctant to condemn all Russians. He asserted that all workers were indebted to Russia for giving them "an actual demonstration of what working people can do."[4] Thus, it was not surprising when Debs, "liberated citizen of the world,"—the title Socialist Party writers gave to Debs after he had been disfranchised—announced that he must work for three causes: raising funds to alleviate starvation due to the famine in Russia, obtaining amnesty for all war prisoners, and the bringing together of organizations that sincerely aimed to abolish capitalism and inaugurate socialism. In spite of Russia's rulers, Debs maintained that the workers of the world had a "sacred and binding" obligation to the poor of that country.[5] In this period, Debs kept himself busy in the office by writing numerous articles on behalf of this cause. "The starving workers and peasants of Soviet Russia cry aloud to us," he wrote, "and unless our hearts are made of stone, we can hear them."[6]

The friendship between Mrs. Curry and Debs had continued since his return from prison. Both suffered from the frustration of indecision and the sense of duty to their respective spouses. When Debs traveled, he wrote Mabel using different code names. The following excerpts from Debs' letters express his feelings for Mabel and the degree of affection that he had for her:

"I wish I could tell you what a grand woman you really are . . . . I love you, my dear, with my whole heart."

"The situation between B and Ura is analogous . . . . I cannot see that all is inevitable—yet, I know that B knows what he can do when his position becomes unbearable, but I cannot think the Gods placed him in that position to make it unbearable for him."

"I can only imagine how much more the trial and pain of waiting is to you, and it is to me . . . . at times I have reached the extremes of endurance. You are truly Juno, Goddess of Beauty."

Another note to "Juno" stated, "I need you. I want you. I must and shall have you. There is but one Juno in all the world . . . . I love her. I reverence and adore her with all my heart."[7]

Although Debs seldom dated these letters, internal evidence indicated they were sent during this period of his life.

The passage of time did not alleviate their suffering. Their letters testify to the pain of their dilemma. Eugene once wrote: "love you awfully, fiercely, terribly and I am glad there's no remedy. I know what madness is." In another: "I can at least understand your situation and your feeling perfectly so . . . . which makes duty so difficult." Time did make further inroads on Debs' health. He began to make visits to Lindlahr Sanitarium in Elmhurst, Illinois, where they advertised steam baths and "naturopathic" cures that promised relief. Katherine also had aged considerably and her health required constant supervision. In the meantime, neither Debs nor Mrs. Curry could make the decision to forsake family responsibilities. In mythology, ironically, Juno not only represented beauty but protected marriage and its sanctity! Debs occupied himself by trying to keep up with the demands for lectures and articles but because of his health hesitated to make definite promises.

The Socialists held their national convention on April 30, 1922, in Cleveland. Debs reluctantly canceled his plans to attend. In addition to renewing friendships within the party, he had hoped to participate actively in planning ways to rebuild the party, but illness prevented him from making the trip. In a telegram to the delegates, he suggested that they reconstruct the party in the sections of the country where the membership had been strong prior to the anti-war resolution adopted by the St. Louis convention in 1917.[8]

After a restless spring in Terre Haute Debs became aggravated with his weakened condition and returned on July 12 to Lindlahr Sanitarium. "I have not been able to gather my strength here," he wrote his friend David Karsner. "I am satisfied that I am going to the right place for repairs," he continued, "and I shall return. . . fit for service again."[9] When reporters greeted him as he got off the train in Chicago, Debs quickly advised them to delay his obituary. After admitting that he was "exhausted nervously and physically," he delivered an impassioned tirade against industrialists whose actions, in his judgment, forced workers to strike. He also castigated craft unionists for not joining industrial unions.[10]

Immediately after his arrival at Lindlahr Debs began a series of "naturo-pathic" treatments, supposedly for his weak heart. Dr. Henry Lindlahr, founder of the clinic, forbade surgery and the use of drugs. Lindlahr claimed that he had invented an "autopathic treatment" that applied the principles of "homeopathy and cataphoresis." In carrying out this ingenious treatment he subjected his patients to alternating warm and cold sprays. He directed his nurses to lower the temperature of the water gradually until the patient could tolerate the coldness. While the patients were immersed in the cold water, attendants manipulated the limbs and Lindlahr administered some electrical current to the water. The electricity, he declared, oxidized "morbid matter." According to this doctor, "it literally burned up the disease miasms in the system."[11] Debs survived the treatments and within a short time he advised Theodore to carry out other parts of the nature cure: ". . . you and Gertrude must eat all of the raw vegetables you can and all the fruit juices, nuts and cereals. Eat only whole wheat or graham bread and use brown sugar—the white sugar and white flour are poison, not food. . . . Sleep with your head to the North. When you have a half-hour of leisure, lie full length in the grass, head to the North, and have the earth's currents of magnetism flow through the length of your body. Snuff cold water up your nostrils one-half dozen times first thing in the morning and three times daily. No one ever has a cold here and constipation is un-known."[12] Debs accepted Lindlahr's advice without reservation. Previously Debs had faith in the use of home remedies, and when these failed to restore his strength he quite willingly followed the quackery of Lindlahr. Perhaps Debs, who thought of himself as a liberal, believed that naturopathic med-icine represented the most advanced application of science to medicine and deserved support.

Debs did not spend all of his time in cold water or in carrying out the various nature cure activities. He refused to see reporters but he enjoyed other visitors. Carl Sandburg lived just three blocks away and came often to see him. Soon after Debs' arrival at Lindlahr, Sandburg wrote Karsner that he had "two or three prize kids that could laugh like running water" and he planned "to put them in Gene's path."[13] Debs mentioned Sandburg's visits in letters to Karsner and Theodore. "Had a wonderful two hours with Carl and his sweet little eleven year old daughter. His visit refreshed me. We sat and poured out our souls to one another. . . Carl Sandburg is one of the really great poets of our day."[14] To Theodore, Gene wrote that during the fourteen years that he had known Sandburg he had appreciated his loyalty.[15] Periodically Dr. Lindlahr would forbid Debs to see visitors, but many people managed to arrange visits. When Rose Pastor Stokes came, she insisted that Debs make plans to tour Russia with her.[16] During this period Mrs. Stokes supported the Communist Party. Although Debs had appreciated the many projects Mrs. Stokes had carried out for the Socialist Party in pre-vious years, he could not agree with her on this issue.

Reporters followed the flamboyant Mrs. Stokes to Lindlahr and besieged Debs for an account of their visit. Debs used this opportunity to declare that "the Communist Party has no place in America." Further he stated, "It has not a single constructive plank in its entire platform. I surely could not endorse any movement that operated under one name and privately under another. That is not necessary in America. Anything that is good, that is truth, has no reason to be kept under cover." In his opinion, the Communists had in the past three years "sought to destroy" those things which the Socialist Party had built.[17] On the same day he sent a telegram to Lenin protesting against the threatened execution of several social revolutionaries that were on trial in Moscow. "In the name of our common humanity," he asked Lenin to free the men and end the "unjust denial of their liberties."[18] If Mrs. Stokes had come to Lindlahr with hopes of getting Debs' support, she was badly mistaken. Debs' attacks did not go unnoticed in the Communist press. J. Louis Engdahl, a former Debs supporter and Socialist, castigated Debs in *The Worker* for complaining to Lenin.[19]

In addition to his concern about the threats from the Communist Party, Debs had to worry about the publication of the *Debs Magazine*. One faction in the party, led by Otto Branstetter who served at that time as Executive Secretary, resented the competition from this publication and the realignment of members behind Debs. Irwin St. John Tucker and W. E. Drake, editors of the *Debs Magazine,* journeyed to Lindlahr to convince Debs to "let the magazine die."[20] Debs knew that Branstetter had been attacking his editors in the party publication, the *Socialist World* and the *Milwaukee Leader* by accusing them of writing the articles that carried Debs' signature. Debs resented this allegation. "It is a damn shame that such spiteful and mean spirited attacks are made by socialists on one another," he confided to his brother. "That's why the party is all split up and doesn't amount to a damn."[21] Later he assured his brother that he would "keep above such party wranglings" and free from "their degrading influence."[22] Never one to fear his adversaries, Debs informed Branstetter that such "puerile performances had no place in our movement."[23]

Continuous pressure from factions within the Socialist Party, plus rumored claims that Debs secretly endorsed communism, finally forced Debs to issue an official statement denouncing communism through the national office of the Socialist Party. In this six page press release Debs not only upheld his continuing belief in socialism but repeatedly called for unity. "The splitting up of the party and the splitting of the splits has reduced us all to weakness and impotency at the most crucial time," he declared.[24] Debs admitted that he hated to break with former comrades who had given loyal service to him and the Socialist Party. He sympathized with those who left the Socialists because they desired a revolutionary party. "If the Socialist Party is not the revolutionary working class party it should be, it can be made so, but if it is held that this is impossible, then how is it possible to achieve that result with the same material, the same comrades, the same ultimate aims by merely adopting another name and marching under another banner?" he questioned.[25] In this statement, Debs did not define what he meant by revolutionary.[26] As the labor unions within the AFL increased in strength, Debs realized that his hope of uniting all workers to overthrow capitalism diminished. In 1922 he continued to advocate a position left of the craft unions, but he held back from endorsing the IWW or the Communists. By placing himself in this position—somewhere between the organized union members and the "Slowcialists" in his own party and the IWW and Reds, as most of them were then labeled, Debs antagonized members of all groups. This was not really a new position for Debs, but the struggle between these groups was more intense and his wide influence irritated organizers in each group. Because Debs had vacillated for years between the extremes within the party without clearly indicating to his supporters why, some admirers of Debs that had joined the Communist Party fully expected him to join with them after his prison sentence. "Debs will learn," wrote the editor of *The Worker* in an article attacking Debs' refusal statement.[27]

While still at Lindlahr, Debs agreed to make his first major address since his prison release. He convinced his doctor that he felt well enough to speak at a dinner in Chicago planned in honor of Jean Longuet, grandson of Karl Marx, who was touring the United States. Debs' remarks at this meeting received much more publicity than his earlier statement against communism.[28] He rekindled old fires with his strong denouncement of the capitalists who started the last war. "The American people were not in favor of that war," he asserted! He also asked his listeners how many soldiers died in World War I to make the new millionaires in this country. Over four thousand people had crowded into Ashland Auditorium to hear Debs reiterate his views on the war. This large audience frequently interrupted Debs with cheers and shouts, making it obvious that they came more to hear Debs than to honor Longuet, the French Socialist. Disregarding his earlier October remarks against the Communists, he must have confused some of his followers when he praised William Bross Lloyd and other Communists serving jail terms and declared that the Soviet Republic was the only good to come out of the war.[29] Debs used this occasion to make these remarks because at that time he opposed both the imprisonment of Lloyd and eighteen other Communists for violation of the Illinois anti-syndicalism law and the trial of alleged Communist workers in Michigan. "I raise my voice in protest," Debs asserted to the crowd. "I despise and defy their laws. . . Because I obeyed my conscience, I lost my citizenship, but I would far rather have it that way than keep my citizenship and lose my conscience."[30]

Longuet followed Debs' lengthy introductory speech with a calmer, quietly delivered attack against Clemenceau, who was also touring America seeking support. Longuet referred to Clemenceau as The Tiger and accused him of awakening bloodlust and war hatred where he asked for the unity of the world's workers.[31] Although the audience within the hall, and the hundreds that stood outside, enthusiastically responded to Debs, most reporters took a more negative view. "Debs speaks to their ignorance and passions and they applaud," one suggested. "If he were capable of one logical thought, he would realize that sovietism has brought more ruin and misery to Russia in a given period than the persecutions under Czarism."[32] Another writer referred to Debs as the Moses of Socialism and chided him for embracing the IWW and the Communist Party under the guise of defending their right to free speech.[33] General John J. Pershing had the final word on Debs' speech when he came to Chicago the month following and told the Association of Commerce that Debs' "seditious sentiments" should not have been permitted.[34]

Three weeks after the banquet speech honoring Longuet, Debs decided his health had sufficiently improved to leave Lindlahr and continue his recuperation in Terre Haute. Since Debs' remarks in the preceding months had reassured Otto Branstetter, party secretary, of his continuing service to the Socialist Party, he convinced Debs that he must go on a speaking tour to rebuild the fast-shrinking party.

Branstetter believed that only Debs could effectively reunite the party. Since Branstetter realized the precarious nature of Debs' health, and the numerous places in which it would aid the party if Debs spoke, Branstetter insisted that he accompany Debs on this tour and handle all arrangements. Branstetter scheduled no more than one speech a day and provided for long weekends and periodic weeks of rest. To each of the local managers Branstetter sent elaborate instructions on how to organize and conduct the meeting. Debs wanted to reach workers who would join the Socialist Party and not just lecture to curious audiences who could afford higher admissions. Debs insisted that general admission not exceed fifty cents and that over half of the seats in every auditorium be held at this price. Box and reserved seats sold for one dollar. In his instructions, Branstetter commanded that no additional meetings be scheduled; no dinners, interviews, or other collections allowed. "Every effort must be made to spare Comrade Debs unnecessary strain and exertion and to protect him from well-meaning but inconsiderate friends," he stated.[35] Because Branstetter anticipated opposition in many towns to Debs speaking, he included instructions on selecting the right kind of hall; on obtaining legal auditorium rental contracts in case the American Legion or Chamber of Commerce later protested; on training ushers and salesmen of Socialist pamphlets and memberships; on preventing the distribution of Communist, Workers Party and other literature or advertising.

In February Debs began this tour by speaking in cities in Ohio. In spite of all the advance planning, some meetings were cancelled because of the controversy over whether Debs should speak. In Cleveland, the City Club membership divided over the issue and a number of members cancelled their membership. When Debs heard of this dissension, he declined the invitation.[36] In a letter to his sponsor, Francis Hayes, Debs assured him that he had "not the slightest feeling of resentment toward those who objected," on account of his opinions. Such protests, he declared, had taught him "the spirit of true tolerance" and he encouraged the "misguided" brothers not to forfeit their own right to be heard within the club by walking out in an attempt to deny him his.[37] In Detroit, the local Communists tried to prevent Debs from speaking, but they failed. At another meeting in that city, Debs chided the Communist hecklers. He confided to Theodore that he could "take care of any of them that come to create disturbance and they know it."[38] In Chicago, Debs spoke to his usual large crowds. Although he granted that the party was "badly smashed and slashed" and totally bankrupt, he told Theodore that he thought his efforts brought results. "We've got a good bunch working, and the bunch is increasing," he commented.[39] After a rest in Terre Haute, Debs continued his speaking tour in Wisconsin and Minnesota that April.

The Wisconsin Assembly countered some of the opposition to Debs in that state by passing a resolution declaring that the rights of free speech had been denied during the war and that all members of the Assembly would attend in a body Debs' speech at the University of Wisconsin on April 18.[40] In this lecture Debs charged that William Howard Taft should resign as Chief Justice of the Supreme Court because he repeatedly favored the steel trust and received a $10,000 annuity from the Carnegie Corporation. The court's recent decision declaring the minimum wage law in the District of Columbia unconstitutional provoked Debs to make this comment.[41] "He is out again—the old agitator," the Madison *Capitol Times* editor declared, "at nearly three score and ten, heedless of his health, perhaps, he is again at war. And his weapons are words and a smile that lights up his lean face, and a lean hand that reaches out over his audience to draw them perforce to the truth as he sees it."[42]

In these speeches Debs repeated pleas for many of his old causes: higher wages; uniting all workers into the Socialist Party; shorter working hours; understanding of Russia because eventually the Socialist workers would regain control from the Communists; abolishing war; freeing all political prisoners; prison reforms.[43] He interspersed with these issues, comments about happenings on the current political scene. In Minneapolis, after making it clear that he did not plan to run in another presidential campaign, he discussed rumors that Henry Ford might consider nomination. Debs argued that Ford knew autos but had little experience that would make him an effective president. He admitted that Ford had gained the respect of many workers. "By treating his employees comparatively well, Ford is prolonging the capitalist regime," Debs warned. "The Simon Legree type of employer is better for the industrial world, because he breeds discontent. . .," he concluded.[44] In other speeches he advocated a bonus for soldiers, especially if the government would take the money from the "war profiteers."[45]

In May and early June Debs delivered a series of addresses in the New York City area. His scheduled speech at a May Day celebration led to a riot among clothing workers who pushed and shoved for a place to hear him.[46] He remained for the annual convention of the Socialist Party in order to oppose any coalitions with the Farmer-Labor Party or the Workers Party of America.[47] During this convention he addressed 15,000 in Madison Square Garden. After stating "I am a Citizen of the World," he continued to demand the release of all political prisoners, especially Tom Mooney, Sacco and Vanzetti, and to repeat his usual issues.[48] In this address he gave no support to the delegates that had been campaigning for him to run for president again. Debs shared with the delegates his concern over the declining membership. Branstetter revealed in his report that only 12,474 members remained in the party—compared to 118,100 in 1919.[49] While in New York, Debs spent many hours visiting with Morris Hillquit planning ways to rebuild the party. He also became concerned with the further infiltration of Communists into unions, particularly the garment workers unions.

In June and July Debs spoke extensively in the Midwest. He continued to meet opposition. In Cincinnati, for example, the Chamber of Commerce persuaded not only the owner of the Music Hall to cancel his contract with Debs' backers, but all other auditorium owners to refuse to rent to Debs. In addition, every suitable hotel in the city closed its doors to Debs. Although Debs sometimes gave up against such odds, he usually adamantly insisted upon his right to speak. Incensed in Cincinnati by the numerous threats against him, he wrote Theodore, "We'll have a packed house and by God I'll tell them the truth as I did in Dayton and the people will stand by me to the finish. I'm in fighting fettle and ready for anything and can face the whole goddamn gang of s.o.b.'s without a flicker. Otto is my bodyguard and he says to tell you that he saved my life once this evening."[50] Since no adequate hall could be rented, Debs spoke three times at the Central Labor Union Building to crowds assembled on the upper and lower floors and from the front steps to several hundred waiting outside. Police surrounded the meeting. While Debs spoke, six volunteer striking steel workers from nearby Covington stood behind him and then escorted him through the crowd.[51]

In August, Branstetter asked the national office to send out revised copies of his directions for planning meetings for Debs. To increase attendance Branstetter planned to have Debs arrive the night before each meeting and hold interviews for both morning and afternoon papers. He also suggested door to door distribution of handbills in addition to handing them out at factories, mines, and businesses at quitting time. Although Branstetter claimed that the meetings had been very successful from a propaganda and financial viewpoint, he lamented that memberships had not increased as Debs hoped. "It is useless to try to get applications for membership or do other organization work after Debs is through, because it is impossible to hold the audience," he admitted in the newsletter.[52] In previous meetings when Debs had stopped in the middle of his speeches to make an appeal for his listeners to fill out the membership applications provided them, many thought he had finished his address and rose to leave. When Debs decided to keep talking while they were supposed to fill out the cards, the audience listened to him and ignored their paperwork. To overcome these problems, Branstetter insisted as conditions to scheduling a Debs meeting for the western tour in September and October that a local organizational meeting be held a week after Debs' speech. Before Debs spoke, the chairman should

174

announce the time and place of this second meeting and proceed to secure on appropriate cards the names and addresses of all interested. Branstetter collected these cards and had the national office immediately send a notice of the meeting and special letter from Debs urging them to join the party.[53] All of this additional advice and activity indicated that fewer and fewer listeners were following Debs into the party.

During the western tour, Debs carried on a lengthy correspondence with William Z. Foster. Debs publicly denounced Foster's Trade Union Educational League, a Communist front organization with headquarters in Chicago. In some early materials sent out by this League, Foster associated Debs' name and early work for unions with the goals of this organization. Debs wanted it understood that he disapproved of the group's "boring from within tactics."[54] Although Debs did not report this to newsmen, Foster had earlier secured from Debs a letter approving the educational work of the League, and thus should have expected such consequences.[55] Naively Debs had expected Foster's work in this organization to not be aimed at building the Communist Party. In early September when the International Ladies' Garment Workers expelled several of Foster's League workers, Debs met with Myer Perlstein, vice-president of the ILGWU, to find out more about the controversy. Perlstein convinced Debs that these League workers took no part in activities to strengthen the union but tried to convert it immediately into a Communist organization.[56] Foster tried to persuade Debs that these men had been unjustly expelled and therefore his organization merited Debs' continued support. Debs asked that both sides meet "to ascertain the real truth of the situation."[57] If a convenient time and place could be arranged, Debs volunteered to attend to help arbitrate this dispute.

Debs told Foster that he knew nothing of the conduct or character of the expelled members, but that he would say privately to Foster that if the expelled members were "like some Communists and members of the Workers' party, happily in minority," he had known, he was not "surprised to hear that they made themselves offensive by their methods. . ." Instead of educating them by "rational means," Debs feared these workers brought about their own expulsion. The same thing will happen again, and more repeatedly under the same circumstances, Debs warned.[58]

Sensing that he could make more rapid gains by not alienating Debs, Foster used Debs' letter to attempt to set up such a meeting.[59] Debs myopically hoped that he could prevent further division in the ranks of labor by mediating such disputes. He never gave up his wish that eventually all workers would unite in one big industrial union, and this partially accounts for his dealings with Foster. Sometime in August, Foster secretly came to Terre Haute and spent several days visiting with Debs. He obviously fooled Debs into thinking that his intentions would benefit all labor. News of this meeting later appeared in *The Chicago News* and the *New York Call*. Foster wrote Debs protesting the interpretation Abraham Tuvim, prominent ILGWU member, had made that "we used the Terre Haute conference to create further division in the needle trades."[60] He further assured Debs that he had not given any stories to the press: "To all of them I replied that it had been agreed that you would issue whatever statements that were to be given publicity, and that you had issued one (*The Chicago News*) such statement."[61]

In mid-October after he finished his western tour, Debs decided to go to New York to look further into the ILGWU dispute and other party matters. He met with Morris Sigman, president of the ILGWU, and other officers and at first tried to persuade them to agree to a meeting. As he listened to these officers, he became irrevocably convinced of Foster's duplicity. "They cited a number of instances to show that where your members could not rule the local by their arbitrary and bulldozing methods, they did all they could to hamper them by inciting the members to strife and factional warfare," he asserted.[62] Belatedly Debs began to doubt Foster and further questioned him about barring applicants that still belonged to the Socialist Party or other parties from membership in the Trade Union Educational League. For the benefit of the officers of the ILGWU, Debs asked Foster why and how it happened that he concentrated his "educational work exclusively in the most radical and progressive unions."[63] In previous correspondence, Foster had informed Debs that Sigman and other ILGWU members had supported Gompers, and so Debs had asked Sigman about this matter. In answer to the charge, Debs replied that the ILGWU officer admitted that it was true, but pointed out that Foster and his followers had aided John L. Lewis and his miners. Debs judged his argument "a standoff with honors equally divided on that point."[64] With this additional information, Debs refused to arbitrate this and further disputes between specific unions and the Communists.

In November Debs became ill and cancelled the rest of his speaking dates.[65] Broken in health, he returned to Terre Haute. Katherine Debs had realized in the past year that she would never be able to dissuade Eugene from his compulsive drive to continue serving the party. Instead of going to Lindlahr for treatment this time, he engaged the services of Dr. Madge Stephens-Patton, a Terre Haute Socialist who combined in her medical practice adjustments with the use of "electronics" and "naturopathic" techniques. Debs saw no need to go to Lindlahr because Dr. Patton offered the same kind of treatment. Although Katherine refused to visit Dr. Patton, she cooked the vegetarian diet this doctor prescribed. For years Debs had been close friends of the doctor and her husband, both considered eccentric by local townspeople.[66] Union friends in Indiana cheered the ailing Debs with the news that they planned to build a state labor hall to be called a "House of Debs" in Indianapolis.[67] Because of controversy and lack of funds this project never materialized. Discouraged with his slow recovery at home, Debs quietly returned to Lindlahr in May.[68] At Lindlahr party officials visited Debs and he helped make plans for the annual convention.

In July 1924, while meeting in Cleveland, the Socialist Party with Debs' approval decided not to conduct a national campaign for president. Debs knew that he lacked the strength for the campaign and that the party lacked the funds and supporters. Unfortunately the leaders in the party were all past sixty, and they had failed to cultivate any charismatic successor. Rather than ignore the campaign, the delegates agreed to endorse Robert La Follette for president and Burton K. Wheeler for vice-president. On July 17, Debs accepted the national chairmanship of the Socialist Party and fall campaign committee. In a letter to party faithful, Debs explained the advantages of the merger of the Socialists with the Progressives. "For the first time, we find that farmer and city worker, the Socialist and trade unionist making common cause in one of the most important elections," he stated. Debs conjectured that this joint effort indicated that the "seed sown by the Socialists" for justice and freedom for labor had "germinated."[69] After assuring the members that the party had helped initiate this movement; that never before had there been such a "readiness to listen to our message," he begged for a contribution, "a dollar if you cannot afford more."

When Foster heard of Debs' endorsement of La Follette, he publicly denounced him and chided him for ever having called himself a "revolutionary Socialist" when he agreed to participate in this "opportunistic debacle." According to Foster, Debs' "surrender to La Follette" indicated that he had left the "camp of revolutionaries" and joined the "opportunists and petty bourgeois reformists."[70] Debs replied that he believed Foster had no right to condemn the Socialists for their action because the Communists had planned to do the same.[71] In this same letter Debs stated that he knew about Foster's activities among the Farmer-Labor membership in Minnesota and the Dakotas. In this organization's convention in St. Paul, Debs alleged that the Communist Party members hoped to dissuade the delegates from endorsing La Follette. If the Communists failed, they "would not split away from it on that issue" in order to "prevent the isolation of the Workers Party from the Farmer-Labor Party forces."[72] However, when the Workers Party contingent lost in their efforts to influence the Farmer-Labor convention, they changed their strategy and later nominated Foster to run for president as a Communist Party candidate.

Debs feared that Foster and his tactics of "boring from within" might succeed and the results under Foster's direction would leave the workers no better off than those in Russia after the revolution. Foster's secrecy and "behind the scenes" approach was alien to Debs' nature. Debs wanted all actions open and subject to referendum at any time by the rank and file—the long standing practice of the Socialist Party. Also Debs knew from his experiences with the IWW that used similar tactics that most American workers would not follow such a movement. The Communists succeeded in the 20's (in spite of Debs' opposition) in infiltrating and securing positions of leadership in several unions. [The depression in the 30's—after Debs' death—accelerated and aided their activities.] Debs felt Foster's Trade Union Educational League created unnecessary tension and disharmony among workers. Foster's activities in the International Ladies Garment Workers Union and the Farmer Labor Party did little to dispel those fears.

As he had from the beginning of his career, Debs at this time—late in his life wanted to achieve unity and a party for workers—one they would control. Under Foster the Communists would control the government and Debs believed the workers suffer the consequences in loss of freedom. Foster didn't offer the solution Debs wanted.

Since Debs could not travel during this campaign, he did continue writing articles praising La Follette and his wife who had been active in past amnesty campaigns.[73] Although Foster was displeased with Debs' interest in a combined labor party, he did not remember that Debs at this time repeated some of the ideas that he stressed in the 1920 campaign.[74] In 1924, Debs envisioned the Socialist Party serving as a guide to "the progressive forces of labor until the American Labor Party is actually achieved."[75] In this campaign the Socialists stated that every member was to be a "loyal and active member of the union of his industry or trade, and to strive for the strengthening and solidification of the trade-union movement." This "Declaration of Principles" published in pamphlet form further maintained that "the duty and the privilege" of the party and its press to "aid the unions in all their struggles for better wages, increased leisure, and better conditions of employment."[76] These statements without reservations certainly contradicted some of Debs' earlier sentiments, and his enemies accused him of selling out to Gompers. In October, Debs left Lindlahr and returned to Terre Haute, but he had to decline countless invitations to speak in the final month of the campaign.[77]

In addition to the burden of declining energy and the struggle with the communists, Debs learned that Mrs. Curry planned to leave Terre Haute. Prior to Professor Charles M. Curry's retirement from Indiana State Teachers College, he accepted an attractive offer to work in the editorial department of Rand McNally Company in Chicago.[78] Mabel Curry acceded to her husband's wishes and reluctantly moved in early 1925 to Chicago. Evidence indicated that Debs corresponded with and probably met Mrs. Curry occasionally when he came to Chicago or she visited friends in Terre Haute.

Accustomed to discouraging election results, Debs ignored the 1924 results and renewed his efforts in 1925 to gain supporters for a united labor party. Although he advocated that the party not consist exclusively of workers, he insisted that those who joined do so with the understanding that it was a labor party, "not a middle-class party, not a reform party, not a progressive party. . . but an open and above board labor party, standing squarely on a labor platform and marshalling its forces to fight labor's political battles for its industrial freedom."[79] In his judgment, no other kind of a third party could succeed. He also advised against designating both industrial and farm labor in naming the party by arguing that both kinds of workers had been exploited by big business. As an indication of his dedication to this new idea, he stated that he wanted to see this party organized rather than the Socialist Party revitalized.[80] Debs eagerly looked forward to the Conference for Progressive Political Action scheduled to begin on February 21. This group, which represented divergent reform and labor interests, hoped to form a permanent party organization to follow up the last campaign. Prior to the meeting Debs declared: "If a bona fide labor party cannot be organized at Chicago, then I hope that no party at all will issue from that conference."[81]

Debs readily consented to speak at this conference. In an address that he prepared more carefully than many he gave, he outlined the problems facing the organization of an American Labor Party and skillfully refuted from his point of view those issues he opposed. For example, he admitted that he had heard considerable talk favoring establishing a non-partisan political organization, but he claimed that such an organization could not serve their purposes. In reply to those assembled who thought the time had not yet come to organize a new party, he rhetorically questioned when that time would come. To support this argument he briefly traced the history of the founding of the Brotherhoods of Locomotive Engineers and Firemen, and pointed out how a few men in each group had the courage to recognize that the time had arrived to organize. He further cited the example of his friend Susan B. Anthony and her uphill struggle, along with Elizabeth Cady Stanton and others, to secure women's rights. "We may not be able to make a very great beginning here," he proclaimed, "but the important thing is that we shall make a beginning."[82]

Throughout this speech Debs recognized the fact that he spoke to an audience composed of more than Socialists, yet he still stressed the socialistic premise of government ownership. He declared that the fundamental question was whether the group favored the nation owning the industries or allowing a "relative few" to privately own the sources and means of wealth. In this speech, Debs frequently provoked laughter and applause. He made fun of the label "progressive": "Rockefeller is a progressive. So is Morgan . . . there is not a term in our vocabulary that has been more prostituted in the last few years." In a more serious mode, he warned that many present "indulged the illusion" that possibly a middle party could attract more supporters, but they failed to realize that such a party could not permanently unite because of conflicting interests.[83] He reminded the group that in the past fifty years no third party had succeeded. "A labor party is the only party that can be organized with any hope of making it." During the rest of this long speech he suggested what this kind of a party could do, including ways of eliminating poverty. In concluding he called for the uniting of the forces present behind this new party: ". . . you will sweep into power and you will issue for the first time in human history the proclamation of the emancipation of the workers and the true civilization of all mankind."[84] Debs had obviously moved his listeners—possibly to the point of taking steps to unite effectively. Dr. Mercer G. Johnson, an official of this conference, described the applause that followed as prolonged and tumultuous.[85] When the clapping ended, a surprised Debs heard John Shepherd, a representative from the Railroad Brotherhoods, introduce a motion to adjourn the conference *sine die*. After some discussion, the motion passed with the Socialist contingent protesting. Evidently much of what Debs said frightened those delegates controlling blocks of votes, and they decided to adjourn before further speechmaking led to motions committing them to action on behalf of this new party. The adjournment dissolved the group and no one succeeded in reviving it that year, probably because they feared that Debs and his socialistic ideas would dominate.

Chapter XIII
A Half-Century Milestone

In spite of his keen disappointment that a labor party had not been formed in February 1925, in the months that followed Debs did not speak against those who declined to accept the idea. He conveniently dropped the subject of forming a united labor party because he faced the decision of what he could or should do next. For a time he occupied himself with speeches at festivities throughout the country honoring the anniversary of his fifty years of service to labor. In these addresses he seemed to be reassuring himself when he declared that he would forever "remain a total stranger to defeat." "Give me your hands, comrades. Mine are outstretched in all directions. I never needed you nor have we ever needed each other as we do now," Debs pleaded.[1] In these rallies Debs reveled in the companionship of supporters, many as old or older than hmself, and retold the struggles he had experienced. Debs claimed that socialism had kept him young and that he looked forward to another fifty years working for labor. Recognizing that the Communists had nothing to offer his followers, and that the LaFollette movement failed to develop into a permanent labor party, he set about trying to strengthen the Socialist Party. The party's need and Debs' own personal need for money were never more acute.

In late March the Socialists called a national convention for Cleveland. Prior to the meeting Debs gave several sales talks that cancelled in cash and pledges the approximately six thousand dollar party debt. In addition, he asked that the party establish a complete printing plant and begin a "bristling weekly."[2] With John T. Whitlock from Illinois, chairman of the finance committee, he organized a "dollar campaign" to try to get the funds needed.

Outwardly Debs maintained this image of hope, but two months later he privately expressed his displeasure over the management and health of the party. In a long letter to Bertha Hale White, secretary of the party, he described the convention and demonstration in Cleveland as "flat humiliating failures compared to what they should have been."[3] Admitting that the day of his speech had been very hot and that local auto races had attracted over fifty thousand people, he protested that so few attended because he knew that 30,000 had cast Socialist Party votes in past campaigns for mayor in Cleveland. He complained that the fifty cent admission had kept workers away and said that the twenty-five cent fee he recommended should have been charged. (In the past year Debs had thought that cutting the admission price would increase attendance.) The convention he judged "the weakest feature of all" and questioned why after "beating the bushes" and spending hundreds of dollars few Socialists attended—"hardly enough for a good local or branch meeting." The convention indicated to Debs that the party was "as near a corpse as a thing can be. . ."[4] He told party officials that the time had arrived to analyze what had happened and take corrective measures. After informing Mrs. White that she should discuss his views with his fellow officers and associates in the national office, he asserted that either there was something wrong with the Socialist Party or there was something "dead wrong" with the management of its affairs.

He wrote Mrs. White that hundreds of labor organizations in the country had succeeded in building up treasuries, and that various Jewish labor and Socialist societies had funds to conduct schools, stores and other enterprises, but "out of the entire lot" the Socialist Party remained a perpetual beggar and "bled" the few "loyal souls" it had to draw upon. Debs complained that in the past seven years "several hundred thousand dollars" had gone into the national office "mainly on my account" and not a dollar had remained there. In this letter, he came as near expressing his regrets for his personal sacrifices over the years as he did in any he ever wrote. "For my brother and myself," he stated, "who have given ourselves wholly to the service of the party . . . we have not received enough to pay our living expenses. During this time I have refused all kinds of lectures that would have made me independent. . ." Ignoring other causes for the party's decline, Debs asserted that mismanagement accounted for it. In saying this he wanted it understood that he accepted his "full share" of the responsibility. "We have been living beyond our means and income," he charged, and demanded that the party economize immediately.

To prevent further deficits Debs suggested strict curtailment of funds. He pointed out the inconsistency of Birch Wilson, member of the executive committee, announcing the party's bankruptcy and inability to meet the payroll at a two dollar a plate dinner in one of Cleveland's finest hotels. Debs reminded Mrs. White that he had not conducted conventions in the expensive hotels when he took over the bankrupt Brotherhood of Locomotive Firemen in 1880. "I shall never again speak at a banquet at two dollars a plate," he promised. Other ideas that he thought would help save money included stopping members of the executive committee voting by telegram and conferring by telephone; employing no paid organizers until funds accumulated; saving $250 a month by moving out of the national office in Chicago into space they could afford. Referring to the earlier six thousand dollar debt that he had "personally agreed to raise the money to pay," he asked why a "new leaf" had not been turned. The new debt indicated that the party had spent the funds sent to headquarters in the "dollar campaign" he and John T. Whitlock, chairman of the finance committee, had sponsored. He called attention to the fact that Whitlock thereafter refused to raise any more money for the national office. "I do not blame him," he asserted; "Whitlock is a shrewd business man." After all of the notes that Debs had signed over the years for the party, he stated that he would not sign another. "It is no use," he lamented. "It is like pouring water through a sieve."

182

The frankness of Debs' next remark must have startled all in the national office who read his letter. "I have been used all of these years as a kind of bait to draw funds to the national office and I have concluded to quit serving in that role," Debs declared. If the party did not financially improve, Debs threatened to resign from the executive committee. "I can see nothing but disaster and ignominy ahead, and I do not propose to lead the party to that kind of an end." He further suggested that they abolish the national office for the next six months, because the ". . . shrivelled little party cannot support a headquarters such as we now have."

Mrs. White replied that she had relayed his instructions to the executive committee and sent Debs the complete financial report he requested. He replied immediately and thanked her for her cooperation but noted that the records revealed "a worse condition" than he expected. After reading the report he said that he was almost persuaded to accept Otto Branstetter's view that they let the party die.[5]

In mid-June Debs started another speaking tour, including conducting a series of regional conferences aimed at rebuilding the party. These meetings, combined with the continuing euphoria generated by celebrations in honor of Debs' first fifty years as a blue-denim stalwart, encouraged Debs that interest in socialism still existed. Conversely he had at the same time a gnawing fear that his efforts failed to make permanent gains for the party and that Branstetter was right. "The great trouble is that the party has lost . . . confidence," he stated. He regretted that his health forced him to take days off and prevented him from doing more organizing work as chairman of the NEC. In these regional meetings Debs hoped to bring the party "to life again," but he had the feeling at times that his "name and prestige have counted for little." Newspaper accounts of his meetings at this time reveal that he attracted large crowds, especially in cities that formerly had active Socialist organizations, but produced meager results. "The eager solicitation, the cheering assurances and the burning appeals I send out fall upon deaf ears and dead souls," he confessed to Mrs. White. Debs suggested that the party had not remained relevant to the times. He wished that the NEC had sufficient writers and speakers to "deal promptly and effectively with the vital world issues which confront us." In his judgment the NEC should long ago have issued definite statements defining the attitude of the party regarding troubles in China and Mexico; Labor Defense Day; the evolution "case in Tennessee which the whole world is talking about." Debs recognized that a viable party had to take a stand on each important issue of the day.

Worried that the present funds for organizing that he had personally asked the Jewish Forward staff to give him would show such insignificant results, he commented to Mrs. White that he would be "eternally discredited" if he failed. In confidence to this longtime party worker, Mrs. White, he alternated between expressions of impending doom and ways to save the party. He proposed three motions for Mrs. White to place in his name at the next NEC board meeting: suspension of the Socialist World since a new weekly publication, the *American Appeal,* had been planned; no further rebates in the dues of the language federation locals; cancelation of the trip of delegates to the International Congress and use of the $800 allotted for paying overdue bills. If the party's financial condition did not improve before September 1, he advised that the NEC discontinue meeting and permit Mrs. White and her associates to manage the national office. Debs could see no sense incurring "enormous railroad and hotel expenses" for NEC meetings "practically barren of results."

After reading Mrs. White's letter from Debs, George Kirkpatrick, publicity director for the party, confidentially informed Morris Hillquit, influential NEC board member in New York City, that Debs was becoming increasingly difficult to manage and that he should expect serious trouble.[6] Kirkpatrick wanted Hillquit to know that the party office and its workers were not entirely responsible for the criticism Debs heaped upon them. He attributed Debs' displeasure to the fact that Debs' pride had been deeply wounded. "The Cleveland meetings opened his eyes. He is thoroughly stung," Kirkpatrick wrote, "but he will not frankly take any of the blame as belonging to him." According to Kirkpatrick, Debs refused to "take his medicine," and was "malicious in his carping."[7] After implying that Debs eagerly sought an alibi, Kirkpatrick warned that he feared Debs would find one "no matter what it may cost individuals and the party" and try to "go it alone." Kirkpatrick elaborated to Hillquit upon Debs' disappointment when he appealed to the supporters of the *Jewish Daily Forward* for $50,000 and received $15,000. Supposedly Debs expected his salary to be taken from this fund and had suggested prior to the appeal that he be paid $7,000 for the year. Kirkpatrick implied that Debs expected to receive a thousand dollars for his Cleveland speech and had asked Mrs. White to make payment to his brother-in-law, Arthur Baur. Kirkpatrick interpreted this as an attempt on Debs' part to conceal from the party membership the fact he wanted such money for a speech "in these days of our poverty." Mrs. White refused to make the payment and asked to bring the question before the NEC committee. Kirkpatrick hinted that Debs would change his mind on this matter before the group met. With a certain kind of clinical deftness, Kirkpatrick told Hillquit that "the time approaches when we must have a new leadership on the platform."[8] "He cannot draw as he did," Kirkpatrick declared, and continued with accounts of comrades complaining of Debs' repetition of old themes and illustrations.[9] Debs had asked Kirkpatrick to assist him on the editing of the proposed new weekly, but he told Hillquit that he now regarded Debs as "so fickle, unreliable, and in a showdown, so egoistic" that he would not assume a position of responsibility with him on the paper. He added two further reasons why he thought Debs was irked: party headquarters would not let him sell the David Karsner biography of Debs at his meetings and refused to commit funds to publish his book of prison experiences. [Debs never succeeded in publishing this book in his lifetime. After Gene's death, Theodore had the Socialist Party in Chicago publish it under the title *Walls and Bars* (1927). This book has been brought out in a new edition by Charles H. Kerr Publishing Company with the support of the Eugene V. Debs Foundation.]

184

Without Kirkpatrick's knowledge, Mrs. White also sent a private letter to Hillquit on the same day explaining her views on the matter. Where Kirkpatrick did not indicate that Debs' current behavior indicated any change from his past actions, Mrs. White, who had worked many years longer in the national office, stated that Debs' letter of complaint represented a "complete reversal of everything he has ever said before and at several NEC meetings and on other occasions here. . ."[10] Regarding money matters, she declared that for some reason Debs had never wanted it to appear that he received adequate payment for his work. She admitted that she had agreed to pay him one thousand dollars after the Cleveland meeting, thinking that the meeting would be a great success. Kirkpatrick either did not know this fact or deliberately did not explain the problem this way to Hillquit. Prior to the earlier tour in New York City in which much less money had been raised than planned, Debs had requested $7,000 for the year but Mrs. White stated he had not pressed for money in light of the poor results. In addition to Kirkpatrick, she mentioned that Comrades Wilson and Berger knew about Debs' request to have the check made payable to Baur. Berger had irritated Mrs. White by warning her not to write the check under these circumstances. "I would resign," she asserted to Hillquit, "before I would conceal or publish a misleading report."[11]

After Mrs. White submitted the items regarding the payment of the $1,000 and the $7,000 for consideration at the next board meeting, Debs replied with a rejoinder which he asked her to circulate to the committee. In order to justify the request for $7,000, he explained how he had used the same amount of money the party had paid him in 1923 for his speech-making and writing efforts. He had allotted one-half for office expenses with an additional fourth for Theodore and a fourth for himself. He suggested that he be paid this way, but Mrs. White reported that Berger again vigorously protested. She viewed this as merely an evasion and declared that his Terre Haute office was not the Socialist Party office! "It is purely a personal matter, and letters dealing with party matters are forwarded here and are taken care of here," she added.[12] The two office set up, which had continued from the early days when Debs served as secretary of the party, had frequently been a source of irritation and duplication. Debs maintained the office as a direct link with his supporters. Perhaps Berger and White perceived a certain irony in Debs' desire to curb expenses in the national office and yet ask for funds to continue his own office.

Mrs. White further complained to Hillquit that she, more than any other party member, had the "unfortunate lot" of saying "no" frequently to Gene. "I can go just so far in opposing him," she confided, for he thought he could draw larger audiences under other auspices. Unless the audience equalled the size of the huge crowd that attended his May 3 rally at Madison Square Garden, Debs thought mistakes in planning had been made. In the past three years, Mrs. White admitted that she had not been able to arrange a second meeting in a city that had not disappointed Debs. "What he does not realize is that his imprisonment is an old story and he is not the drawing card he once was," she kindly but emphatically stated.[13] Her efforts to convince Debs that he should speak on new issues resulted in few changes. Since the summer commitments had been made for Debs, she suggested that the NEC not meet until fall, but that the committee plan to depend less on Debs and seek other lecturers. In her judgment, plans for the *American Appeal* needed further study if Debs served as editor. "Gene's psychology is all wrong—the old Appeal days and methods are of the past," she opined. The paper needed a new leader with "real force" but she pointed out that it would be difficult to pay for such a person, if in addition, the organization had to pay "a salary such as Gene will expect."[14]

The letters from Kirkpatrick and White indicated that Debs did test their patience. Debs obviously did not confide in them the fact that he had borrowed money from his brother-in-law during the past two years and anxiously hoped to repay him.[15] Although Oscar and Arthur Baur did not endorse their brother-in-law's political views, they knew that he would amply repay his debts. Since Debs had frequently borrowed money from the Baur brothers from the earliest days of his union activities and Democratic Party campaigns, it was consistent for Debs in his later years to continue seeking loans from them. They served as a family loan company and made it easier for Debs to get credit. Since 1923 Debs had not received any money from the party, yet during that time he had been seriously ill for six months and his medical and living expenses continued. Any speaking he had done had been under the auspices of the party, and he had been paid little in return. Kate had inherited a modest amount of money some five years previous, and Theodore's wife also had inherited several thousand dollars years before. But Debs resented his having to live on Kate's resources or his brother having to depend upon others when he still worked actively for him and the party. Rather than bother Kate with money matters, he arranged for Arthur Baur to pay bills when they became due. In better days, Debs' income covered these necessities, but the simple fact became apparent that his lecturing no longer could provide for both his private needs and the party's. In addition, the party no longer gained much revenue from pamphlet sales or from other orators. During this period the party lacked speakers, and both White and Kirkpatrick continually urged Hillquit to use his international contacts to secure European Socialist speakers—as if this would remedy the multiple problems the party faced in a changing United States.

The regional conferences held in Minneapolis on June 20-21, St. Louis, July 4-5; San Francisco, August 1-2; Chicago, August 29-30; New York City, September 19-20; plus numerous rallies, including state picnics in Milwaukee on July 19 and Seattle on August 8, did produce enough funds to enable the party to continue with plans to publish a weekly.[16] Publicly Debs spoke at these meetings in optimistic terms, seldom alluding to the party's problems. After the meetings he met with friends and with missionary zeal tried to re-establish in their minds the idea that permanent reforms could only be made through socialism. "He tried to analyze the capitalist society by portraying the various steps in the evolution of the machine," one former supporter wrote, but "scientific analysis was not his forte."[17] Another said that Debs was as "emotionally exuberant as ever" but failed to convince those that had left the party that "bourgeois reform elements" had not succeeded in destroying the party.[18]

Debs did add a new issue to his speeches: a rousing defense of Bartolomeo Vanzetti and Nicolo Sacco. Although he had supported their cause from the beginning, he became more concerned as the case dragged out in courts. When Debs spoke on their behalf at these rallies, his old vigor seemed to return and his audiences momentarily forgot his age and the fact he repeated himself on other issues such as industrial unionism and capitalism vs. socialism. Both Vanzetti and Sacco appreciated his appeals, especially when he prompted listeners to send money for their legal fund. Debs visited the two men in prison and assured them that they would eventually be released.[19] Vanzetti wrote Debs about each turn of events in their trial and fight for freedom.

In September 1925, Debs decided to go to New York City to continue his agitation to free Sacco and Vanzetti and to visit with Reverend Norman Thomas, a young Socialist running for mayor of that city. Debs endorsed Thomas and predicted that this minister would not "yell for blood" if war ever threatened again.[20] In October Debs returned to help Thomas with his campaign. They appeared together at numerous meetings.[21] In order for Debs to get some rest, Thomas scheduled his major addresses every other day: October 11 at Hunts' Point Palace; October 13 in the Bronx; October 15 at the Brooklyn Academy of Music. Both in the earlier August visit and in this later one, Communist demonstrators heckled Debs and threw anti-Socialist leaflets from the galleries. Debs also continued to receive threatening letters as he had throughout his life. One wrote, ". . . if you don't shut up, you will be or you'll wake up in Hell. Beware for you are playing with fire when you provoke the American Eagle. . ."[22] Another in scribbled handwriting warned: "Debs as you are an in grate to the wellfare of the business of this countrey I propos to put astop to youre lawlas acts by Sending a bullet through you miserabel heart at the very first opportunity. The corts has Saved men for Shooting law a biding and good men. You are nothing but a law braker and I am going to take my chances. I am after you."[23] As he had in the past, Debs ignored these messages.

When Debs' health permitted, he continued his activities for causes he thought worthy. The other national officers postponed any board meetings during the summer and fall of 1925, possibly because they lacked ready answers to the problems before them. The executive committee experienced great difficulty in finding a business manager for the proposed weekly. Numerous prominent party workers turned down the job. Finally Murray E. King of Indianapolis accepted, but he had little training for the position.[24] Since Debs raised the necessary funds for starting the paper, and had experience in publishing, he accepted the duties of editor. Debs recognized that he lacked the stamina to edit the paper unless he could find an assistant. According to Kirkpatrick, Debs asked him in a specially arranged meeting to serve as his "writer-in-chief." Infuriated with this proposal, Kirkpatrick emphatically told Debs that he knew little about newspaper writing and would not accept.[25] "Gene is definitely expecting or planning to do very little writing," Kirkpatrick tattled to Hillquit, chairman of the committee charged with starting the paper. "With equal definiteness Debs is planning that someone shall serve him," he informed Hillquit.[26]

This arranged visit between Debs and Kirkpatrick took place in Galesburg, Illinois, another city where Debs spoke to raise funds for the weekly. Evidently Debs had written earlier to Hillquit and informed him that he planned to resign from all fund raising activities and serve only in a nominal way with the weekly. This move frightened both Hillquit and Kirkpatrick because headquarters still needed more dollars to guarantee the publication of the weekly and they had no other revenue-raiser available. Kirkpatrick decided to go visit Debs at Galesburg and attempt to change his mind. In the meantime Debs answered Hillquit's letter requesting him not to resign and agreed that he would make no announcement of it until the December 19 meeting of the NEC. He regretted quitting and felt "guilty of desertion at a time of the party's greatest need,"[27] but feared that if he continued he would collapse. Interestingly Debs did not inform Kirkpatrick of his statement to Hillquit.

Debs did agree to meet with Kirkpatrick a week later for an important meeting at Chicago party headquarters. Debs met with Arthur Schlesinger and B. C. Vladeck, who represented the New York *Jewish Daily Forward* supporters. While these men met, Kirkpatrick sent Hillquit a running account of the day. At that time the New York group had set a $10,000 goal to support the weekly. Although Kirkpatrick had written in the past that Debs had to be replaced or better managed to suit the party's needs, he now confided to Hillquit that if Debs gave any indication of abandoning the project, Vladeck would refuse support. Obviously Debs remained the best hope of reviving the party in the eyes of this group. Kirkpatrick predicted to Hillquit that "if the paper begins vigorously," more money would come from the *Forward*. "So much depends upon Gene. Surely he must talk victory and he must let his name stand," he declared. In a note at the bottom of the letter, he indicated that Debs cooperated: "All is well—apparently."[28] This letter serves as striking evidence of the strategy that officers of the party played with Debs—a game of use him when helpful but ignore him when convenient. In late December the first issue of the *American Appeal* appeared with a column by Debs.[29] Another task had been accomplished and Debs asked to retire. When the NEC committee met, they took no official action on his resignation. They knew that Debs would handle his own bookings thereafter and write a column for the weekly, but that King and others would have to direct it. In addition, both Mrs. White and Kirkpatrick resigned from the headquarter's staff at this same meeting. Mrs. White had been in ill health and Kirkpatrick decided to take a business option while he still had the opportunity. Possibly these resignations from longtime staff members made it all the more important that the NEC keep Debs with the party under any conditions to maintain some semblance of continuity to the "Jimmy Higginses" the party depended upon.

Chapter XIV
Setting the Record Straight

Early in 1926, weary from all of the haggling with party officials, and discouraged with his lack of success in rebuilding the party, Debs carried out his often mentioned wish to retire. He realized that he lacked the strength to continue the rigorous routine of continually speaking and writing. The publication of the *American Appeal* buoyed Debs' spirits, and he hoped it would serve as a rallying point for the dwindling party. After such an active life, Debs could not simply quit all of his activities. He used part of his new leisure time to write long letters to friends and to respond to writers who wrote about people or political events that concerned him. In these letters, he went to great length to explain his views, and, in a sense set the records straight from his point of view. Debs never intended to write his autobiography, but his letters and articles written in retirement provide some additional information about how he interpreted various issues.

Debs' letter to Haldeman-Julius, an old colleague in social agitation, typified his desire to clarify his opinions. In an article about pre-war radicals, Haldeman-Julius praised Debs and Darrow and condemned Upton Sinclair for leaving the Socialists during the war. Debs disagreed with his remarks. He protested to Haldeman-Julius that he overlooked the fact that, although Sinclair had supported Wilson's early war plans, he had later changed his mind and had made amends to the party. Debs further noted Sinclair's leadership in groups protesting Debs' imprisonment and the incarceration of other anti-war dissenters. Darrow had consistently supported Wilson and the war, but he also opposed confinement of political prisoners after the war. "For my part," Debs appealed to Haldeman-Julius, "I want neither condemned. I recognize in them . . . great qualities of mind, heart and soul; men who achieved great and lasting good in the service of humanity."[1] Although he admired Darrow, Debs admitted that he had never been able to predict his actions. He pointed out that he had failed to get Darrow to endorse LaFollette in the 1924 campaign. "He is not of the classifiable kind," he declared. "He is neither Republican, nor a Democrat, nor a Progressive, nor anything else in politics." In spite of the fact that Darrow usually endorsed Democratic candidates, including John W. Davis in 1924, and never had backed a Socialist ticket, Debs appreciated Darrow's legal efforts which he declared "exposed the rottenness of capitalist misrule."[2]

In recognition of Debs' service to labor and socialism, B. C. Vladeck, the manager of the *Jewish Daily Forward* who had raised funds to start the *American Appeal*, decided to direct a "Debs Testimonial Fund" drive. In earlier years, Debs had refused this kind of charity, but when the first $5,000 check arrived, he wrote Vladeck to express "Thanks too deep for words."[3] With this check, Debs received a note stating to use it "exclusively for yourself for personal needs."[4] Later Debs received another $5,000 from this fund, but he shared $2,000 with party headquarters, indicating that $500 be used for the newspaper.[5] According to Theodore, this money enabled Debs to pay his bills. He steadfastly refused to use Kate's money—even to remodel the porch on their house.[6]

In March, Debs announced that he planned to take an extended vacation to Bermuda and possibly Cuba and Mexico. During the winter, Kate had suffered from a severe flu attack and he thought that a warmer climate would help her.[7] News of his possible departure from the mainland prompted editors to comment that he would not be permitted to return to this country since he had been disfranchised. Anticipating this possibility, Debs asked his lawyer friend, Hillquit, to help him regain his full citizenship rights.[8] In reply, Hillquit quoted several law cases and concluded that the statutes of Indiana disfranchised a person only during the period of imprisonment. Hillquit argued that since Debs was a citizen from Indiana at the time of his conviction, Section 6877 of the Indiana Code applied to his case.[9] Berger who had been returned to the House of Representatives by his Milwaukee supporters introduced a congressional resolution to restore Debs' citizenship, but Hillquit disapproved of this action.[10] Other congressmen informed Berger that Debs had not applied for a pardon. Debs adamantly informed reporters that he had no such intention. "I committed no crime," he declared, "and if I apply it would serve as an acknowledgment that I was wrong when I stood my ground for the right of free speech in the United States."[11]

Debs replied to Hillquit that he appreciated his interpretation of the Indiana law, but informed him that he had not been permitted to register by his local election board and refused admission to the voting booth. He repeated to Hillquit President Harding's words during their personal visit after his release from Atlanta. "The restoration of your citizenship is a matter for after-consideration," the President had stated.[12] This after-consideration had failed to materialize, Debs noted. He added that his requests to President Coolidge and his attorney general, plus the head of the Department of Justice had also failed to regain him his citizenship. As long as these powers in Washington ignored his requests, Debs knew that he would not succeed. He had consulted several lawyers in Terre Haute, plus Clarence Darrow, and they all agreed.[13] Short of begging the President for a pardon by personally applying, Debs saw no way to solve the dilemma. In the meantime, Debs continued with his plans to take a trip outside the country. [In September 1975 when Congress restored General Lee's citizenship, Indiana's Senators Birch Bayh and Vance Hartke introduced a bill asking for similar consideration for Debs. In 1976 the bill passed in the Senate but the House sought an opinion from the Justice Department. In 1977 Senator Bayh requested a ruling from Attorney General Griffin B. Bell, who replied in a letter to Bayh on August 30, 1977, that Debs never had been deprived of his citizenship. "The statute under which he was convicted did not authorize loss of citizenship," Bell wrote, "and there does not appear to be any sentencing order which would have deprived him of his citizenship."]

Hillquit suggested to Debs that he visit Bermuda instead of Cuba and Mexico, since he had vacationed there and recommended the climate. Debs accepted this advice and a week later visited overnight with Vera and Morris Hillquit while waiting to catch the boat. Although Hillquit assured the Debses that they would not have to worry about returning, newspaper reporters pestered for interviews and speculated upon the matter. Perhaps a trip to the southern part of California or some part of the Southwest would have had equal health benefits, but Debs obviously wanted to leave the country and insisted upon testing the extent of his freedom. Since Kate had always avoided the limelight, she did not particularly appreciate the notoriety.

Since the time Debs turned down the gift of a European trip from the Brotherhood of Locomotive Firemen, he had wanted to travel outside the United States. At that time, his sense of duty prevented him from doing it. Now at seventy years of age, he lacked the strength and resources to tour Europe. The two day boat trip to Bermuda over rough seas was far from pleasant, and both Debses became seasick.

The Chief of Police and his Sergeant greeted Debs upon his landing. They conducted a long and detailed investigation. After quoting all applicable laws, they threatened the Debses with deportation for any violations.[14]

Shortly after their arrival, Theodore requested some additional articles for the *American Appeal*, but Debs refused. Since both he and Kate had not been well, Debs replied that he did not have the time, energy, or a typewriter. In addition, the Immigration Inspector paid two visits to the Debses during the first week of their vacation. "There will be rest for me when I am put away for good and not before," he confided to his brother.[15]

After the first week, the local authorities permitted the Debses some rest. Eugene wrote Theodore that they found the St. George Hotel comfortable. Evidently Debs continued his field work, because he requested that Theodore forward to a St. Louis woman he had just met five of his articles that had been printed as pamphlets.[16] It would have been too much to expect Debs not to proselytize for the causes he had so long advocated whenever he got a chance!

On April 20, the Debses started their return trip to New York, because Eugene had a speaking engagement in Pittsburgh on May 1.[17] His departure prompted further newspaper comment, but he landed in New York without incident.[18] His niece, Marguerite Debs Cooper, met them and took the elderly couple to the home of his sister Emily Mailloux for some additional rest. In Pittsburgh Debs spoke again of the war and told of his difficulties during his recent vacation. He repeated his plea for funds and public support of Sacco and Vanzetti. Exhausted from the trip, he returned to Terre Haute, where he spent the next several weeks in bed.[19] Letters to and from old friends helped to pass the time.

When Debs arrived home, a letter from his friend, Sinclair Lewis, who at that time lived in Kansas City, awaited him. Lewis had visited Debs on two previous occasions in Terre Haute, staying each time for several days. Lewis, who knew Debs and his brother well, invited them to come to Kansas City for a visit.[20] Lewis had also met Debs at other times when both happened to be speaking in the same city. Each developed a mutual admiration for the other. In this letter, Lewis spoke of "our novel", a book he proposed to write with Debs as the central character. In previous conversations, they had visited at great length about this book and even had selected a title, "Neighbors".[21] Lewis assured Debs that "you know that some day I will do it." He continued, "And I am now starting on the nearest novel to Neighbor—the real approach to Neighbor—the other novel of which I told you at such great length—the novel about preachers." Lewis predicted to Debs that this book, later called *Elmer Gantry*, would "be a sweet and sanctified novel filled with praise for all of the capitalistic preachers."[22] In the letter, Lewis included notes from Ethel Barrymore, then appearing in a touring company in Kansas City, and L. M. Birkhead, a Kansas City Unitarian minister who was helping Lewis with his book. After finishing her acting roles in the evening, Ethel wrote that she would join Birkhead and Lewis for supper and that in their conversations they often discussed Debs. Ethel informed Debs that in trying to give a "certain sincerity to art" she "loved him" for the example his life had set for her. She boldly asserted that Debs' expression of meaning via his life was far greater than her efforts or what Lewis tried to express in his novels and Birkhead in his preaching.[23] In his note, Birkhead predicted that by the time Lewis finished with the preachers of Kansas City, "their morals and economics will be corrupted beyond repair." He declared that Lewis and Debs had similar goals: "to free the human race from a lot of its damned foolish ideas."[24] These letters pleased Debs, who found praise important since he had to decline Lewis' invitation and no longer had the strength to rush out and join Lewis or any other friends. He answered each of their letters, including one to Edwin Markham who later joined Lewis in Kansas City.[25]

Debs also continued his correspondence with Carl Sandburg. At this time, he read Sandburg's *Lincoln* and wrote him at length praising the research and comprehensiveness of the work. Sandburg replied that he appreciated his comments and stated that "Sometimes I hope to do an extended sketch of you that will have some of the breath and feel of Lincoln."[26] Debs' expectations that these two promising young writers might write books about him buoyed his spirits, but he did not spread the news.

During the heat of the summer, Debs found it increasingly difficult to maintain his strength, but he wanted to improve so that he could do more for Sacco and Vanzetti. His heart condition required larger prescriptions of digitalis and more frequent visits to Dr. Marge Patton, his physician, who continued to advise additional naturopathic remedies. In mid-August she suggested that Debs return to Lindlahr for a complete rest and series of treatments. Debs protested and said that he needed a couple of weeks to write additional columns for the weekly and do a special leaflet on behalf of Sacco and Vanzetti. "They have suffered for six and a half years," he told Dr. Patton. "One of these men is a poet and an idealist. I visited them while East. Those men would not hurt an insect. They would not think of killing a human being."[27] According to Dr. Patton, Debs forgot about his office call for medicine and spoke about these imprisoned men for thirty minutes while tears coursed down his cheeks.

Debs kept his word and wrote "Sacco and Vanzetti: An Appeal to American Labor," which had a wide circulation.[28] In this persuasive leaflet, Debs traced more carefully than in many of his writings the details of the case. He wrote objectively about the sequence of events but revealed his pessimism for the fate of the men when he interpreted the meaning of the events. "Sacco and Vanzetti were framed and doomed from the start," he stated. "Not all the testimony that could have been piled up to establish their innocence beyond a question of a doubt could have saved them in that court," he asserted.[29]

Before leaving for Lindlahr and complying with Dr. Patton's advice, Debs accepted an offer from *Colliers* to state his views in an article on a variety of questions sent to him. Debs recognized the opportunity that this magazine with a large circulation provided him, especially since he seemed concerned about clarifying his views to the public. Although the magazine only published part of his replies, he spent considerable time drafting his answers and discussing them with Theodore. He gave his opinions on questions ranging from what reasons explained the increase in savings bank deposits; Henry Ford's scale of wages; League of Nations; to what he thought of modern man and morals. Arthur Robinson, the writer who submitted the questions to Debs, deliberately phrased many of them to find out if Debs' ideas had changed and if Debs would admit that progress had been made toward solving some of the problems he had agitated about.[30] With candor, Debs agreed that some conditions had improved in the country: that more people had savings accounts; greater earning power; a higher standard of living than Europeans. However, other conditions needed attention. He countered each argument showing improvement in the status quo, by quoting figures from the National Bureau of Economic Research showing that 78% of the citizens had incomes less than $1,600 a year when $1,800 was needed for a minimum standard; by pointing out that automated machines meant an increasing absentee ownership and investment with little concern for the resulting unemployment; by insisting that labor's advances had been the result of organization and not generosity from management. He granted that Socialists had changed plans, methods, and tactics as industrial, political and social problems changed but affirmed that the goal remained—"the establishment of a Socialist Cooperative Republic."

In this article Debs had the chance to express further views on a variety of his favorite topics, including Ford and the League of Nations. Although Debs admired the ability of Ford to create a mass produced automobile that many could afford, he objected to his paying higher wages than comparable industries and then forbidding unions. "He has developed the most profitable exploitive process in industrial America," Debs declared. Since the League of Nations represented rival nations that had not solved their differences, Debs stated that he feared this organization could not prevent war. If the United States "had sufficient faith in its own moral rectitude to completely disarm," Debs believed that then this country could compel general disarmament by the force of its moral example. According to Debs, modern man was "undeveloped" morally and intellectually because he had to spend all of his time securing a living.

Debs encouraged women to continue their efforts to escape man's dominion by seeking equal employment rights. "It does not matter to me how a woman dresses or what she does in private, so long as she pleases herself," he asserted. He thought that men who feared that women with "new ideas, new conceptions and new values" would go astray, unconsciously paid a sad compliment to their own wives or mothers.

Modern morals, he insisted, reflected modern economics, for he believed that economic relations largely determined conduct toward one another. In his judgment, morals could not be inculcated or improved by statutory enactment or judicial sentence. Optimistically he predicted that morality would improve, but not until poverty and misery were reduced. "A woman can still earn more money in self-degradation in five minutes than she can by a week of honest work," he asserted. In addition, he pointed out that a prize fighter earned more in a few minutes with his fists than the greatest genius could command in a year. These comments indicated that he recognized that morality reflected the values people uphold.

Throughout, his answers repeatedly reminded his readers of the increasing influence of the machine upon modern life. Debs wanted his readers to realize that the "application of the machine to industry has recreated and is reshaping the destiny of the modern world." Debs saw no limits to the development of machines nor to the harnessing of the forces of nature to serve man. If operated under a socialistic system, he predicted, modern machinery could have a great emancipating power and could eventually aid, not only men who worked with their hands, but all classes of people.

After completing this writing assignment, he wrote a few additional columns for the *American Appeal* and shipped more of his papers and books to Rand School in New York City. On August 24, 1926, Debs wrote to Mabel Curry. In one of the few letters he dated, he addressed Mabel as "B".......... one of the code names they had used years before. The brief note included this line: "my heart keeps calling, calling you. Be patient yet a little while." This letter indicated that although Mabel left Terre Haute, she never left Debs' thoughts and that each remained devoted to the other.[31] On August 29, the NEC met in Chicago, but Debs' health forced him to cancel his plans to attend. When the NEC passed a resolution for another campaign for funds, Debs immediately sent a check for $100 in his and his brother's name.[32]

In the third week in September, Dr. Patton again urged Debs to go to Lindlahr, where she thought he might recover more quickly. Theodore agreed to accompany him. Upon their arrival in Chicago, Debs, though quite ill, insisted on visiting the *American Appeal* office to check on the progress of the weekly. Finally, Theodore got him to the hospital. For a few days, Gene seemed to relax, but his strength waned. He suffered from a combination of rheumatism, kidney trouble and heart spasms. On October 9, Debs felt better and asked to go for a ride to the Elmhurst Post Office. He wanted to mail a letter that he had written to Sacco and Vanzetti in which he enclosed another $10.00 for their defense fund.[33]

Although Theodore wrapped his brother well, Eugene started to chill, and that evening he suffered a heart attack. Theodore called Kate to his bedside. In a few days, Debs rallied and asked each day to be taken in a wheel chair to the sun porch so that he could visit other patients. During these visits Debs tried to cheer up other patients. Cecile Oehlert, a patient, overheard Debs say to a despondent patient that no sick person should be discouraged, because their souls remained free. To emphasize his point, Debs recited Henley's "Invictus". Mrs. Oehlert asked for a copy of the poem and Debs dictated it to Theodore. She interrupted Debs to ask if he would write the last verse for her. Although frail, he complied and wrote:

> It matters not how strait the gate,
> How charged with punishments the scroll,
> I am the master of my fate;
> I am the captain of my soul.[34]

Debs had given his last speech.

The next day, Debs was too weak to leave his bed. After going into a coma on October 16, Debs died on October 20. The doctor who filled out his death certificate listed the cause as chronic myocardites.[35] Theodore and Kate made plans for returning his body to Terre Haute.

Upon hearing in Terre Haute of Gene's death, the Central Labor Union wired Kate and asked that his body lie in state at the Labor Temple. The next day, when the train arrived in Terre Haute, Percy Head, president of the local labor council, stepped forward and greeted the family. "You will have to give him to us for awhile," Head stated, "you know he belongs to us."[36] Six laborers lifted Debs' simple grey cloth covered casket to their shoulders and took his body to the Labor Temple.

That evening and throughout the following day, thousands of people filed past his bier. Finally, at midnight on the second day, the crowd diminished, and Kate asked that his body be brought home to await the funeral the next day. On the day of the funeral, special trains arrived from St. Louis and Chicago carrying mourners and baggage carloads of flowers. Others came by car from the nearby coal mining towns of Jasonville, Sullivan, Linton, Vincennes, Bicknell and Hymera. The grief and homage of the workers who admired Debs can be sensed in this anecdote reported in the newspapers of the day. When his niece, Marguerite Debs, opened the house to visitors the morning of the funeral, an old miner from Clinton came forward with two geranium blooms. He asked if they were appropriate, and Marguerite smiled and escorted him into the house and placed his flowers in her uncle's hands.[37] Crowds streamed through the house until time for the funeral.

The front porch served as a platform for the service and the people gathered on the nearby lawns. In the main address, Norman Thomas attributed greatness to Debs because he possessed an "unusual combination—a prophet and a lover of mankind".[38] Other speakers included such prominent Socialists as Morris Hillquit, Victor Berger, Seymour Stedman, William H. Henry, and William Cunnea. After the services, six old friends who were still members of the local Brotherhood of Locomotive Firemen carried his body to the train for a trip to Indianapolis for cremation.[39]

The next day Kate had his ashes placed in a lot near the entrance of Highland Lawn Cemetery in Terre Haute. She hoped eventually that Debs' friends would erect a large monument in his honor. From this lot, a Debs monument could be seen from the highway. Kate's request irritated members of Debs' family, for they intended to bury Gene with his parents and sisters in the large family plot near the back of the cemetery.

Controversy followed Debs to the grave. In New York and other eastern cities, Socialists planned memorial services. In several of these same cities, the Communist Party held separate service or deliberately interrupted the Socialist Party services. The Communists used Debs' passing as a further means of harassing the Socialists. One party editor referred to the Communists as jackals and rebuked them for attempting to claim Debs in death when he had repeatedly refused to endorse their party in life.[40] Another problem developed when Kate Richards O'Hare started to collect a $200,000 memorial trust fund for Deb's widow. After the funeral Mrs. O'Hare visited with Mrs. Debs and secured her permission for the drive. During her life, Mrs. Debs was to receive the interest from this fund, and upon her death, the principal was to be converted into some kind of a memorial.[41] When the first checks arrived, Theodore angrily protested. He went to Kate and discovered that she had already received $250 which he asked her to give to him so that he could return it. Mrs. O'Hare had announced the fund in the *Ripsaw,* which she and her husband published in St. Louis. Theodore demanded that the drive end and that money not be solicited from poor people. He assured Mrs. O'Hare that Kate did not lack funds.[42] Reluctantly, Mrs. O'Hare cancelled the drive, but she protested to Theodore because of the embarrassment. Later, Theodore agreed with New York Socialists, including Hillquit and Vladeck, that any memorial to Debs should continue his work. Together they raised money and started a radio station in New York City which used Debs' initials for the call letters: WEVD.[43] Mrs. Debs abandoned plans for a monument and erected two small limestone headstones on their cemetery lot.

After Theodore visited Kate Debs to persuade her to stop the O'Hare fund drive, he never spoke to her again. When Theodore read in the local paper that his brother's will had been filed for probate, he sent Kate a letter asking why a will dated January 10, 1907, had been filed. Theodore informed Kate that Gene had told him that he had written a new will in the summer of 1926 and "that practically everything belonging to him at the time of his death, including his home—which you should be allowed to occupy during your life—should pass to the National Socialist Party."[44] He added that Gene had remarked again about the will at Lindlahr shortly before his death and expressed "evident satisfaction that this joint will had been made . . ."[45] Kate Debs never answered the letter.

Since Theodore remembered Gene saying that Nellie and Arthur Baur witnessed both wills, he later wrote Arthur just to inform him that the family knew about the second will.[46] Theodore took no legal steps to force Kate to probate the later will. Debs' estate was valued at $15,000 which included the house appraised at $8,500.[47] This figure included the money Debs had received from the *Jewish Forward* fund, but not his $5,000 share of his father's estate which had never been settled. Later, Theodore sold his father's store and lots and sent Kate her husband's share with interest.[48]

Kate lived alone in the old home that she loved. She seldom left the house except to take her evening meal at the Deming Hotel. She usually sat alone and said little to other diners. She occasionally rented a room to a professor at the nearby normal college. Upon Mrs. Debs death in 1936, she willed the home to her brothers and sisters. They sold it and eventually a fraternity purchased it. In 1959 a Debs Foundation, formed by Indiana State University faculty members and labor leaders throughout the country, organized and purchased the house. Today the home has been restored and opened to the public as a memorial to Eugene V. Debs. In 1967, Secretary of the Interior Stewart Udall visited the home and designated it as a national historic monument.

Chapter XV
In Retrospect

After Eugene's death, Theodore closed their downtown office. He moved the desks and cabinets to the basement of his home. Theodore carefully tied up the copies of speeches and essays that Debs kept in the pigeon holes of his desk. He wanted Eugene's desk to remain as it was on his last day in the office. The desk, cabinets and their contents remained in Theodore's basement until moved to the restored Debs' home in 1967.

Until his death in 1945, Theodore continued to correspond with old comrades and others about Eugene and his ideas on labor. Younger Socialists began to accept the leadership of Norman Thomas. In an interview, Thomas stated that he found Debs a difficult man to follow because Debs elicited such devotion from his followers. With admiration for Debs, Thomas said that he never tried to compete or become a second Debs. Rather, Thomas planned his own strategies and hoped the oldtimers would join in the agitation.[1] In letters to Theodore, former members of the executive committee and other party stalwarts complained of the differences in party administration. These writers especially feared that eastern intellectuals would dominate the party and alienate the workers.[2] Theodore encouraged former supporters to remain loyal to the party—even when the party continued to show diminishing results at the polls.

Since Debs prided himself upon his skills as a spokesman, some evaluation should be made of the skills and the strategies he used in his persuasion. In a speech before a large crowd of Philadelphia workers, he once stated: "I look into your faces. I catch your spirit. I am simply the tongue of the working class, making this appeal from the working class."[3] An interviewer once asked Debs his earliest ambition. He replied, "I wanted to be an orator. In my boyish estimate, the power of the speaker was infinitely greater than that of the writer."[4] Usually Debs prepared his speeches en route "with a pen, because a machine is too cold."[5] While traveling, he avidly read magazines and newspapers and made many clippings. He made use of these clippings in his speeches; underlined always with a blue pencil the parts he intended to utilize; and when finished with the clippings, mailed them home to Kate who placed them in his scrapbooks for possible future use.[6] In retrospect, Debs should be evaluated in this chapter as to whether or not he succeeded as the tongue of the working class.

Because Debs took seriously his role as the voice of laborers, he almost compulsively felt that he had to fulfill a speaking engagement or writing assignment. Even late in life when he lacked strength and began too frequently to repeat himself on some issues which were no longer vital to his audiences, he continued to accept opportunities to speak and write. By the end of his career as a spokesman for labor and socialism, Eugene V. Debs had delivered an estimated six thousand speeches, and had written countless articles, pamphlets, and letters.[7]

He used his voice and pen to aid workers in important strikes, union organizational battles, five Socialist presidential campaigns, cases defending imprisoned workers, free speech contests, and in other controversial issues ranging from women's rights, birth control, child labor, to the threat of automation. Throughout these fifty-two years of agitating, Debs kept his enthusiasm for the causes that he thought just. He never thought of himself apart from the blue-collared class he represented. During Debs' lifetime, no other figure in the American labor movement or Socialist Party attracted any more attention or had more intense followers. Samuel Gompers and other non-industrial union officials had larger organizations back of them and wider public support, but these labor leaders never incited the public enthusiasm or devotion that Debs received from his adherents. Within his own party, no other Socialist could as effectively placate, instruct, or lead the shifting minority factions. In summarizing and assessing Debs' strengths and weaknesses as a charismatic leader who agitated against the status quo at the time when this country was changing from an agricultural nation into an industrial one, an analysis will be included of the persuasive techniques that he used, the role that he played in his party, and the influence that he had upon certain men and issues. Influence can be defined as a stimulus to action or to thought. It also means to affect other people or a course of events.

In evaluating Debs' career, it must be remembered that he never posed as an intellectual. His failure to do so endeared him to countless thousands of men who carried dinner pails, but irritated theoreticians within the party. Workers saw in Debs a humble man—one who had ascended from their ranks—a man they could trust. When Debs quit high school at fourteen, he entered the practical world and gave up the academic. In spite of his father's early insistence upon his reading the classics, Eugene read few great books in later life. He did read major newspapers to keep abreast of current events, but his book reading consisted mostly of volumes that people sent to him. Socialist writers such as Herron, Spargo, Hillquit and others supplied Debs with their books which he read. In 1911, the Department of Education at the University of Wisconsin asked a number of prominent speakers, including Debs, to state their views on oratory. Debs admitted in his essay that his own education and speech training had been limited. "I had no time for either," he said, "and have often felt the lack of both."[8] Shortly after he left school, Debs tried to overcome these deficiencies by memorizing parts of orations and poems, by studying a set of *Appleton's Encyclopedias,* and by attending Garwin's Business College. No one could judge the agitator illiterate, but Debs' self-education resulted in few changes in his philosophy. Debs quickly became involved in his youth in a maelstrom of historical changes, and because of his convictions and courage to speak out, he emerged a leader. But he never took time from his writing and speaking to stand back and appraise objectively the changes that America had undergone. Each project or campaign so completely occupied his waking hours, that he had little time to study. His long speaking trips meant that correspondence often never caught up with him and that at these times, he did not have the time or energy to worry about what the men in the national office of his party or those on the executive committee were thinking. But at other times, he used his travels to personally investigate party matters and conduct interviews for information. Since he travelled far more than any other member of the executive committee of the Socialist Party, he had an advantage when the board discussed the status of the party. Periodically, he announced plans to take off a year for study and travel around the world to view socialism at work, but some strike case, or party need for money from his lecturing would prevent him from ever taking this rest and study. Both his speeches and articles had a redundant quality, and aside from the value of repetition in his speeches, both needed vigorous editing.[9]

The materials that Debs used in his oral and written arguments reflected both the shortcomings of his education and the values of his first hand experiences among laboring people. Although Debs' logic lacked rigorous discipline in the development of his arguments, his keen sense of the importance of key issues made him a prophet for certain causes. Rather than construct tightly knit arguments, Debs articulated from his experiences the truth that prompted workers to demand changes in the status quo. He often rambled from one experience to another without adequate transition. Debs weakened his arguments by overusing generalizations and various propaganda devices. In both his speaking and writing, he often failed to present the facts and figures that might have proved the assumptions that he made. Many times, he reduced the solution of a problem to two choices and ignored other possible causes and answers. Many of Debs' listeners did not care or notice whether he documented his charges. Crowds cheered when he called John D. Rockefeller, George Pullman, or Andrew Carnegie typical capitalists and compared their incomes to the wages of ordinary workers. Most of Debs' listeners failed to realize that he used examples and extreme figures that made the contrast greater. The following excerpt, similar to some that have been cited for other purposes in this book, typified Debs' frequent use of overstatement, especially when upbraiding "capitalists". In a talk to steel workers, Debs declared, "The capitalist does no useful work. . . . He lives in a palace in which there is music and dancing. . . . He is the man who furnished the funds with which politics are corrupted and debauched."[10] In spite of his overstatements, some editors praised Debs for his logic and concluded: "There is more truth in his views than is good for this great republic."[11] After hearing Debs address twenty-five thousand at a Milwaukee Socialist picnic, Lincoln Steffens commented: "There is nothing demagogic about that speech. It was impassioned, but orderly; radical, but granting the premises, especially those advocating socialism as the only answer to any economic or political problem the government encountered, logically reasoned."[12] Many workers between 1875 and 1925 appreciated Debs' remarks about strikes and the expansion of business and thus granted his "premises" without reservation.

Since Debs seldom used notes when he spoke, he quoted few statistics, and then only of a most general nature. The speech Steffens heard was no exception. Rather than marshal an impressive array of facts, Debs kept repeating his ideas in terms the listeners understood. He substituted verbal imagery for facts. Even in his writings, he did not use a large number of statistics. From 1895 to 1908, he used more statistical evidence than he did in his later more militant speaking and writing against World War I. When he did use figures to support his ideas, he gleaned them from government documents, annual reports of corporations, and reports of special investigations, as when, in speeches to railroad workers in 1906, he cited a report of the Interstate Commerce Commission that showed the growth in numbers of railroad employees from 779,608 to 1,296,121 in 1904, with approximately 1,400,000 workers in 1906.[13] He later used these figures to illustrate the rapid gains of the industry compared to the slow economic and social gains of the workers. Speaking on prison labor before the wealthy gentlemen's Nineteenth Century Club at Delmonico's in New York City, Debs effectively cited an investigation in South Carolina that revealed that "out of 285 prisoners employed by one company, 128, or more than 40 per cent, died as the result, largely of brutal treatment." Another company, The Tennessee Coal and Iron Company, supposedly leased convicts to force the wages of miners down to the point of subsistence.[14] But Debs' listeners would have had difficulty checking his proof because he did not indicate what wages were before or after the employment of convicts. He seldom documented the sources of the few facts that he used. In a 1908 speech, he announced that "according to the reports furnished us, twenty per cent of the workingmen of this country are now out of employment."[15] No mention followed of who provided the reports. In the famous Canton, Ohio, speech, which led to his arrest for opposing World War I, Debs stated two figures: "That the 121 federal judges owed their appointments to corporate connections; and that 52 percent of the arable land had been held out of production by landlords, speculators and profiteers."[16] On one occasion, Debs did prepare an impressive array of figures, but the judge denied his request to deliver them. In his speech to the jury in Cleveland, Debs asked the judge if he could give evidence of profiteering during the war. The judge ruled that such facts had no bearing on his indictment.[17]

For proof, Debs also made frequent use of comparisons, especially in his anti-war speaking. In his speech before the jury in Canton in 1918, Debs hypothesized that history proved the views of minorities eventually triumph. He proceeded to support each of his contentions with some event in history that he thought analogous to his stand against the war. Later, in his last major speech before his incarceration in the Atlanta prison, he made this statement: "Abolitionism was the Bolshevism of that day."[18] In this analogy, Debs disregarded the point that Bolshevism and abolitionism have more differences than likenesses. In this same address before the Cleveland Socialist Party, Debs said, "I have faith in the Man of Galilee. Twenty centuries ago, he spoke to the common people. . . . They said he preached dangerous doctrines. He was a Bolshevist." Again the comparison represented an oversimplification. In other comparisons, Debs reasoned that if men were fit to be political equals, they were also fit to be economic equals, and concluded that if they were economic equals, they would be social equals. Debs sincerely believed that such a Utopian transformation in human beings would take place under the system he proposed.

Rather than rely on documents and figures, Debs based the strength of his arguments upon the experiences that he had had and the accounts others related to him. He often mentioned stories that he had heard of injustice, poverty, and corruption. Before and after every speech, staunch supporters beseiged Debs to tell him their personal ordeals. Whenever he returned to Terre Haute to write articles, a constant stream of workers came to visit him and tell him of their experiences. Daily he received letters with reports of injustices against workers. One danger in this method of collecting evidence was that the informants filled their stories with emotional judgments. Debs had little chance to check their authenticity. He wove these stories into a chain of examples which served as support for his assertions and extended illustration became the rhetorical plan or organizational pattern for his writings and addresses. For example, a partial list of illustrations that Debs used in a speech to steel workers, later published both in the party press and as a pamphlet, follows: "It has not been a great while ago that the operators on the Missouri, Kansas, and Texas Railroad appointed their committees. . ."; "We had another case on the Great Northern and Northern Pacific system when the telegraph operators went out on strike . . ."; "Here in Chicago, you have witnessed the defeat of one section after another of the army of organized labor. . ."[19] After each of these statements, Debs proceeded to give a detailed account of what had happened. In this manner, Debs related to his listeners and readers his firsthand knowledge of the labor situation. "When I travelled over the Southern states thirty-five years ago organizing the workers, oh, what a desolate, unpromising situation it was! I made my appeal to unions wherever I went to open their doors to the colored workers upon equal terms with the white workers, but they refused," Debs told an audience of black workers in New York in 1923. "Poor as most of them were, they still felt themselves superior to the colored people," he stated.[20] Following this general statement about his experiences in trying to improve racial relations in the unions, Debs proceeded to recall specific incidents in Atlanta, Georgia, Montgomery, Alabama, Louisville, Kentucky, and other places where he had observed prejudice. [Debs' interest in Blacks will be discussed later in this chapter.] This accumulation of examples enhanced his logical appeal to his listeners, but his use of them created a loosely arranged speech or article. Debs' rapid fire delivery of his speeches made his lack of organization less noticeable to his audiences, but his articles, lacking the vocal mode of emphasis, rambled.

Debs effectively turned these illustrations into strong emotional appeals. He would extend these examples into a plea for change, making it difficult to tell where the anecdote ended and Debs' persuasion began. His sensitive, sentimental nature made it easy for him to overstress this appeal. Reverend John Hayne Holmes, who knew Debs well, said "Debs could be fierce and furious. Unforgettable were his bursts of wrath when moved by some torture of the body or degradation of the soul. It was this that made his oratory of such surpassing power. He had but to hear an injustice visited upon helpless workers to unleash his spirit in a dreadful passion of resentment."[21] These excerpts taken from his speeches, articles, and letters illustrate his sentimental nature and his "spirit in a dreadful passion"—a passion that endeared him to many workers.

"Labor, at least that part not reduced to the dullness and servility of 'The Man with the Hoe', will arouse and unify in the next year or two and take cognizance of the trend of the economic development from which there is now evolving a new and progressive trade unionism. . . Such alleged leaders as Arthur and other high officials who are on terms of intimacy with the oppressors of labor and whose leadership consists in keeping labor in chains will be ignominiously retired. . . In the campaign of 1900, the Socialist Party will surprise the country; in 1904, if it does not carry the country, it will take second place, and in 1908, it will sweep into power in spite of hell and all its furies. What will it do to the trusts? In the language of the Bowery, 'Oh, not a thing!' But you insist on an answer. . .[22]

"Most of you are children of the poor; few of the rich, but you all are children of a common father, and all sisters and brothers in the great family of humankind. If you think you are better. . . your young minds have been tainted by wrong examples and wrong education."[23]

"To talk about reforming these rotten graft infested unions, which are dominated absolutely by the labor boss is a vain and wasteful use of time."[24]

"The greatest misfortune of the average workingman is that he is so easily satisfied. He is so strongly inclined to be content. Give him a miserable job; a two-by-four boss to wield the hunger whip over him; a place to sleep and enough to eat to circulate his blood and keep him in working order, and his ambition is satisfied. I want to do what little I can to reach him and rouse him. I am an agitator. . . The capitalists want no agitation—they are on top, they rule, they own, they have, they want to remain where they are, they protest against change. Don't you know that by change, you have everything to gain and nothing to lose? Marx expressed it over a half century ago. He said, 'You have a world to gain and nothing to lose but your chains.' "[25]

"In bourgeois wars the revolutionary elements are shoved into the first line trenches to shoot off one another's heads and at the same time shoot the head off the revolution, and thereby restore the status quo for another indefinite period."[26]

"I wish you could have heard my speech. Billy Sunday is here and I took him on the line—stripped him stark naked and the crowd went wild as I showed him for the kind of charlatan he is. See papers. They give a fair report. . . I'm giving war hell— peeling the hides off the patriots. . ."[27]

These quotations not only indicated Debs' sentimental nature and intense feelings but the somewhat aggressive direct manner in which he identified himself with the workers he hoped to influence to change society.

When Debs used these emotional appeals, he effectively employed a number of persuasive devices. While he had never studied techniques of persuasion, he discovered via experience the ways to get his blue denim followers to respond. Although the following remarks appeared in a pamphlet copy of a speech which Debs delivered to an audience of children at Pullman, Illinois, years after the strike, they typify his intensive use of appeals to fair play, happiness, security, honesty, freedom, pride, honor, loyalty and other basic human needs. In using these appeals, notice how Debs again related to his listeners by reflecting upon his experiences: "In my railroad career I had occasion to go out to the coal camps to visit the miners in their miserable, wretched hovels. I saw them so poorly fed and clad that my heart ached when I saw their little children in the street." Attempting to enlist the children in the ranks of socialism, he appealed to their sense of duty, self-respect, achievement, and opportunity: "They try to withhold the truth from you children who are the next generation and will rule the world in the future. I would have you know the meaning of socialism because it is a great thing. In this field you will find opportunity for those fine abilities we have seen displayed this afternoon. You have ability and want to extend it in useful service." Promising that socialism would change conditions. Debs concluded with appeals to fear and honor: "I hope none of you children will have to go to jail, but if you do I am sure you will go as cheerfully as I went there. They cannot punish us if we are true to ourselves."[28]

Debs could effectively combine a series of parallel negative statements into a strong emotional appeal. For example, when speaking to an audience surrounded by policemen, Debs censured the striking workers: "Don't strike a blow. Don't object to having your job taken away from you. Don't mind such a small thing as seeing your wife starving or your children hungry and perhaps homeless, about to be evicted because the rent cannot be paid. Just remember that you ought to be a law-abiding citizen and allow them to die."[29] Before a banquet crowd in Schenectady, New York, Debs charged: "If you belong to the party of the future, then this is your party. If you prefer democracy to despotism; peace to war; brotherhood to brutehood; if you have a system in which all would be properly clothed and fed, in which all would cooperate, instead of being rivals; if you would humanize humanity and civilize civilization; then this is your party."[30] In many other speeches and articles to laborers he frequently used this same negative approach: "You are not very intelligent now. If you were those two old parties would not be as powerful. . . If you weren't so foolish, you would have put yourself in a position to have a fair share. . ."[31] Only a spokesman such as Debs who commanded the respect of the workers could have made such statements without incurring their resentment. A Socialist writer succinctly summarized Debs' persuasion when he wrote: "Debs is essentially the evangelist of the Socialist movement. He understands how useless is the academic attitude in missionary work. He comprehends the psychology of the multitude, and he reached their reason through their hearts."[32] Norman Thomas stated essentially the same thing: "Debs wasn't the intellect of the Party but he was emphatically the heart of the Party."[33]

Debs knew that he had the ability to move an audience and, perhaps as a result, spent too little time throughout his life on the preparation and organization of his speeches. He disliked the arduous task of writing and rewriting. His prepared scripts differed little in style from stenographic reports of hundreds of his extemporaneous talks. Those addresses written in his office or home library contained more quotations from literary men and various government documents than those he composed enroute, but even these excerpts lacked analysis or adequate documentation. For each of the presidential campaigns, he drafted two or three basic outlines, and then varied these as he used them on the campaign trail. In one town he would discuss unemployment, and perhaps child labor in the next. Debs liked to wait and "let the crowd inspire" the speech that he delivered. Debs confided in his friend, Edwin Markham, his antipathy toward organizing his ideas on paper when he said "writing is like giving birth to a rough-shod colt."[34] Frequently the spokesman declared that he preferred the platform to the desk, and found speaking easier than writing.

Debs often failed to keep the central idea in focus, instead losing it in a series of collateral theses. As a result, his ideas lacked clear subordination and transitional signposts to guide his readers or listeners. Internal summaries would have helped his organization and given greater clarity to his long involved sentences. Debs had the ability to make individual remarks quite clear, but too often he developed them in isolation from his main contention. Part of the reason for this discursiveness can be attributed to Debs' habit of dictating his writings to his brother, Theodore, as he paced about the room. Although Eugene discussed ideas with Theodore, he seldom received criticism from him. Since they so frequently experienced the same events; heard the same informants; read the same sources, they rarely disagreed. Without Theodore's services, Eugene never could have delivered so many speeches, written so many articles, or continued his numerous agitating activities. Theodore handled the calendar and selected the letters that needed answers. He also brought to his brother's attention the assignments for speeches and articles he thought Eugene should accept. At a reception in

Boston for Debs, Horace Traubel paid tribute to Theodore when he stated: "No one can really claim knowing Debs without knowing Theodore."[35] Theodore, who possessed a quick temper, tried to guard his brother against many exhausting outside demands and attacks by critics, but he often failed to get Eugene to conserve his strength and not engage in long disputes or discussions after his lectures.

Aside from his role as an essayist, pamphleteer, and speaker for the causes of labor and socialism, Debs skillfully played another role as leader and member of the National Executive Committee [N.E.B. in earlier years] of the Socialist Party. Periodically he served as chairman of this group, in addition to running five times as presidential candidate. In the early struggles within the party hierarchy, Debs realized that neither he nor the Socialist Party movement had much to gain from these fights. He recognized the strength in the combined factions but knew that no leader could entirely satisfy the wishes of such diverse and strong personalities as Berger, Hillquit, DeLeon, Herron, and others, who led the various factions. After all the internal squabbling ended, Debs perceived that someone had to unify the party, and secure the funds and lead the campaign for votes. In the early conventions that Debs attended, he became embroiled in the arguments. Aside from the fact that he had little patience for Socialists who wasted their energies fighting one another instead of the capitalists, Debs discovered that after the conventions, he had a difficult time uniting the party. By adopting the strategy of avoiding the convention scene, he irked his opponents, but he developed a method whereby he emerged as leader without increasing personal animosity between himself and his opponents. In order to do this, Debs had to know that he had the support of the "Jimmie Higginses" and that certain delegates would represent his views. His continual writing and speaking had made him the best known figure in the party and thus he had the assurance that when official party actions, which required approval by a national referendum, were taken, he could win. Debs cultivated support from the rank and file party members rather than the executive committee. Debs also never failed to have on the convention floor ample spokesmen for his views. Prior to each convention, key delegates came to him or wrote to secure his opinions. Debs wrote letters to other delegates and asked them to make sure certain items were included or not included in the platform.[36] He consistently advocated an aggressive platform that demanded immediate government control by workers, for he feared Berger and his "Slowcialists" would take a more moderate stand. Ideas Debs advocated for changing this government into a socialist nation do appear in the platforms. Only in 1920 did he publicly protest against a platform, and he did so then because he felt the planks on the past war were too weak. Delegates who visited Debs knew that Debs would run and countered rumors that he would not. Berger and Hillquit forces often ran other candidates in opposition to Debs, but they lost after a few ballots and succeeded only in compromising upon a vice-presidential candidate. Theodore Debs attended a number of the early conventions as an official delegate from Indiana and certainly represented his brother's interests. Debs often had been designated as a state delegate, and thus could have exercised his option to attend if he ever wanted to change his strategy. The fact that he might attend intrigued reporters and younger delegates, but older party stalwarts knew better. In a letter to his wife, Hillquit commented on the persistent rumors in the newspapers that Debs might attend a convention. He assured her that Debs would find ample reasons to avoid the event.[37]

Although Debs avoided the national conventions, he attended many of the executive committee meetings. His correspondence contains many letters to committee members in which he sought further information about business items prior to these meetings. Theodore tried to make sure that when Debs traveled, letters concerning party matters would reach him. Debs took time to answer these letters or directed Theodore to make specific replies. It cannot be said that Debs did not know what was going on in his party. Too many letters, both in Debs' manuscripts and in those of other prominent party officials who corresponded with one another, indicate that he had a vital concern in party direction and that other officers cared whether he favored an idea or not. When Debs could not attend board meetings, he often sent telegrams or letters explaining his ideas. After the bitter fight over Barnes as campaign manager in 1908, Debs found himself at odds with the national office staff. Berger did little to discourage this kind of conflict since several office appointments, including Barnes, respresented his interests. Partly because of this mutual distrust, Debs maintained his own office in Terre Haute and never closed it.

Debs read Marx's *Das Kapital* in 1895 during his Pullman Strike jail sentence. He later did read more of Marx and biographies about him.[38] Debs never made pretensions of expanding Marx's socialistic theories. More frequently in his writing or speaking Debs quoted other writers that he admired, especially Hugo, Shakespeare, Longfellow, Markham, Holmes, and Whitman—all literary figures. In his defense of socialism, he usually ignored both the translated works of Marx, Engels, and Kautsky, and the tracts of Herron, Hunter, Seidel, Berger, Hillquit, Walling, and other prominent American Socialists. This annoyed scholars in the party. V. F. Calverton, a party writer who frequently opposed Debs, asserted that "Debs was not a theoretician. He was innocent of subtlety, and ignorant of logic. He spoke from the heart rather than the head. His Marxism, if it could be called such, was more instinctive than intellectual."[39] On the one hundreth anniversary of Marx's birth, Debs wrote an essay honoring Marx. In this article Debs stated that it would be "reckless imprudence" for him to think that he could do justice to Marx the "revolutionary inspirer and leader." Rather than write about Marx's ideas, Debs chose to write about "Marx the Man," but he first noted that "no pen or tongue" could do Marx justice.[40] Interestingly, Debs avoided on this occasion, as he had in his other writings, any detailed analysis or comments that might have indicated the depth or precision of his knowledge of Marx's socialist theories. In the following quotation Debs does reveal his admiration for Marx and summarize what he thought of him:

"Karl Marx as a scientific and scholarly investigator, writer, and author in the field of economic, political and social research stands pre-eminent before the world. As the triumphant awakener of the long-asleep and the revolutionary leader of the long-enslaved masses of mankind he towers before us a titan and without a peer in history. But it is in his character as a man that he stands supreme and challenges the respect and love, the admiration and emulation of the modern world.

Had Marx, the Man, been weak, Marx the scientist and scholar would never have aroused, inspired and set into motion the masses by his masterly genius and fulfilled the world with the fame of his immortal achievement.

Stern, inflexible, self-forgetting, and rigidly scrupulous and honest he presents to us today the inspiring figure of a man.

. . . Had he but consented to negotiate, to bargain, to compromise with the ruling powers, he and his loved ones would never have been driven into the desert and compelled to bear in cold and hunger and tears the bitter bread of poverty and exile. But Karl Marx was immeasurably above and beyond temptation; his lofty character disdained all dickering and temporizing; he stood . . . inflexible as granite in his moral rectitude . . . he would not, could not pervert or prostitute his ideas and ideals, the children of his brain and soul. . ."[41]

All evidence available indicates that Calverton's judgment was accurate. The quotation above does indicate that Marx's steadfastness to his beliefs influenced Debs.

A number of prominent men admired Debs, not for his teaching of doctrine but for his persuasive impact over blue-denim audiences. Debs preferred agitation to theory building. In an interview with Lincoln Steffens, Debs stated with some seriousness that when the Socialist Party got close to electing a man to take over the White House, he would step aside.[42] In an interview Norman Thomas spoke of Debs' ability to hold audiences with "a language and style a little florid for our time."[43] Thomas stated that he admired Debs but had a difficult time in the beginning because audiences expected him to be like Debs. Upton Sinclair, who knew Debs and heard him speak on several occasions, wrote: "I was impressed—very warm kind man. . . . Debs never used a note. He knew his speeches as an actor does. They were his life . . . He spoke with fire and fervor; his enemies would say he ranted. He put his whole soul into it."[44] Although Claude Bowers, the historian, never agreed with Debs' politics, he summarized Debs' appeal to workers when he wrote: "Debs' oratory was good, and many passages of his speeches had a literary flavor. He was a phrasemaker, and his humor and gentle irony brought cheers and laughter. His voice was pleasant, and his charm in conversation was transmitted from the platform."[45]

Perhaps another reason why Debs ignored theory was that his opposition within the national executive committee prided themselves on this knowledge. From the time that Debs broke with Berger over the colonization scheme, the two men seldom agreed. Others who had positions of influence and did some writing, such as Frederick Heath and John Spargo, also sided with Berger. When Debs abandoned the colonization idea, he never regained a position of prominence on deciding theoretical matters. Debs left the theoretical disputes to DeLeon, Berger, Hillquit, and others. In order for Debs to continue to lead his party it was not necessary that he intellectually mastermind it. In fact, he increased his support among the common workers by talking about problems they confronted rather than lecturing them on political theory. What theory Debs did use he translated into terms the workers could follow.

Sometimes Debs aggravated his party's officials by openly supporting ideas and people more militant than the executive committee wanted to endorse. He also sometimes forced his party to take a firmer stand of support for freedom of speech and assembly for anarchists such as Emma Goldman and for William Haywood and to help free imprisoned I.W.W. leaders. In this sense he served as a conscience to his executive committee opponents, as he continually prodded them to not sit back and become satisfied with the progressive legislation that began to enter the law ,books. Debs' impatience with the step-at-a-time philosophy and gradual takeover of political reins by concentrating on electing office holders a few at a time was well known. He wanted more immediate changes and feared the workers would accept some concessions without pressing on to change the system that he thought caused these problems.

Just how radical was Debs? In his own time Debs was perceived to be radical by a majority of Americans. Anyone who dared speak out as Debs did against well-established tycoons like Pullman, Rockefeller, Hill, or Carnegie, and presidents from Theodore Roosevelt to Woodrow Wilson invited "image" trouble. Within his party Debs carried out the leadership role of a radical because he wanted to abolish the private ownership of property. In Debs' party the term radical meant one who intended to go to the roots of society and change society to benefit all, not merely reform aspects of it. Debs insisted as a Marxist that the social structure had to be changed and the people placed in control of the economy. Debs never wavered from this essential radical demand that capitalism had to be replaced because he believed only socialism could give the workers this kind of economic control. This would require extreme changes in the established order in America and Debs accepted that challenge.

In most controversies with labor, the press in Debs' time certainly supported management and inflamed public opinion against leaders of strikers. The same was true of anti-war speakers. Some writers define a radical as one who disagrees with the establishment and will try to correct it by any possible means, including extreme or drastic measures to bring about the changes desired. Debs did try to correct the status quo but not at the expense of any available means. Debs above all was a remarkable, compassionate human who left that impression with others, even his enemies. He had little stomach for violence and bloodshed. However, Debs by his remarks created part of the confusion over his radicalness. He sometimes with pride used the label radical when referring to himself or spoke of the need for radical actions when the time was right. For example, in an essay, "Reorganizing the International," Debs stressed the need for infusing the "true revolutionary spirit" into the party and warned of "impending disaster" if that spirit were lacking in the days to come." He declared "There is never a danger of being too revolutionary; the danger that always threatens is in not being revolutionary enough, to the discouragement and disgust and final loss of the virile, active, energetic and inspiriting element that is the very life and soul of the organization. . ." In that same essay, he spoke of the need to rebuild the Socialist Party after the war (WWI) ended and strengthen it by making it "truly militant" so the party would be "equal to every opportunity and to any test or crises that fate or fortune may have in store for it."[46]

In another article "Sound Socialist Tactics" Debs explained his stand on radical actions. The essay, like references in his speeches exemplified the way in which Debs tended to talk on both sides of the issue of radical actions in an effort to achieve party harmony. First he stated that Socialists essentially agreed on fundamental principles but "as to tactics there is wide variance." He next referred to a paragraph in a pamphlet titled "Industrial Socialism" by William D. Haywood and Frank Bohn. This paragraph which follows had become quite controversial among Socialists and also the press: "When the worker, either through experience or study of socialism, comes to know this truth (i.e. socialism must replace capitalism and wage slavery), he acts accordingly. He retains absolutely no respect for the property 'rights' of the profit-takers. He will use any weapon which will win his fight. He knows present laws of property are made by and for the capitalists. Therefore, he does not hesitate to break them." Debs wrote that "For my part I believe the paragraph to be entirely sound." But his explanation doesn't support that statement!

Note in this next paragraph how Debs endorsed potentially radical actions in the opening sentence but then backed away from any desire to carry them out.

As a revolutionist I can have no respect for capitalist property laws, nor the least scruple about violating them. I hold all such laws to have been enacted through chicanery, fraud and corruption . . . But this does not imply that I propose making an individual lawbreaker of myself and butting my head against a stone wall of existing property laws. That might be called force but it would not be that. It would be mere weakness and folly.

In a further statement he made this interesting remark:

"If I had the force to overthrow these despotic laws, I would use it without an instant's hesitation or delay, but I haven't got it, and so I am law abiding under protest—not from scruple—and bide my time.

Here let me say that for the same reason I am opposed to sabotage and to 'direct action'. I have not a bit of use for 'propaganda of the deed'. These are the tactics of anarchist individualists and not Socialist collectivists."

This 1912 article better than any other explained Debs' views on radical actions. After Debs had contended that he didn't take such actions because he felt they were foredoomed to failure because he lacked the force and support to carry them out, he gave further reasons. He feared that using force could have a boomerang effect on Socialists. "The blow he strikes reacts upon himself and his followers," he warned. He admitted that the "frenzied deed of a glorious fanatic like old John Brown seems to have been inspired by Jehovah himself" but cautioned that it happened in a past century and wouldn't work in his time. In Debs' judgment only when "acute situations arise and grave emergencies occur, perhaps with life at stake," could violence be justified. Debs advised that the Socialist movement couldn't predicate its tactical procedure upon such exceptional instances. "My chief objection to all these measures is that they do violence to the class psychology of the workers and cannot be inculcated as mass doctrine," he declared. To him, guerilla warfare, bomb planters, midnight assassins, and such warfare played into the hands of the enemy. "Such tactics appeal to stealth and suspicion and cannot make for solidarity," he wrote. "The very teaching of sneaking and surreptitious practices has a demoralizing affect," Debs concluded. Furthermore, he declared he didn't want the Socialist Party to attract and become a haven for dynamiters, safe blowers and "every spy or madman."

Also, Debs discussed the Industrial Workers of the World and asserted that their principles of industrial unionism were sound but that their tactics had stymied their growth. "The American workers are law abiding . . . direct action will never appeal to any considerable number of them while they have the ballot and the right of industrial and political organization," Debs concluded. To achieve Debs' goal of a socialist system, he stressed the importance of educating the workers to the advantages of an economy they controlled and directed. In this respect Debs remained consistent in his advice—it differed little from the advice he gave workers in his first years as a railroad organizer and editor-speaker. Near the end of this provocative essay, Debs lessened the impact of what he had said by suggesting that Haywood and Bohn had not meant the blackjack, lead pipe, and sawed-off shotgun when they stated the "use of any weapon which will win the fight."[47] This remark begged the question and indirectly showed Debs' inability to make a clean break with Haywood and Bohn. Debs grew weary of the internal fighting within the I.W.W. but didn't hold Haywood responsible—the man who had the greatest influence in that organization. Another reason why Debs never made a complete separation with the I.W.W. was his hope that eventually differences would be settled that the I.W.W. would gain greater strength and become the economic arm of the socialist movement and the Socialist Party the political arm. Debs cherished the idea of industrial unionism spreading throughout this country and from its founding in 1905 hoped that the I.W.W. would accelerate that movement. He believed that workers needed to join together in industrial unions and then vote together as Socialist Party members to effectively defend their interests.

Other examples could be cited that prove that Debs in all cases stopped short of taking or advising violent actions. He confused the public by talking about revolution and the revolutionary spirit in generalities. He remained a man who hoped to reason out problems and solve them. He hoped educating the workers would lead to a peaceful overthrow via the ballot box. He had naive faith in the ballot box! Idealogically he kept left of Berger who called Debs and his followers "impossibilists" but not so far left as to embrace those who advocated radical actions. Debs was sort of a romantic but he controlled his actions. His behavior was essentially pacifistic. Debs defied injunctions in early strikes but he did not destroy factories or railroads or try through violent means to escape or prevent his arrests. He challenged the government in his anti-war speaking but he never destroyed or advocated the destruction of government property. Although Debs was totally involved emotionally in his hate of World War I and its proponents, he never suggested in any speech or writing that his followers impede the war efforts by direct intervention methods.

This position on radical tactics which Debs explained in 1912 he adhered to in the years that followed. The public often misconstrued his later support of I.W.W. leaders in court trials as endorsement of them. In 1918, he again explained his point of view in an essay, "The I.W.W. Bogey." He stated, "I think I may claim to be fairly well informed as to the methods and tactics of the I.W.W.—with some of which I am not at all in agreement." (Note how the word "some" raised again the question of which ones Debs might have meant!) Debs' strong plea in this article is that the "hundreds of I.W.W.'s and Socialists now in jail are entitled to be fairly tried."[48] Regardless of the charges or radical tactics, Debs wanted justice within the American judicial system until socialism replaced it. His stand was much like we find the American Civil Liberties Union taking today in controversial cases. Another factor affecting Debs' image as a radical was his endorsement of the revolution in Russia. This made him a radical in part of the public's eye. But Debs changed his views within a short time when he discovered the workers in Russia were no better off under communism and denounced the new Communist Party leaders. Since Debs had contacts with the I.W.W., the Communists, and other dissenters, many people found it satisfying to assume that Debs believed as they did. Debs got a chance to defend himself from such charges in the Socialist press but not in the newspapers and magazines that the masses read. Debs served his followers as a radical reformer and agitator against the status quo but not one who advocated illegal means. Debs used propaganda of the word, not propaganda of the deed.

Because of the techniques that Debs used and the role that he played in the party in creating a pressure group for change, certain of his ideas were followed and had an impact upon the course of history. Certainly his dynamic leadership as a labor spokesman helped many workers gain the right to organize and to strike if necessary to receive safer working conditions, higher wages, and welfare benefits. His vigorous opposition to women and children working in factories, and to all employees working excessive hours, started in the 1880's—long before he became a Socialist. The industry-wide plan of union organization that predominates in America today had its first strong advocate in Debs. Gompers opposed every move in this direction. When Gompers later said that labor should enter the field of political action, Debs noted his belated entry: "In arriving at this conclusion Mr. Gompers is about a quarter of a century behind his more intelligent followers. . . I never knew Mr. Gompers to risk his throat or breastbone in the leading of any great strike or ever go within the range of any injunction or a Gatling gun."[49] Behind Debs' terse comment is the fact that Debs often led the way on political issues; he created the propaganda and persuasion and other labor leaders, often within the A.F. of L., later followed. Debs' strong stand with the I.W.W. and its leader, Bill Haywood, slowed progress on the industrial union issue, because workers hesitated to join forces with Haywood. In January 1969 when the railroad brotherhoods of Trainmen, Firemen and Enginemen, Conductors and Brakemen, and the Switchmen finally merged into the United Transportation Union, the officers announced that Debs' ARU dream of one big union had been achieved.[50] Other men spoke on these issues and deserve credit, but few would deny that Debs' strong voice had an effect. Debs advocated in the Socialist Party most of the planks he upheld as a Populist. He often took what was considered at the time the most radical stand on an issue. This aggressiveness attracted many to pay some attention to issues they might have ignored. Although the majority of Americans judged Debs' overall solution of socialism wrong, they eventually adopted ideas that he championed into their own political platforms.

Debs vociferously opposed a fellow Hoosier, Albert Beveridge, on the issue of imperialism. His opposition to the imperialistic movement typified his interest in other causes. He championed the underdog and conducted a vigilant campaign to secure justice for minority interests. This constant support of causes that in the beginning represented minority views became one of his important contributions to history. By speaking against presidential decisions of Cleveland, Roosevelt, and Wilson, Debs furthered the legal rights of minority groups. Many citizens thought his denunciation of World War I and the Espionage Act was not patriotic, but perhaps it helped to prevent Americans from becoming as intolerant of dissent in World War II. Debs understood war hysteria and gave in his "Canton Speech" a timeless condemnation of super-patriots. In Debs' opinion, citizens "who wrapped up in the American flag; who made the claim that they were the only patriots, who had their magnifying glasses in hand, who scanned the country for some evidence of disloyalty, so eager to apply the brand to men who dared to whisper opposition," constituted a far greater danger to democracy than those who opposed it.

Other issues Debs supported included women's right to vote, judicial and prison reforms, birth control, and equal opportunities for Blacks. Margaret Sanger got Debs to write items for her birth control publications. She asked for permission to quote his statements at "open meetings, knowing the weight it would have with the intelligent people of this country."[51] Debs' support in the Sacco-Vanzetti case represented his keen interest in justice, although some editors charged that he sought publicity by endorsing "other anarchists."

Debs consistently opposed all discrimination toward Blacks but he had little success in securing jobs or a large role for them within the Socialist Party. Repeatedly Debs advised union officers and Socialist locals to admit Blacks on an equal basis. Before Debs became a Socialist, he came to the conclusion that Blacks could make their greatest gains through organization into unions. In an 1896 speaking tour throughout the South as a Populist he stated "the only solution for the Negro laborer was organization."[52] After joining the Socialists, Debs held to this view but substituted the word party for union in his thinking and speaking. Debs saw the struggle that Blacks faced as parallel to the struggle White workers faced. By combining forces to overthrow "wage slavery" he thought both would be freed via socialism. Economic equality supposedly would solve social and racial inequality.

The official Socialist Party attitude essentially followed the same premises and although Debs made stronger comments from time to time on behalf of Blacks, he never succeeded in rallying the officers of the party to lead a fight for Black rights. Probably to keep peace within the party Debs took a "middle of the road" stand on this issue in the early years to encourage party growth but later his views changed and he did become more direct and militant on the subject. Within the executive committee of the party the Black issue caused dissention. The "Rights" led by Berger did not want to get involved and thought Southern as well as some Northern workers would not join the party if it meant equality with Blacks. Berger once declared "There can be no doubt that the Negroes and mulattoes constitute a lower race—that the caucasian and indeed even the mongolian have the start on them in civilization by many thousand years—so that the Negro will find it difficult ever to overtake them. The many cases of rape which occur whenever Negroes are settled in large numbers prove, moreover, that the free contact with the whites has led to further degradation . . ." Such sentiments by party officials made Debs' task of securing admittance of Blacks into the party all the more difficult. In the Socialist Party Unity Convention in 1901, the party after a long floor fight did adopt a resolution introduced by William Costley, one of three Black delegates, declaring the party's support for Blacks and urging them to join.[53] This resolution remained the only one for years that specifically directed attention to Black support. Only William Walling among the leaders in the Socialist Party made a strong stand for Black rights. This popular writer and close friend of Debs helped found the N.A.A.C.P. Another Socialist, Charles Edward Russell, aided the N.A.A.C.P.

In 1903 the executive committee of the party in which Debs certainly had a voice denied Louisiana a state charter until they removed a specific clause forbidding Blacks to join except in separate locals. Their attitude was that the party's statement declaring itself open to all on an equal basis regardless of race or creed had to be upheld and that anti-Black statements or plans for separate locals invited unnecessary criticism and problems. Louisiana removed the offensive clause, however locals for Blacks continued and some letter writers in the Socialist press advised them for the North as well.[54] Aware of this controversy Debs wrote in 1903 that Blacks deserved "absolute equality with his white brother and where this was not the case the genius of unionism was violated and investigations will disclose the fact that corporate power and its henchmen are back of it." He continued by declaring that "what the Negro wants is not charity but industrial freedom and then he will attend to his own education." Next Debs made this remark that revealed his thinking at this time: "There is no Negro problem apart from the labor problem. The Negro is not one whit worse off than thousands of white slaves who throng the same labor market to sell their labor power to the same industrial masters."[55] Unfortunately Debs ignored the fact that discrimination and widespread poverty among Blacks made their life conditions worse than Whites.

In another essay written the same year Debs again recognized the merits of the Black's cause but offered generalizations for solutions. After stating that the "whole world is under obligation to the Negro, and that the white heel is still upon the black neck is simply proof that the world is not yet civilized," Debs declared again that "there is no Negro question outside of the labor question—the working class struggle." To him the capitalists stood on one side and the workers "white, black, and all other shades" stood on the other side. He cited Marx's remark "workingmen of all countries unite" as reason for all races to join together. "The question of social equality would disappear when the Negro had economic freedom," he declared.[56]

Between 1904-1915, Debs continued individual acts of kindness and support of Blacks. He noted from time to time in his speeches and writings examples of gross discrimination against Blacks in law cases and how management used Blacks in strikes against Whites. He told union officials they asked for this abuse by Black workers because they didn't organize them and accept them as equals in their unions. The party reaffirmed its general statement on race in 1904 when it passed by a referendum this statement, "Every person, resident of the United States, of the age of 18 years and upward, without distinction of sex, race, color, or creed who has severed his connection with all other parties is eligible for membership."[57] On questions of race, Debs would refer to this official measure and sometimes quote it in his messages. Debs assumed equality would come with socialism. Theodore Roosevelt noted that the Socialist Party did not wholeheartedly accept Blacks and all immigrants and asserted that "if the leaders of the Socialist Party would force their followers to admit all Negroes and Chinamen to real equality their party would disband." Debs replied to Roosevelt that the "party admits to membership on terms of equality of men and women of all races. And this platform has been approved by rank and

216

file."[58] But the rank and file had little power and less leadership to enforce the party's general statement. In his 1912 speech of acceptance of the presidential nomination, Debs repeated, "There are no boundary lines to separate race from race, sex from sex, or creed from creed in the Socialist Party."[59]

Debs liked and encouraged Reverend George W. Woodbey, a Black Socialist orator and writer. Woodbey's ideas closely paralleled Debs on the race issue. "I am about as much of a slave now as I was in the South, and I am ready to accept any way out of this drudgery," he wrote. Woodbey, a former slave, "wished to be free from slavery of Capitalism." According to Woodbey, the Socialists followed "in the footsteps of the Abolitionists."[60] He wrote a widely circulated booklet on *The Bible and Socialism* in which he maintained that the two were compatible. He believed that the Bible taught that man should make things better on earth as part of earning his reward in the hereafter.[61] Woodbey, like Debs, made no demands upon the National Executive Committee to do more for Blacks. He wrote a very popular pamphlet advising Negroes to vote for Socialists. The party press highly recommended it and sold over 30,000 copies in its first year. It ranked in the top ten pamphlets in 1914.[62]

Gradually Debs changed his views and made statements in particularly the *National Rip Saw* that indicated that he knew the plight of Blacks was not improving and that more attention should be paid to their needs. When a young Black was sentenced to a reformatory for refusing to salute the flag, Debs declared that he knew of no particular reason why a Black should do so after "being stolen from his native land and . . . . robbed of his franchise, stripped of his citizenship and reduced to the level of merchandise."[63] Debs saw repeatedly how politicians managed to control Blacks voting. "The colored people are free in name only and most of them are deprived of the ballot. The politicians who do not openly despise them cunningly contrive to control their votes," he wrote.[64] Nothing enraged Debs more than lynchings. He wanted all citizens to do more "when innocent Negroes are lynched by blood thirsty white mobs." "When one reads of these crimes in the high noon of what one calls the Christian civilization in the supposedly most advanced nation on earth, one is painfully impressed with our white degeneracy," Debs asserted. He suggested that a man "who is really white" should take off his hat when he meets a Black and apologize to him for the crimes of his race.[65] At the time of the release of "Birth of a Nation" Debs criticized its treatment of Blacks. "The whole history of the Negro race is one of shameless exploitation and degradation for which the white race can never atone in time nor eternity," he asserted. He suggested that our histories have been written by Whites and that Blacks had no hand in them or they might have told the story differently. He denounced the Ku-Klux-Klan, white supremacy, and sexual exploitation by white men of black women that had resulted in four million mulattoes. "Intelligent Negroes will not be deceived," he declared, "the progress they have made is mainly due to themselves. They owe little to the white race . . ."[66]

In 1918 the congressional platform of the Socialist Party in the last of twelve principles and demands declared with Debs' endorsement that Negroes were the victims of lawlessness, including hanging and burning, widespread political disfranchisement and loss of civil rights and "They are especially discriminated against in economic opportunity."[67] Debs wrote several articles on behalf of Blacks in this year. In one he asserted that the "Negro is entitled to exactly the same economic, political, social, and moral rights that the white man has." Until this happened Debs admonished that our "talk about democracy and freedom is a vulgar sham and false pretense." Declaring that the Negro was his brother, Debs stated "the color of his skin is no more to me than the color of his eyes. He is human and that is enough." Debs said he would refuse any advantage over Blacks and this had to be the attitude of the Socialist movement if it hoped to win the Negro "to its standard and prove itself worthy of his confidence and support."[68] In another essay Debs noted that crimes by Whites against Blacks had only been partially atoned for and that complete restitution could never be made. "Never do I see a Negro but my heart goes out to him . . . my Black brother for the crimes perpetrated upon his race by the race to which I belong," he confessed.[69]

Late in life, Debs gave an important address to a Negro audience in which he summarized many of the mature views that he held on the race question. In this speech arranged by A. Phillip Randolph, then editor of *The Messenger,* a Black journal advocating socialism for workers, Debs traced his arguments over the years and reaffirmed his unequivocal support of Blacks and their rights. He declared that Blacks had just as much potential and capability of development as Whites and that "all he needed" was a chance and "he has never had that chance." After stressing that Blacks needed to build self-respect, he advised that they could compel respect "only when you respect yourselves. As long as you are willing to be the menials and servants and slaves of white people, that is what you will be." Through organization of all Blacks and improving their education Debs said conditions had to change. He wanted better housing for Blacks. "The rich are not worried about housing conditions," he noted. "Give a colored man the same chance, the same opportunity that you give a white man, and he will register as high upon the mental and moral thermometer of civilization," Debs declared to the attentive audience. After praising *The Messenger* Debs stressed the importance of Blacks having their own press to develop their political power.[70] In the year Debs died he wrote an article on how Blacks had seldom received equal and fair treatment in court cases. He cited a trial that lasted fifteen and one-half minutes of a Black charged with rape in Kentucky. In his judgment this "15½ minute" treatment characterized far too many trials for Blacks. This next remark summarized Debs' attitude and sympathy for Blacks: ". . . it makes all the difference whether God Almighty gave you a white skin or a black one . . ."[71] No longer did he state that Blacks were "not one whit worse off" than Whites or that simply becoming Socialists would erase the problems for Blacks. Over the years Debs had changed into one of the most articulate and knowledgeable defenders of Blacks.

Although Debs recognized the problems that disturbed the status quo, he offered few specific solutions. His one overall answer was that socialism would cure all social, economic, and political problems. In his earlier years, he advocated cooperation, arbitration, and craft union organization, but when these suggestions failed to bring immediate results he endorsed strikes, industrial unionism, and socialism.

Debs' early experiences provided the material for his ideas on labor, socialism, and war. As a boy he had few luxuries, and lived among poor people. His watching injured Civil War veterans on their way to Terre Haute hospitals left a permanent impression and distaste for war. As a youth he supplemented these experiences with avid reading of Hugo's accounts of war, poverty, and revolution. His experiences as a paint scraper, fireman, clerk, and politician provided the material for the rest of his premises. From this background, Debs extracted these arguments: (1) Poor working conditions demand correction to save lives. (2) Workers who are injured, ill, unemployed, or old need welfare benefits. (3) Laborers without industrial unions fail to receive a fair return for their work. (4) Capitalists control social, political, and economic affairs for profit and socialism will end this exploitation. (5) War is futile. Debs believed that anyone who upheld these ideas could further labor's cause by speaking on behalf of them. In 1895 he expressed this conviction in a letter to a Terre Haute friend who lamented that the local committee could not find a suitable replacement for Debs as orator on Labor Day. "All men who wear the badge of labor are representative speakers on that day," he asserted, "not orators, perhaps, as the term is accepted to mean, and yet orators in fact, from whose lips fall thoughts that breathe and words that burn."[72] In his own rhetoric, Debs found "thoughts that breathe" in these simple arguments and "words that burn" by appealing to the strongest emotions that motivated his blue-denim listeners. By stressing hazards to health, inadequate savings for old age, children working to avoid starvation, and a lack of time or money for aesthetic interests, he made the workers aware of the pains and limitations in their lives. He incited in his followers anger, enmity, fear, shame, pity, and indignation against their employers, or others responsible for their plight.

In addition to the political issues that Debs influenced, he had an effect upon a large number of young writers and other men who became famous. These same individuals influenced Debs. It is difficult to appraise the degree of this influence from comments these men made regarding Debs. Darrow, who always admired Debs, gave up a promising career as a corporation lawyer to defend him in the Pullman trial. He later defended a number of strikers—the same ones that Debs supported in his writings and speeches. "There may have lived sometime, somewhere, a kindlier, gentler, more generous man than Debs, but I have never known him," Darrow wrote. "He was the bravest man I ever knew. He never felt fear. He had the courage of the babe who had no conception of the world. . ."[73] Frank Harris, the editor of *Pearson's Magazine* stated that Debs interested him at one time more than any other living American. "The humanity in him was so profound, the sympathy with the suffering and oppressed so sincere," according to Harris, that he hesitated to describe Debs until he knew him.[74] After hearing Debs speak Lincoln Steffens declared: "I don't know how to give you my impression of this man. . . I could hardly credit it myself. . . Gene Debs was the kindest, foolishest, most courageous lover of men in the world."[75] When Harding freed Debs from prison, William Allen White wrote: "Debs was pardoned for the same reason he was jailed; because he was a man of charm and eloquence whom it was dangerous to have out fighting the war when we were in the war, and also whom it is dangerous to have in jail now when we are at peace."[75] Jack London proclaimed Debs a hero and wrote a widely read pamphlet, "The Dream of Debs."[77] During his Cleveland trial Max Eastman, the poet, essayist, and editor of *The Masses,* wrote several articles in Debs' defense.[78] Eastman described Debs as follows: "Debs was present with entire spirit and concentration in every minutest motion that he made. His tongue would dwell upon a 'the' or an 'and' with a kind of earnest affection for the humble that drew the whole accent of his sentences out of the conventional mold, and made each a special creation of the moment. He was tall and long of finger like a New Hampshire farmer, and yet just as vivid, intense, and exuberant with amiability as the French. A French Yankee is what he was."

Following the agitator's arrest for his Canton speech, Ruth LePrade collected a series of tributes to Debs from various poets.[79] In his tribute, Louis Untermeyer suggested that some simple, patriotic crown of thorns should suffice. Sandburg declared that an ignorant government in America had locked up Debs. Riley repeated his widely known poem about Debs. The last lines read:

> And ther's Gene Debs—A man 'at stands
> And jest holds out in his two hands
> As warm a heart as ever beat
> Betwixt here and the Jedgment Seat.

These various quotations do suggest that Debs not only bemused but charmed and impressed people with his courage and humane concerns. Eugene Field, who started a lifelong correspondence with Debs when he entered Woodstock Jail, wrote: "If Debs were a priest the world would listen to his eloquence and that gently, musical voice and sad sweet smile would soften the hardest heart." The booklet included other tributes, including statements from Edwin Markham, Helen Keller, Upton Sinclair, and Ruth LePrade. In another letter Shaw wrote, "What a country! Afraid of Debs and proud of Dempsey! It's too silly."[80]

Although Sinclair Lewis twice started a novel about labor with Debs as the hero, he never finished it. In 1947 Irving Stone wrote such a novel.[81] Lewis called Debs "John the Baptist of American socialism." After a visit with Debs at Lindhlar shortly before he died, Lewis wrote Upton Sinclair, "Gene is the Christ spirit. He is infinitely wise, kind, forgiving, yet the devil of a fighter."[82] Frank DeWitt Talmage claimed that of all the speakers he had heard, none came closer to his idea of Abraham Lincoln than Debs.[83] Another Hoosier poet, Max Ehrmann, defended Debs against his critics and insisted that "he had won a place in American history as one of its greatest orators."[84] Ehrmann first heard Debs speak at Harvard. Students came to see the "monster" speak, according to Ehrmann, but left two hours later greatly impressed. Later John Clark Redpath, organizer of a famous Chautauqua lecture bureau, told Ehrmann that he believed that Debs was one of the most masterful orators that had ever been reared on American soil.[85] Booth Tarkington said "politically and generally I'm old Republican, yet among the highest respects in my life is that which I still retain for the memory of Eugene Debs."[86] John Dos Passos wrote in his poem honoring Debs; "He was a tall shamblefooted man, had a gusty sort of rhetoric that set on fire the railroad workers in their pine boarded halls."[87] All of these writers noted Debs' sincerity and intense desire to shape a better world for workers.

Debs inspired other prominent men to act on his behalf. The former president of Indiana University and later of Stanford University, David Starr Jordan, like scores of others, sent letters and telegrams to Secretary of War, Newton D. Baker, and to President Wilson urging a general amnesty for political prisoners. Jordan later informed President Harding of his belief that "so long as Debs is in jail for voicing his opinions, the rest of us are in a degree stopped from expressing ours. Unless persons who disagree with me are free to speak their minds, I am not free either."[88]

In 1962 when the Debs Foundation started work to preserve Debs' home in Terre Haute, Albert Schweitzer wrote: "I regarded him as a profound and noble man. It moves me deeply that people think of him."[89]

Eugene V. Debs played an active role in American public affairs for over half a century. No other labor leader or Socialist gained the same prominence or attracted as many auditors and readers. Debs saw a certain praise in the title agitator. He admired Socrates, Christ, Henry, Lincoln, Phillips, and Ingersoll because he believed they had been the agitators of their day. Throughout his life Debs adhered to a belief in the value of agitation. "Intelligent discontent is the mainspring of civilization. Progress is born of agitation," he stated. "It is agitation or stagnation. I have taken my choice."[90] In addition to his concern for labor issues, Debs hated waste and thought capitalism made inefficient use of natural resources. "You will see that private interests are the enemies of the public wealth; that trusts and corporations deliberately pollute . . . Socialist production will be limited by what it can consume," he promised.[91] Walter Hurt described Debs as the true reformer because he advocated change in the worker's environment and not the individual. "Debs is admirably equipped for social agitation," Hurt declared, for "he received his education in the school of rugged experience."[92]

In his role as labor-Socialist agitator, however, Debs lacked adaptability. Once he took a stand on an issue he seldom changed. As the Democratic and Republican Parties adopted various planks of the Socialist platform, he moved further left. Debs' contemporaries, Bryan and Roosevelt, quickly sensed the need for some of the changes that he advocated. Roosevelt made repeated promises of trust regulation and labor reforms, but ironically his conservative successor, Taft, executed most of the changes. Debs found all of this frustrating and insisted that revolutionary socialism offered a quicker answer. Debs vacillated on such issues as the I.W.W., but when forced to choose between endorsing anarchistic tactics and more moderate means, he chose the latter. He never publicly announced when he left the I.W.W.—just stopped paying dues.

Many of the preceding comments indicated the strengths and weaknesses of Debs who served as a charismatic leader of a badly divided Socialist Party. How much Debs deserved blame for the decline of the Socialist Party is a much more difficult question to answer. Some might say that his long service to the party prevented other leaders from emerging or delayed the training and grooming of an effective replacement. Others justifiably could say the party would have declined faster without his devotion and unifying talents. The party received its highest percentage of electoral support in 1912 and declined thereafter. Several factors, including some beyond Debs' control, aided this decline. By 1914, arguments over preparation for World War I began to divide the intellectual leadership of the party. Eventually almost all of the liberal intellectuals in the party abandoned it and many never returned. Wilson succeeded in convincing the likes of Robert Hunter, Upton Sinclair, J. Phelps Stokes, Mother Jones, William English Walling, Allen Benson, George Herron, John Spargo, and other important socialists to support the war. Also to Wilson's credit, because of his liberal ideas and his promises of reform, he attracted to the Democratic Party new members that in the past years might have joined the Socialist Party. The reform movement had partially succeeded and this diminished the rush of new members into the Socialist Party to seek redress for their grievances.

The growth and success of the A.F. of L. trade union movement under Samuel Gompers also had affected the growth of the Socialist Party. Gompers in a sense bored from within the capitalist system and carved out a place for workers and demanded that management recognize their rights. His approach never alienated or frightened management the way Socialists did. Debs derided him for this soft approach, but the facts are that as the A.F. of L. membership increased, the Socialist Party membership declined. In part the Socialist Party failed because it never won wide support from organized labor. Not enough rank and file workers endorsed the socialist cause. Workers chose—and so did management—the A.F. of L. as a less drastic alternative than the Socialists who also demanded a new form of government.

In industry there were also tremendous technological advances. New machines not only produced thousands of additional products but reduced their cost and made them available to more people. The industrial expansion brought more jobs, safer machines and working conditions and a new kind of prosperity. All of these reasons made socialism less appealing and necessary to workers. Debs' opponents could clearly point to monetary gains for workers in agriculture and industry.

The Socialist Party after 1912 also lost strength, never to be regained, in the agricultural and mining areas of this country. The loss of members in rural regions was only partially made up with growth in urban areas, notably in the northeastern part of this country where large numbers of European immigrants came to work in factories. They organized foreign language federations. Earlier in his life when the party needed money, Debs would line up a series of speeches and rallies in the midwest and southwest, but near the end of his life, Debs most frequently campaigned for funds in the East, especially among Jewish workers. Legislation favoring farmers and liberalizing of credit (Federal Reserve Act of 1913 made mortgages to farmers and the Federal Farm Loan System Act of 1916 made loans for seed and equipment) also worked against Socialist Party organizers in rural areas. Thus prosperity in both industrial and agricultural areas—a rising standard of living—certainly contributed to fewer party memberships after 1912. According to voter records the Socialist Party peaked with six percent of the total vote in 1912, but it is impossible to know how many votes were never counted. Socialist publications after elections contained numerous reports from members throughout the country protesting that their votes had not been counted or had been reduced in number. Even Debs wrote letters to Terre Haute editors asking officials why so few Socialist votes had been tallied in wards where friends had sworn they voted for him. The Democrats and Republicans had poll watchers but the Socialists failed to use them and protect their rights.

The decline of early successful papers and magazines that supported socialism and flourished in the Midwest hurt the party's cause. By 1912, the amazingly successful *Appeal to Reason,* published in Girard, Kansas, had a diminishing subscription list. No replacement equalled its impact although the *Ripsaw* staff tried, under the leadership of Frank and Kate Richards O'Hare. Debs wrote some of his most perceptive essays for this publication —articles that revealed his mature thoughts on a wide range of topics. The growth within the Socialist Party of language federations between 1912 and 1921, many with their own foreign language newspapers, helped bolster party membership for a time. However, the new recruits never equalled those who departed. The *Jewish Daily Forward* had an impact on its readers in New York and enviorns but it never served as the rallying party instrument on a national level that the *Appeal* had in past years.

Fundamentally the Socialist Party never came to grips with a basic question: whether to overhaul capitalism or overthrow it? Thus party leaders remained eternally divided and members of the executive committee worked at cross purposes. Berger approved and led the step-at-a-time approach while Debs sporadically led those who wanted to replace the old system with a socialist system, but he vacillated between advocating revolutionary and evolutionary means and never clearly and unequivocally took a stand on the issue. Hillquit essentially tried to keep peace between the two and their supporters, yet on key issues he would side with Berger and placate Debs into taking a moderate stand. A clear cut decision on this question would have aided the party and prevented many contradictory stances within the party. Division over this basic question often left Debs straddling both sides of the fence (for example, supporting the I.W.W. and then later ignoring it) and confused potential followers. The Socialist Party leaders believed in political action, not direct action. Socialists never made a real confrontation, or for that matter, had support for a general strike that might have forced such a confrontation. A direct confrontation like what developed in the '60's in this country would have aided the Socialists but those factors never coalesced in Debs' time.

It must also be stated that Debs believed, and rather naively so, that capitalism contained the seeds for its own destruction and that time would favor the socialists. Debs often spoke and wrote of the day this demise would occur but in the practical world of politics after 1912 he should have realized that counter forces such as reform legislation and an improved standard of living made this unlikely to happen. In a sense he did realize it, somewhat late in life, beginning with his disagreement over the platform for the campaign of 1920. From then on, he prodded the party's spokespersons to address themselves more directly via official party statements on current critical issues but it didn't happen. Why? The pleas came too late in the day for saving the party by a leader who had grown old serving the cause but not leading it. The executive committee then as in previous years had its fighting factions and the three principals—Berger, Hillquit, and Debs remained loyal to their supporters. Compromise and unity of purpose never became the theme of the party! Debs never assumed or took the responsibility for "shaping up" the party and clarifying its directions. The party failed to develop strong state organizations, except in Oklahoma and Wisconsin. North Dakota socialists moved into the Farmer Labor Party in order to control successfully the state for a time. They elected their own governor and created a state bank, crop insurance and state elevator that operates yet today! Better organized "grass roots" support throughout the country would have aided the party and helped to maintain it. Every state had an organization but too few had strength. No one really led or devoted full time to the organization and direction of the party and helped to focus its goals. Berger kept himself busy publishing and editing several newspapers and running the party in Milwaukee. Hillquit administered a growing law practice in New York City. Debs spent his time in endless fund-raising efforts for the party, aiding and sometimes directing numerous strikes throughout the country and writing and speaking for a variety of causes. Debs' writings and speeches rarely focused upon party direction and what his role as the central and best-known figure should have been. One can only conjecture on the outcome if Debs had played his role differently within the party. It may very well have made little difference because the forces of disunion within the party were formidable. Berger certainly was not a weak opponent and a confrontation by Debs might have permanently split the socialist forces. It must also be noted that DeLeon offered with his Socialist Labor Party a clear choice for the more radical element. DeLeon provided a party platform that remained consistent and militant throughout the years, yet DeLeon's party after 1900 never had much influence and certainly not the membership of the Socialist Party.

Norman Thomas followed Debs and ran for president six times, but his different style of leadership failed to increase membership and rebuild the party. Only at the time of the depression in 1932 did the party revive and Thomas' voter support increased, but it did not equal Debs'. The arrival of Franklin Roosevelt in Washington and his reforms ended the brief party revival. This again would indicate that prosperity and reforms did more, as they had in Debs' time, to keep the voters within the framework of the two established parties than encourage the growth of a third party. Even in the turmoil of the sixties, the Socialist Party failed to regain a wide following. In 1976, Frank Zeidler, former successful three term mayor of Milwaukee from 1948 to 1960, ran for president on the Socialist ticket but with no delusions of success. In an interview he stated "Jimmy Carter is popular because he is a fresh face. Politics is like a drama. The actor can be good or evil as long as he doesn't weary the audience." Zeidler blamed the more recent wars for the declining strength of the Socialist Party." We lost our young people in the war," he declared. "They were our future. We had a power base here; that base was built carefully. I tried to build and expand, but I did not succeed."[93] Ironically Debs could have made a similar remark. Debs would have empathized with Zeidler. Debs did have more success in his time than his followers and he had the satisfaction of knowing that the opposition adapted many of his ideas.

In recent years Debs' ideas on prison reform have attracted renewed attention. A reprinting of *Walls and Bars,* his book on reforms needed in our penal system, quickly sold thousands of copies. Debs often stated what he called his prison creed:

> While there is a lower class I am in it.
> While there is a criminal element I am of it.
> While there is a soul in prison I am not free.

Debs believed prisoners could be reformed if they received treatment that humanely helped them solve their problems. "The inmates of prisons are not irretrievably vicious and the depraved element they are commonly believed to be," he wrote. In writing the book Debs hoped to let the public know what a mismanaged "corrupt, brutalizing and criminal breeding system" they supported. He wrote the book after the Bell Syndicate of New York, a newspaper firm, severely edited twelve articles they requested. Debs insisted that the prison "as a rule to which there are few exceptions, is for the poor," and that the prison problem was "directly co-related with poverty." He believed the prison served as an incubator for crime, especially influencing first offenders. In his judgment, first offenders received overly harsh and long sentences. The atmosphere of fear within prisons where guards watched constantly and swung clubs or carried guns depressed Debs. Also he found the "maddening monotony" of the daily routine one of the most inhuman features of prisons.

When prisoners secured their release, Debs asked the state to give far greater help in rehabilitation, including support of their families until such time as they found jobs and had made the adjustment to the external world. Debs thought criminals were "simply the victims of social injustice in some form," and when the cause was ascertained and removed by giving the "victims" human treatment in "terms of love and service their criminal psychology" vanished. Debs pleaded that prison management be taken out of politics and that all who worked in prison be trained for it. Debs wanted prison employees to use the "redeeming power of kindness" rather than the "destructive power of brutality." Finally Debs advocated to wardens that prison populations be organized upon a basis of "mutuality of interest and self government," plus the removal of all clubs, guns, and guards, except those chosen by the inmates from their own ranks.[94]

Throughout his long career Debs insisted that the purpose of his life was to educate, organize, and emancipate the working class, and not to gain fame. "It was this passionate sympathy for my class that gave me all the power I have to serve it," he declared. As the "tongue of the working class," he advised those who aspired to master "the art of oratory first of all to consecrate themselves to some great cause. I simply had to speak and make people understand."[94] In his role as spokesman for labor and socialism, Debs distinguished himself and left behind a legacy of ideas that command respect.

Chapter Notes

Chapter 1 Notes—Pages 13 to 22

1. When Marguerite Bettrich's parents died, her grandfather, David Stubert, raised her. Stubert had fought under Napoleon. Daniel's illustrious family contained many prominent military, political, and professional members. Emily Debs Mailloux and Theodore Debs discussed the family dispute in letters December 1, 1926, and December 13, 1926. Theodore Debs MSS., Indiana State University Library, Terre Haute, Indiana. All MSS. in the Indiana State University collection were placed there in August 1967. These MSS, gift of Marguerite Debs Cooper, hereafter will be referred to as ISU MSS.

2. "Wedded Fifty Years," Terre Haute *Express*, September 14, 1899.

3. Letter to writer from Walter Reiz, August 29, 1964. Mr. Reiz knew Mr. Debs well and lived near Debs' home.

4. Harley Pritchett interview November 20, 1960. (Mr. Pritchett was born in 1860. He was alert and remembered dates accurately.)

5. Debs MSS., Tamiment Library, New York University, 7 East 15th, New York, New York, Scrapbook 3, p. 63. Debs left his scrapbooks and books to this library that was part of the Rand School of Social Sciences, a Socialist training school. Hereafter the Tamiment collection referred to as Debs MSS. New York University acquired this collection and has moved it to their new Bobst Library.

6. Marguerite Debs Cooper interview June 16, 1963. Also confirmed in a search through Church Records 1850-1870, St. Joseph's Church, Terre Haute, Indiana. Mrs. Cooper, niece of Eugene V. Debs, provided valuable family background information to me.

7. Coleman, *Eugene V. Debs, A Man Unafraid* (New York: Greenberg Publishing Co., 1930), p. 11. He probably read it in the diary David Karsner kept when he stayed in Terre Haute in 1918 as a guest of Debs. Karsner MSS., New York Public Library, New York City.

8. "Debs' Welcome Home," Terre Haute *Express*, November 24, 1895.

9. David Karsner, *Debs His Authorized Life and Letters* (New York: Boni and Liveright Publishers, 1919), pp. 110-114.

10. A. R. Markle, "Gene Debs' Hundredth Birthday," Terre Haute *Star*, November 6, 1955.

11. C. C. Oakey, *History of Greater Terre Haute and Vigo County*, Vol. I (Chicago: Lewis Publishing Co., 1908), p. 346. See also H. Metzger, a seminary classmate of Debs, letter to Debs, July 16, 1921, and Debs' reply, July 26, 1921. Debs commented upon Treplo's death in the Civil War. ISU MSS.

12. W. H. Wiley, *Public Schools in Terre Haute: 100 Years of History*. Vol. I. Bound privately. p. 37. References in the book were checked to determine that this volume was written in 1900.

13. Martha McKinney, "Early Schools in Terre Haute up to 1889—from 'Unpublished Notes of W. H. Wiley.' " Unpublished pamphlet on file at Fairbanks Memorial Library, Terre Haute, Indiana, pp. 4-5.

14. George Scott interview November 16, 1960. (Mr. Scott, born early in 1862, practiced law until 1960.)

15. Wiley, p. 41.

16. H. W. Beckwith, *History of Vigo and Parke Counties* (Chicago: H. H. Hill and N. Iddings Publishers, 1880), p. 134. The textbooks used in other courses in Debs' school included: *Goodrich's Readers, McGuffey's Spelling Book, Ray's Arithmetic, Butler's English Grammar, Davie's Algebra, Mitchell's Geography, Cuter's Physiology,* and *Wilson's Outlines of History.* In 1863 Hayes replaced *Goodrich's Readers* with *McGuffey's Readers* and added *Smith's Astronomy.*

17. Old Seminary Folder, Vigo County Historical Society, 1411 South Sixth Street, Terre Haute, Indiana.

18. Beckwith, p. 133. Most of Terre Haute's private schools closed because they could not compete with the free tuition in public schools.

19. Debs MSS., scrapbook 3, p. 62.

20. Dated September 7, 1868. Found in vault, School Administration Building, 667 Walnut, Terre Haute, Indiana.

21. Ralph Nickless interview November 10, 1960. (Barber and union supporter of Debs.)

22. Coleman, p. 21.

23. "Minutes of City Teachers Institutes 1867, 1868, 1869, 1870." Vault School Administration Building.

24. *Ibid.,* November 9, 1867, pp. 27-28.

25. Wiley, p. 74. Also in Vol. II, section on "Exams," n.d., n.p.

26. *Superintendent's Reports 1869-1875,* "Curriculum." Bound and stored in vault of Wiley High School, 215 South Seventh Street, Terre Haute, Indiana, n.p.

27. Program Philomathean Literary Club, July 1, 1869. Files Vigo County Historical Society.

28. Floy Ruth Painter, *That Man Debs* (Bloomington, Indiana: Published by Graduate Council, Indiana University, 1929), p. 186.

29. "The Two 'Genes': A Talk with Debs," *Chicago Tribune,* September 5, 1896; Debs MSS, Scrapbook 3, p. 49.

30. "Minutes of Teachers Institutes," January 8, 1870, p. 97.

31. Collections of Graduation Programs, 1870-1875. Vault of Wiley High School.

32. Coleman, p. 14. Ray Ginger, *The Bending Cross* (New Brunswick: Rutgers University Press, 1949), p. 11. Coleman erred when he stated Debs quit school because "Kindly Abbie Flagg had little more knowledge to impart to Gene." Before Debs quit, he had advanced beyond the usual courses Abbie taught. Also the records listed four other teachers for the same grade. Ginger oversimplified Debs' reasons for dropping when he stated the curriculum offered only a rehash.

33. *Superintendent's Reports 1869-1875.* The following courses were available:

Courses: Terre Haute High School, 1870

3rd Year	4th Year
Geometry 1st, 2nd.	U. S. Constitution 1st.
Trigonometry 2nd.	Bookkeeping 1st, 2nd.
Natural Philosophy 1st.	Logic 1st, 2nd.
Botany 2nd.	Chemistry 1st.
Latin or German 1st, 2nd.	Rhetoric 2nd.
General History 2nd.	English Literature 2nd.
	Moral Philosophy 2nd.
	Composition 2nd.
	Political Economy 1st.
	Astronomy 2nd.
	Electives: Greek, Analytical Geometry

34. E. V. Debs, "The Secret of Efficient Expression," *Distinguished Contemporary Orators and Lecturers,* compiled by University of Wisconsin (c. 1919).

35. Coleman, p. 14; Debs' Scrapbook 3, p. 49.

36. Beckwith, p. 286. Garwin's became the largest business school in the state and stressed combining practice with theory.

37. In E. V. Debs to parents, East St. Louis, Illinois, September 21, 1874, ISU MSS.

38. *Ibid.*

39. Debs to parents and sister, October 3, 1874.

40. *Ibid.*

41. E. V. Debs to Eugenia Debs, October 8, 1874.

42. "Death Notices," *Terre Haute Gazette,* October 16, 1874; Debs MSS., Scrapbook 3, p. 49.

43. Coleman.

44. In a November 13, 1930 letter to David Karsner, Theodore Debs discussed his brother's job with Hulman's and how he injured himself while working there. Hulman liked Debs and defended him in later years. Theodore Debs MSS., ISU Library.

45. *Ibid.*

46. "Debs! Welcome Home," *Terre Haute Express,* November 24, 1895. In an interview with an *Express* reporter, Debs reminisced about his early aspirations and meeting with Ingersoll.

47. *Terre Haute Gazette,* February 3, 1878.

48. Eugene V. Debs, "Recollections of Ingersoll," *Pearson's Magazine,* April 1917, p. 302.

49. Scott interview. Scott attended the lecture and remembered Debs' laudatory introduction of Ingersoll.

50. Ruth Crawford, "An Interview with E. V. Debs," *Terre Haute Star,* November 7, 1926. Debs later gave this set of books to the Terre Haute Labor Temple. They have been returned to the Debs Foundation Library.

51. Karsner, p. 127.

52. E. V. Debs "Susan B. Anthony: A Reminiscence," *The Socialist Woman,* January 1909, p. 3.

53. *Ibid.*

54. Mabel Kennon, "E. V. Debs in Rochester," undated clipping in Debs' Scrapbook 3, p. 3. A "Letter to Editor," *Rochester Herald,* November 22, 1899, by John R. Morrison tells of Debs visiting with Miss Anthony after a lecture in her home city, Rochester. After congratulating Debs, Miss Anthony remarked, "You have evididently studied your subject pretty well, but you will never get socialism until we women have the right to vote." Debs replied, "You will never get the right to vote until we get socialism. . ."

55. Allan L. Benson, "The Socialist Candidates," *Pearson's Magazine,* August 1912, p. 118.

56. Souvenir Wedding Program, Jean Daniel and Marguerite Debs 50th Celebration. Debs MSS., Emeline Fairbanks Memorial Library, Terre Haute, Indiana.

Chapter 2 Notes—Pages 23 to 34

1. Ruth Crawford, "Interview with E. V. Debs," *Terre Haute Star,* November 7, 1926. The charter Debs signed on this night hangs in the library of the restored Debs' home in Terre Haute, Indiana.

2. Pritchett interview, November 16, 1960.

3. Crawford, "Interview with E. V. Debs."

4. Eugene V. Debs, "Review of Early Days of Unionism in the City of Terre Haute," *Terre Haute Tribune,* March 2, 1913.

5. Minutes of Vigo Lodge No. 16, Vol. I, 1875-1878, Debs' MSS., Eugene V. Debs Foundation Library, 415 North 8th Street, Terre Haute, Indiana.

6. Examples found throughout the minutes. Minutes, Vol. 2, 1879-1883, pp. 7, 9, 25.

7. *Ibid.,* p. 38.

8. *Ibid.,* Vol. 1, p. 37.

9. *Ibid.,* p. 57.

10. *Ibid.,* p. 87.

11. *Ibid.,* Vol. II, p. 85. Debs seldom spelled out the members' first names. Since the city directories list several men for most of these family names, it was impossible to identify all of them accurately.

12. *Ibid.,* pp. 43, 49.

13. *Ibid.,* p. 127.

14. *Ibid.,* p. 12.

15. Letter to Theodore, January 27, 1876, Theodore Debs MS., ISU Library.

16. *Ibid.,* September 14, 1877.

17. Records, Vigo County Court House, Second and Wabash, Terre Haute, Indiana. An editorial in *The Saturday Evening Mail,* Terre Haute, May 22, 1879, discussed the party dispute and praised Debs for refusing to follow his party.

18. Eugene V. Debs, "Serving the Labor Movement," *The Call Magazine,* October 1, 1922. Debs discussed this campaign in this article. See also Terre Haute *Express* and *Gazette,* November 6, 1881 for election figures.

19. Interviews with Mrs. Marguerite Debs Cooper, August 12, 1969, and Harley Pritchett, November 16, 1960.

20. *Journal of the House of Representatives of the State of Indiana,* Fifty-Fourth Session of the General Assembly (Indianapolis, Indiana: Wm. B. Burford, Contractor Printer, 1885), pp. 53, 54.

21. *Ibid.,* p. 136.

22. *Ibid.,* January 20, 1885, p. 185.

23. "Appeal to Negro Workers," Speech at Commonwealth Casino, 135 Street and Madison Avenue, New York City, October 30, 1923.

24. Eugene V. Debs, "Serving the Labor Movement," *The Call Magazine,* October 1, 1922.

25. Debs MSS. Untitled clipping of an article that Debs wrote for a Socialist paper in New York in April of 1902, Tamiment Library.

26. Debs became editor in July, 1880. The library in the Debs' home in Terre Haute contains a complete set of the magazine—a gift from the Brotherhood.

27. Eugene V. Debs, "Unionism and Socialism," *Debs, His Life, Writings and Speeches,* Bruce Rogers, editor (Girard, Kansas: Appeal to Reason Press, 1908), p. 119.

28. Eugene V. Debs, "The University Oratorical Report," *The Coming Nation,* July 8, 1911.

29. See Annual Reports of Bureau of Labor Statistics, first published in 1885; Phillip S. Foner, *Labor Movement in the United States* (New York: International Publishers, 1955), p. 12.

30. *Ibid.*

31. "Railroad Labor Statistics," *Fifth Annual Report of the Commissioner of Labor,* 51st Congress, H. R. Exec. Doc. No. 336 (Washington, D.C. 1890), pp. 131, 145. Also reprinted in Foner, p. 248.

32. *Ibid.,* p. 52; see also the Annual Reports of the Bureau of Labor Statistics published by Government Printing Office, Washington, D.C., especially reports covering railroad, mining, etc. accidents in each state. Some tables begin in 1883. Especially helpful is the *Index of Labor Reports* published by the Bureau for all reports prior to 1902 with location of accident figures listed on pp. 11-14.

33. "The America of Debs," *Eugene V. Debs Centennial* (New York: Socialist Society, USA, 1956), p. 11.

34. Similar conditions existed in mining. Adolph Germer, close friend of Debs and active union organizer in Southern Illinois, wrote the author March 16, 1964: "At the age of eleven I went to work in the coal fields of Illinois. The rate was 6¢ per hour; 60¢ for 10 hours work. In 1894, the miners organized a local and went on strike. That strike failed and 51 of us were fired. We moved to another field, began work and began to organize. By 1897, we had built a union strong enough so we could make some demands of the coal operators. We called a strike and after five months we received recognition and an eight hour day. . . . We had many bloody battles with the imported strike breakers and hired thugs. In one such skirmish at Virden, Illinois, four men from my local at Mt. Olive were killed." Debs spoke in this area at the time of the second strike. See also Germer MSS., Wisconsin State Historical Society, Madison.

35. Debs MSS., Tamiment Library, an unmarked newspaper copy of a speech. Internal evidence indicated the place: Staub's Opera House, the date, May 12, 1896, somewhere in the South.

36. H. C. Bradsby, *History of Vigo County,* pp. 611-612. Bradsby interviewed Debs and followed his work.

37. "Unionism and Socialism," p. 125.

38. David A. Shannon, "Eugene V. Debs: Conservative Labor Editor," *Indiana Magazine of History,* December, 1951, p. 141.

39. "A Grand Brotherhood," Philadelphia *Times,* September 22, 1885.

40. Bradsby, p. 612.

41. *Ibid.,* p. 637.

42. Ralph Donham letter to Debs Foundation Library, June 20, 1964. He discussed Miss Harper's work on the magazine. Later, Miss Harper worked for women's rights and wrote a biography of Susan B. Anthony.

43. "Coming Labor Leader," *Chicago Herald,* April 28, 1893.

44. Eugene V. Debs, "Railroad Federation," *Commoner and Glassmen,* Pittsburg, Pennsylvania, September 28, 1889.

45. Eugene V. Debs, "Federation," *United Labor,* Denver, Colorado, August 30, 1890.

46. "Debs Declines Re-election," *Cincinnati Enquirer,* September 16, 1892; September 20, 1892.

47. Ginger, p. 92.

48. Crawford, "Interview with E. V. Debs."

49. Ginger, p. 96.

50. Speech delivered August 30, 1893, and printed in the *Firemen's Magazine,* October 1893, pp. 875-879.

51. Printed in Chicago, n.d., n.p., 32 pp. In Terre Haute, Bert Viquesney, a friend of Debs, printed many of the pamphlets he used during this period. Since Mr. Viquesney didn't own a linotype machine, he had the copy set in the composing room of the *Terre Haute Star.* Letter to writer from Roy J. Owen who worked for Viguesney's, November 30, 1964.

52. *You Railroad Men,* pp. 5-6.

53. Speech at Spokane, Washington, March 13, 1894. Newspaper clipping in Theodore Debs' Scrapbook, Fairbanks Library, Terre Haute, Indiana, p. 13.

54. See the *St. Paul Globe,* Moorhead, Minnesota *Watch,* and *Grand Forks* (North Dakota) *Herald* for articles complaining about rates, April 15 to 25.

55. "Injunction Issued: President Debs Arrives," *St. Paul Dispatch,* April 15, 1894

56. Report of speech in *St. Paul Globe,* April 21, 1894.

57. See for examples the *Minneapolis Tribune* and *Minneapolis Journal* from April 20 to May 2 for articles covering the strike.

58. For a sample of papers supporting the ARU and Debs, see these North Dakota papers: *Dickinson Recorder, Grand Forks Herald, Benson County News, Jamestown Capital, Sargent County Teller, Devils Lake Inter-Ocean, Casselton Reporter, Larimore Graphic, Grafton News;* Minnesota papers—*Minnewaukan Siftings, Moorhead Watch, Barnesville News* and *St. Paul Globe,* from April 15 to May 2.

59. "Strike Complete," *Fargo Forum,* April 27, 1894.

60. "The Debs House," *Moorhead Watch,* May 19, 1894.

61. "No Sympathy," *Fargo Forum,* May 1, 1894.

62. Editorial, April 25, 1894.

63. "Strike Conference," *St. Paul Globe,* May 1, 1894.

64. "Great Northern Strike Settled," *Daily Pioneer Press,* St. Paul, Minnesota, May 2, 1894.

65. "Great Strike Off," *St. Paul Globe,* May 2, 1894; "Strike Settled," *Fargo Forum,* May 2, 1894; "Echoes of the Strike," *Dickinson Recorder,* May 2, 1894.

66. "Greeted by Parade of Labor Unions at the Depot, Praise For His Successful Handling of the Great Northern Strike," *Terre Haute Star,* May 4, 1894.

67. *Ibid.* The arbitration committee consisted of five prominent Twin City businessmen, headed by Charles A. Pillsbury. *The Daily Pioneer Press,* St. Paul, listed points in favor of the strikers. The *St. Paul Evening Post,* May 2, 1894, also stated that the ARU gained 97.5% of its requests.

68. *Terre Haute Tribune,* May 4, 1894.

69. "Settlement Signed," *Fargo Forum,* May 16, 1894.

70. *Ibid.*

71. Comment made to Grace Brewer, letter to writer, July 19, 1965. Grace Brewer worked several years as Debs' secretary.

1. "E. V. Debs' Lecture: The Distinguished President of the ARU at the Metropolitan Opera House," *Grand Forks Daily Herald* (North Dakota), March 8, 1895.

2. *Report and Testimony on the Chicago Strike, 1894*, by United States Strike Commission appointed by the President (Washington, D.C.: Government Printing Office, 1895), p. 130.

3. *Ibid.*, p. 129.

4. *Ibid.*, p. 87. Space in this biography does not permit a longer account of the complex Pullman Strike but the writer recommends Almont Lindsey's book, *The Pullman Strike: The Story of a Unique Experiment and of a Great Labor Upheaval* (Chicago: University of Chicago Press, 1942). W. F. Burns, a railroad switchman, tells the strike story from a worker's point of view in his book, *The Pullman Boycott* (St. Paul: McGill Printing Co., 1894.)

5. "Debs' Telegrams," The *Tacoma Daily News*, Tacoma, Washington, July 3, 1894. This newspaper carried numerous accounts of the effects of the strike in the western part of the United States.

6. "Confidence is Restored," The *Tacoma Morning Union*, July 18, 1894.

7. Nym Crynkle, "The Central Figure of the Great Railroad Strike as viewed by Nym Crynkle," Chicago newspaper clipping in Debs' Scrapbook, Tamiment Library, July 1, 1894, p. 1. Other publications such as *The Critic*, July 7, 1894, p. 40, contained anti-Debs articles.

8. Letter from E. A. Lee to E. V. Debs, April 12, 1920. Debs MS., Indiana State University Library.

9. Chicago newspaper clippings, Debs' Scrapbooks, July 7, 1894.

10. Michael Brennen's "Annual Report of Chicago's Chief of Police," issued March 21, 1895.

11. Letter from Grace Brewer, July 19, 1964. Mrs. Brewer was Debs' secretary from 1907 to 1913.

12. Editorial, *New York Tribune*, July 14, 1894.

13. *The Nation*, September 13, 1894.

14. Copy in Debs MSS., Indiana State University Library.

15. Debs gave this Marx autographed copy to Walter Reiz who has it in his library in Terre Haute.

16. Letter to Kautsky, December 4, 1925. Reprinted in *New Leader*, December 14, 1935.

17. List in Debs' Scrapbook 3, p. 41. Debs MSS., Tamiment Library.

18. In a letter to Theodore on May 19, 1920, Debs discussed his meeting with Harvey, T. Debs MSS., ISU Library.

19. Unidentified newspaper clipping, Debs' Scrapbook 1, p. 173.

20. Jean Daniel Debs MSS., ISU Library, January 11, 1895.

21. *Ibid.*, January 14, 1895.

22. *Ibid.*, January 27, 1895.

23. "Debs Teaches School in Jail," *Chicago Journal*, July 1, 1895.

24. Letter from Debs to *The Tribune*, Evansville, Indiana, August 19, 1895.

25. Copy in Debs MSS., ISU Library, October 29, 1895.

26. Several letters in Debs MSS. mention his work on the speech; Rogers, p. 41. Separate meetings celebrating Debs' release were held throughout the country.

27. Pritchett interview, May 14, 1962. Mr. Pritchett worked in Chicago at the time and accompanied Debs and Theodose throughout the day.

28. *The Chicago Chronicle* contacted Judge Woods in Indianapolis and reported "No Comment," November 23, 1895, p. 3.

29. "Liberty," Speech reprinted by Standard Publishing Company, Terre Haute, Indiana, n.d., p. 7. Newspaper copies of the speech in the *Cincinnati Commercial Gazette* and *The Chicago Chronicle* on November 23, 1895, agreed with this reprint.

30. *Report and Testimony on the Chicago Strike,* 1894.

31. "Railway Managers Hot," *New York World,* November 14, 1895.

32. See records at Graceland Cemetery, Clark and Irving Park Street, Chicago.

Chapter 4 Notes—Pages 41 to 58

1. "Fourth Biennial Report of Convention Brotherhood of Locomotive Firemen," submitted by Eugene V. Debs, Grand Secretary and Treasurer, Moore and Langen Publishers, Terre Haute, 1894.

2. "Pastors' Opinions: What Lansing Clergymen Think of Mr. Debs' Lecture," *Lansing Tribune,* Lansing, Michigan, February 3, 1899, p. 1.

3. *Ibid.*

4. *Ibid.* Some reporters reacted negatively, and Debs may not have clipped as many of these, but the presence of the Nym Crynkle type indicated that he wanted these, too.

5. "The Debs lecture," *The Fargo Daily Forum and Republican,* Fargo, North Dakota, March 7, 1895. The reporter spoke of Debs' late arrivals and his success in building ARU locals.

6. Eugene V. Debs, "The Problem of Labor," June 1895, pamphlet, Debs' MSS.

7. "Debs on Future of Labor," *St. Louis Chronicle,* September 14, 1895.

8. Eugene V. Debs, "Liberty's Anniversary," *Twentieth Century,* July 4, 1895.

9. "Echoes of the City," *The Fargo* (North Dakota) *Daily Forum and Republican,* March 6, 1895; "E. V. Debs Lecture," *Grand Forks Daily Herald* (North Dakota), March 8, 1895. See also Debs' Scrapbooks, Tamiment Library in New York City for other speech clippings that mention women's right to vote.

10. "Debs Backs Populists," *Coming Nation,* August 2, 1895.

11. Unidentified newspaper clipping of a speech in Debs' Scrapbook, Emeline Fairbanks Library, November 1, 1895.

12. *Ibid.*

13. Another clipping, Spokane, Washington, March 15, 1895.

14. Henry Demarest Lloyd MSS, Wisconsin State Historical Society, Madison.

15. "Debs Declines," *St. Louis Post Dispatch,* July 25, 1896.

16. Debs MSS, Scrapbook I. This remark refuted some of Debs' critics who maintained that he supported socialism from the time he left Woodstock and wanted political offices.

17. "Populist Convention," *St. Louis Union Record,* July 25, 1896.

18. *Ibid.*

19. "Debs Declines," *Ibid.*

20. Eugene V. Debs, "The Truth About Bryan," n.p., n.d., p. 231, Debs' Scrapbook II, Tamiment Library.

21. Unidentified newspaper clipping, Debs MSS., Scrapbook 3, May 12, 1896. Speech presented somewhere in the South, possibly Tennessee. The next day Debs spoke in Chattanooga, and then went on to Atlanta, Georgia.

22. Debs on "Future of Labor," *St. Louis Chronicle,* September 14, 1895.

23. E. V. Debs, "From Obscurity to Fame," (Obscurity reference to Wayland). *Appeal to Reason,* September 5, 1903.

24. "Debs Will Lead," *Chicago Dispatch,* October 31, 1895. In the Socialist Labor Party Newspaper, *The People,* August 12, 1894, DeLeon wrote that Debs would probably flounder for a while but that eventually he would join the socialist ranks.

For further background on DeLeon and his influence on socialist thought see Howard Quint's excellent chapter "DeLeon Molds the Socialist Labor Party" in the *Forging of American Socialism* (Columbia: University of South Carolina Press, 1953), pp. 142-174. Ira Kipnis' chapter "The Socialist Labor Party" in *The American Socialist Movement* 1897-1912 (New York: Columbia University Press, 1952), pp. 6-24; McAlister Coleman's Chapter "The Pioneers" in *Eugene V. Debs: A Man Unafraid* (New York: Greenberg Publishers, 1930), pp. 188-195.

25. Lloyd MSS, Wisconsin Historical Society, Letter from Debs, February 1, 1896.

26. "Debs Comes Out for Socialism," *Chicago Record,* January 1, 1897.

27. "Social Democracy Born in Jail," *St. Louis Chronicle,* August 29, 1900.

28. Eugene V. Debs, "The Socialist Party and The Working Class," Indianapolis, September 1, 1904. Opening campaign speech as Socialist candidate for president.

29. Eugene V. Debs, "The Social Democracy," *New Time,* August 1897, p. 74. See also "Debs' Great Scheme," Philadelphia *Enquirer,* May 1, 1897.

30. "E. V. Debs' Commonwealth Plan," editorial, *Boston Herald,* April 19, 1897; "Debs Writes on New Scheme," *Cincinnati Post,* June 3, 1897.

31. "Debs' Manifesto on Co-operation," *New York Press,* April 27, 1897.

32. Robert P. Porter, "Debs' Commonwealth," Philadelphia *Enquirer,* May 1, 1897; May 8, 1897.

33. "Debs Plans for Colonies," *New York Journal,* April 15, 1897; James Creelman, "Debs' Policy Defined," *New York Journal,* June 22, 1897.

34. Creelman, *Ibid.* See also *The Outlook,* June 26, 1899, p. 480.

35. "Debs Outlines New Political Party," *Milwaukee News,* July 31, 1897.

36. *Ibid.*

37. "Debs' Great Scheme: Requests Union Pacific Lands," Philadelphia *Enquirer,* June 18, 1897.

38. Dorothy Richardson, "Women in Debs' Colony," *Milwaukee Sentinel,* July 25, 1897.

39. *Ibid.* Miss Richardson interviewed Debs before he gave a speech on the colony plan in Milwaukee.

40. "Miners are Marching," *Chicago Record,* July 22, 1897.

41. "Debs' Advice to Miners," *Wheeling Intelligence,* Wheeling, West Virginia, July 22, 1897.

42. "Debs Stirs Up Miners," *Chicago Dispatch,* July 22, 1897.

43. Interview with Walter Reuther, November 20, 1964.

44. "Looks Like a Battle Royal to the Finish," *Pittsburg Dispatch,* July 24, 1897.

45. An account of the stroke later appeared in *Motorman and Conductor,* July 1898.

46. "Circular on Strike: Issued by United Mine Workers," Columbus, Ohio, August 20, 1897.

47. "Government by Injunction," *Railroad Locomotive Journal,* August 5, 1897.

48. "Debs Denounces the Courts of the Country in Pittsburg," *Cleveland Citizen,* August 6, 1897.

49. "Calls It Murder: E. V. Debs Declares Sheriff and His Men are Criminals," *Chicago Chronicle,* September 11, 1897. This article discusses the investigation that followed the incident.

50. "Brutal Want in Huts of Miners," *Chicago Journal,* August 23, 1897.

51. "Says McKinley Should End It," *Chicago Journal,* August 24, 1897.

52. "Evangelist of Labor: E. V. Debs' Masterly Effort in Pleading the Cause of Miners," *Columbus Evening Press,* Columbus, Ohio, August 5, 1897.

53. "Strike Ends," *United Mine Workers Journal,* September 16, 1897.

54. Eugene V. Debs' Report to National Executive Committee, mailed from Nashville, Tennessee, October 2, 1897; copy in Marguerite Debs Cooper MSS., Indiana State University Library, Terre Haute, Indiana. (Mrs. Cooper is E. V. Debs' niece.)

55. *Ibid.* For further information on the formation of the Socialist Party see Daniel Bell's essay in Donald Drew Egbert and Stow Persons' book *Socialism and American Life* (Princeton University Press, Princeton, N. J. 1952) pp. 213-405.

56. "Interesting Talk with Eugene Debs," *Marion Chronicle*, Marion, Indiana, April 20, 1899.

57. "Interview with J. A. Wayland," *Kansas City Star*, December 6, 1896. See also ISU MSS, for letters from Wayland that indicate the respect Debs had for Wayland's opinions.

58. Quote from the telegram Debs sent to memorial services for Bellamy. John Clark Redpath read it. Printed in *Boston Constitution*, June 9, 1898. Also see Debs' Scrapbooks 2-5 in Tamiment Library.

59. "Debs Bolts Social Democracy Convention," *Chicago Dispatch*, June 11, 1898.

60. "Schism Ends the Meeting," *Chicago Chronicle*, June 11, 1898.

61. "Debs Goes Out. Platform of New Party," *Chicago Chronicle*, June 12, 1898.

62. "Debs' Social Democrats in Hard Straits," *Chicago Dispatch*, July 17, 1898.

63. "Want Debs' Party to Put Up a Ticket," *Chicago Dispatch*, August 20, 1898.

64. "Debs Retires," Special to *New York World*, June 29, 1898.

65. "Laboring Man Not Conscious of His Power," *Omaha World Herald*, December 15, 1898.

66. Eugene V. Debs, "Social Democracy," *National Magazine*, October 1898, p. 103.

67. "Judge P. S. Grosscup Here," *Topeka State Journal*, June 27, 1898.

68. "Socialism is Not Solution," *Chicago Tribune*, December 18, 1898. The 492 votes represented 50,000 members; the 1,923 votes represented 200,000 AFL members.

69. "Labor Never So Well Off," Unidentified newspaper clipping, November 21, 1899, Debs MSS., Scrapbook, Volume 4, p. 173.

70. "New Party Urged by Dr. Rainsford," *New York World*, March 23, 1899. Convention also discussed in *New York Tribune*, March 22, 1899.

71. William B. Hesseltine, *The Rise and Fall of Third Parties* (Washington, D.C.: Public Affairs Press, 1948), p. 36.

72. Ira Kipnis, *The American Socialist Movement* 1897-1912 (New York: Columbia University Press, 1952), Chapters I-V discuss party feuds. See also Howard Quint's *The Forging of American Socialism* (Columbia, South Carolina: University of South Carolina Press, 1953), especially Chapters V-XI.

73. "Labor and Liberty," *Linton Call*, Linton, Indiana, March 3, 1899.

74. "Debs Here," *Saginaw News*, Saginaw, Michigan, February 6, 1899.

75. "Speech to Women's Club of New Orleans," Algiers Hall, May 28, 1896. Copy in Debs MSS., E. Fairbanks Library.

76. Published later as a pamphlet by Debs in April 1899. He delivered the speech on March 21, 1899. Copy in ISU MSS.

77. "Mary Elizabeth Lease's Report of the Meeting of the 19th Century Club and the Impression Made," *Debs Herald and Souvenir*, n.p., n.d. (circa 1900), copy ISU MSS.

78. Editorial following a Debs' lecture, *Daily Morning Sun*, Springfield, Ohio, February 22, 1899.

79. "Debs Speaks," *Saginaw, Michigan News*, February 6, 1899.

80. Carl Bode's *American Lyceum* (New York: Oxford University Press, 1956), carefully traces the growth of lyceums in the country and their decline in the period before the Civil War.

81. "Call Convention for S. D. P. in 1899," *Chicago Record*, October 27, 1899.

82. *Ibid.*

Chapter 5 Notes—Pages 59 to 65

1. "Will Amalgamate Socialist Labor Party—Willing to be Absorbed," *Indianapolis News*, Indianapolis, Indiana, March 7, 1900.

2. "Debs Did Not Desire Honor: Pressure Necessary," *Indianapolis News*, March 9, 1900.

3. *Ibid*. "Debs is In Favor," March 6, 1900.

4. *Ibid*. See Howard Quint, *The Forging of American Socialism*, (Columbia: University of South Carolina Press, 1953), for details on party history; Harriman polled 5,600 votes in California, p. 344.

5. "Debs Forced to Take It," *Indianapolis Press*, March 9, 1900.

6. *Ibid.;* Kipnis, p. 87; Ginger, p. 210; H. Wayne Morgan, *Eugene V. Debs: Socialist for President* (New York: Syracuse University Press, 1962), p. 36.

7. See Debs' Scrapbook, Volume 3, for clippings of many of his speeches during this campaign, Debs MS, Tamiment Library.

8. "The National Platform of Social Democratic Party of America," March 1900, Debs' MSS., Tamiment Library.

9. "The Speeches of Eugene V. Debs and Prof. George D. Herron Delivered at Opening of National Campaign, Central Music Hall, Chicago, September 29, 1900." (Social Democratic Party, 126 Washington Street, Chicago, n.d.).

10. *Ibid.*

11. Editors often urged listeners who had heard Debs speak to not waste their votes. For example, the Quincy, Illinois, *Journal* editor in an essay, "Debs' Mistake," March 15, 1900, wrote: "Debs will draw masses of labor to his ticket and thousands of votes will be uselessly wasted. . ."

12. "The Speeches of Eugene V. Debs and Prof. George Herron," *Ibid.*, p. 7.

13. "Mr. Debs Is In The City," *Leader Democrat*, Springfield, Missouri, October 20, 1900.

14. "Debs at Taunton," Old Fellows Hall, October 28, 1900. Reported in *Boston Globe*, October 29, 1900.

15. "All Laboring Men Slaves," *Boston Herald*, October 29, 1900, p. 1.

16. *Boston Globe*, October 29, 1900.

17. "Socialists Are At War," *Chicago Chronicle*, August 8, 1900.

18. "Debs To Step Down," *Chicago Chronicle*, July 15, 1900; "Withdrawal of Debs," *Saginaw Evening News*, July 23, 1900; "Editorial: Debs to Run," *Ibid.*, July 25, 1900.

19. "Two Candidates for the Presidency," *North American*, Philadelphia, Pennsylvania, October 26, 1900, p. 1.

20. Letter from Morris Stempa to writer, April 8, 1961.

21. *Boston Globe*, October 29, 1900.

22. David Karsner, *Debs His Authorized Life and Letters* (New York: Boni and Liveright, 1919), p. 179, quoting from *World Almanac;* Morris Hillquit, *History of Socialism in the United States* (New York: Funk and Wagnals, 1903), p. 308.

23. David A. Shannon, *The Socialist Party in America* (New York: The Macmillan Co., 1955), p. 4.

24. E. V. Debs to Theodore Debs, November 9, 1900, Theodore Debs MSS., ISU Library.

25. *Ibid.*

26. *Ibid.*

27. *Ibid.*

28. Hillquit MS., March 29, 1901, State Historical Society of Wisconsin, Madison.

29. *Ibid.*, May 27, 1901.

30. *Ibid.*

31. Hillquit to Simons, May 24, 1901.

32. Simons to Hillquit, May 27, 1901.

33. *Ibid.*

Chapter 6 Notes—Pages 67 to 77

1. Morris Hillquit, *History of Socialism in the United States* (New York: Funk and Wagnalls Company, 1903), p. 308. Mr. Hillquit identified with the Springfield faction and served as chairman of several of the sessions. "Debs Telecom Starts Some Talk," *Terre Haute Gazette*, July 31, 1901.

2. See articles in *Indianapolis Journal* and *Indianapolis Gazette,* July 30, 1901.
3. "A Talk With Debs," *Terre Haute Express,* July 31, 1901.
4. "Open Letter," *Social Democratic Herald,* July 27, 1901; Howard Quint, *The Forging of American Socialism* (Columbia: University of South Carolina Press, 1953), p. 337.
5. "Proceedings of the Socialist Unity Convention, Indianapolis, July 29, 1901;" *Social Democratic Herald,* August 17, 1901.
6. "Debs is Shelved," *Terre Haute Express,* July 30, 1901.
7. "Debs Telegram Starts Some Talk," *Terre Haute Gazette,* July 31, 1901.
8. "Has Debs Been Shelved? A Telegram Sent Him," *Terre Haute Gazette,* July 30, 1901.
9. "A Talk with Debs," *Terre Haute Express,* July 31, 1901.
10. "Proceedings of the Socialist Unity Convention," p. 182; Quint, p. 383.
11. "Comrade Debs is Pleased," *The Worker,* August 11, 1901.
12. Collection of Debs' lecture leaflets, owned by Marguerite Cooper, Theodore Debs' daughter. Loaned to writer. Now in ISU Library.
13. "The Terre Haute Spellbinder on Carnegie Libraries," *Indianapolis Union,* April 6, 1901.
14. "Crimes of Carnegie: E. V. Debs Protests Against Condoning Crime in Name of Philanthropy," *New York People,* April 7, 1901.
15. Debs to Germer, April 13, 1903, Debs MS., ISU Library; original in Germer MSS., State Historical Society of Wisconsin Library, Madison.
16. Letter to Germer, March 4, 1904, *Ibid.*
17. "Miners Denounce Debs in Resolutions Today," *Terre Haute Gazette,* April 15, 1904.
18. Debs to Germer, August 1, 1904, Germer MS. at Madison.
19. *Ibid.*
20. "Labor vs. Capital," *Kansas City Journal,* January 10, 1904.
21. *Ibid.*
22. "Organized Labor is a Mob," *Boston Globe,* January 31, 1904.
23. *Ibid.*
24. *Ibid.*
25. See Scrapbook 4, Tamiment Library.
26. Reprinted in *International Socialist Review,* January 1904, p. 392.
27. "A Blow to Union Labor Says Eugene V. Debs," *Fort Worth Register,* Fort Worth, Texas, October 10, 1903.
28. "The Negro Question by E. V. Debs," *American Labor Journal,* Butte, Montana, July 9, 1903.
29. *Ibid.*
30. Printed in November issue of *International Socialist Review,* p. 212.
31. Printed in same magazine, January 1904, pp. 391-397.
32. *Ibid.,* p. 393.
33. Eugene V. Debs letter to *Indianapolis World,* May 23, 1903.
34. Theodore Debs MSS, loaned to writer by Marguerite Debs Cooper. Theodore wrote thirteen essays on Eugene's life titled "Sidelights in the Life of Debs" but never published them. Copies in possession of writer. In 1976 the Eugene V. Debs Foundation of Terre Haute printed the essays, thanks to a grant from Marguerite Debs Cooper.
35. *Ibid.*
36. *Ibid.*
37. *Ibid.*
38. *Ibid.*
39. *Ibid.;* interview with Marguerite Debs Cooper, April 20, 1967; examination of Eugene V. Debs' Scrapbooks, Tamiment Library, New York City.
40. Interviews with Ed Whalen and Mrs. Harry (Clarabel) Dickey, April 20, 1967. Mrs. Dickey worked in the Moore-Langen firm for many years. Mr. Whalen is the present manager, See also Debs MSS, ISU Library, for printing orders and bills.
41. Letters to writer from Owen, November 30, 1964.
42. Hillquit's MSS, State Historical Society of Wisconsin Library, contain many letters from Harriman.
43. *Ibid.,* February 11, 1903.
44. *Ibid.*
45. *Ibid.,* January 28, 1903.

46. *Ibid.*, June 22, 1903.

47. *Ibid.*

48. *Ibid.*, February 1, 1904.

49. *Ibid.*

50. Letter from Debs, October 29, 1903.

51. *Ibid.*

Chapter 7 Notes—Pages 79 to 90

1. "The Years Progress," *The Worker*, May 1, 1904.

2. Seymour Stedman, "The American Socialist Movement, Its Recent National Convention," *Wayside Tales*, August 1904, p. 127.

3. *Socialist Party, Proceedings of the National Convention*, 1904, p. 21.

4. Stedman, p. 130.

5. *Ibid*, pp. 123-130.

6. *Ibid.*

7. "The Socialist Party and the Working Class," opening speech 1904 campaign (Terre Haute, Indiana: Standard Publishing Company, 1904).

8. *Ibid.*, p. 8. See also Indianapolis newspapers, September 2, 1904.

9. *Ibid.*, p. 24.

10. *Ibid.*, p. 28.

11. Bruce Rogers, *Debs His Life, Writings and Speeches* (Girard, Kansas: Appeal to Reason Press, 1908), p. 69.

12. Upton Sinclair, "The Socialist Party," *The World's Work*, XI, April 1906, p. 7431.

13. *Ibid.* Letter to writer from George N. Caylor, October 3, 1961. Mr. Caylor related how the rallies for the campaign speeches were organized and admissions and pamphlets sold.

14. "Republicans and Democrats Scored: Eugene V. Debs Speaks for the Betterment of the Laboring Man," *Terre Haute Star*, November 8, 1904; letter from Roy J. Owen to writer, November 30, 1964. Mr. Owen heard the speech and stated that Debs had the audience in tears one moment and laughing the next.

15. William E. Walling, "The Labor Vote," *The Independent*, pp. 1188-1190.

16. Sermon delivered in Baltimore Cathedral, February 4, 1906. Quoted in Karson, p. 225. See also "Come Let's Reason Together," *Appeal to Reason*, March 10, 1906. This controversy continued and Morris Hillquit, prominent New York Socialist theoretician and John Ryan, a Catholic priest, wrote a series of articles in *Everybody's Magazine* defending their views. In 1913, these essays were published as a book, *Socialism: Promise or Menace* by the MacMillan Company.

17. Letter from Roosevelt to Charles Gettemy, February 1, 1905, in E. E. Morison, editor, *The Letters of Theodore Roosevelt* (Cambridge, Massachusetts: Harvard University Press, 1951), IV, p. 1113.

18. Roosevelt to White, July 30, 1907, *Ibid.*, V. 736.

19. December 31, 1904, Hillquit MSS., State Historical Society of Wisconsin, Madison.

20. See "Proceedings of the First Convention of Industrial Workers of the World" (New York, 1905).

21. Joyce Kornbluh, *Rebel Voices, an IWW Anthology*, "One Big Union," (Ann Arbor: University of Michigan Press), p. 7. See also Paul F. Brissenden's *The I.W.W. A Study of American Syndicalism* (New York: Columbia University Press, 1919), p. 79.

22. See "Speaking Dates," *Appeal to Reason*, June 28, 1902; also *Rocky Mountain News*, Denver, Colorado, June 3, 1902.

23. Eugene Debs, "A Valiant Foeman (Hagerty)," *Social Democratic Herald*, August 15, 1903.

24. Robert E. Doherty, "Thomas Hagerty, The Church and Socialism," *Labor History*, Winter 1962, p. 38.

25. March 27, 1905, Hillquit MSS., State Historical Society of Wisconsin, Madison.

26. April 28, 1905, *Ibid.*

27. "Speeches of Eugene V. Debs and Daniel De Leon at the Organization of the Industrial Workers of the World," (New York Labor News Company, n.d.). Speech also found in the IWW Convention *Proceedings,* 1905, pp. 142-145.

28. *Ibid.* Copy of speech in possession of writer.

29. See Marc Karson, *American Labor Unions and Politics,* 1900-1918 (Carbondale, Illinois: Southern Illinois University Press, 1958), for further comments on this meeting.

30. Germer to Allan Swimm, Editor of *CIO News,* July 6, 1950. Germer served in 1950 as a CIO Director of Organization.

31. Printed as a pamphlet. Delivered November 23, 1905. (Chicago: Charles Kerr and Company, n.d.)

32. "Class Unionism," address to steel workers in South Chicago, November 24, 1905 (Chicago: Charles Kerr and Company, n.d.).

33. *Ibid.* Debs frequently warned against a hasty change to socialism. In an interview in 1900 he stated: "In many areas socialism is not possible, and I would not precipitate it by a single hour." "Social Democracy Born in Jail," *St. Louis Chronicle,* August 29, 1900.

34. *IWW Songbook* (Chicago: Industrial Workers of World, 1909).

35. "Industrial Unionism" lecture at Grand Central Palace, New York City, December 10, 1905. Copy in possession of writer.

36. "The Million Voiced Protest," *Appeal to Reason,* February 9, 1907, p. 1. See also "Debs on Deck," *Appeal to Reason,* January 19, 1907. Debs wanted to arouse sympathy for these three prominent agitators who he thought would be hanged unless public sentiment prevailed. He stated this as his reason for joining the *Appeal* staff.

37. "Interview with E. V. Debs," *The Saturday Spectator,* Terre Haute, Indiana, July 27, 1907.

38. Eugene V. Debs, "Fourteenth Anniversary of 'The Coming Nation'," *Appeal to Reason,* April, 7, 1907. See also item on Debs in *Girard Press,* March 28, 1907.

39. Letter from Grace Brewer to writer, July 19, 1964. Other letters of interest between Debs and the Brewers are found in the Brewer MSS., Wayne State University Library, Detroit, Michigan.

40. *Ibid.*

41. "Why Have an Appeal Meeting," pamphlet circulated by the *Appeal to Reason* Lecture Bureau, Girard, Kansas, 1907.

42. "Bryan and the Commoner," *Appeal to Reason,* March 30, 1907, p. 1.

43. *You Railroad Men,* and other sources.

44. "Roosevelt and His Regime," *Appeal to Reason,* April 20, 1907, p. 1.

45. Comment reprinted in *Appeal to Reason,* May 4, 1907.

46. "Debs Not To Go To Boise For Trial," *Appeal to Reason,* June 8, 1907.

47. "Not Guilty the Verdict. Keynote of Darrow's Address," *Appeal to Reason,* August 3, 1907.

48. Clipping from a New Orleans paper, May 28, 1896. Debs MSS., Emmeline Fairbanks Library, Terre Haute, Indiana.

49. "E. V. Debs Flays Capitalists in a Stirring Address," *Detroit Times,* January 12, 1906.

50. "Speech to Steel Workers," November 24, 1905, reprinted in *Appeal to Reason,* December 16, 1905.

51. "Canton Speech," September 14, 1918, Debs MSS., Tamiment Library.

52. Remark in many speeches and in "Debs Centennial Issue," *The Socialist Call,* October 1955, p. 13. Also found at Tamiment Library in Castleton MSS. in a letter from L. B. Woodstock, M.D., who heard Debs say it in Scranton, Pennsylvania.

53. Unionism and Socialism," Terre Haute, Indiana, Standard Publishing Company, 1904, p. 12.

54. David A. Shannon, "Eugene V. Debs Conservative Labor Editor," *Indiana Magazine of History,* XLVII (December 1951), pp. 141-146.

55. "Unionism and Socialism," p. 15.

56. Term first applied to Debs during his speaking tour in Michigan in 1899. The Bay City, Michigan *Chronicle* first used the phrase. Many other labor writers later used the same comparison to Phillips.

57. Copy found in Debs MSS., Tamiment Library, New York, n.p., n.d.

1. "Platform of the Socialist Party," *Appeal to Reason,* October 17, 1908, p. 2.

2. *Ibid.*

3. "Speech Nominating Debs," *Appeal to Reason,* May 30, 1908, p. 2.

4. In January 1907, Debs had a "rheumatic attack" and throat infection. He went to Cincinnati to a throat specialist for treatments. Debs discussed the illness in a letter to the *Appeal to Reason,* January 19, 1907.

5. Debs to Karsner, quoted in Karsner's book, p. 186. Karsner MSS., New York City Public Library.

6. *Proceedings of the National Convention,* 1908, pp. 160-161. Debs received 159 votes. Thompson 14; Carey 16; Simons 9. Debs' supporters knew he would run. Robert Hunter, delegate to the convention and prominent writer on social issues, came to Terre Haute and persuaded Debs to run a third time. Hunter convinced Debs that William Haywood might run and that the Socialist party would lose everything. See unpublished memoirs of Hunter, Lilly Library, Indiana University, Bloomington, Indiana.

7. "Speech to Friends at Girard," *Appeal to Reason,* May 23, 1908; *Terre Haute Tribune,* June 7, 1908, p. 17. Speech later printed as a pamphlet called "The Issue," (Chicago: Charles Kerr & Co.) n.d.

8. "Eugene V. Debs Honored. But Not By His Home Folks," *Terre Haute Tribune,* June 7, 1908, p. 17.

9. "The Socialists Deify Debs," *New York Sun,* June 1, 1908, p. 1; *New York Herald,* same date, p. 5.

10. See *Appeal to Reason,* June to August issues, 1908, for Debs' speaking assignments.

11. "From Debs to *Appeal,*" July 18, 1908.

12. "Master of the Machine," Special to *Appeal,* July 25, 1908, p. 3.

13. *Ibid.*

14. *Ibid.*

15. Speech reprinted as pamphlet. Given August 12, 1908 (Chicago: Charles Kerr & Co.).

16. Letter from George N. Caylor, Newton, Pennsylvania, to writer, on October 5, 1961. Socialist organizer and promoter for Debs in Philadelphia in 1908. Later a close friend of Debs' and visited Debs in Terre Haute on several occasions.

17. "The Socialist Special," *Appeal to Reason,* August 1, 1908, p. 1.

18. "Red Special," *Appeal to Reason,* September 19, 1908, p. 3. This issue contains itinerary of train. See also Otto McFeely's article, "Campaigning With Debs," *Wilshire's Magazine,* December 1908, pp. 4-5, for details on Barnes' planning and fund raising.

19. "Party Notes," *Appeal to Reason,* September 19, 1908. Lapworth and Simons delivered many fund raising speeches for the train. Lapworth as a foreign Socialist had an especial appeal.

20. "The Socialist Special," August 1, 1908, *ibid.*

21. "Stops Debs," *Chicago Record Herald,* August 31, 1908. See also "Red Special on its Way," *Appeal to Reason,* September 5, 1908: "When the Red Special made its appearance at the depot thousands of social revolutionists cheered continuously. Even representatives of the Chicago capitalist press were present with pencil and camera to see the great train and its decorations."

22. Faith McAllister, "Across Iowa in the Debs Red Special," *Des Moines Daily News,* September 3, 1908.

23. "With Debs on His Special," *Kansas City Star,* September 2, 1908.

24. "Ten Thousand Paid to Hear Debs Speak," *Kansas City Journal,* September 3, 1908.

25. "St. Joseph," *Appeal to Reason,* September 19, 1908.

26. "On to the Coast," *Appeal to Reason,* September 19, 1908.

27. "Red Special on Its Way," *Appeal to Reason,* September 5, 1908.

28. *Ibid.,* September 19, 1908.

29. "Collect the Dinner Pails," *Appeal to Reason,* August 8, 1908.

30. Letter to the *Appeal*, September 19, 1908.

31. Clippings from *Denver Post, The Times,* and *The Republican,* September 5, 1908, Debs' Scrapbook, Tamiment Library.

32. "Debs Expounds Socialism to His Denver Admirers," *Daily News,* September 5, 1908, p. 7.

33. "Grand Junction," *Appeal to Reason,* September 19, 1908.

34. Letter to Readers, September 19, 1908. For another summary of the campaign see "The Socialist Party in the Present Campaign," *American Review of Reviews,* September 1908, p. 299.

35. Letter to *Appeal,* September 11, 1908.

36. *Ibid.* See also James Creelman's article, "America's Trouble-Makers," *Pearson's Magazine,* July 1908, pp. 3-5. Creelman warns his readers about Debs and the increasing Socialist agitation. "The movement is too real, too tremendous, too intelligent to be successfully dealt with by misrepresentation," he wrote.

37. "Debs Draws Splendid Hearing," *San Bernardino Daily Sun,* September 9, 1908, p. 1.

38. "Debs Attacks Judge Grosscup; Rude Interruption for Presidential Candidate," *The Berkeley Independent,* September 12, 1908, p. 1.

39. "Greek Theatre Packed," *The World,* Oakland, California, September 19, 1908.

40. *Miners Magazine,* September 1908; Karsner, p. 197.

41. *Pioneer Press,* St. Paul, Minn., September 21, 1908. Debs expressed in a milder tone some of these ideas in "The Socialist Party's Appeal," an article which appeared in *Independent,* October 15, 1908, pp. 875-880.

42. "The Socialist Party's Campaign," *The Public,* October 2, 1908, p. 635.

43. Carl Sandburg to Paula Sandburg, letters from Manitowoc, September 22, 1908; from Green Bay, September 24, 1908; from Oshkosh, September 27, 1908. *The Letters of Carl Sandburg,* edited by Herbert Mitgang (New York: Harcourt, Brace & World, 1968) pp. 77-79. Toledo, Ohio, September 29, 1908.

45. *Ibid.*

46. "Thousands Hear Debs and Hughes," *Cleveland Plain Dealer,* September 30, 1908, p. 1.

47. "Casino Rink Packed to Limit: Debs Made Fine Address Void of All Ranting and Raving," *Erie Dispatch,* Erie, Pennsylvania, October 1, 1908.

48. "Editorial," *Evening Times,* Rochester, New York, October 2, 1908.

49. "Debs Speaks Here in a Sea of Red," *New York Times,* October 5, 1908, p. 2.

50. "Crowds Wildly Welcome Debs," *The Sun,* New York, October 5, 1908, p. 3.

51. *Ibid.*

52. *Ibid.*

53. *Ibid.*

54. "Debs Here on Red Special, Talks to Two Big Meetings," *New York American,* October 5, 1908.

55. *Ibid.*

56. Reported in *Times, Sun, New York American.*

57. "Red Flags Wave in Fanueil Hall," *Boston Post,* October 6, 1908, p. 12.

58. "Candidate Debs Greeted With Great Enthusiasm," *Boston Journal,* October 6, 1908.

59. *Ibid.*

60. "Debs Brings a Cloud of Red Fire," *Providence Journal,* Providence, Rhode Island, October 8, 1906, p. 2.

61. "Reds Greet Debs With Cheers at the Opera House," *New Haven Palladium,* New Haven, Connecticut, October 9, 1908.

62. "Debs Speaks at Smith Theatre," *Bridgeport Telegram,* Bridgeport, Connecticut, October 10, 1908.

63. Caylor letter to writer.

64. "Debs Gets a Warm Reception in City," *Public Leader,* Philadelphia, Pennsylvania, October 12, 1908, p. 14.

65. *Ibid.*

66. "On Board The Special," *Appeal,* August 8, 1908.

67. Special news item reported in *Philadelphia Ledger,* October 12, 1908. See McFeely's article previously cited in footnote 18 for details of Debs' October speaking, including his invitation to Taft to speak with him.

68. "Eugene V. Debs On What the Matter is in America and What To Do About It," *Everybody's Magazine,* October 1908, pp. 455-70.

69. "Three Big Crowds Hear Debs," *Milwaukee Sentinel,* October 31, 1908. Since Debs caught colds easily, Theodore kept a dry shirt backstage and Debs quickly changed before he went outside.

70. "Halls Too Small for Debs' Crowd," *Milwaukee Free Press,* October 31, 1908.

71. Interview with Schubert Sebree who heard the speeches, April 20, 1962.

72. "Debs Stirs Home Folks," *Terre Haute Star,* November 3, 1908, p. 1. Same newspaper gives accounts of other candidates' speeches.

73. Various figures are argued; all range between $30,000-35,000. The most complete account of expenditures appeared in the *Socialist Party Official Bulletin,* September-November, 1908.

74. Same cost figures in *Terre Haute Star,* November 3, 1908, p. 10.

75. "Interesting Election Results," *Current Literature,* December 1908, p. 588. "The Socialist Showing," *The Nation,* December 3, 1908, p. 541; Kipnis, p. 212, also discusses election.

76. "Debs, The Apostle of Failure," *American Federationist,* September 1908, pp. 736-740.

77. See Part II, Chapter I, "Socialist and Social Reformers," (New York: The Macmillan Company, 1909), p. 209.

78. *Ibid.,* p. 211. See also the discussion on the problem the Socialists faced with reforms in other parties in W. E. Walling's *Socialism As It Is,* "Reformism in the United States," (New York: The Macmillan Company, 1915), p. 175. Walling supported and followed Debs' career. Debs wrote of reforms in an article, "The Socialist Party's Appeal," *Independent,* October 15, 1908. On p. 88, he asserted, "There is no middle ground possible and it is this fact that makes ludicrous those sporadic reform movements typified by the Populist and Independent parties."

79. Alexander Trachtenberg, "The Heritage of Debs," Pamphlet (New York: International Publishers, 1928), p. 11.

80. Steffens, p. 455.

Chapter 9 Notes—Pages 127 to 145

1. "Special from Debs," *Appeal to Reason,* January 25, 1908; also March 14, 1908, issue discusses Debs' trip in an editorial. In 1907 the Goldfield miners struck when the mine owners constructed "change rooms" to prevent stealing of gold ore. Debs resented these rooms and saw the owners' adoption of script in 1908 as just another method of harrassment.

2. "Susan B. Anthony," *The Socialist Woman,* January 1909, p. 3.

3. December 7, 1909. Letter found by writer in Jack London's MSS., Box 15, Huntington Library, San Marino, California. London knew both Debs and Walling. Evidently Walling sent Debs' letters to London.

4. *Ibid.*

5. Eugene V. Debs to William Walling, December 13, 1909, London's MSS.

6. Berger to Hillquit, December 6, 1909, Hillquit MSS., State Historical Society of Wisconsin, Madison.

7. Eugene V. Debs to Morris Hillquit, February 19, 1909, Hillquit MSS., Tamiment Library, New York, New York.

8. *Ibid.*

9. *Ibid.*

10. February 26, 1909, Hillquit MS.

11. *Ibid.*

12. *Ibid.*

13. Victor Berger to Hillquit, February 13, 1910, Hillquit MSS.

14. Letter from Hunter to Adolph Germer, March 18, 1910, Germer MSS., State Historical Society of Wisconsin, Madison.

15. Letter to writer from Morris Stempa, April 8, 1961. Mr. Stempa worked in the city at the time and accompanied Debs to the speech. Other informants told the writer this story but they did not know the place or year.

16. Elizabeth Gurley Flynn, *Debs, Haywood, Rutenberg* (New York: Workers Library Publishers, 1939). Another account of Debs' activities in this year appeared in "Debs Censored by the Ministers," *The Miners Magazine*, December 23, 1909, p. 5. See also Flynn folder of correspondence to Debs, ISU MSS.

17. "Working Class Politics," Speech in Riverview Park, September 18, 1910. Reprinted by William Cherney, *International Socialist Review*, November 1910, pp. 257-58.

18. Morris Hillquit, *Socialism in Theory and Practice* (New York: The Macmillan Company, 1909), p. 354. James Robb in a letter to writer, December 8, 1964, related how Debs would come to his father's West Terre Haute home in 1910 and speak to local unionists and advocate the necessity for industrial unions in basic industries. Debs consistently recommended industrial unionism, even to the Mexicans who revolted under Diaz. See Debs' article, "The Crises in Mexico," *International Socialist Review*, July 1911, pp. 22-24.

19. "Danger Ahead," *International Socialist Review*, February 1911, p. 413.

20. *Ibid.* These same ideas appeared in speeches that he gave at this time.

21. "Official Vote Now In," *Appeal to Reason*, January 7, 1911, p. 3.

22. Morris Hillquit, *History of Socialism in the United States* (New York: Funk and Wagnalls Company, 1910), p. 351. This book was a revised edition of his 1903 book.

23. *Ibid.*, p. 353. For example, the *Jewish Daily Forward* sold 100,000.

24. "Historical Sketch of the Socialist Movement," (New York: The Macmillan Company), p. 320.

25. *Ibid.*, p. 335.

26. The Macmillan Company published the 1906 book; B. W. Huebsch Company of New York published the 1909 and 1911 books; Harper and Brothers the 1918 work. Spargo also published numerous pamphlets and other books that ignored Debs.

27. *Sidelights on Contemporary Socialism*, p. 75.

28. *Ibid.*, p. 110.

29. Ghent's publisher: John Lane Company, New York City, 1910.

30. Charles H. Kerr and Company Co-Operative, Chicago, 1908, printed Reynold's book and The Macmillan Company copywrited Walling's book in 1912.

31. Walling, p. 204.

32. In a letter to Morris Hillquit, February 14, 1907, Herron explained the family's part in founding the school. Mrs. Rand had intended to give the money to Iowa College where Herron had taught, but his liberal views led to his dismissal. Hillquit MSS., State Historical Society of Wisconsin, Madison.

33. Catalogs of Rand School, MSS. in Tamiment Library, New York City. The library occupied one floor of the old school building.

34. Eugene V. Debs, "Sound Socialist Tactics," *International Socialist Review*, February 1912, p. 481.

35. *Ibid.*, Haywood and Bohn had published in 1912 a pamphlet, "Industrial Socialism" which caused this further dissension.

36. "The National Socialist Convention of 1912." *International Socialist Review*, XII, June 1912, p. 807.

37. *Ibid.*, "Socialists Open Convention," Indianapolis News, May 12, 1912.

38. "Tar and Feathers for Ben Reitman—Emma Goldman's Aid," *Indianapolis News*, May 15, 1912, p. 1.

39. "Party Ban on Violence," *Indianapolis News*, May 18, 1912, p. 1.

40. "Socialist Waiver on Direct Action," *Indianapolis News*, May 16, 1919, p. 1; "Berger Sounds Campaign Cry," *Indianapolis Star*, May 13, 1912, p. 3. J. L. Engdahl, "Socialism vs. Syndicalism," *Twentieth Century*, September 1, 1912, p. 399; "Engdahl States the Vote: 191 for; 91 against."

41. "The National Socialist Convention of 1912," p. 827. "Reds and Yellows in Socialist War. Workers and Intellectuals in the Party are Striving for Control," *Indianapolis News*, May 14, 1912, p. 1.

42. E. V. Debs to John Spargo, July 12, 1912, Debs MS., Indiana State.

43. "Socialists Pick Debs and Seidel to Head Ticket," *Indianapolis Star*, May 18, 1912, p. 1; "Debs and Seidel Socialist Ticket," Indianapolis News, May 18, 1912, p. 1.

44. "Socialists Fix June 16 to Open Campaign Fire in Chicago Amusement Park," *Indianapolis Star*, May 20, 1912, p. 1; Ginger, p. 311. Mr. Ginger erred when he claimed the campaign opened in St. Louis on June 29.

45. Letter to James M. Reilly, who served as secretary of the 1912 convention, August 7, 1912. Debs ISU MS.

46. *Ibid.*
47. Cartoon by W. W. Kemble, *Harper's Weekly*, September 21, 1912.
48. "Eugene V. Debs' 'Address of Acceptance,'" 1912. Pamphlet published by National Committee, n.d. or place of speech listed. This speech was given possibly on May 29, in Girard, Kansas, for Debs stayed there until late May when he returned to Terre Haute. The content of this speech differed from the "opener," and no evidence indicats that Debs gave this address in Terre Haute. In this same pamphlet is a copy of Seidel's letter of acceptance, and the 1912 platform. The Seidel letter is not the same as the acceptance speech reported in Indianapolis newspapers at the time of his nomination. *International Socialist Review*, October 1912, pp. 304-307, also published Debs' speech.
49. *Ibid., p.* 3.
50. *Ibid, p.* 5.
51. Ryan Walker MSS., Lilly Library, Indiana University. Walker also served as a campaign speaker. In writing to Debs he seldom used his name. He would draw a picture of Debs, perhaps quote a line from some speech of Debs' and address the letter to the town where Debs happened to stop on his tours. Debs claimed he received his letters. Also, on the front of post cards, Walker would list reasons why the post office employees should support socialism.
52. "This Is Our Year," Debs MSS., Tamiment.
53. Autographed copy from Oneal to Debs, published by National Rip-Saw Company, St. Louis, Missouri. Copy in possession of writer.
54. "This Is Our Year," *Ibid.*
55. *Ibid.*
56. *Ibid.*
57. "'Debs Says Roosevelt Never Had a Principle," Chicago Press release, *Indianapolis News,* 17 June 1912), p. 9.
58. William Hesseltine, "The Bull Moose Movement," *The Rise and Fall of Third Parties* (Washington, D.C.: Public Affairs Press, 1948), p. 27.
Press, 1948), p. 27.
59. See Report of Committee, dated August 3, 1977. Copy in Debs MSS., Indiana State Library. See also Debs' letters to James M. Reilly, August 7, 1912; and to George Goebel, August 13, 1912.
60. May 31, 1912. The letter is not to Ryan Walker but is found in his MSS. Evidently Warren sent the letter on to Walker. Both opposed Barnes.
61. Berger's views on this matter appeared in the August 3 issue; Debs' letter to Berger dated August 10, 1912, Debs MSS., ISU Library.
62. Walker MSS., August 5, 1912, letter.
63. *Ibid.* The only "left" on the National Committee in 1912 was Haywood. Debs never seemed to get his supporters on this important committee.
64. July 26, 1912, letter, Debs MSS., ISU Library.
65. "The Fight for Freedom" speech; published in *Labor and Freedom* (book); *The Voice and Pen of Eugene V. Debs* (St. Louis: Phil Wagner, 1916), p. 165.
66. *Ibid.,* p. 154.
67. *Ibid.*
68. Reprinted in *Labor and Freedom*, pp. 167-168.
69. *Ibid.,* p. 172.
70. Figures also found on p. 5 of Oneal's pamphlet. Debs could have borrowed from this source, but Nearing frequently wrote Debs.
71. "Capitalism and Socialism," p. 175. Elsie B. Harris, who joined the campaign tour at Fergus Falls gave a detailed report of the next month's campaign in "Debs in the West," *International Socialist Review,* October 1912, p. 351.
72. Ray Ginger, *The Bending Cross* (New Jersey: Rutgers University Press, New Brunswick, 1949), pp. 311-12.
73. "Debs: Lover of Men," *Unity,* November 15, 1926, p. 165. Speech delivered in Carnegie Hall.
74. "Socialists Arrange For Large Overflow Audience," *Terre Haute Star,* November 1, 1912, p. 14; "Complete Plans for Big Debs' Meeting," *Terre Haute Star,* October 29, 1912, p. 18; "Debs Stayed In Bed To Rest Up For Tonight's Meetings," *Terre Haute Tribune,* November 4, 1912, p. 1.
75. "Debs: Lover of Men." *Op. cit.*
76. *Ibid.*
77. "The Socialist Vote," *Literary Digest,* November 23, 1912, pp. 943-44.
78. "Socialist Vote in Indiana," *Terre Haute Star,* November 9, 1912, p. 9.

79. "Debs Asserts Charge in Indictment is False," *Idianapolis News*, November 25, 1912. "E. V. Debs Indicated in Kansas Court," *Terre Haute Tribune*, November 24, 1912.

80. "Gene Debs' Generosity Used to Victimize Him," *Christian Socialist*, February 1, 1913.

81. "Eugene V. Debs, *'Why They Are After the Appeal'*," *National Rip Saw*, January 1913. He maintained that for six years the government had been investigating. A previous court trial against Warren cost $12,000.

82. "E. V. Debs Arrested by Deputy Marshals," *Indianapolis News*, January 24, 1913.

83. Letter to the writer, March 16, 1964. See also Debs' letters to Theodore dated May 17, May 18, and May 23 for further details on committee's work. Debs MSS., ISU Library.

84. Interview with A. Germer, October 12, 1964; "Report to Socialist Party Clears Governor Hatfield of Charges," *New York Times*, June 4, 1913, G. H. Ambler, *History of West Virginia* (New York: Prentice Hall, 1933). Includes an account of how the mine owners harrassed the workers, p. 453.

85. "Charges Against Debs Dropped," *New York Times*, May 8, 1913; see also issues of *Appeal to Reason* during May 1913.

86. "Debs Says He Has Paid Off Debt of ARU," *New York Times*, October 30, 1913. Late in the campaign of 1912, Debs had mentioned that the debt would soon be repaid in several speeches.

87. "Blames Public, Not Girl," *Indianapolis News*, July 4, 1913.

88. "E. V. Debs Defends His Action in Taking an Outcast Woman Into His Home," *New York Journal*, July 16, 1913; "The Woman That Debs Took Into His House," *Los Angeles Herald*, July 24, 1913, "Debs Action a Challenge to Christianity," *Tribune*, Tampa, Florida, July 20, 1913; "Eugene Debs, The Church and Woman of the Underworld," *Detroit Times*, July 18, 1913.

89. "Debs to Play Ranchman," *Indianapolis News*, September 24, 1913. Also see clippings from Colorado newspapers in Debs' Scrapbook No. 2, Tamiment Institute Library. Also his letters to Theodore, 1913 file, Debs MSS., ISU Library.

90. Riley had several strokes—the first in 1910. He died in 1916. After the stroke, Debs visited Riley every time he passed through Indianapolis. Debs' Scrapbook contains many clippings on Riley. Riley always brought him a copy of his newest book of poems.

91. Debs to Hillquit, December 20, 1913, Hillquit MSS., Tamiment Library.

92. March 5, 1913, Debs MSS., ISU Library.

93. *Ibid.*

94. Debs to W. H. Thompson, June 26, 1913, Debs MSS., ISU Library.

95. *Ibid.*, June 3, 1914.

96. See Theodore Debs MSS. in letters to close friends written after Eugene died, *Ibid.*

97. Debs to John Brown, June 26, 1913. Brown had been a principal leader in strikes in West Virginia.

98. *Ibid.*

99. Victor Berger to Morris Hillquit, October 23, 1913, *Ibid.* In a second letter to Hillquit on February 13, 1914, Berger claimed O'Hare's election was a fluke and urged Hillquit to run, admitting that Hillquit had a better chance than he did. Interestingly he refers to Debs as the "Sitting Judge."

100. Debs, "Gunman and the Miners," *International Socialist Review*, September 14, 1914, p. 161. See also in same magazine Debs, "Revolt of the Railroad Workers," June 1914, pp. 736-38. Some unions did collect guns. In Adolph Germer's MSS., State Historical Society of Wisconsin, Madison, are a few letters about the matter.

101. Letter to Editor by E. V. Debs, *Terre Haute Tribune*, February 13, 1913. He particularly denounced our involvement in Mexico.

Chapter 10 Notes—Pages 147 to 158

1. Speeches of E. V. Debs, Social Democratic Candidate for President, and Professor George D. Herron, Central Music Hall, Chicago, September 29 (Chicago, 1900), p. 2.

2. "Debs Talks of Trouble in Terre Haute and Mexico at I. U.," *Indianapolis News*, June 2, 1914.

3. "Debs Speaks at Lafayette," *Indianapolis News*, December 6, 1915.
4. Debs to Upton Sinclair, June 12, 1916, Sinclair MSS., Indiana University, Lilly Library.
5. "In Whose War Will I Fight," *Appeal to Reason*, September 11, 1915, Debs stated that the only justifiable war would free the working class.
6. *Appeal to Reason*, August 25, 1915. This newspaper had three hundred thousand subscribers at this time.
7. "Letter of Acceptance," *American Socialist*, April 2, 1916.
8. "E. V. Debs Will be Elected on Socialist Ticket Predicts J. Gerber," *New York Times*, November 3, 1916.
9. Letter from Debs to Hoan, August 17, 1916, Eugene V. Debs MSS., Tamiment Library, New York, New York.
10. Interview with Schubert Sebree on March 10, 1962, Terre Haute, Indiana. In 1920, with Debs in prison, Sebree ran for the same congressional post.
11. Letters from Mrs. Maynard Shipley, May 11, 1964, and George Caylor, October 3, 1961, confirmed this.
12. "Editorial," *National Rip-Saw*, XIII (October 1916), p. 3; Ray Ginger, "The Bending Cross," *A Biography of Eugene Victor Debs* (New Brunswick, New Jersey: 1949), p. 336; Claude Bowers, *My Life* (New York, 1962), p. 101. In 1916, Bowers spoke for the Democrats in the district. He described meeting Debs in Bowling Green, Indiana.
13. Schubert Sebree MSS., Eugene V. Debs Foundation Library, Terre Haute, Indiana.
14. "Editorial," *Appeal to Reason*, April 21, 1917.
15. In several letters to Rose Pastor Stokes between the years 1917 and 1921, Mrs. Curry discussed the college administration's attitude toward her activities. There are nineteen letters from Mrs. Curry in Mrs. Stokes' papers that discuss her work for Debs and her feelings for him. These letters were in a private collection that John M. Whitcomb of Cambridge, Massachusetts, gave to Yale University.
16. Mrs. Curry did not always date her letters but internal evidence indicated that she wrote it in 1917.
17. *Ibid.*
18. Interview with Marguerite Debs Cooper, September 20, 1969.
19. Mabel Curry to Rose Pastor Stokes. February 6, 1919.
20. David A. Shannon, "Eugene V. Debs, Conservative Labor Editor," Indiana Magazine of History, XLVII (December 1959), pp. 141-146.
21. Bowers, p. 102.
22. Letter from Goebel to writer, April 18, 1961.
23. Clyde R. Miller, "The Man I Sent to Jail," *Say,* Alumni Quarterly of Roosevelt University, Chicago (Winter, 1954), p. 71.
24. McAlister Coleman, *Eugene V. Debs, A Man Unafraid* (New York, 1930), p. 287.
25. In former national Socialist conventions, Mrs. Prevey always had been a staunch supporter of Debs for president. Debs often had visited her home for brief rests during his speaking tours.
26. All excerpts, including the introductory remarks. are taken from the first carbon MS. of this speech as recorded by a government agent June 16, 1918, in Nimisilla Park. Copy in possession of the writer.
27. He discussed in detail the cases of Tom Mooney and Francis J. Heney. Heney, a government-appointed investigator, was shot in a San Francisco court room. Heney had given information that supported the union's side in that city's battle.
28. Miller, p. 9.
29. Eugene V. Debs, *The Heritage of Debs: The Fight Against War* (Chicago, 1935), p. 12.
30. The official indictment did not cite specific remarks. It listed points under the amended Espionage Law that Debs supposedly violated. In fact, the Attorney General in Washington told officers in Cleveland: "The case is by no means a clear one. All in all, the department does not feel strongly convinced that a prosecution is advisable." O'Brian to Wertz, Department of Justice Central File, National Archives; David A. Shannon, *The Socialist Party of America* (New York, 1955), p. 115.
31. The formal indictment came on June 20. Debs was not arrested until he returned to Cleveland, Ohio, on June 30 to give a speech in West Side Park, Coleman, p. 288.

32. "Debs Asserts He Is With Government in the War," *Indianapolis News*, June 18, 1918.
33. "Debs Makes Defense of His Canton Speech," *Indianapolis News*, June 24, 1918; *Terre Haute Tribune*, June 24, 1918.
34. "Debs Out On Bail, Pleads Not Guilty," *New York Times*, July 2, 1918.
35. Twenty-year old Miller later regretted his actions. The article (previously cited) by him was his attempt to "set the record straight." He later admired Debs for his courage and convictions. He sent the Debs Foundation in Terre Haute a letter and a copy of this article on May 20, 1963.
36. *New York Times*, September 12, 1918, described Debs during the delivery of this speech: "Debs alternately faced the jury, the court, and lastly the spectators. He spoke with few gestures. . ."
37. Max Eastman, "The Trial of Eugene Debs," *Debs and the War* (Chicago, 1922), pp. 44-57.
38. *Writings and Speeches of Eugene V. Debs*, edited by A. M. Schlesinger (New York, 1948), p. 433. Same speech appears in numerous Socialist party pamphlets.
39. *Ibid.*
40. The twelve jurors averaged over seventy years of age, and they all had assets of more than $50,000. Seven were retired businessmen and farmers. Ginger, p. 364. See also the *New York Times*, September 23, 1918, quoting Rose Pastor Stokes' description of the jury in a speech she delivered on Debs' behalf in New York's Beethoven Hall: "It looked to me as though most of them had gone to sleep before the Civil War. The only slaves they knew were colored. . . no appreciation of the . . . wage slave."
41. "Statement to the Court," Schlesinger, p. 437; also in numerous Socialist pamphlets printed from 1918-1922 in an attempt to secure Debs' release.
42. Debs used this statement in an article in *The Masses* in 1913, and on the title page of a collection of his speeches and writings called *Labor and Freedom*, published privately by Phil Wagner, St. Louis, 1916. Ginger, p. 374.
43. *Ibid.*, p. 439.
44. "Debs Gets Ten Years in Federal Prison," *New York Times*, September 12, 1918.
45. "Terre Haute Socialist Is Found Guilty," *Terre Haute Tribune*, September 13, 1919.
46. Letter undated but written during September 1918. See also her letter to Stokes, November 18, 1918.
47. Hoyt Hudson reported on his Cleveland speech in *The New Justice*, April 1, 1919; see also "Debs Praises Bolsheviki" in *Indianapolis News*, March 13, 1919; "Debs Defies Despots," *Duluth Truth*, Duluth, Minnesota, March 28, 1919.
48. "Toledo Speech Investigated," *New York Times*, November 30, 1918. *The New Republic*, May 3, 1919, pp. 13-15, featured an article on Debs' case. E. Freund stated that the Espionage Law ceased to be effective, or needed, when the war ended.
49. Beard's, *The Rise of American Civilization* (New York: Macmillan Co., 1927), p. 670. Although Beard had been identified with the Socialist Party, he left it to support the war.
50. "Debs Says Washington and Jefferson were Bolsheviki," *Indianapolis News*, December 23, 1918.
51. May 16, 1919.
52. *Ibid.*
53. *Ibid.*
54. June 14, 1919.
55. *Ibid.*
56. See letters in the Library of Congress, Attorney General's Files, 1919, Washington, D. C.
57. Interview with Dr. Eugene Dyche, Terre Haute, son of the prison warden, April 28, 1961. Dyche recounted his father's respect for Debs as a model prisoner. Zerbst was warden during the first part of Debs' term, and Dyche during the last.
58. Frank Harris to E. V. Debs, August 17, 1920, Debs MSS., ISU Library. See also several other Harris letters in 1920-22 file for an account of his efforts to free Debs. See also Herron's MSS., Lilly Library.
59. Theodore Debs MSS., ISU Library, contains letters from these men and others who worked for Debs' release. Debs also stated: "Woodrow Wilson is an exile from the hearts of his people. The betrayal of his ideals makes him the most pathetic figure in the world. . ." *New York Times*, February 2, 1921.

60. "Are We Losing Our Liberty? Is the Incarceration of E. V. Debs an Act of Statesmanship?" *Billboard*, August 30, 1919. See also, David A. Shannon in *The Socialist Call*, Debs Centennial Issue, October, 1955, discussed the pressures on Wilson to free Debs, pp. 14-18.

61. "Ex-President Taft on Eugene V. Debs," *Pearson's Magazine*, January 1920, p. 680.

62. "Debs in 1920," *The Socialist Review*, June 1920, p. 1. Karsner stated that he "convinced Debs to accept," and the delegates to agree.

63. "Debs Nominated by Socialist Convention," *New York Times*, May 14, 1920. Oscar Ameringer of Wisconsin said in his nomination speech of Stedman that he was the only man the Socialists could nominate: "He knows as a lawyer just what to say, and say it well, and keep out of jail at the same time." See also "E. V. Debs' Statement," *New York Times*, May 15, 1920.

64. Excerpts from "Acceptance Speech," Federal Penitentiary, Atlanta, Georgia; May 29, 1920, printed in Alexander Trachtenberg's *The Heritage of Gene Debs*, pp. 46-48.

65. Hillquit to Debs, June 30, 1920, Hillquit MSS., Tamiment Library.

66. Debs to Hillquit, July 16, 1920, Debs MSS., ISU Library.

67. Copies of each in possession of the writer. "The Issue" differed from the others in that it was printed by the "Backboners," a workers' group that met weekly in Chicago, and not by the party.

68. Sam Castleton MSS., Tamiment Library, New York. Mr. Castleton, Socialist party leader in Texas, acquired six of Debs' handwritten prison news releases.

69. "Total Votes Received; Votes for Debs," *New York Times*, November 4, 1920. In 1912, Debs received six per cent of the votes cast. Although more people voted for Debs in 1920, the fact that women voted for the first time lowered his percentage of the total vote.

Chapter 11 Notes—Pages 159 to 166

1. In a letter to William E. Sweet, Denver, Colorado, dated December 7, 1931, Theodore Debs recalled comments Eugene made about Moore. J. E. Dyche had played a prominent role in Republican politics in Oklahoma during the 1920 campaign. Harding rewarded him with the prison appointment.

2. Undated letter from Eugene to Theodore written at time Debs met Moore in prison, Theodore Debs MSS., Indiana State University.

3. *Ibid.*, Sam Moore wrote an unpublished essay describing their friendship. Debs MSS., ISU Library. There are also other letters in this collection from Moore.

4. *Ibid.*

5. Sweet, *Ibid.*

6. Debs sent this item to Theodore, dated November 13, 1921. Theodore Debs MSS., ISU Library.

7. Moore, *Ibid.* Theodore Debs MSS. contain two unidentified clippings from newspapers on Byrne's remarks. In 1926, Moore received a parole. He found it difficult to find work in Chicago. In a letter to Theodore dated July 31, 1927, he stated, ". . . there is as much prejudice here against the colored man as in the South."

8. Sinclair supported Wilson in the early part of the war but later changed his mind. Sinclair strongly opposed the prison sentences given to those who opposed the war. Darrow consistently supported Wilson and the war but deplored the sentencing of antiwar advocates.

9. "Victor Berger Escapes Punishment," *The Outlook*, February 12, 1921; "Debs Stays Put," *The Outlook*, February 16, 1921, p. 245; "Debs Pardson Refused," *The Independent*, February 12, 1921.

10. Editorial, "A Soap-Box Jail," *New York Times*, February 3, 1921.

11. After Debs' release *The New York Call* reported his visit. See article "The World a Poorer Place For Two Years With Debs in Jail," December 24, 1921, p. 2. The *New York Times* in an article on December 24, 1921, incorrectly stated that President Harding ordered a review of the case on April 1, and had Debs come to Washington to visit Daugherty.

12. "Form B. Department of Justice," Theodore Debs MMS., ISU Library.
13. Letter from David Clark to T. Debs, February 13, 1927, *Ibid.* Clark, who knew Debs well, accidentally met him on the train and rode to Atlanta with him. He insisted that Harding wanted Debs to flee since Harding regarded Debs as a "white elephant" from Wilson.
14. "Jail Doors Forced Open by Labor's Two Year Fight," *New York Call*, December 24, 1921.
15. Eugene V. Debs to Theodore Debs, April 26, 1921, Debs MSS., ISU Library.
16. Clipping and attached note found in Theodore Debs MSS., *Ibid.* Often Eugene Debs would send Theodore Debs clippings from various newspapers and attach notes. He seldom dated them.
17. Letter to Spurgeon Odell, Minneapolis, Minnesota, June 17, 1921. Villard MSS., Houghton Library, Harvard University, Cambridge, Massachusetts.
18. July 21, 1921, *Ibid.*
19. *Ibid.*
20. July 22, 1921, *Ibid.*
21. Curry to Odell, July 25, 1921, *Ibid.*
22. Copy of the letter dated July 28, 1921, sent to Theodore Debs.
23. "Favor Debs in Prison," *New York World*, August 10, 1921.
24. "Minute Men Disbanded," *Debs Freedom Monthly*, September 1921, p. 17.
25. See Curry to Stokes MSS., especially letters dated October 4, 1919 and November 4, 1919.
26. Theodore Debs to President Harding, August 31, 1921. Copy of telegram in T. Debs MSS., ISU Library.
27. *Ibid.*
28. August 30, 1921, Karsner MSS., New York Public Library, NYC.
29. *Ibid.*
30. October 6, 1921, *Ibid.*
31. The American Civil Liberties Union on July 7 protested against these harassing activities, often backed by the American Legion, but they continued throughout the summer. Various newspapers carry accounts of these events and the *New York Call*, December 24, 1921, contains a detailed account of many of these raids. Speakers, for example, were usually taken to some isolated rural area and left—miles from the platform and audience they planned to address.
32. "Forgiveness Without Repentence," *New York Times*, November 5, 1921.
33. "American Legion Protests to President Harding Against Leniency," *New York Times*, November 25, 1921.
34. "Eugene Victor Debs Freed," *New York Call*, December 24, 1921; "History of the Case," *New York Times*, December 24, 1921.
35. "Harding Frees Debs. No Restoration of Rights," *New York Times*, December 24, 1921.
36. "Rejoicing Sweeps Prison When Debs Is Ordered Freed," *New York Call*, December 24, 1921. David Karsner wrote the article and helped Debs pack.
37. "Debs Faces the World," unpublished manuscript dated 1922 found in Karsner's MSS., New York Public Library. See also Karsner's article, "Prison Release," *New York Call*, January 14, 1922.
38. "Debs Free: Called to Capital," *Indianapolis Star*, December 26, 1921.
39. *Ibid.*
40. Letter to Hillquit, March 4, 1926, copy in Debs MSS., ISU Library.
41. *Ibid.*
42. *Ibid.*
43. "This Christmas Will Be My Happiest," *New York Call*, December 24, 1921.
44. *Ibid.*
45. *Ibid.*
46. Interview with Marguerite Debs, August 14, 1967.
47. *Ibid.*
48. "Throng of 50,000 Welcome Debs Home: Cheers Greet Socialist Leader in Terre Haute," *New York Times*, December 29, 1921. Terre Haute and Indianapolis papers carry similar accounts of the homecoming.
49. Beard's, *The Rise of American Civilization* (New York, 1927), p. 670. Although Beard had been identified with Socialist causes from time to time, he supported the war.

50. "Debs Says Washington and Jefferson were Bolsheviki," *Indianapolis News,* December 23, 1918.

51. May 16, 1919.

52. *Ibid.*

53. *Ibid.*

54. June 14, 1919.

55. *Ibid.*

56. See letters in the Library of Congress, Attorney General's Files, 1919, Washington, D. C.

57. Interview with Dr. Eugene Dyche, Terre Haute, April 28, 1961.

58. Frank Harris to E. V. Debs, August 17, 1920, Debs MSS., ISU Library. See also several other Harris letters in 1920-22 file for an account of his efforts to free Debs.

Chapter 12 Notes—Pages 167 to 180

1. "I.W.W. Repudiates the New Red Party," *New York Times,* December 28, 1921.

2. *Ibid.* O'Neal also wrote many articles and a book on the Communists. He knew many of the Socialists who became Communists.

3. Debs in an undated letter in Theodore Debs MSS. collection discussed these visits.

4. "These Things We Must Do," *Appeal to Reason,* April 15, 1922.

5. *Ibid.* In this period Debs often referred to himself as "liberated citizen of the world."

6. "Debs' Appeal for Russia," *Debs Magazine,* May 1922, p. 16.

7. Mabel Curry kept Debs' letters and before her death entrusted them to their mutual friend, Rosalie Goodyear, a poet who wrote for several socialist publications. She had frequently corresponded with Debs. These letters remained in a private collection and were read by the writer. In 1975 Lilly Library at Indiana University acquired these manuscripts.

8. "Message to Annual Convention of Socialist Party," *New York Times,* April 30, 1922.

9. July 12, 1922. Karsner MSS., New York City Public Library.

10. "Delaying Obituary Says Debs in Chicago," *Chicago Daily News,* July 14, 1922.

11. "Nature Cure," Lindlahr Publishing Company, 513 Ashland Boulevard, Chicago, 1909. Copy found in Debs MSS., ISU Library.

12. Letter to Theodore, August 12, 1922. Theodore Debs MSS., ISU Library.

13. Karsner included Sandburg's comments in an article, "Here, There and Everywhere," that he published in *New York Call,* July 18, 1922.

14. Letter from Debs to *New York Call,* August 16, 1922.

15. Letter August 5, 1922, Theodore Debs MSS., ISU Library.

16. "E. V. Debs Repulses Soviet," *Christian Science Monitor,* July 28, 1922.

17. *Ibid.*

18. Reprinted in *New York Call,* July 28, 1922.

19. August 12, 1922.

20. Letter from Debs to Theodore, August 22, 1922, Theodore Debs MSS., ISU Library.

21. *Ibid.*

22. Letter to Theodore, September 11, 1922.

23. *Ibid.*

24. "Review and Personal Statement of Eugene V. Debs," Special Press Service, National Office Socialist Party, October 5, 1922.

25. *Ibid.*

26. "The Statement of Eugene V. Debs," *New York Call,* October 8, 1922.

27. "Debs Issues a Statement," *The Worker,* New York, October 21, 1922.

28. "Debs Defies U. S. Policy," *Chicago Tribune,* November 27, 1922; "Debs in First Talk Since Cell Opened," *Terre Haute Star,* November 26, 1922.

29. "Debs Defies Laws; Thousands Laud Him; First Public Utterance Since Release," *New York Times,* November 27, 1922.

30. *Ibid.*

31. "Debs and Longuet," *Debs Magazine,* December 1922, p. 3.

32. "Single Track Minds," *Chicago Tribune,* November 29, 1922.

33. "Chicago Gives Debs Ovation," *Los Angeles Times,* November 26, 1922.

34. "Debs Denounced by General Pershing," *New York Times,* December 7, 1922.

35. "Conditions Which Must Be Observed in Arranging the Debs Meeting," mimeographed brochure, National Office Socialist Party, Chicago, 1923, 8 pp.
36. "Abandons Speech in City Club of Cleveland," *New York Times*, February 14, 1923.
37. Eugene V. Debs to Francis Hayes, February 12, 1923, MS., ISU Library.
38. Eugene V. Debs to Theodore, Chicago, Illinois, March 5, 1923, *Ibid.*
39. *Ibid.*
40. "Wisconsin Assembly Praises Debs," *New York Times*, April 19, 1923.
41. "Debs Here to Speak, Says Supreme Court is Swayed by Steel Trust," *The Capitol Times*, April 18, 1923.
42. *Ibid.*
43. After two months of touring, the National Office of the Socialist party issued a manuscript of Debs' usual speech for press releases. Numerous reviews in newspapers revealed that he essentially followed this general outline and modified it only for comments on local conditions or current events. Copy in Debs MSS., ISU Library.
44. "Debs Not a Candidate: Opposed to Ford," *Minneapolis News*, April 23, 1923.
45. "Debs Favors Bonus," *Minneapolis News*, April 22, 1923.
46. "Schedules Speech at May Day Cause Riot. . .," *New York Times*, May 2, 1923.
47. "Annual Convention of Socialist Party. . .," *New York Times*, May 21, 1923.
48. "Launch Debs Boom for Presidency," *New York Times*, May 23, 1923.
49. *Ibid.* See also *New York Call* articles on convention, June 17, 1923.
50. Eugene V. Debs to Theodore, June 21, 1923, from Cincinnati, Debs MSS., ISU Library.
51. Theodore Debs, "Eugene V. Debs in Cincinnati," *St. Louis Labor*, June 19, 1926.
52. "To the Committee in Charge of the Debs Meeting," National Office of Socialist Party, Chicago, Illinois, August 15, 1923.
53. *Ibid.*
54. "Debs and Foster Break," *New York Times*, September 6, 1923.
55. Eugene V. Debs to William Z. Foster, September 12, 1923, MSS., ISU Library. In this letter Debs spoke of his earlier writing approving the League.
56. *Ibid.*, the *New York Times* article mentioned in footnote 54 also discussed Perlstein visit.
57. *Ibid.*
58. *Ibid.*
59. William Z. Foster to Morris Sigman, president of the ILGWU, October 25, 1923.
60. Foster to Debs, September 22, 1923, Debs MSS., ISU Library.
61. *Ibid.* Foster mentioned these newspapers but did not give dates.
62. Eugene V. Debs to Foster, November 8, 1923, Debs MSS., ISU Library.
63. *Ibid.*
64. *Ibid.*
65. "Eugene V. Debs is Compelled to Cancel All Lecture Dates," *Schenectady Citizen*, Schenectady, New York, November 30, 1923.
66. Interviews with Schubert Seebree, August 11, 1967; Marguerite Debs, July 20, 1968. Other elderly Terre Hauteans interviewed often used the term "quack" to describe Dr. Patton.
67. "Funds Being Sought to Build House of Debs in Indianapolis," *New York Times*, December 16, 1923.
68. "Heart Bad, Debs Enters Sanitarium," *Chicago Herald Examiner*, June 1, 1924. Article states Debs arrived two weeks ago.
69. Mailed by Socialist party national office, 2653 Washington Blvd., Chicago in July 1924. Copy in Debs MSS., ISU Library.
70. William Z. Foster to Eugene Debs, July 30, 1924, *Ibid.*
71. Eugene Debs to William Z. Foster, July 23, 1924, *Ibid.*
72. *Ibid.*
73. "Mrs. Robert La Follette," *Labor*, St. Louis, Missouri, July 26, 1924.
74. "Debs Tells Hapgood that He Sees Broader Socialist-Labor Party," *New York American*, October 9, 1920. Norman Hapgood, the biographer, went to Atlanta and interviewed Debs for a series of articles.
75. Eugene V. Debs to Nomination Committee, July 15, 1924. Copy Debs MS., ISU Library.
76. "A.B.C. of Socialism," Socialist Party, Chicago, 1924.
77. "Calling for Debs," *Terre Haute Tribune*, October 2, 1924.
78. Professor Curry's resignation at the end of the first semester 1924-25, is noted in William O. Lynch's *History of Indiana State Teachers College 1865-1945*, p. 311.

79. Eugene V. Debs, "The American Labor Party," *Socialist World,* January 1925.
80. *Ibid.*
81. *Ibid.*
82. Speech copy in Minutes and Journal of Conference for Progressive Political Action. Debs MSS., ISU Library.
83. *Ibid.*
84. *Ibid.*
85. In the Minutes, Johnson made notations of the crowd's reactions. He later served as chairman of this group, known as the CPPA, from 1926-1928.

Chapter 13 Notes—Pages 181 to 188

1. "Gene Debs—50 Years In Service to Labor," Chicago *Socialist,* March 7, 1925. The first of these celebrations took place at party headquarters on February 27. Similar remarks are found in numerous talks.
2. Eugene V. Debs letter to party members, March 24, 1925, Debs MSS., ISU Library.
3. Debs MS., June 3, 1925.
4. *Ibid.* All short quotes that follow appeared in same letter.
5. Eugene V. Debs to Bertha Hale White, June 29, 1925. Other quotes that follow appeared in same letter.
6. June 8, 1925. Hillquit MSS., State Historical Society of Wisconsin, Madison.
7. *Ibid.*
8. *Ibid.*
9. *Ibid.*
10. June 8, 1925. Hillquit MSS., State Historical Society, Wisconsin, Madison.
11. *Ibid.*
12. *Ibid.*
13. *Ibid.* Mrs. White made reference to the 15,000 people that paid to hear Debs speak at Madison Square Garden. An additional estimated 10,000 sought admission. The event commemorated the 25th anniversary of the founding of Workmen's Circle, a Jewish fraternal organization. See "25,000 Storm Garden to Hear Debs on War," *New York Times,* May 4, 1925.
14. *Ibid.*
15. In Theodore Debs MS., ISU Library, several of Theodore's letters to Arthur Baur, written after Eugene's death, indicate full repayment came in settling Eugene's estate.
16. "New Socialist Publication; American Appeal Out," *New York Times,* December 31, 1925.
17. Letter to writer from J. A. McDonald, May 10, 1964. McDonald heard Debs again at the San Francisco meetings.
18. Letter to writer from Mrs. Maynard Shipley, February 28, 1964. Maynard had been Debs' campaign manager in the 1916 Congressional election; he also saw Debs in San Francisco.
19. Debs MSS., at ISU Library contain several letters from Sacco and Vanzetti. Possibly Debs visited these men twice but no specific dates are mentioned in their letters —only comments about their visits. One visit was definitely in the late summer of 1925, perhaps prior to Debs' New York visit or right after it.
20. "Will Speak for Reverend Norman Thomas," *New York Times,* August 22, 1925.
21. "Debs at Rally Asks Votes for Thomas," *New York Times,* October 12, 1925. "Debs, Purcell Share Ovation by Socialists," *New York Tribune,* October 12, 1925.
22. Sent to Debs in Terre Haute from New York City in 1925; no name except "An American for America." Debs MSS., ISU Library.
23. Unsigned note in Debs MSS., *Ibid.*
24. King to E. V. Debs, October 20, 1925, Debs MSS., ISU Library Hillquit's MSS. contains several letters from men declining the position. Some frankly stated they would not risk their present jobs for this job that could easily fail to last.
25. George Kirkpatrick to Morris Hillquit, November 19, 1925, Hillquit MSS., State Historical Society of Wisconsin, Madison.
26. *Ibid.*
27. Eugene V. Debs to Hillquit, November 19, 1925.
28. Kirkpatrick to Hillquit, November 21, 1925.
29. "New Socialist Publication-American Appeal Out," *New York Times,* December 31, 1925.

1. Debs to Haldeman-Julius, January 4, 1926. Carbon in Debs MSS., ISU Library.
2. *Ibid.*
3. Debs to Vladeck, February 15, 1926, *Ibid.*
4. Vladeck to Debs, February 13, 1926, *Ibid.*
5. "Eugene V. Debs Passes From Life of Service, Achievement and Glory," *American Appeal*, Chicago, October 23, 1926.
6. Theodore Debs to Elizabeth Taylor Chedron, December 5, 1936, Theodore Debs MSS., ISU Library.
7. Debs to J. A. C. Meng, March 12, 1926. Debs MSS., ISU Library.
8. Debs to Hillquit, February 24, 1926, *Ibid.*
9. Hillquit to Debs, March 1, 1926, *Ibid.*
10. "U. S. Representative Berger Moves for Restoration of Citizenship," *New York Times*, March 11, 1926.
11. "Refuses to Apply," *New York Times*, March 12, 1926.
12. Debs to Hillquit, March 4, 1926. Debs MSS., ISU Library.
13. *Ibid.*
14. E. V. Debs to Theodore Debs, March 31, 1926. Theodore Debs MSS., ISU Library; also "Warned Against Speeches or Propaganda in Bermuda," *New York Times*, April 8, 1926.
15. *Ibid.,* (Theodore Debs Ms.)
16. April 8, 1926, *Ibid.*
17. Theodore Debs to Marguerite Debs Cooper, April 20, 1926, *Ibid.*
18. "Puzzled As to Status Here," *New York Times*, April 23, 1926; "Cannot be Excluded as An Alien," *New York Times*, April 15, 1926.
19. "Illness," *New York Times*, May 3, 1926.
20. April 8, 1928, Debs MSS., ISU Library.
21. *Ibid.*
22. *Ibid.*
23. April 8, 1928, *Ibid.*
24. April 8, 1928, *Ibid.*
25. Lewis to Debs, May 16, 1925, *Ibid.*
26. Sandburg to Debs, May 18, 1926, *Ibid.*
27. "Debs Praised by Woman Physician," Interview in *Terre Haute Post*, Terre Haute, Indiana, October 22, 1926.
28. Various printings were made of this leaflet and circulated by groups working on behalf of Sacco and Vanzetti. Copy in Debs MSS., n.d. but it came out in September, 1926.
29. *Ibid.*
30. Debs MSS. include a copy of the questions and answers. Since Debs' answers are more complete and include his handwritten changes, the quoted excerpts that follow have been taken from this copy and not from Robinson's article, "The Great Dreamer, An Interview with Eugene V. Debs," which appeared in *Collier's*, November 20, 1926, pp. 11-12.
31. Mabel Curry MS, Lilly Library, Indiana University at Bloomington. This is the last dated letter Debs wrote to Mabel before he died.
32. "Eugene V. Debs Passes from Life of Service. . .," *loc. cit.*
33. Last receipt he recorded in his checkbook, Debs MSS., ISU Library.
34. The copy of the poem was photographed and reprinted in several Socialist publications. It appeared first in an article, " 'I Am the Captain of My Soul,' Quotes Debs as Last Expression of His Life," *American Appeal*, October 23, 1926. Legend often states that Debs rallied from a coma a few minutes before he died and spoke these lines, but actually he did so several days before for Mrs. Oehlert. Marguerite Debs was at his bedside and agreed. Interview, August 13, 1967. The legend of Debs dying reciting "Invictus" is found in several biographies of Debs.
35. Copy of Certificate found in Theodore Debs' Scrapbook 5, p. 54, Tamiment Library, NYC.

36. "Thousands in Last Farewell to Debs," *American Appeal,* October 30, 1926. "Debs Funeral to be Held Saturday," *Terre Haute Tribune,* October 21, 1926.

37. "Thousands in Last Farewell," *Ibid.*

38. "Speakers Pay Glorious Tribute to Debs," *American Appeal,* October, 26, 1926.

39. Pallbearers now worked for Pennsylvania Railroad: Vernon Morris, Harry Stinson, John Ryan, Edward Heinig, Charles Beard and Samuel Anderson.

40. "Jackals", *New Leader,* October 30, 1926; "Radicals Wrangle Over Honors to Debs," *New York Times,* October 23, 1926.

41. Theodore mentioned the fund in letters to various Socialists but explained it in detail to Arthur Baur in a letter dated December 2, 1927, T. Debs MSS., ISU Library.

42. *Ibid.*

43. "Eulogized at opening of Radio Station WEVD, *New York Times,* October 21, 1927.

44. Theodore Debs to Kate Debs, November 9, 1926, T. Debs MSS., ISU Library.

45. Theodore Debs to Arthur Baur, December 2, 1927.

46. Left $15,000 Estate," *New York Times,* November 7, 1926, same item carried in *Terre Haute Post* and *Terre Haute Tribune* on November 5, 1926.

47. Theodore Debs to Kate Debs, no date, but around 1928, carbon in Theodore Debs' MS.

Chapter 15 Notes—Pages 199 to 226

1. Interview with Norman Thomas, August 5, 1966.

2. See Theodore Debs Correspondence, ISU Library, 1926-1945.

3. "Fight to the Last," Speech to Labor Lycum, Philadelphia, March 19, 1910. Debs MSS., Tamiment Library.

4. Waldon Fawcett, "A Talk With Debs," *Illustrated Express,* April 16, 1896, p. 38. (A clipping of this interview without further documentation was found in Debs' Scrapbook 2 at Tamiment Library.)

5. *Ibid.*

6. See Debs' Scrapbooks at Tamiment Library and the ones at Indiana State University Library.

7. This number is based on a careful study of Debs MSS., including his datebooks; interviews and correspondence with people who worked with him, especially Grace Brewer who served as Debs' typist for several years. Also various labor and Socialist publications frequently carried lists of Debs' speaking engagements.

8. "The Secret of Efficient Expression," reprinted in *Coming Nation,* July 8, 1911. Debs also included the essay in his book, *Labor and Freedom,* pp. 15-22.

9. Ray Ehrensberger, "An Experimental Study of the Relative Effectiveness of Certain Forms of Emphasis in Public Speaking," *Speech Monographs,* vol. 12, 1945, pp. 94-111.

10. "Industrial Unionism," Address delivered at Grand Central Palace, New York City, December 10, 1905. Also widely circulated as a pamphlet. Debs Ms.

11. Clipping, *New Orleans Picayune,* 1896, Theodore Debs' Scrapbook. E. Fairbanks Library, Terre Haute.

12. "Eugene V. Debs on What the Matter Is in America and What to Do about It," *Everybody's Magazine,* October, 1908, p. 457.

13. "Railway Employees and the Class Struggle," speech reprinted in *Appeal to Reason,* February 3, 1906.

14. "Prison Labor," March 21, 1899, Debs MSS., ISU Library.

15. "Unity and Victory," speech to State Convention of the A. F. of L. in Pittsburg, Kansas, August 12, 1908, Debs MSS., ISU Library.

17. "Address to Jury," *Writings and Speeches of Eugene V. Debs,* edited by A. M. Schlesinger, Jr. (New York: Hermitage Press, Inc., 1948). This speech also appeared in many Socialist publications following delivery to the court on September 8, 1918.

18. "Last Speech Before His Voice Was Silenced," Cleveland, Ohio, March 12, 1919. Also published by the Socialist Party as a pamphlet.

19. "Class Unionism," Delivered South Chicago, November 24, 1905, Debs MSS. Tamiment Library.
20. Eugene V. Debs, "Appeal to Negro Workers," Commonwealth Casino, 135th Street and Madison Avenue, New York City, October 23, 1923. Typescript of Speech, Debs' MSS., Tamiment Library.
21. Letter to writer, June 14, 1962.
22. E. V. Debs, "The Worker and the Trusts," *Terre Haute Gazette*, September 30, 1899.
23. E. V. Debs, "Suffer Little Children," *Party Builder*, December 13, 1913, p. 5.
24. E. V. Debs, "Progressive Unionism," *Chicago Socialist*, December 23, 1905, p. 2.
25. E. V. Debs, "The Forbidden Speech," Philadelphia Labor Lyceum Hall, October 11, 1902. Printed by Socialist Party and circulated without a date around 1904.
26. E. V. Debs, "The Crying Need of the Day," Leaflet published by Socialist Party, n.d. but after 1922.
27. E. V. Debs to Theodore Debs, letter referring to his speech in Buffalo, New York, May 3, 1917, Theodore Debs MSS., ISU Library.
28. "Eugene V. Debs to the Children." Speech in Chicago, May 3, 1923, Debs MSS., ISU.
29. "Fight to the Last." Note how Debs elaborated and added one emotional threat after another—each a more dramatic appeal than its predecessor. He overused this propagandistic device of card stacking.
30. "Debs Banquet Surpasses All Expectations," *Citizen*, Schnectady, New York, December 18, 1925.
31. "Appeal to Negro Workers," at Commonwealth Casino, New York City, October 23, 1923.
32. Walter Hurt, "Debs and Sullivan," *The Social Builder*, May, 1918, p. 14.
33. Letter to Writer, January 3, 1961.
34. Debs' Scrapbooks, Tamiment Library, n.p., n.d. This newspaper clipping contained a discussion of a visit between Debs and Markham. Markham had attended a New York City speech of Debs and a reporter interviewed them afterwards.
35. "Life Story of Eugene V. Debs," *Omaha Free Press*, October 10, 1923. Also several interviews with Theodore's daughter, Marguerite Debs Cooper, on the relationship and working habits of the two men.
36. See Debs' Correspondence prior to any major conventions, Debs MSS., July 12, 1908, ISU Library.
37. Morris Hillquit to Vera Hillquit, Hillquit MSS., Wisconsin State Historical Society Library, Madison, Wisconsin.
38. Eugene V. Debs, "Marx the Man—An Appreciation," *The Ohio Socialist* Newspaper, April 5, 1918.
39. *Common Sense* (magazine) July 1933, p. 22. Debs' library contained personally autographed copies of works by the Socialists mentioned.
40. Debs, "Marx the Man—An appreciation," *The Ohio Socialist* Newspaper, April 5, 1918.
41. *Ibid.*
42. Lincoln Steffens, "Eugene V. Debs on What the Matter is in America and What to Do About It," *Everybody's Magazine*, October 1908, pp. 455-470.
43. Interview April 23, 1960 and letter to writer, January 3, 1961.
44. Letter to writer, March 11, 1961.
45. Claude Bowers, *My Life* (New York, Simon and Schuster, 1962), p. 55. Bowers lived in Terre Haute for several years and knew Debs personally.
46. *The National Rip Saw*, December 1915, p. 16.
47. *International Socialist Review*, February 1912, p. 481.
48. *International Socialist Review*, February 1918, p. 395.
49. Eugene V. Debs, "Political Action," *Chicago Socialist*, June 30, 1906.
50. The first convention of the merged railroad unions met in August 9, 1971 at Miami Beach. See article describing merger: "Historic UTU Convention Set, Luna and Gilbert Dropping Reins," *Labor*, July 17, 1971.
51. Letter from Margaret Sanger to E. V. Debs, October 17, 1921. Debs MSS, ISU Library.
52. "Debs Speaks at Knoxville, Tennessee" *Chicago Choronicle*, May 12, 1896; "Debs Speaks," *The News*, Chattanooga, Tennessee, May 13, 1896.
53. "Proceedings of Socialist Unity Convention," manuscript in Harper Library, University of Chicago, pp 125-132. Berger's Milwaukee paper, *Social Democratic Herald*, May 31, 1902, carried the remark.

54. Eraste Vidrine, "Negro Locals," *International Socialist Review*, January, 1905, p. 389.

55. "Debs on Color Question," *Appeal to Reason*, July 4, 1903; See also an article by Debs for the *Indianapolis World*, June 30, 1903, a Black newspaper.

56. E. V. Debs, "The Negro in the Class Struggle" *International Socialist Review*, November, 1903, p. 258.

57. National Constitution of the Socialist Party, adopted at Chicago Convention, May 1-6, 1904. Endorsed by referendum August 4, 1904.

58. "Debs Reply to Roosevelt," *Appeal to Reason*, May 1, 1909.

59. Speech of Acceptance, 1912. Reprinted in Socialist Campaign Book, Published by National Headquarters of Socialist Party, 111 North Market Street, Chicago.

60. Reverend G. W. Woodbey, "What and How to Do It or Socialism vs Capital ism," *Wayland's Monthly*, August, 1903. Whole issue devoted to Woodbey's ideas on how socialism could take over capitalism.

61. Reviewed by A. M. Simons, *International Socialist Review*, February, 1905, p 508.

62. "Why a Negro Should Vote Socialist Ticket," *Party Builder*, March 21, 1914. Woodbey corresponded with Debs and each admired the other. See Debs' MSS., ISU Library.

63. E. V. Debs, "Unmitigated Barbarity," *National Rip Saw*, June, 1915, p 3.

64. E. V. Debs, "The Color Line," *National Rip Saw*, April, 1916, p 3.

65. E. V. Debs, "The Crime of Lynching and White Supremacy," *National Rip Saw*, January, 1917, pp 3-4.

66. "Eugene V. Debs on Birth of a Nation: Who is Responsible for the American Mulatto," *National Rip Saw*, March, 1916, p 27.

67. Congressional Platform of Socialist Party, National Office, Chicago.

68. Eugene V. Debs, "The Negro: His Present Status and Outlook," *The Intercollegiate Socialist*, May, 1918, pp 11-14.

69. Eugene V. Debs, "The Negro: His Present Status and Outlook," *Public Ownership*, Baltimore, Maryland, June 15, 1918, p 1. (Although titled the same as previous article they differed.)

70. "Appeal to Negro Workers," speech at Commonwealth Casino, New York City, October 30, 1923.

71. Eugene V. Debs, "Black Persecution," *American Appeal*, February 20, 1926, p 4.

72. Letter to Edward H. Evinger, August 29, 1895; Bruce Rogers, ed., *Debs His Life Writings and Speeches* (Girard, Kansas: Appeal to Reason, 1908), p. 65.

73. Clarence Darrow, *Story of My Life*, p. 73.

74. Alexander Marky, "Saving the Life of Gene Debs," *Pearson's*, October, 1924, p. 17.

75. Steffens, *Everybody's Magazine*, October 1908.

76. Quoted in an article, "Much Loved, Much Hated Gene Debs," *Milwaukee Journal*, June 15, 1949.

77. Published by Charles H. Kerr, Chicàgo, n.d. Contrary to some published reports London and Debs never met although they corresponded. See London MSS., Huntington Library, San Marino, California.

78. "Greek Drama in Cleveland," (a Report on Debs' Trial) *Heroes I Have Known* (New York, Simon & Schuster, 1942), pp. 56-57. "The Trial of Eugene V. Debs," *The Liberator*, November 1918.

79. Published privately by Upton Sinclair, ca. 1919.

80. Shaw to J. Mahlon Barnes, July 28, 1921. Copy in Debs MSS., ISU Library.

81. Irving Stone eventually wrote such a novel, *An Adversary in the House* (Garden City, New York: Doubleday and Co., 1947).

82 Mark Shorer, *Sinclair Lewis. An American Life* (New York: McGraw Hill, 1961), p. 337.

83. *The Saturday Spectator*, Terre Haute, Indiana, July 27, 1907.

84. Bertha K. Ehrmann "Reminiscences of Max Ehrmann," *Indiana Magazine of History*, XLVI, 249.

85. *Ibid.*

86. James Woodress, *Booth Tarkington* (Philadelphia: Lippincott and Co., 1955), p. 111.

87. John Dos Passos, *U.S.A.: The 42nd Parallel* (Boston: Houghton Mifflin and Co., 1960), p. 26.

88. Edward McNall Burns, David Starr Jordan (Stanford University Press, 1953). The remark is taken from a letter to Ruth LePrade, April 17, 1920, in Jordan's papers, Hoover Library, Stanford University.

89. Letters from Lambarence, May 21, 1962, Debs Foundation MSS., in Debs' home. Sweitzer was a cousin of Debs' mother.

90. "The Issue." Copy in possession of writer.

91. E. V. Debs, "The Real Debauchers of the Nation," originally in *Success Magazine,* reprinted in *Chicago Socialist* newspaper, July 21, 1906.

92. "Debs the Dreamer," *Eugene V. Debs: An Introduction* (Williamsburg, Ohio: Progress Publishing Co., n.d.), pp. 24-25.

93. Roger Simon, "Socialists' Last Hope Runs a Quiet Campaign," *Chicago Sun Times,* April 2, 1976.

94. *Walls and Bars* (Chicago: Charles H. Kerr, 1973).

95. "Secret of Efficient Expression," p. 19.

Index

abolition of Senate, 91
accidents, 20, 25, 77-28
Adams, Samuel, 93
agitator, 26, 28, 40, 54, 62, 93, 140, 161, 221
American Appeal, 184, 186, 188, 188-189, 191, 194-195
American Civil Liberties Union, 161, 213
American Federation of Labor, 44-45, 54-55, 80, 83, 84, 93, 161, 170, 214, 222
American Labor Party, 177-179, 181
American Legion, 162, 164
American Railway Union, 29-34, 36, 39, 40-42, 46-47, 53, 60, 83-84, 89, 97, 142, 214
amnesty, 160-162, 167, 189
Anthony, Susan B., 22, 127, 179
anti-war, 147-149, 150-158, 159-161, 210
Appeal To Reason, 57, 79, 83, 85-90, 92, 93, 95, 130, 132, 141-142, 147, 161
Atlanta Prison, 156, 161
automation, 42, 93, 99, 194-195

Baker, Charles, 151
Baker, Newton D., 221
ballot, 42, 44, 62, 82, 212
Bancroft, George, 153
Barnes, J. Mahlon, 77, 93, 134, 137-139, 162, 208
Barrymore, Ethel, 192
Bartholdi, August, 14
Baur, Arthur, 142, 184, 186-187, 197
Baur, John, 26, 27
Baur, Nellie, 197
Baur, Oscar, 186
Bayh, Birch, 190
Beard, Charles A., 155
Bell, Theodore, 97
Bellamy, Edward, 52
Benson, Allen, 222
Berger, Victor, 38, 43, 47-48, 53, 55, 59-60, 63, 64, 67, 69, 76, 83, 91, 104, 128-129, 130-131, 132-134, 138-139, 143, 144-145, 160, 184-186, 190, 196, 207-208, 210-212, 223-224
Bermuda, 191
Beveridge, Albert J., 61, 214
birth control, 215
Birth of a Nation, 217
blacklisting, 35, 37-39, 52
Blacks, 72-73, 76, 89, 140, 159, 203, 215-219
Bohn, Frank, 83, 132, 210-212
"boring from within", 44, 71, 177
Bowers, Claude, 150, 209
Branstetter, Otto, 170-172, 174, 183

Brewer, George, 87
Brewer, Grace, 87
Brotherhood of Carmen, 31, 214
Brotherhood of Carpenters & Joiners, 23
Brotherhood of the Cooperative Commonwealth, 47
Brotherhood of Locomotive Engineers, 31, 179, 214
Brotherhood of Locomotive Firemen, 23-26, 28-31, 53, 74, 179, 182, 191, 196, 214
Brotherhood of Railroad Brakemen, 26, 214
Brown, John, 212
Bryan, William Jennings, 43, 60-63, 87, 93, 95-96, 100, 101, 102, 104, 134-135, 222
Buffalo Switchmen's Strike, 29
Burleson, Albert S., 158
Burns, William E., 47
Bush, Ned, 10
Butscher, William, 64, 67
Byrne, J. Fr., 160

Calamity Howler, 89
Call, The, 161
Calverton, V.F., 208
Cannon, Joseph, 95
Canton speech, 150-155, 202, 214
Carey, J. F., 59-60, 67, 91
Carnegie, Andrew, 70, 82, 201, 210
Carnegie Steel 29
Carr, Ellis, 92
Carter, Jimmie, 225
Castleton, Sam, 163
Catholic, 15, 82-83
Caylor, George, 102
Central Lyceum Bureau, 86
Chappell, C. H., 40
Chautauqua, 70, 86
childhood, 13, 22, 215
child labor, 88, 97, 135, 140, 204-205, 214
Christian Socialist, 92, 137
(See also George Herron)
Cigar Makers Union, 33
citizen of the world, 165, 167, 171, 173
citizenship, 190
City Clerk, 24-25
Civil War, 16, 22, 215
Clemenceau, Georges, 171
Clemons, C. G., 68
Cleveland, Grover, 37, 40, 62, 72
Colliers, 193
Columbian Lyceum Bureau, 86
The Coming Nation, 57
Communist Party, 129, 167, 169-171, 173, 175-177, 181-182, 187, 196, 213

Congressional campaign, 147-148
contempt of court, 153
Coolidge, Calvin, 190
Cooperative Commonwealth Colony,
  46-48, 51-52, 62, 69
corruption, 93
courts, 92, 160
Cox, Helen, 142-143
Cox, James M., 157
Cox, Jesse, 53-54
craft unionism, 29-34, 82, 84, 168, 171
Creel, George, 92
Crinkle, Nym, 36, 38
Cuba, 55-56
Cunnea, William A., 196
Curtis, Jennie, 35-36
Curry, Charles, 148, 178
Curry, Mabel Dunlap, 148-150,
  154-156, 160, 162, 162-163,
  165-168, 178, 195

Darrow, Clarence, 37, 81, 88, 157,
  160, 189-190, 219
Das Kapital, 38, 208
Daugherty, Harry M. (Atty. Gen.),
  157, 160-162
Davis, Henry G., 81
Davis, John W., 189
death, 195-197
Debs (Mailloux) Emma, 14, 191
Debs, Eugenia, 14, 20
Debs Freedom Monthly, 163
Debs Foundation, 197
Debs, Gertrude (Mrs. Theodore), 70,
  148, 150, 166, 169, 186
Debs, Jean Daniel, 13-15, 19, 21-22,
  38-39
Debs, Katherine Metzel, 26-29, 67, 70,
  74-75, 85-86, 142-143, 149,
  150, 155-156, 163, 165-166, 168,
  176, 186-187, 189-191, 194-197, 199.
Debs, Louise, 14-15, 17
Debs Magazine, 170
Debs, Marguerite Bettrich
  (Mrs. Jean Daniel), 13-16, 19-22, 38
Debs, Marguerite (Cooper), 70, 150,
  166, 191, 195-196
Debs, Marie, 14, 26
E. V. Debs Publishing Company, 56
Debs Minute Men, 163
Debs Testimonial Fund, 189
Debs, Theodore, 14, 20, 24, 38,
  59-60, 62-64, 67-70, 72, 73-75,
  94-96, 98, 101, 133, 142, 144,
  148, 149-150, 154-157, 159-165,
  167, 169-170, 173-174, 182, 184-186,
  189-192, 194-197, 199, 206
debt of ARU, 41
De Leon, Daniel, 44-45, 55, 59-60, 62,
  64, 83-84, 128-129, 143, 207, 225
Deming Hotel, 197

Democratic Party, 24-26, 42, 44, 62,
  80, 91, 94, 98, 101, 134-135,
  186, 222-223
Dempsey, Jack, 162, 220
De Pew, Chauncey, 61
disenfranchisement, 189-190
  (See also "Citizen of the World")
Dos Passos, John, 221
Drake, W. E., 170
drinking, 23-24, 48-50, 57, 138, 148
Duches, Lena, 19-20
Dyche, J. E., 159, 164

Early, Jacob and Samuel, 13-14
Eastman, Max, 150, 153, 220
Eckert, George, 38
editing, 24-29, 85-91, 93, 95, 130-132,
  147
education, 15-19, 21, 27, 199-201
Edwards, A. W., 31-32
Ehrmann, Max, 221
eight hour day, 71-72, 75, 81,
  93 (4-5 hr. day), 134
election returns, 63-64, 82, 157-158,
  222-224
Emmett, Robert, 15
Engdahl, Louis J., 160, 170
Engels, Friedrich, 208
Espionage Act, 152, 155, 162, 214
estate, 197
Ettor, Joseph, 133, 137
evolution, 183
evolutionary socialism (see also
  Slowcialists), 80, 84, 103, 127-128,
  132-133, 137, 171, 193-195, 207,
  210, 215

Fairbanks, Charles, 81
Farmer Labor Party, 161, 173, 177
federal troops, 37, 127
Field, Eugene, 220
Firemen's Magazine, 24-27, 29, 89
Flagg, Abbie, 15-19
Flynn, Elizabeth Gurley, 129
Ford, Henry, 173, 193-194
Foster, William Z., 174-178
Franklin, Benjamin, 93, 153
free speech, 132-133, 136, 151, 154,
  160, 171, 173, 210
Frick, Henry, 29

Garrison, William Lloyd, 62
Garwin's Business College, 19, 200
General Managers Association, 36, 40
George, Henry, 38, 44
Germer, Adolph, 70-71, 84, 142, 160
Ghent, W.J., 131
Gibbons, Cardinal, 82
Giovannitti, Arturo, 133, 137
Goeble, George, 64, 92, 133, 139, 151
Goldman, Emma, 133, 210

Gompers, Samuel, 44-45, 55, 84, 94, 104-105, 161, 176, 178, 199, 214, 222
Goodwin, Roy M., 47
Great Northern, 31-34, 35-36, 42, 140
Greenbaum, Leon, 69, 76
grocery store, 14
Gronlund, Lawrence, 38
Grosscup, Peter S., 97

Hagerty, Thomas, Fr., 83
Haldeman-Julius, E., 189
Hanaford, Ben, 77, 79, 81, 91-92, 94
Hanna, Mark, 63, 71-72
Hapgood, Mary Donovan, 56
Harding, Warren G., 158, 159-165, 190, 219, 221
Harper, Ida Husted, 22, 29
Harris, Frank, 157, 219
Harriman, Job, 59-60, 76
Harrison, Benjamin, 29
Hartke, Vance, 190
Harvey, W. H. "Coin", 38
Hatfield, Henry D., Gov., 142
Hayes, "Uncle" Benny, 15, 17
Hayes, Max, 60, 77
Haywood, William (Bill), 83, 85, 87, 89, 94, 105, 132, 143-145, 152, 161, 210, 214
Head, Percy, 165, 195
health benefits, 97
Heath, Frederick, 53, 57, 59, 210
Henry, Patrick, 21, 221
Henry, William H., 196
Herron, George, 61, 67, 92, 132, 157, 200, 207-208, 222
High, Fred, 157
Highland Lawn Cemetery, 196
Hill, James J., 31-34, 210
Hill, Joe, 84, 143
Hillquit, Morris, 46, 64, 69, 76-77, 82-84, 100, 106, 127-129, 130, 132-134, 137-138, 143-144, 145, 157, 161, 174, 183-185, 187-188, 190-191, 195-197, 200, 206-208, 223-224
Hoan, Daniel W., 147
Hogan, Ben, 34
Hogan, Dan, 133
Hogan, James, 47
Holbrook, Josiah, 57
Holmes, John Haynes, 140, 204
Holmes, Oliver W., 208
home, 28, 85, 105, 141, 166, 196-197
House Bills 91 & 92, 25
Howard, George W., 33
Hughes, Charles Evans, 99
Hugo, Victor, 13, 15, 75, 208, 215
Hulman, Henry, 23, 25
Hunter, Robert, 128-129, 222
Hurt, Walter, 221

illness, 159, 167-169
imperialism, 61-62, 81
income tax, 91
Indiana General Assembly, 25-26
Indiana State Normal (University), 16, 148, 178, 197
industrial growth, 27
industrial unionism, 29-53, 80, 82-84, 91, 168, 212-213
Industrial Workers of the World (IWW), 79, 82-86, 89, 91, 130, 132-133, 136, 143-144, 152, 161, 167, 171, 177, 212-213, 222
Ingersoll, Robert, 21, 56, 75, 221
injunction, 31, 36-38, 44, 50, 81, 91, 93, 127
insurance for workers, 97
International Ladies' Garment Workers Union, 175-176
International Socialist Bureau, 128, 129, 144
International Socialist Review, 64, 73, 80

Jefferson, Thomas, 61, 62, 93, 153, 155
Jewish Daily Forward, 129, 130, 184, 188, 189, 197
Jewish unions, 45, 74, 129, 223
Jimmie Higgins, 79, 92, 94, 132, 141, 188, 207
Johnson, Mercer G., 179
Jones, Mother (Mary), 50, 63, 92, 130, 142, 222
Jordan, David Starr, 221
Journal of Knights of Labor, 45
Juno, 167-168
Justice, 85, 89

Karsner, David, 21, 157, 163, 164-165, 168-169, 184
Kautsky, Karl, 38, 208
Keliher, Sylvester, 41, 47
Keller, Helen, 220
Kerr, Charles, 128
King, Murray E., 187-188
Kirkpatrick, George, 183-185, 129-130, 187-188
Knights of Labor, 45
Kollantai, Madame Alexandra, 148
Kruse, William, 160
Ku Klux Klan, 217

labor conditions, 27-28, 42, 48-49, 50
Labor Lecture Bureau, 70
labor legislation, 25, 91
Landis, Kenesaw, Judge, 97, 160
La Follette, Robert, 139, 177, 181, 189
Langen, E. O. and E. J., 56, 76
Larkin, James, 148
Lawrence (Massachusetts) Strike, 132, 136
Leach, Joshua, 23
leadership, 199-200, 206-215, 222-225

League of Nations, 193-194
Lease, Mary Elizabeth, 56-57
lectures, 87, 88, 92, 96, 99,
    104, 134, 135, 140, 142, 172-176,
    181-183, 199-202, 204-206,
    209-210, 219
"Lefts," 91-92, 133
leisure time, 24, 42
Lenin, Vladimir Ilyich, 170
Le Prade, Ruth, 220
Lewis, John L., 176
Lewis, Sinclair, 191-192, 220
Lincoln, Abraham, 61, 163, 221
Lindlahr, Henry, 169
Lindlahr Sanitarium, 168-169, 172, 176,
    178, 193, 195
Lloyd, Henry Demarest, 30, 40, 43-44,
    45, 48
Lloyd, William Bross, 171
London, Jack, 220
London, Meyer, 161
Longfellow, Henry W., 208
Longuet, Jean, 171-172
Lovejoy, Elijah, 62

Macnider, Hanford, 164
Mailloux, Emily (Emma), Debs, 14,
    191
Mailly, William, 53, 76, 79
Markham, Edwin, 92, 192, 204,
    206, 220
marriage, 26-27
Marx, Karl, 38, 46, 57, 61,
    84, 131, 140, 171, 208-209
Messenger, The, 218
Meyers, John, 190
Midland Lyceum Bureau, 86
military conscription, 148
Miller, Clyde, 151-153
Milwaukee Leader, 170
minority rights, 214
Mitchell, John, 70-71
Moliere, 18
Mooney, Tom, 174
Moore, Sam, 159-160
Moore, T.S., 56, 76
morals, 194
Morgan, J. P., 179
Morgan, Thomas J., 62-63
Moskowitz, A. W., 152
Moyer, Charles, 83, 85, 87

McCartney, F. O., Reverend, 60
McGuire, P. J., 23
McHenry County Jail (Woodstock, Ill.)
    37-38, 44, 56
McKinley, William, 44, 51, 60-61, 63
McKeen, Frank, 18

NAACP, 215-216
National Association of
    Manufacturers, 72

National Executive Board [committee],
    64-65, 83, 128, 132, 137-139,
    142, 167, 181-186, 188, 194, 206-207,
    209, 215
nationalization, 53
Naturopathic cures, 168-169
Nearing, Scott, 140
Negroes (See Blacks)
"Negro & His Nemesis", 73
"Negro in the Class Struggle," 73
New York Call, 129-130

Occidental Literary Club, 21
Oehlert, Cecile, 195
O'Hare, Kate Richards, 92, 130,
    145, 150, 196
O'Neal, James, 167
one big union (O. B. U.), 84
Old Seminary School, 15-18
Oneal, James, 136
orator, 20-21, 199-202, 204-206,
    209-211, 219, 225
Order of Railway Telegraphers, 26
organizing unions, 23, 26, 28, 45-47
Otis, James, 93
Owen, Ray J., 76

pacifist (See Ch. 10) 147, 210
Paine, Thomas, 70, 93, 153
Palmer, A. Mitchell, 155, 157
pardon, 156, 190
Parker, Judge Alton, 81
Parry, David N., 71-72
Parsons, W. W., 16
party conflicts, 59, 62, 63-70, 76-77,
    91-93, 130, 132-134, 144, 181-183,
    206-208, 210
Patton, Dr. Madge Stephens, 176,
    192-195
patriots, 101
peace resolutions, 162
People, The, 45
Perlstein, Myer, 175
Pettibone, George, 85, 87
Philippines, 55-56, 61, 147
Phillips, Wendell, 22, 62, 89, 221
Pillsbury, Charles, 32
Pinkerton detectives, 29, 70, 90
platforms, 52, 60-63, 68, 80, 91-92,
    132, 134-135, 157, 177-179,
    206-207, 217, 223
political prisoners, 152, 155, 161-164,
    173, 189-190
Populist Party, 42, 44-46, 53, 55, 82,
    134, 214-215
poverty, 106, 135
presidential candidate, 43, 59-61, 63-64,
    79, 82, 105, 157
Prevey, Marguerite, 151-152
prisons, 141, 156, 159-160, 164, 166,
    173, 184, 187, 205, 215, 226
Pritchett, Harley, 14, 39-40
Private Soldiers and Sailors Legion, 161

Progressive Party, 176-179
Progressive Thought, A Radical Monthly, 57
prostitutes, 24, 135, 142, 194
Pullman, George, 35-37, 40, 201, 210
Pullman town, 36-38, 205
Pullman Strike, 35-38, 40-42, 89, 136, 205

race prejudice, 72-73
radical, 209-214
Rainsford, Rev. W. S., 55
Rand, Carrie, 131-132
Rand School of Social Science, 131-132, 194
Railway Times, 47, 57
Randolph, A. Phillip, 218
Redpath, John Clark, 221
"Red Special", 93-106, 134, 136
Reed, Myron, 47
referendum, 177, 207
reforms or reform movements, 91, 105-106, 134
Reitman, Ben, 133
religion, 14-15, 92
Republican Party, 42, 44, 53, 62, 80, 94, 96, 97-99, 105, 134-136, 223
Reuther, Valentine and Anna, 49
Reuther, Walter & Victor, 49
revolutionary socialism, 45, 55, 80, 84, 97, 103, 127-128, 130, 132-133, 177, 204, 207, 210
Reynolds, Stephen, 81, 96, 103, 131
"Rights" (See also evolutionary socialism & Berger), 91-92, 215
Riley, James W., 143, 220
Rip Saw (National), 147, 196
Robinson, Arthur, 193
Rockefeller, John D., 82, 92, 145, 179, 201, 210
Roosevelt, Theodore, 63, 81, 82, 87, 96, 98, 100, 103, 134, 134-135, 137, 139, 151, 210, 222
Russell, Charles Edward, 216
Russian Revolution, 152, 157, 160, 167, 178, 212
Ruthenberg, Charles, 151
sabotage, 212
Sacco, Nicolo and Vanzetti, Bartolomeo, 165, 174, 186-187, 191-192, 194, 215
safety, 20, 24, 25, 27, 213
Sandburg, Carl, 98, 169, 192, 220
Sanger, Margaret, 215
Sanial, Lucien, 45
Schlesinger, Arthur, 188
Schweitzer, Albert, 221
Scott, George, 16
Sebree, Schubert, 148
Seidel, Emil, 134, 208
Shakespeare, William, 208
Shaw, George Bernard, 162, 220
Sheperd, John, 179

Shepperd, J. I., 141
Shipley, Maynard, 148
Sigman, Morris, 175-176
Simons, A. M., 64, 68, 80, 82, 91, 94, 96, 128
Sinclair, Upton, 81, 100, 147, 156, 160, 189, 209, 220, 222
"Slowcialists" (See also evolutionary socialism), 128, 132, 136, 171, 207
Social Democracy of America Party, 52, 53, 57-60, 62-64
Social Democrat, 47, 70
socialism, 45-46, 54, 61-62, 65, 68, 80, 82, 84, 91-106, 130, 134, 157-159, 167-169, 171, 181-183, 186, 194, 200, 204-208, 210-217
Socialist Cooperative Republic, 193
Socialist Labor Party, 44, 59-60, 62-63, 64, 83, 128, 144, 210
Socialist Party, 44-47, 55, 59-61, 67-70, 89-106, 130-133, 134, 136, 139, 142, 143-145, 147-148, 151, 157-158, 167, 168, 170-174, 176-178, 181-188, 193-200, 206-208, 210-218, 222-224
Socialist summer camps, 92-94
Socialist Trade and Labor Alliance, 44-45
Socialist World, 170
Solomon, Pierre, 18
Sovereign, John R., 45
Spargo, John, 128, 131-134, 138, 200, 210, 222
speaker (see also lectures), 20-21, 199-202, 209-210, 219, 225
Standard Publishing Company, 75
Stanford University, 98
Stanton, Elizabeth Cady, 179
state representative, 25-26
Stedman, Seymour, 53, 62-64, 91, 157, 196
Steffens, Lincoln, 104, 106, 201-202, 209, 220
Steiner, Virgil, 153
Stempa, Morris, 63
Steunenberg, Frank Gov., 85
St. John, Vincent, 143
St. Joseph's, 15
St. Louis, Belleville & Southern Illinois Railroad, 19-20
St. Stephen's Episcopal Church, 26
Stokes, J. Phelps, 149, 222
Stokes, Rose Pastor, 101, 148-151, 153-156, 163, 169
Stone, Irving, 220
strikes, 28-29, 31-36, 40, 46, 48, 51, 70-71, 89, 97, 127-130, 135, 140, 142
Sue, Eugene, 13
Sunday, Rev. Billy, 205
Supreme Court, 85-86, 160
Switchmen's Mutual Aid Society, 26

264

Taft, William Howard, 93, 97-101,
    103-106, 134-137, 140-157, 173, 222
Talmage, Frank DeWitt, 220-221
tariff, 43, 81, 99
Tarkington, Booth, 221
Terre Haute Central Labor Union, 195
Thomas, Norman, 187, 196, 199,
    206, 209, 225
threats on life, 187
"Tongue of the working class," 199, 210
Trautman, William, 83
trials, 37-38, 40
Trommer, Marie, 101
trusts, 93, 105
Tucker, Irwin St. John, 160, 170
Tuvim, Abraham, 175
Typographical Union, 33

Udall, Stewart, 197
unemployed, 98, 106, 135
United Socialist Democratic Party, 62
United Mine Workers, 26, 70, 142
United Transportation Union, 214
Union Pacific, 31, 33, 48
University of Wisconsin, 200
Untermann, Ernest, 84
Utopia, 203

Vanzetti, Bartolomeo (See Sacco)
Versailles Treaty, 162
Vigo Lodge #16, 23-25
Villard, Oswald Garrison, 162
violence, 33, 37, 49-51, 143-144, 210
Vladeck, B. C., 188-189, 196
Voice of Labor, 83
Volkzeitung, 129
Voltaire, 18
Vorhees, Daniel, 26
Vandalia Railroad, 18
Viquesney, Bert, 56, 76
votes (for Debs), 63, 82, 105, 141,
    148

wage slaves, 84
Wagenknecht, Alfred, 151
Waite, "Bloody Bridles", 38-40
Walker, Ryan, 135

Walling, Wm. English, 127-128,
    131, 143-144, 208, 215, 222
Walls and Bars, 184, 226
war profits, 152
War, World War I, 145-158, 214
Warren, Fred, 87, 92, 128, 137
    141-142
Washington, Booker T., 72
Washington, George, 153, 155
Watson, Tom, 44, 46
Wayland, J. A., 44, 52, 57, 85-88,
    93, 141
welfare benefits, 213
Westenhaver, Judge D.C., 153-155
Western Federation of Miners, 26, 47,
    83, 85
West Virginia Coal Miners' Strike
    (1897), 48, 63, 81
WEVD, radio station, 196
Wheeler, Burton K., 177
White, Bertha Hale, 181-182,
    183-188
White, William Allen, 82, 220
Whitlock, Jim, 182
Whitman, Walt, 10, 103, 208
Wiley, W. H., 17-18
will, 196-197
Wilshire, Gaylord, 68, 130
Wilson, Birch, 182, 185
Wilson, Noble, 148
Wilson, Woodrow, 134, 140, 147,
    152, 156-163, 189, 210
Woodbey, George W., 217
Woods, William A., 37, 39-40
Woodstock Jail (see McHenry
    County Jail)
Work, John N., 150
Worker, The, 170-171
Workers' Defense Union, 161
workers utopia, 46-48
working conditions, 193, 204-205
women's rights, 21, 42, 48, 73, 88,
    89, 98, 101, 127-131, 135, 140-141,
    178, 194, 214

"You Railroad Men," 30
Zerbst, T. G., 157, 159-161
Zeidler, Frank, 225

Among the works available from
Charles H. Kerr Publishing Company:

WALLS AND BARS, by Eugene V. Debs

THE PULLMAN STRIKE, by William H. Carwardine

THE AUTOBIOGRAPHY OF MOTHER JONES, Third Edition

LUCY PARSONS: AMERICAN REVOLUTIONARY,
    by Carolyn Ashbaugh

THE ROADS THEY MADE: WOMEN IN ILLINOIS HISTORY,
    by Adade M. Wheeler with Marlene S. Wortman

CRIME AND CRIMINALS: ADDRESS TO THE PRISONERS
    IN THE COOK COUNTY JAIL, by Clarence Darrow

Published by the Eugene V. Debs Foundation:

SIDELIGHTS: INCIDENTS IN THE LIFE OF EUGENE V.
    DEBS, by Theodore Debs

Published by the Illinois Labor History Society:

TOURING PULLMAN, by William Adelman

HAYMARKET REVISITED, by William Adelman

Write for our list
Charles H. Kerr Publishing Company
600 W. Jackson Blvd., Suite 413
Chicago, Illinois 60606